AUTOMATED SOFTWARE QUALITY MEASUREMENT

AUTOMATED SOFTWARE QUALITY MEASUREMENT

Computer-Assisted Information Resource Management of Applications in IBM Mainframe Environments

Keith A. Jones, Ph. D., C. Q. A.

VNR VAN NOSTRAND REINHOLD
_____ New York

I(T)P   Van Nostrand Reinhold is a division of International Thomson Publishing. ITP logo is a trademark under license.

Printed in the United States of America.

Van Nostrand Reinhold
115 Fifth Avenue
New York, NY 10003

International Thomson Publishing
Berkshire House
168-173 High Holborn
London WC1V7AA, England

Thoman Nelson Australia
102 Dodds Street
South Melbourne 3205
Victoria, Australia

Nelson Canada
1120 Birchmount Road
Scarborough, Ontario
M1K 5G4, Canada

16 15 14 13 12 11 10 9 8 7 6 5 4 3 2 1

Dedicated to the memory of my father,
Dr. Charles C. Jones,

Whose career ranged from Industrial Engineer for GTE
to Arkansas State University Professor of Constitutional Law;
Who had his own pragmatic American TQM philosophy:

"Anyone can do anything better and faster,
if you just give them the opportunity to learn how."

PREFACE

The idea for this book first originated when I was working for the U.S. Environmental Protection Agency at the National Center for Toxicology Research, designing a system known as IMPACT (Interactive Management Planning And Control Tracking), back in the early 1980s. This system has long since been made obsolete by many newer and better technologies, but one of the most important technologies upon which it was based is just as timely today as it was over a decade ago. That technology is system log audit trails, which was originally designed to record timestamps of all CPU internal operating system events.

During the early days when system logs were first introduced, it was difficult to read them, and this difficulty limited their usefulness. However, in the early 1980s, several major innovations were also introduced, which served to make mainframe system logs, such as IBM's SMF, both accessible and usable for a wide variety of applications beyond the basic system performance management applications for which they were first designed—including chargeback billing, project management accounting, and, more recently, Automated Software Quality Measurement. Among the most important of these innovations were the SAS programming language and two system log management products based on SAS programming language: MICS and MXG.

The purpose of this book is to explore the potential applications of system logs, and their related technology, in their potential role as handy tools that can assist in the Continuous Quality Improvement processes inherent in Total Quality Management programs designed to enhance the efficiency and effectiveness of any information data center operation. This book is written for the technical manager as well as technical analysts and programmers interested in applying this technology, and vendor products based upon this technology, in their everyday practice. This book should be especially useful to data center quality assurance personnel as a guidebook for the practical applications of system logs as a source of software development productivity, performance, and process quality measurements.

This book is the result of personal experience in developing and applying Automated Software Quality Measurement techniques based on processing of SMF and other system log data over the course of the past decade, as ASQM has progressed from an obscure art to a fully leveraged technology that is the basis for a growing number of commercial vendor products. As the concepts of ASQM are presented in this book, some examples of related vendor products that are currently available will be highlighted with examples in order to reinforce the concepts and offer some indication of the usefulness of procuring such products for your data center.

It should be noted that each of the products highlighted in this book is undergoing rapid development, and ongoing developments in the related ASQM and system log technology and standards dictate that these products will continue to change at an accelerated rate. For this reason it is advisable that any data center manager or analyst interested in procuring any of these products should contact the vendor directly in order to obtain the most recent literature and vendor examples of the product. All addresses and phone numbers for the highlighted products are listed in the appendix of the book, and most of the vendors will send a PC-executable demo diskette as well as product literature.

Dr. Keith A. Jones, C. Q. A.

ACKNOWLEDGMENTS

This book could not be possible without the cooperation of the many vendors whose products are highlighted throughout the book. Among the many individuals who have provided critical assistance in the selection and preparation of product demonstration figures are: Dean Veraegher, of Legent Corp.; Karin Chandler, of Compuware Systems; Beverly MacDonald, of Programart; Elizabeth Wilson, of Eden Systems; Mark Levin, of KPMG Peat Marwick; Wink Swain, of SAS Institute; Paul Kellar, of Quality America; and special thanks to Barry Merrill of Merrill Consultants.

Acknowledgment must also be made to American Airlines, where these products have been demonstrated and applied for the past five years. Special acknowledgment must be made to the management of American Airlines, which is well deserving of its reputation for being among the first (and foremost) to implement the "cutting-edge" of new information systems management technology such as ASQM. This extends to the very top of the AMR Information Systems organization, as Max Hopper was one of the first (if not the very first) to spread the maxim "you can't manage what you can't measure"; and the president of SABRE Computer Services (SCS), Tom Kiernan, who spearheaded the introduction of the Total Quality Management movement to American Airlines in the form of the SCS Quality Through Leadership (QTL). Important contributions to the realization of the vision of QTL, and ASQM applications of the TQM movement at American Airlines, have been made by a large number of SCS management, including Bruce Parker, Terry Jones, William Davis, Bill Coyne, Dalton Wiley, Bill Arend, Jim Culver, and Kieran Major, as well as such farsighted senior analysts as Bill Miller, Vince Garroutte, Rick Sharon, and Ron Johnson.

Special acknowledgment is due to my wife, Grace, and daughters Andrea and Alana, who missed daddy for a year of evenings and weekends while this book was being written, to Lauralee Reinke, of Context Publishing Services, who formatted a difficult and complicated manuscript, and to Alan Rose, president of Intertext Publications, who "discovered" this project and had the foresight to see it through from the earliest planning stages.

CONTENTS

1

MEASURING ALL
THE THINGS THAT
COMPUTERS MANAGE

Most business professionals have heard the caveat: "You can't manage what you can't measure." An application of this bit of wisdom to data processing might be expressed as: "You can't manage computer software if you can't measure all the things that computer operating systems do."

Everything that happens in a computer is automatically measured or logged by its operating system. Every operating system—from MVS to VM to VMS to OS to DOS or OS/2—is equipped to make a system event record, or audit trail, to log each and every instruction and its outcome. These audit trails are known as *system logs*, and are the most important source of diagnostic and performance data for measuring the quality of computer systems—and the application software that they execute.

There are many proven strategies available to systems programmers that can minimize resources to capture, store, and analyze the system log data in a way that more than justifies the expense and effort to do so. However, it is first of all essential that both the management of the computer center, as well as the top-level organizational decision makers, are fully aware of the potential benefits that such system event log audit trails can provide.

Although the initial justification for such automated software quality measurement may be based upon cost savings, the long-term benefit is in better-quality applications software that is more responsive to current business needs. This chapter explains how system logs work; relates system logs to marketing data needed by a business; and discusses how system logs can be captured, stored, and analyzed automatically by the computer itself.

THINGS COMPUTERS MUST MEASURE IN ORDER TO
MANAGE THEMSELVES

The computer's operating system is a collection of programs and subprograms which are loaded centrally in the main processing control unit and which must be constantly accessible in memory in order for the processor to function. In a very basic sense, the operating system *is* the computer, since it encompasses all of the things that we normally think of as a computing device. The operating system both measures and manages everything computers do. The operating system is thus both the "soul of the machine," and what we can regard as the "mind of the machine," since it is both the essential part of a computer, as well as the part of the computer which makes each unique.

Every operating system must, in a practical sense, perform a common set of basic functions which are expected of all computing devices. Yet every kind of computer has been given a unique personality by the vendor that created it, in the sense that each individual operating system is equipped with special characteristics or specifications that make it particularly well suited to handle a specific set of activities or tasks. This functional specialization depends on unique hardware qualities.

These unique qualities are generally referred to as the *architecture* of particular operating systems, and individual specifics of how a computer applies that architecture is known as its *configuration*. Entire families of computer systems have hardware architecture specifications that allow selection from a wide variety of possible operating systems and allow configuration of the individual computer unit to support a myriad of possible functions and organizations. In most cases, it is now also possible to configure a computer with more than one operating system, which may process alternatively or simultaneously—depending on the way in which a computer can be most effectively used by its operators. This multiple-processing capability of modern computing system architectures creates a greater flexibility, which is offset by a greater complexity; and this makes computers more difficult to control.

Increasingly, computing architectures are designed with the assumption that they must be able to simultaneously handle both online as well as batch processing, in both centralized as well as distributed network capacities. This increases the need for complex and specialized methods of handling input/output operations for the central processing unit and data storage devices. It also has resulted in complex arrangements to measure address placements and cross-linkage of functional areas within the operating system, and the programs and data that it controls. However, for the most part such complex organizational innovations of operating system design are but variations on a theme. The basic functions of operating systems have not changed substantially even across the four generations of computers that evolved over the past three decades and have basically involved dialectic reversals in emphasis from central to distributed architectures.

BASIC FUNCTIONS COMMON TO ALL COMPUTER OPERATING SYSTEMS

The essential functions of all operating systems existed in the earliest automated computing devices, and can still be regarded as fundamental functions despite the architecture or technology that is involved in the context of each new type of computer system which is introduced. The functional *primitives* (the basic elements of operating system design) fulfill an important and necessary role in assuring *upward compatibility*—or true universality—of one generation of computer technology to the next. These basic operating system functions can be generally defined as:

- Task Supervision
- Scheduling Supervision
- Program Management
- Storage Management (both Real and Virtual)
- Distributed Resource Management (both Attached and Network)
- Recovery Management (including Interrupts and Terminations)

Although some vendors will argue that their operating systems are much more complicated, these are in a practical sense the most basic functional areas into which all other, more specialized operational processes can be categorized. Each hardware architecture has specialized characteristics that must be understood, especially in multiple operating system environments that can have confounding interactions. Nonetheless, these are all the areas which are required to achieve a basic understanding of system logs by data center managers as well as applications software programmers. Unfortunately, the potential benefits of system logs are still not widely recognized as a major productivity tool for use by the entire business enterprise.

METRICS ASSOCIATED WITH BASIC COMPUTER OPERATING SYSTEM FUNCTIONS

It should be understood that each of the basic functional areas of the operating system involves a particular set of metrics that are associated with that function. These measures are generated as part of the process wherein each function is performed, and are used by computers to provide feedback which an operating system uses for self-regulation.

Task supervision primarily involves *timestamps*, which are used to show when an action was requested and when the task and its associated tasks actually began, as checkpoints to confirm that the task was still being actively performed and, finally, when the task was actually completed. Scheduling supervision involves expected start times, durations, and amounts associated with critical resources needed by each task. Program management involves the identification and sequencing of the *standard operating procedures* that interrelate tasks into coordinated activities required to achieve a particular procedural output or objective. Storage management involves amounts of temporary and permanent *space* that will be needed in order to perform particular tasks, at particular times, and with particular performance specifications, methods, or manner of output. Distributed resource management involves remote monitoring of specifically named and addressed devices and related resources. It involves both the timestamps that record when particular process events began and ended at remote network nodes (or branch points), as well as the traffic (or volumes of data that traversed each regional domain of the network during specified time periods). Recovery management relates to the validation values, or range of permissible variance from critical measurements, generated by other functional areas of the operating system, and the special operating procedures that should be initiated if an undesirable measurement is detected. All of these areas work together to regulate and supervise computer processes.

OPERATING SYSTEMS AS THE SILENT SUPERVISORS OF COMPUTER SYSTEMS

Both host mainframe computing systems and distributed network systems can be conceptually understood and used to optimize performance efficiency if these six basic operational areas are fully accounted for. Automated supervision is necessary to detect shifts in statistical characteristics routinely associated with these basic operational areas, and extends to each individual user environment that has been configured to the extended computing system architecture.

Each of six operational areas is associated with a number of available system monitoring instruments and measurement types that can be routinely captured and accumulated. Thus, the status and trends that characterize the health of the computer system in each of the six areas are automatically tracked. These functions correspond to a healthy business.

Each of the operating system functions corresponds to a basic function found in every viable organization. Tasks must be defined, set up, assigned, and monitored to their conclusion. The scheduling of resources is needed to complete each task and involves planning that includes tracking both the current and future availability of necessary resources, the routine assignment of resources to tasks, and the reassignment of resources to inventory pools after they are no longer needed. Programs and procedures that control the linkage between tasks that result in achieving specific goals or objectives must then be initiated and routinely reevaluated to determine the effectiveness of the overall activity. It is necessary to make decisions about revisions in procedures and whether it is possible or necessary to adopt an alternative program or procedure in order to better accomplish the same objective or goal. Distribution involves both the protocols, or standardized process plans, by which different interconnected parts of the system interact, as well as the rules for resolving routine workflow problems to the timely assignment of necessary resources. Storage processes involve the availability of a place to maintain inventory of the completed product or a temporary place to complete a particular task or work effort. Recovery can involve both the process of determining whether something may be wrong, as well as what to do about it. This can include a temporary slowdown to proceed with caution or a complete shutdown, which may or may not have a defined procedure to determine what needs to be done next.

An example of how these functions are incorporated into one comprehensive advanced host mainframe operating system, IBM's *Multiple Virtual Storage* (MVS), is shown in Figure 1-1.

HOW OPERATING SYSTEMS LOG THEIR DATA
PROCESSING ACTIVITIES

Operating systems can also be understood by a correspondence to the functional subsystems in living organisms, since a computer operating system has for all intents and purposes evolved based upon a functional understanding of the interrelated processes that make up the human body and especially the human neurophysiological system. The procedural computing models that were developed during the 1950s by Von Neumann, Wiener, and others all tied back to schemas and models that were analogous to human neurophysiology and mental processes; computers were after all an attempt to create a machine which could do some equivalent of human mental work or at the very least be an amplifier of mental capability.

These efforts were referred to as *psycho-cybernetics*, the science of designing computing machines with human capabilities and characteristics, and included the early frameworks for what has recently been revived as the basis for artificial intelligence and neural network technology. The original direction of computer development was oriented toward processes entirely based on the outcome of statistically oriented computations. This early work was overshadowed by process models which were more procedural in nature. However, even though statistical computations were replaced by process-oriented controls as the predominant method of supervising internal computer operations, measurement of computer activities remained a fundamental part of operating system design. Relationships of computers to human systems are also the basis for most regulatory system control design options.

Every action that is taken by an operating system program or subroutine is held in a register during the course of that action, and then each activity is logged, or a counter is incremented to a current value in a log in the master system control workspace area. These internal system statistics and measurements

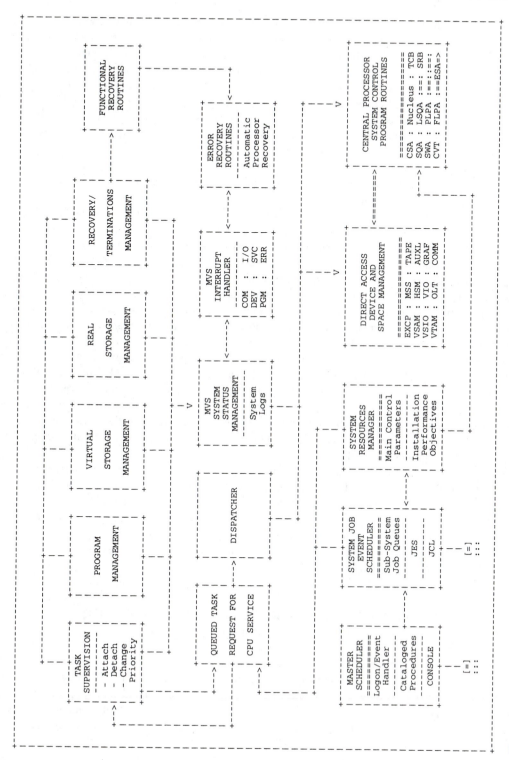

Figure 1-1 Basic Functional System Architecture for IBM Multiple Virtual Storage (MVS) Operating Systems

are used by the computer to regulate itself and to support operational supervision. Every operating system function has an associated set of parameters and a corresponding normal range of parametric values related to measurement of these basic functions. This is analogous to the normal range of values that have diagnostic value in the practice of human medical science. These baseline values normally fall within a range that is defined and documented by the vendor for each individual computer architecture and its operating systems. Yet the variability of each parameter for each installation is determined by a number of factors controlled by the computer's human operators and users and, in a more fundamental sense, by the manner in which system programmers have defined installation parameter controls to each of the operating systems that have been configured for an environment.

It is a traditional duty of the system programmers involved in providing technical support for a computing environment to monitor and regulate operating system installation parameter values in order to fine-tune the system and, in the case of some more critical parameters, to make the system operational. These parameters are coded into tables or macro files and are the master controls defining each computer installation configuration and driving the automated functions that make up the operating system. They are analogous to the parameters in the batch process *Job Control Language* (JCL), or online processing tables that applications software programmers use to control the processing of particular application programs on the system. Both types of parameter specification files can be used to make software operate more efficiently by changing the values for each available parameter option up or down or to take advantage of available alternative methods to control a particular operating system.

These parameters each correspond to special subroutines and macro programs which make up the operating system. To the extent that these parameters are defined, the computing system will operate under the constraints that have been defined by the systems and application programmers. To the extent that they are left undefined, each parameter has either a default value or an algorithmic method for assigning a default value based on other related programmer-defined parameters or vendor-defined characteristics of the computer architecture. In most cases, the operating system will use these functional parameters to monitor and control the computer system as a whole. These are the measurements that a computer must make in order to manage itself, and they have become essential to what we think of as automation in computing system devices.

Due to the importance of measurements to functional control of computer operating systems, there is an understandably high correspondence to characteristics we regard as the essential factors defining the quality of computer systems and software. These parameters can be used by programmers to customize operating systems by overriding the default values used by its system-internal programs or subroutines. The metrics that are associated with these parameters are used by operating systems to automatically supervise and manage all of its operations—and ultimately define how well a system is perceived to operate by its customers, a primary determinant of quality.

HOW BUSINESS OPERATIONS USE COMPUTER OPERATING SYSTEM LOG DATA

In a practical sense, these basic functional areas all correspond to supervisory areas in the management of a business organization—which routinely monitor operations to improve the efficiency and viability of the organization. Just as systems and applications programmers monitor and modify operating system parameters to control the efficiency of a computer's operation, the management of a data center, as well as management outside of data processing, can use automatically collected system measurements.

These metrics can improve their decision-making concerning the planning and management of data centers, as well as the organization as a whole. Although the level of detail and summarization will vary substantially for each of these areas, it can be assumed that the same categories of data which are used to monitor and manage an organization's computer system environments can be used to provide a consistent and far-reaching basis for organizational analysis and decision-making. This data can provide centralized control of the organization in a manner that results in more consistent quality of products and services and improved economies of scale to achieve progressive improvements in the efficiency of any business organization. It is also a key to restoring American productivity in the coming Information Age.

The automated accumulation of operating system log data into historical baseline performance databases can prove to be an extremely useful and effective source of data for *Total Quality Management* (TQM) and *Continuous Process Improvement* (CPI) programs, both for a data center and the business organization it supports. Although the use of automated capture, accumulation, and analysis of such computer operating system log data has not been a major strategic element of winners of the coveted Malcolm Baldridge Quality Award in its earliest years, it is certain to play a role in Total Quality Management and Continuous Process Improvement programs of future winners.

Although TQM and CPI have received considerable attention since they were first identified as being fundamentally similar to the Statistical Process Control techniques taught by Demming, and identified as similar to methods used by the Japanese to improve quality (and achieve their near-global domination of most high-tech manufacturing industries), there has been very limited attention directed toward the potential usefulness of operating system logs as an automated source of raw data about data processing operations—which can be used to improve the quality of a data center operation and customer service.

Even less attention has as yet to be directed toward the potential usefulness of this data source to the analysis of an organization's critical business processes and operations. With the increasingly important role of computer information systems and networks in the daily operations and management of contemporary business, and the increasing importance of computer system efficiency to the overall viability and competitiveness of a business, there is certain to be a growing emphasis on this technology in the future.

The enormous wealth of data that IBM and the other American vendors have designed into their operating system logs can conceivably provide the basis for a new informational Industrial Revolution. It is conceivable that many of the same management methods and measurement techniques developed by American industrial managers to make the United States the world's most productive industrial nation early in the century might similarly be applied to a new generation of industry to recover the productivity advantage of American workers, which may have been only temporarily lost to Japan and other nations.

The enormous detail in IBM's and other American computer systems' audit logs does not exist in such variety or abundance in the operating systems of computers designed by competitors to America's last remaining contemporary area of industrial dominance, software design. In fact, most Japanese computer system designers have streamlined an IBM-equivalent system log detail capability out of their own operating systems, assuming that this functionality is not worth the substantial process overhead and CPU memory involved in logging each operating system activity, let alone the storage costs to record all process activity data that is logged by our operating systems. This has been the basis of some criticism of IBM and the other American operating system designers in the past. But IBM has felt justified in providing this level of detail precisely because their data center operation customers have asked for each available system statistical measurement over the course of the thirty years that IBM's 370 operating systems architecture has evolved. In this case, it is the American manufacturer who has listened directly to its customers, and it is the Japanese manufacturer who has been making assumptions about predominant desires of the marketplace without direct feedback from its customers.

The significance of robust operating system logs to the continued dominance of the American computer industry is critical. The potential value of automated computer audit trails to the success of the TQM movement in streamlining American business operations is also critical. The Japanese would probably prefer that Americans were limited in system audit log capability to the level and relative obscurity the Japanese design into operating systems.

In any case, as each year passes, American consumers ask IBM and other vendors for more, not less, operation system audit log detail, especially in the areas that have grown most recently in importance: distributed network processing and personal computer workstations.

It is always the option of the management and technical support staff of each individual data center to decide exactly how much or how little of the system log audit detail to keep for short-term, tactical analysis and how much to accumulate for more long-term, strategic forecasting. However, as data center organizational management becomes more aware of how valuable the system log data can be in terms of optimizing the overall business operations and streamlining the process of everyday business, more and more data centers are summarizing critical performance indicators for use by business process analysts to improve the quality of business products and services of the entire organization. Many value-added benefits can be realized by investment in the software and staff for the support of proprietary data stores of critical system performance indicators, in addition to direct benefits to the data center.

LINKING OPERATING SYSTEM LOG DATA TO LOWER BUSINESS PROCESS COST

Perhaps the best demonstration of the value of the systematic accumulation and analysis of system log data to an entire business organization can be provided in a case study of the actual benefits achieved by an actual business organization. These results were achieved within a single month following the commitment to apply system log audit trail data using automated capture and analysis methods. The analysis methods were consistent with TQM techniques taught by analysts from such Malcolm Baldridge Award winners as the Xerox Corporation and Florida Power and Light.

The success demonstrated by the following examples was compiled from the actual experience typical of a Fortune 500 firm with an annual computer services budget of several hundred million dollars a year and annual business revenues of several billion dollars per year at the time when the project began. Although the examples involve a single company of substantial size and growth rate, the results are fairly typical and somewhat on the conservative side. These were similar to figures on potential returns of fully implemented and integrated quality and performance management programs published by computer industry vendors and analysts such as the Gartner Group and Auerbach, publishers of DataPro Reviews. These results are not limited to large companies; even greater percentages of savings have been achieved by some smaller companies which have focused on a fewer number of process problems.

The following success stories were accomplished following the summarization of the three previous years of IBM/MVS *System Management Facility* (SMF) system log tapes into an integrated series of summary performance databases of critical baseline statistics. These historical databases were prepared in less than three months of effort by a single programmer, with most of the man-hours involving supervision of the batch processing of *Statistical Analysis System* (SAS) programs in the MXG Library (purchased from SAS Institute at a price less than $1,200 at the time the effort began).

The total investment to buy the product and process the three previous years of data amounted to about $10,000. The investment required in order to achieve the same results could have been higher or lower at other companies based upon the relative expertise of the performance analyst doing the work. Cooperation and level of communication from areas presenting test case problems to the performance analyst and system resource commitment of the data center operations management, as well as the prevailing system unit costs and economics of the data center, also impacted the results.

However, the margin for potential return on investment is quite large once the performance databases are built. In fact, the Fourth Generation SAS statistical language tools affiliated with the vendor MXG product enabled a fairly typical SAS language programming yield of fifty-five function points of application program sourcecode within the first month reporting was attempted. Use of MXG program utilities included with its source libraries yielded twelve more reporting applications.

This product yield was achieved in a fairly consistent manner in follow-on application enhancements and new report writing projects by other programmers—with SAS application product yields equivalent to over five times greater efficiency than the national average for high-level procedure language programming. This resulted in programs added to in-house software inventory with a value equivalent to more than five times the original investment in the databases.

The actual expenses related to the investment were fully recovered within the first month that the data was available for use. Total net savings estimated at $30 million were documented as a result of this demonstration project, with major benefits enjoyed by both the data center operations and the entire business organization. The direct benefit to the data center operation was about one-half of the dollar amount recovered by the project. This dollar amount represented a total net savings that was equivalent to a 5 percent reduction in the yearly operating expenses of the data center. The average cost of a comprehensive TQM program has been estimated by the Gartner Group's studies of Malcolm Baldridge Award winners as approximately 2 percent of the involved functional business unit's net yearly operating expenses. Thus, the net savings resulting from even a basic demonstration of the benefits of automated system audit log performance analysis was able in this particular case to more than pay for a comprehensive TQM program before it was implemented and was also able to assure a significant source of data for a TQM program as it geared up and progressed to realize its greatest benefits.

The categories of system log record types that were selected for accumulation in the performance database included: CPU usage times, DASD and tape device mount times and I/O's, hardcopy output spooled print lines, execution start and end times, CPU memory sizes, data buffer sizes, data set storage allocation statistics, remote terminal usage statistics, task completion codes, and user account identification for all of the MVS batch jobs, IMS transactions, TSO sessions, and related programs executed within an entire MVS multiprocessor supported environment. The statistics, units of measure, and performance measurement variables were selected based on recommendations by vendors and publications by prominent industry analysts to be used as basic examples of the type of automated system log quality metrics found most immediately useful to most organizations.

A large part of the success achieved in this demonstration project was the result of the relatively rapid programming effort enabled by the SAS database language. Each application required only one or two days to design and program, based on a fairly reasonable knowledge of SAS language and a fairly general knowledge of the business processes involved in the operations of the company and of its data center. Greater or lesser results have been obtained by other companies using MXG and similar system log performance database management and reporting products. These include the powerful MICS Performance Database and are dependent on the creativity and commitment applied to the use of the tools. However, discussions with vendors and other SAS customers indicated these results are fairly typical.

Among the list of successfully demonstrated applications of this initial attempt—using three years of system log history data in a large-scale, integrated MVS environment—were the following:

Elimination of a Bottleneck in Completing a Critical Process

The most critical problem that can be addressed by system log data is a process bottleneck which directly threatens ongoing cash flow or potential revenues of the business organization. This type of problem must be solved immediately carrying the highest priority of all process performance problems. It can arguably pay for the investment in performance history databases all by itself, due to the benefit of stability in the business organization and ultimate savings gained as related to risk management. Although they are rarely designed exclusively for this purpose, it is the common experience of data centers building performance databases that the first requests from customers of the computer center for performance analysis involve solving a revenue or cash flow related bottleneck. In this particular case the problem related to a gradually worsening delay in the completion of a batch process which had a critical deadline and needed to make a routine scheduled data transmission to Europe to meet a bank clearinghouse cutoff time for posting credits to business accounts. Every time the batch process finished late, posting of the past day's accounts rolled over to the next day; because of the volume of transactions and special contractual penalties involved, several thousand dollars would be lost to the business. The batch process had been completing on schedule for several years with no significant losses, but over the course of only a few months, the process began to finish late increasingly often and eventually was late every day. Due to the size of the losses involved, a massive manpower effort had been directed to analyze the problem in order to eliminate the bottleneck. Nothing had been changed in any of the programs or procedures in the process jobstream, and the late completions were determined to be unrelated to any increase in the volume of transactions, since the problem continued to occur regardless of whether the daily process volume was relatively high or low. Without more detailed data about the individual steps in the process it was not possible for the data center to determine where the bottleneck was actually occurring and what to do about it. Over two months of painstaking analysis had yielded no results. Since the demonstration performance databases had just been created, it was decided that what was needed was an analysis of all steps in the jobstream with regard to start times, waits for resources, and elapsed time to process. In less than two days of programming to extract the desired data about the individual job steps and programs involved in the entire process flow, it was determined that in every case there was a time span of only a few seconds between the end of one job step program and the start of the next program's execution. In addition, an analysis of CPU efficiency statistics for each program indicated that they were all running at the best possible performance level. However, there was one job step in the process that had extremely long waits for resources, and the waits were growing to the point of several hours of inactivity during the course of processing the step. The waits were not reduced even on days when the volume was lower than usual. An analysis of the dataset activity records of the system log revealed that one of the working files processed by the program step was being accessed at the same time during the job step by another offline program that was attempting to off load and back up the same data. When this data was provided to the data center operations, it was an easy matter to change procedures to make sure the problem program could not be executed against the working dataset until all of the critical jobstream programs had been completed and the final accounting data was being transmitted to Europe. This solution was presented to data center customers, who accepted the problem as resolved. They determined that several million dollars in annual revenues had been saved and were understandably pleased with the availability of the new performance data. However, they were also understandably concerned that the same problem could happen again elsewhere in the system environment, perhaps with even greater risk exposure or revenue losses in the future. They were also motivated to require a more reliable assurance that related processes would complete on time, every time, so that they could adjust their ongoing business plans accordingly. This concern led to a series of meetings in which the new data and the process involved in identifying the bottleneck was explained and documented using TQM methods. However, in spite of the fact that they were pleased by the new level of process diagnostic detail that had become available as a result of the performance databases, the data center customers openly voiced a great deal of difficulty in understanding all the pages of process timestamp data that had been used in tracing the events. Yet, the timestamp data was to the data center staff a simple, straightforward single-threaded operational process flow. In order to understand the process that the customer used in troubleshooting and fixing a bottleneck in the workflow of their own business process area, TQM methods were used to diagram and document a customer workflow process using the customer's own charting conventions. The data center performance analyst identified available system log measurements that were analogous to measures the customer used to manage his own business area. As a direct result of this effort, which took place in a series of only four one-hour weekly meetings, it was not only possible to define—to the customer's full understanding and satisfaction—the problem-solving process by which similar process bottlenecks could be resolved, but it was also possible to design a time-line diagramming format similar to the Gant charts used by the data center customers to manage their own workflow. This was then used by the data center to report the ongoing performance of similar time-critical processing using the new system log data. This format was used as the design for a new SAS time-line reporting program, based upon SAS statistical libraries, with only a few days' effort and placed into routine production before the end of the month. An example of this report format is shown in Figure 1-2, and SAS program sourcecode examples to produce similar reporting of time plots related to a critical operational production data process are given in Appendix C.

Finding Resource-Intensive Programs in Routinely Processed Jobs

This particular application is the most commonly used involving performance data produced by processing of system logs. A large number of SMF system log measurement variables are intended primarily to help identify the job execution steps and programs which are the most inefficient consumers of system resources. Because of the large number of tradeoffs involved in the fine-tuning of computer systems (such as CPU versus I/O, memory versus storage, paging versus swapping, etc.), it is not always a simple matter of a descending sort routine to rank the batch jobs or online programs that use the most CPU, storage, or I/O resources. Instead, it is usually necessary to apply ratios or weight-assignment algorithms that take into account two or more interrelated functions of the operating system, and thus account for how efficiently a program or process task is making use of the overall system within the time frame and working set of other programs that it normally processes with. By looking at several such performance ratios it is possible to apply heuristic rules of thumb used to achieve objective system quality improvements based on vendor diagnostic troubleshooting and fine-tuning manuals. The individual ratios and measurement variables upon which they are based hold meaning for a technical support staff, within the context of expected baselines derived from vendor manuals. However, the large number of system metrics involved have little meaning to data center management and even less meaning to the management of data center customers. Therefore, it was an early experience that the most resource-intensive programs would have to be reported to management in a form that provided both critical performance statistics and a basic conclusion as to what the combination of those numbers could generally mean. The methods used in knowledge, rules-based expert systems were implemented in a simple form using SAS language select statements. A format was prototyped and approved for routine

```
     OVERNIGHT PRODUCTION PROCESSING TIMEPLOT SUMMARY OF SERVICE LEVEL AGREEMENT (SLA) PERFORMANCE

                       ** IF TIME SPAN TOO SHORT TO PLOT, STARTED (S) + ENDED (E) = X **

                                                                       CUSTOMER  : EURTRANX
                                                                       COMMITTED : GROUP 1-A
                                                                       DEADLINE  : @11:59:59

=====   =======   =======  =====   =======   ======   MIN                                      MAX
SLA_#   BATCHJOB  PROGRAM  DATE    STARTED   ENDED     TIME                                     TIME
=====   =======   =======  =====   =======   ======   0:00:01                               23:59:01

A-049   ABC00235  TAPGEN   22OCT   0:53:59   0:54:55   X
A-049   ABC142G2  TAPESEND 22OCT   1:20:22   2:13:13   +S-E*
A-052   ABC02730  ABCFICH  22OCT   1:55:46   2:18:21   SE*
B-08D   BAR27037  BAR228   22OCT   0:06:51   2:50:26   S----E*
G-027   GOV14005  TAPGEN   22OCT   2:00:30   2:51:48   S-E*
C-029   CAN08698  CAN020   22OCT   4:10:29   4:14:03          X
                                                              |
                                                              +
C-029   CAN42955  CAN829   22OCT   8:02:50   8:18:21          +-----SE
C-029   CAN24340  TAPGEN   22OCT   8:32:20   9:03:42                SE*
A-055   ABC01995  ABC488   22OCT   8:13:04   9:04:10               S-E*
                                                                   S---E
E-002   PAY02275  EURTAPE  22OCT   7:00:05   9:05:11              S---E
E-002   ABC00168  EURTRAN  22OCT   8:54:37   9:36:00              S-E
                                                                 +-X*
F-002   FAR02275  FARTAPE  22OCT  11:00:07  11:05:11                SE
                                                                    |
E-002   CAR00570  EURSEND  22OCT  10:39:27  10:39:27               +---S-------E
F-002   FAR00168  FARTRAN  22OCT  12:45:23  15:12:56                      S-------E
F-002   FAR00570  FARSEND  22OCT  15:23:12  16:34:23                           S--E <!>
```

Figure 1-2   Sample SMF Software Process Quality Measurement Time Plots of Accumulated Waits Impact on Service-Level Agreement

production to report whether programs were properly tuned, and, if not, what was the most likely performance problem indicated for further analysis. This format was integrated into a new data center function to provide support to the fine-tuning of application programs, involving both changes to JCL and maintenance changes to program sourcecode in order to make them process more efficiently. This new function resulted in the recovery of several million dollars of savings per year. Due to the ease of maintenance of the SAS programming language, the rules for the program-tuning analysis reports (which came to be known as the "QA-Auto" reports) were easily modified as new performance ratios and diagnostic baselines were made available in new releases of the vendor-tuning manuals. Eventually, this new application program's fine-tuning function became so successful that it was determined to be more cost justified to invest in several vendor products providing highly specialized analysis of some fairly exotic (but resource-critical) application performance factors. However, it was likely that both the management of the data center and its customers were not willing to approve investment in highly sophisticated products until after they had been able to participate in the design of the in-house "QA-Auto" reports and become comfortable with the capability of SMF system log detail data to precisely characterize the use of specific system resources and the value of specialized tuning ratios to improve the efficiency of individual programs and the overall system environment. The original QA-Auto reporting programs were thus eventually removed from production; however, the programs were moved to in-house software inventory as reusable sourcecode examples which came to be used in the on-demand reporting of special program performance characteristics not yet available from the specialized application-tuning vendors. Examples of this QA-Auto format are shown in Figures 1-3 to 1-5 and are based on SAS program coding techniques related to the generation of basic, expert system knowledge rules shown in Appendix C.

Reducing the Volume of Input/Output for Blocked Datasets

This is also one of the most common initial uses of a performance database, and often one of the most beneficial. In many cases, the most efficient way to store and retrieve record-oriented data is to *block* the records into fixed packet sizes or use a consistent number of records per packet block. In this way, the system only has to make one I/O operation for a large number or block of data records, rather than having to issue one I/O request for each and every record that is processed. This is an easily understood concept that is easily implemented by virtue of selecting a blocked storage method and a suitably high *blocking factor* at the time when the dataset file is first allocated. This allocation is stamped to the dataset file's overhead area known as the *Data Control Block* (DCB). It cannot be easily overridden without going through a reallocation of the dataset using an operating system utility program provided by the vendor. There are limits to the number of records that can be blocked together; and there are also optimally efficient block sizes—which are not always the highest number possible—and are dependent upon the system's architecture, the operating system, the access method selected by the programmer, and most importantly, the unique specifications of each individual data storage device where the data will be archived or actively processed. Over the life cycle of an application system or individual program (which may in many cases exceed five or even ten years) there may be a change in the most commonly configured storage hardware devices every one or two years. Often these changes take place without changing optimum block size in the JCL or in the catalogued dataset file allocation tables. They may even be hard coded into the DCB code definitions in some programs; and programs may continue to be processed with block sizes that are not optimally efficient, or, in some cases, even with blocksizes that can cause one I/O per record, or even multiple I/O's per record in extreme cases, to be changed. In addition, depending on the rigors of the data center configuration and change control function, the

APPLICATION SOFTWARE PRODUCTION JOBS QA-AUTO SOFTWARE PRODUCT TUNING ANALYSIS MTD BASE RANK BY IO DATA INEFFICIENCY

RANK	PGMR	JOBNAME	PRODUCT	AVG WAIT TO EXEC	AVG TAPE I/O TIME	AVG BLKS TAPE I/O	AVG BLKS DASD I/O	TOT PGM ABENDS	TOT PGMS IN JOB	AVG PGM SWAPOUTS	AVG I/O REWRITES
1	TRIMPY	ABC221	BACCTG	21:13:03	15:26:42	530,078	2,837	0	6	435	2439
2	UNKNOWN	TR033	TRANIX	16:57:21	12:36:26	202,848	12,482	0	5	7	1909
3	TRIMPY	ABC219	BACCTG	12:40:40	6:40:21	226,400	80,910	0	8	239	1117
4	WILSON	BAC173	BACSRS	11:13:31	9:30:38	1,919,634	905,133	0	14	3822	1090
5	WILSON	BAC171	BACSRS	17:53:12	6:44:18	6,968,082	153	0	4	1328	1084
6	WILSON	BAC141	BACSRS	10:56:08	5:31:59	1,409,208	9,138	0	57	364	683
7	MADDEN	SAL060	SALYR	12:06:30	4:27:32	646,095	6,788,133	0	2	0	674
8	WILSON	BAC172	BACSRS	22:50:25	8:01:11	7,610,784	64,659	0	8	300	656
9	LANTZ	AXT008	AXTDXS	6:06:14	4:22:29	1,616,982	8,307	0	12	346	594
10	KEENEN	DAR206	DARCS	5:09:12	0:15:44	16,212	738,742	0	26	29	576

Figure 1-3   Sample SMF-Based "QA-Auto" Diagnostic Reporting for MVS Batchjobs

APPLICATION SOFTWARE PRODUCTION JOBS QA-AUTO SOFTWARE QUALITY TUNING ANALYSIS WEEKLY JOB DIAGNOSTIC TROUBLESHOOING

OBS	WEEK ENDING	AVERAGE ENDTIME	CPURATE X*S370	PRODJOB ACCOUNT	AVG CPU EXECTIME	AVG TAPE USG TIME	AVG TAPES	TIMES RUN	AVG PGMS	AVG WAIT TO EXEC	**** Q A AUTO **** ===== ANALYSIS =====
				PRODJOB ACCOUNT=ABCAPP1							
1	10/19/92	7:47	U*13.76	ABC091	0:00:28	1:25:36	16	5	34	0:38:54	-- TPMNT OVERLOAD --
2	10/19/92	6:27	K*06.78	ABC148	0:02:03	0:20:49	1	5	32	0:35:25	-- I/O CONTENTION --
3	10/19/92	7:18	U*13.76	ABC212	0:03:24	0:00:00	0	5	70	0:26:11	-- PRINT OVERLOAD --
4	10/19/92	23:51	U*09.78	ABC332	0:02:14	2:36:54	5	2	7	0:14:05	==> RUNNING LATE <==
				PRODJOB ACCOUNT=BETAPP1							
5	10/19/92	0:59	U*13.76	BET117	0:11:49	1:07:17	2	27	2	0:00:48	// RUNTIME FASTER \\
6	10/19/92	0:58	U*13.76	BET115	0:15:41	1:05:14	2	20	2	0:00:21	// USING LESS CPU \\
7	10/19/92	8:53	U*09.78	BET053	0:00:50	0:00:00	0	5	14	0:09:28	-- PRINT OVERLOAD --

Figure 1-4   Sample SMF-Based "QA-Auto" Diagnostic Reporting for MVS Programs

APPLICATION SOFTWARE PRODUCTION PGMS QA-AUTO SOFTWARE QUALITY TUNING ANALYSIS WEEKLY PGM DIAGNOSTIC TROUBLESHOOING

OBS	WEEK ENDING	AVERAGE ENDTIME	CPURATE X*S370	PRODUCT PROGRAM	PROGRAM STEPNAME	PRODJOB ACCOUNT	TIMES RUN	AVG PGM CPUTIME	AVG WAIT TO EXEC	AVG PGM SWAPOUT	AVG I/O REWRITES	**** Q A AUTO **** ==== ANALYSIS ====
					PRODUCT=IREDR							
18	10/19/92	14:48:18	Z*09.86	IRE0012	IRE00325	IREDR1	5	0:13:41	1:45:57	14	164	\\ AWAITING SPACE //
19	10/19/92	19:07:17	U*13.76	IRE0024	IRE07005	IREDR2	21	0:15:37	1:50:09	108	128	!! USING MORE CPU !!
					PRODUCT=IRAXR							
20	10/19/92	15:45:01	X*03.10	IRA0234	IRA00115	IRAXR1	29	0:00:05	0:10:30	12	0	=> NEARING LIMITS <=
21	10/19/92	17:32:20	K*06.78	IRA0434	IRA05215	IRAXR2	27	0:00:05	0:10:30	12	0	// RUNNING FASTER \\

Figure 1-5 Sample SMF-Based Production Processing Batch Jobs and Programs "QA-Auto" Knowledge Rules-Based Diagnostic Reports

optimum block size allocations for either test or production environment programs can be overlooked—or, due to the complicated optimization formulas issued by some vendors, not properly calculated in the first place. These formulas are often so complex that most data centers will assign system programmers to test the formulas against each new storage device to be certain that the calculations provided by the vendor produce the most efficient method of blocking data. In any case, a large number of studies by user groups of IBM and other vendors' operating systems has determined that this is the most common area where the inefficient use of computer systems occurs. Therefore, one of the first uses of the new performance database was to read SMF Type 14 dataset activity records in order to build a dataset allocation database. The database was built with the logical record length, access method, and block size of each dataset name routinely processed in the production environment, as well as the calculation of statistics to indicate average volume-per-period time. This data was then used with QA-Automation rules to assign the most efficient block size depending on record length, access method, and the storage device type on which the dataset was most often stored or processed. In this case, the dataset volume statistics, in terms of the average number of I/O blocks or EXCP events processed, were combined with system chargeback pricing data in order to determine the average cost of processing each dataset-per-period time. Then, the efficiency of I/O processing for each dataset was calculated based on the number of records currently blocked, compared to the number of records that could be moved with each I/O operation if the dataset was blocked with optimum efficiency. The typical data center surveyed in the user group studies cited inefficient block sizes for more than half of its datasets. This level of inefficiency indicated that 50 percent or more of the datasets were blocked between 10 to 100 times lower than optimum blocking factors. It should not be uncommon then to achieve an incredible reduction in the demand and need for large numbers of storage devices if block sizes are routinely optimized across the entire data center. In this case, the original analysis of the I/O inefficiency yielded over $5 million of potential savings, which was somewhat above the numbers found by vendor user group surveys. However, this analysis was conducted during a period when a major portion of the storage devices had been upgraded to a new vendor model, and most of the planned block size maintenance had not yet been done. This particular analysis was conducted six months later and it was determined that the magnitude of inefficiency had been more than reduced by half. These QA-Automation reports covering potential cost savings from dataset/block size optimizing were then routinely produced and made the focus of several concentrated efforts to optimize dataset block sizes and keep them optimized as part of each new storage device upgrade. After six more months, the level of nonoptimized datasets had dropped to less than 10 percent of previous levels. It then remained fairly consistent due to decisions not to optimize some dataset allocations because it would involve changing program sourcecode and limit exportability of critical programs across operating systems in some cases. The total savings in this case were estimated at over $3 million per year once the problem was permanently brought under control. The savings were used to eventually cost justify several advanced vendor products that are capable of performing the QA-Automation report functions and automatically changing JCL and DCB allocations to dynamically set the optimum block size for each new storage device. The original QA-Automation potential method is based on research by Sun Oil using MXG and is now the basis for many vendors' automated, storage-optimizing tools.

Finding Dominant Cause of Repeated Program Abend Dumps

One of the most labor-intensive aspects of diagnosing the cause of a production program abend dump, or other abnormal termination of processing, involves determining what other programs were executed at the same time or may have also terminated shortly before or after the application program in question.

This is a fairly common labor-intensive process that is automated based on cross-checking the system log abend codes and recovery action flags in the SMF Type 30 job accounting records. This type of application of system logs can be particularly complicated if there is multiprocessing linkage across multiple parallel host CPU processors. In this case, the time plot report format, and procedure to locate and document critical process bottlenecks, was adapted for use by graphically sequencing each program abend to occur during a given twenty-four-hour period. The time plot was sorted to show commonality across all host processors over time, as well as on individual CPU processors. This was done to save time when researching the most likely cause of each of the abends that occurred within the same time period and to avoid looking up the critical CPU processor weight (as a relative multiplier of the IBM 370 benchmark), which determines the power of the CPU upon which a program was processing at the time it abended. This is an important diagnostic to determine if it is the same CPU or equivalent that the program is normally processed on and whether the CPU was sufficient for the performance group to which it was defined and the workload of other programs it was running with at the time that the abend occurred. Although in some cases it is also necessary to know the IBM action codes that precede and follow an abend code in order to be 100 percent certain of the cause of an abend, analysis determined that in over 95 percent of all cases a standard cause assigned automatically by the abend code was able to diagnose the primary reason that the abend happened. This was sufficient so that statistical profiles were developed that characterized the most common types of errors that were routinely occurring. TQM methods were then used to rank, analyze, and solve the most common types of errors that had been occurring due to lack of standards or improper procedures, as well as to identify the programs with routinely repeated errors that required maintenance. This report was determined to be capable of reducing the need for a staff of six operations problem analysts to research and resolve program abends down to only one, and it demonstrated potential for a 95 percent reduction in the time needed for application programmers to assign an initial problem determination from two hours to one-half hour. This yielded a net savings in programmer labor of over ten man-years per annum, which amounted at the time to over $1 million saved per year. The report was eventually supplemented with additional specialized vendor products to provide abend diagnostic detail and in-house operations analysis systems to document final analysis and resolution of the problems. An example of this report is shown in Chapter 3, along with a discussion of SMF error tracking.

Notifying Programmers of Other Programmers' Changes to JCL

Although most data centers have rigorous standards and procedures to assure that every change to resources processed within their production environments are coordinated across the entire data center organization, it is an unfortunate reality that as a data center becomes increasingly large, an increasing number of changes will be made without notifying every other impacted area. If there is a notification, it may not be detailed enough or it may not be acknowledged until after the change has taken place. In this case, a daily pass was made of the SMF Type 14 records in order to build a file of every DCB and JCL parameter that was in effect the last time the dataset was updated or accessed. This file was then compared to the previous daily version of the file in order to identify any dataset that had changes in any DCB or other JCL parameter value, indicating both the previous and current value of the changed parameter. A report format was designed and routinely processed, and a TSO notification process was devised to automatically send e-mail to all areas which routinely access that dataset or use a program that may be executed by the new JCL members. This confirmed that they were aware of the change and have completed any changes they need to make in order to accommodate it. This new procedure reduced the labor-intensive notification process by at least one hour for each change, which amounted to a yearly labor cost savings of at least $1 million when the report was implemented. An example of the report is shown in Figure 1-6 and related SAS code is given in Appendix C.

Verifying System Development Projects Are Still on Schedule

One of the most difficult and labor-intensive activities of system development project management is status reporting. Such reporting confirms that each step of the development process is completed as scheduled according to the project plan of record and estimates how much of the project has been completed and how much remains to be done. The SMF system logs help automate this process, as well as provide an automated validation to project status reporting which may not be already automated. This occurs by daily scans of the activity of application development programmers as they compile new programs and as they test the programs either in a batch or online testing environment. These daily scans can be accumulated into weekly summary files, and statistics can be reported to indicate the number of times that each programmer on each project has compiled new programs. The system logs can also provide data as to how many successful compiles were made, as well as the number of failed program compiles and successful compilations which received warning messages. It is also possible to determine the size and complexity of the program modules that were compiled, and—together with the successful compile counts and program size—the actual programs that are completed can be compared to estimates of the number and size of programs that were expected to be produced. Similarly, if the proper standards and job accounting necessary to automatically track development projects are enforced, it is possible to track the testing of programs in order to determine the difficulty that may be involved in implementing the new programs to production, as well as some indications of the individual differences between programmers. By building baseline history performance databases of average times from the new program's original assignment by application programmer, which include the average number and development time until a program is successfully compiled and the number and expected length of time to test the program, valuable data can be accumulated about the application development process for each individual type of software product. This data can also be used to help evaluate differences between alternative methods and the use of new technologies, as well as other productivity-related factors weighing upon the application development process. In this case, it was only possible to develop basic reporting of the number, date, and success ratio of compiles by project and manager area, as well as the number, date, and completion code of each test by a programmer. This data was sufficient to demonstrate potential reduction of up to four hours per week of labor-intensive information gathering about projects in progress and had the potential to save over $1 million per year in management support labor costs. This report was put into routine production and integrated into a global design for a comprehensive Total Project Management System, designed to use information of this nature—in combination with TQM methods—to improve the process of estimating and planning system development projects. This data is also of critical value to the preparation of the benchmarking methods and report formats which are discussed in Chapter 7.

Eliminating Delay in Loading an Online Database for Update

In this particular demonstration application, the number of data buffers for online transactions were compared to the wait times required to perform the updates, the total elapsed process times, and the volume of transactions processed. This was done in order to plot the most efficient number of buffers and to make decisions regarding the best online parameters for the database control tables. The data from

```
                              SAS
                        COMPARE PROCEDURE

                COMPARISON OF CURRXDCB IWTH PREVXCDB

      ** CHANGE IN DSORG, LRECL OR BLKSIZE ALLOC SINCE PREVIOUS PROCESS CYCLE **
```

FUNCTION	PRODUCT	JOBNAME	DDNAME	DSNAME	VARIABLE DSORG	COMPARE DSORG
SUPPORT	TERABLD	BDK024	BDLLOG	TERABLD.BDL024.A01	PS	DA
SUPPORT	TERABLD	BDK032	BDLLOG	DBA.BDL032.A01	DA	PS
SUPPORT	TERABLD	BDK036	BDLLOG	DBA.DBL036.A01	PS	DA

FUNCTION	PRODUCT	JOBNAME	DDNAME	DSNAME	VARIABLE LRECL	COMPARE LRECL	DIFF	% DIFF
FAXDIV	FACDOC1	FAX016	FAX012A	FY.FAX016EA(0)	170	178	8	4.71
FAXDIV	FACDOC1	FAX016	FAX012A	FY.FAX016EB(0)	66	74	8	12.12
FAXDIV	FACDOC1	FAX016	FAX012A	FY.FAX016EC(0)	88	106	18	20.45
FAXDIV	FACDOC1	FAX016	FAX012A	FY.FAX016ED(0)	52	54	2	3.04

FUNCTION	PRODUCT	JOBNAME	DDNAME	DSNAME	VARIABLE BLKSIZE	COMPARE BLKSIZE	DIFF	% DIFF
PAYROLL	PAYROLL1	PAY034	SYSUT2A	FY.PY004A59(0)	23400	6200	-17200	-73.51
REVENUE	STAX1	ST006A	DY002202	FI.ST006A03	6216	23352	17136	275.68
REVENUE	STAX1	ST006B	DY002203	FI.ST006A02	6216	23352	17136	275.68
REVENUE	STAX1	ST006C	DY002204	FI.ST006A04A.TOTALS	6218	23408	17290	282.61
REVENUE	STAX1	ST006D	DY002205	FI.ST006A05A.TOT(0)	6218	23408	17290	282.61
REVENUE	STAX1	ST006E	DY002206	FI.ST006A07(0)	6228	23472	17244	276.88
REVENUE	STAX1	ST006F	DY002207	FI.ST006A08.A01	6228	23472	17244	276.88

Figure 1-6   Sample SMF-Based Production Software Quality Configuration Control Audit Report of JCL or DCB Parameter Changes

the performance database made it possible to reduce online response times, as well as to reduce the overall time it took to process an equivalent volume of transactions processed before tuning in one working day prime shift by several hours after tuning. This reduction in process time and the impact it had on reducing turnaround time, resulted in a reduction in wait time to the data center customers—thus, realizing a substantial savings of data center resources, as well as a reduction in labor costs of the customers.

Finding Excessive Paper Usage and Optimizing of Reports

This application involved two *ad hoc* reports which were considered a one-time activity; the program to produce the reports was placed in the in-house software inventory for production upon demand. One report ranked the hardcopy print jobs involving the greatest number of spooled printlines. Analysts were assigned to contact customers to determine whether they were using the entire report and to recommend alternative output solutions allowing for the selective viewing and printing of only the most important pages or placing the reports on a less expensive media for permanent data archival. Another report cross-referenced the number of spooled printlines to the number of page-ejects for the report (both were available from the SMF data), as well as cross-referencing to offline files which logged the number of boxes of paper physically loaded to printers logged on the SMF for each individual logical printer address that received spooled printlines. A ratio between the number of printlines per page-eject for each report and for each printer was used in order to rank reports and printers in terms of relative print density. (This was done in order to identify reports and printer nodes where a high volume of pages were ejected blank or with only a very few number of lines.) Reports and nodes ranking high on the list were assigned for maintenance in order to attempt to consolidate report pages onto a single page and reduce most page-ejects to a single line-feed. This activity produces over $1 million a year in annual savings and is now part of the routine resource recovery function along with application-tuning.

Identifying the Savings Potential from a New Storage Device

In this exercise, a file was built of all the datasets in routine production based on a scan of the SMF Type 14 data access activity records and the Type 30 job accounting records. For each dataset, an average value was calculated for the number of EXCPs, or blocks of data I/O accessed using the current storage device, and the number of blocks of data permanently allocated for each dataset. These two numbers were used to calculate a ratio indicating the volatility of I/O activity for the dataset. This ratio was ranked and the top datasets segmented up to several possible conversion levels. The chargeback cost of the permanent allocation of the datasets, as well as the average number of EXCPs was combined to get an approximate storage related cost for the old device. The cost of the new device was factored against the current storage cost using the ratio of the purchase price of the two devices. After factoring the recovery ratio from the rate assigned by the chargeback pricing system for use of the old device, and the new pricing rate of expected recovery proposed for the new device, a reliable estimate was obtained of potential savings from the proposed purchase of the new storage device, determining how many units to purchase as well.

Eliminating Excessive Tape-Waits for Critical Datasets

This application involves sorting all the tape-mount wait times, tape block I/Os, and total elapsed tape-mount times for all production batch jobs in order to rank the job steps which have both the highest and lowest ratio of tape-mount delays adjusted for volume of tape data transfer. The tape datasets ranking lowest are examined in order to determine if it might be more appropriate to convert the tape dataset to DASD, since the volume is so low and possibly not worth the delay for a tape-mount. Tape datasets ranking the highest were assigned for analysis to determine if the cause for the tape-mount delay is routinely operational (in other words, if it happens in the same area and shift), or if there is an obvious problem with the JCL with regard to inappropriate buffers or other parameters which may have been missed prior to the implementation of the job to production. If there does not appear to be any problem with the JCL, a cross-reference of datasets requested by multiple jobs within the same time period, as well as datasets that are within the same job (as other datasets that are requested by multiple jobs within the same time period), is automatically generated by a program that reads the SMF Type 14 dataset access activity records. This activity has also become part of the routine resource recovery area function and routinely results in production window scheduling changes and improvements in JCL that save over $1 million per year in tape device access costs.

Customer Demographic Survey and Technology Needs Assessment

This activity involves the routine summary of the TSO and *ad hoc* batch customer's usage of individual programs and vendor products. This is done in order to determine changes in their terminal work behavior and the percentage of their average workday-per-network terminal logon ID involving the use of particular programs. This data is used to determine the number of customers using each product, by area, the amount of time, and the percentage of the workday—as well as the time period within the workday—when they use particular products. By corresponding the data to job category codes from employee information files, it is possible to profile the average usage of each product and type of product by customer area. This data is then available for use in estimating the need for training services and determining the impact of proposing alternative products or new technology to the customers. Also, by merging the data with workload factors to compare the labor and system resources associated with alternative products, it is possible to estimate in advance what the impact will be on customer labor and system resources. This report resulted in a set of databases and procedures which were developed into an entire system for managing product impact. The total savings were incredibly large, with over $1 million within the first year that this new report was prototyped.

Finding Customer Areas That Need Attention to Terminal Needs

A simple report was developed to track the number of repeated online abends, time-outs, or access security violations that came from the same terminal line number and recorded on the SMF system log within a given period of time. This evolved into a series of reports and automated notifications that were sent via e-mail to various areas responsible for handling potential customer problems, such as training needs or audits and security. The savings from this particular report were originally nominal and were consolidated into some functional prototypes which were later evolved into larger comprehensive systems, consolidating this report into existing systems for customer support and audits.

The variables and record types selected for this demonstration project represented less than 1 percent of the total system log variables and record types available as supported by the MXG vendor. Once the performance history databases had been built by the application programmer's submission of *ad hoc*, on-demand batch jobs to load archived SMF log tapes, programs based on the MXG vendor program libraries were adapted for routine, scheduled submission from a batch production automated console environment. Additional MXG-based performance application reports continued to be developed monthly as they were needed.

Since some, but not all, of the performance variables overlapped with the job accounting data collected routinely by a corporate data center chargeback system, and with CPU performance variables routinely collected by a systems-tuning group, some of the original demonstration variables were not routinely loaded directly from SMF log tapes and were instead collected offline from the chargeback and CPU-tuning databases. Incidentally, these variables were based on products purchased from other vendors utilizing the SAS database language, which possesses special technical advantages over all other methods of reading and loading system log data. The decision was made to continue licensing the specialized system log management products for their *ad hoc* analysis reports. Some of these products are highlighted later in this chapter.

Eventually, based upon the substantial success of the original demonstration project at realizing a respectable level of savings for both the data center and the entire business organization, the decision was made to replace all of the various vendor products for managing specialized SMF system log types with a single, fully integrated system log management facility that could centralize all of the performance data in one place. This decision helped to further reduce the costs of managing the SMF data by more than 50 percent. This decision served to ensure that a single vendor would be solely responsible for all of the maintenance that kept the input log load data structures abreast of the most current release of each new operating system log (traditionally a monumental task due to the enormous number of variables in system logs). It also helped to assure that all the calculations and analyses based upon the MVS system log data were consistent and more readily accessible to the corporate and data center analysts requesting them.

HOW TO CAPTURE AND ACCUMULATE
SYSTEM AUDIT LOG DATA

In order to build historical system performance databases for use by the data center and organizational business analysts yielding the continual improvement of quality in everyday business operations, it is necessary to automatically capture the operating system audit log data on a daily basis. Once captured, the data will be accumulated into files summarized on a weekly, monthly, quarterly, and yearly basis according to levels of detail and the priority of business units most critical to the organization being served.

The first step needed for establishment of any comprehensive automated software quality measurement program is to become acquainted with the system programmer library and handbooks which describe the architecture and internal functions of the operating system that will be logged. Every operating system has a series of technical manuals, with contents that range from instructions for installation of operating systems to procedures for routine tuning. Almost every one of these manuals will have sections describing the role that system logs can have in these efforts. It is necessary to have all the manuals relating to system programmer functions available to the application programmers who will support the automated software quality measurement function. In many cases, they must be aware of the impact that the routine tasks performed by systems programmers can have upon the system log data. Regardless of the operating system that is involved—from IBM's MVS to VM to DOS to OS/2, from DEC's VMS to AT&T's UNIX—it is always necessary to first read the system programmer's operational procedures manual in order to understand fundamental functions of system log generation modules, as well as the specifications of the system log records created by that operating system. Every system log record is different, and they can range from the extremes of eighty-character fixed card images with less than 10 record types (in the case of IBM's VM Accounting Records), to the irregular variable length records making up IBM's *System Management Facilities* (SMF) logs, currently available with over 100 separate record types. Basic record types in VM Account logs are shown in Figure 1-7. A summary of the major SMF record types as they are used in the MICS Performance Database product is shown in Figures 1-8a to 1-8i, with related operations and network records shown in Figures 1-9a and 1-9b.

The only thing that is common among all system logs is that they are always record-oriented, although the methods that must be used to keep and separate the record types are also largely unique to each individual type of operating system and its system programming procedures. In every case, the intricacies of the individual system log must be understood in the context of the overall operating system that it is based upon. Unless a vendor product is used to administer the changes in the system log record layout, each change in the operating system by the hardware vendor will require changes in programs written to read the system log. SMF is the system log that is demonstrated in this explanation of automated software quality measurement techniques, because it is by far the most complex operating system log, but also because it has incidentally been the focus of the most activity by commercial vendors that specialize in automated system log management products. All of the techniques that are used in managing and analyzing the SMF system log can be easily applied to all other system logs. A point which is reinforced by the fact that all major system log management vendors who support SMF analysis normally *throw in* the code needed to use their software performance analysis programs to analyze other operating systems logs at no cost or at nominal cost. Once an application programmer has learned the steps to load and analyze SMF, all other system logs are easily mastered.

A diagram to demonstrate SMF operations is shown in Figure 1-10.

The IBM System Management Facility is a system log that collects and records a variety of system- and job-related data. System-related SMF records involve information about the system configuration, status, active tasks, I/O, CPU paging, and system workloads; the job-related records include information on the relative usage units of CPU time, channel, device, file, and output process activity of each batch job, program step, or online session. SMF runs in its own MVS operating system address space. Because the SMF address space contains its own control blocks and buffers, an installation can restart or reload SMF without requiring the restart or reload of the entire operating environment. SMF also provides exits that allow installations to add routines to the control program to perform specialized processing. An installation can even design and code its own unique SMF records, which can be captured to monitor and collect statistics on any activity or function that is controlled by the operating system. This includes any new software application or environmental facility that runs under that operating system.

IBM routinely adds new SMF records for such major strategic facilities as CICS, IMS, or DB2. However, some vendors and individual data centers have written their own SMF record exits for products such as ORACLE and NOMAD. User-defined SMF system exits specify a record format and method of measuring specific events as they occur, such as the time when an event takes place or the number of times that a condition is met. These user-written exits can also be used to *kick off* automated processes, such as the cancellation of invalid jobs or sessions in order to enforce local host installation standards.

Because of the volume of data that is recorded by operating systems in the system logs, and because of the extremely high speed at which the operating system log functions take place and the fact that the system logging functions are regarded as being less essential than the actual processing of data by a computer, it is normally the case that a very large amount of the data in the system log will be null,

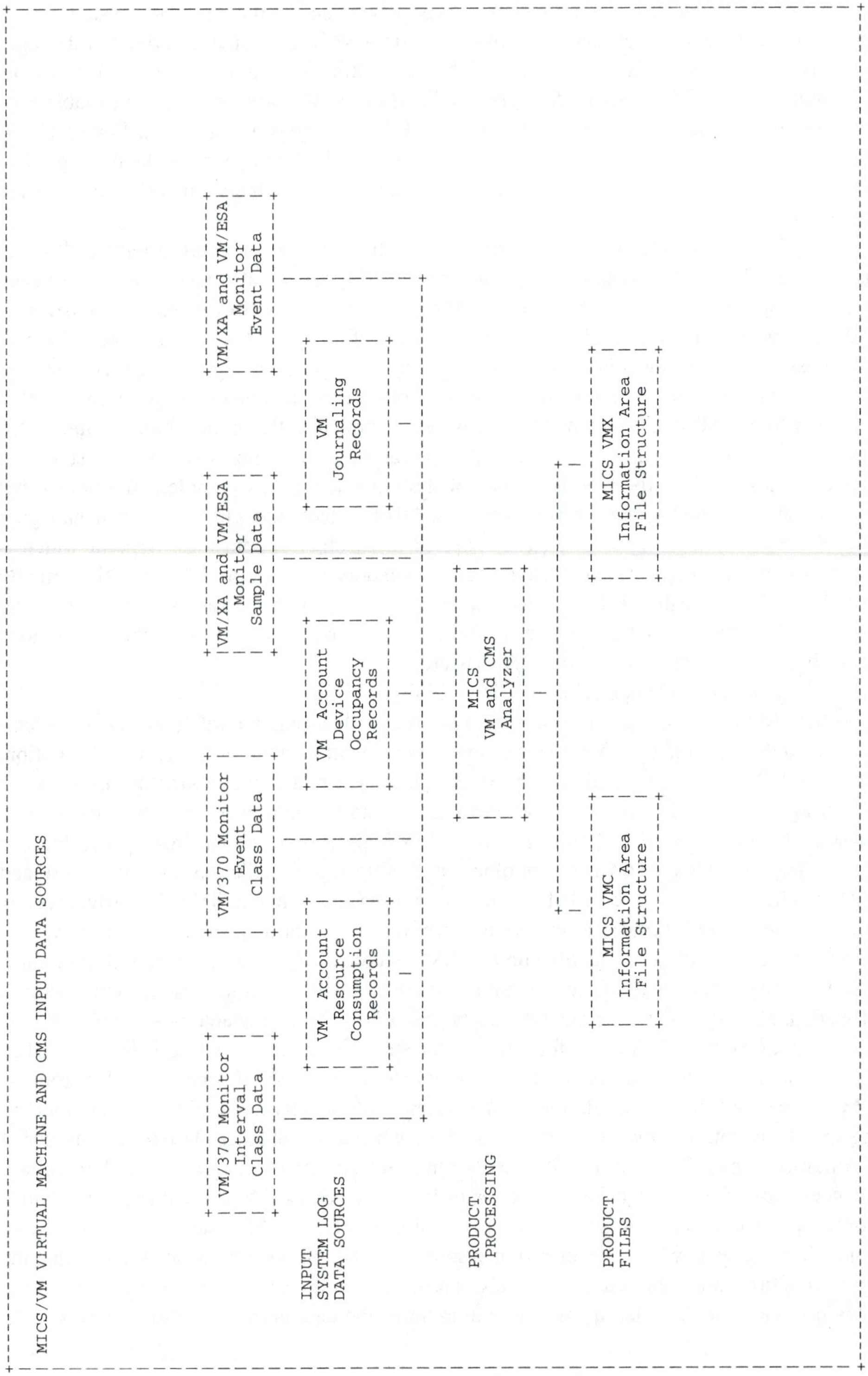

Figure 1-7   VM System Log Input to MICS Performance Database

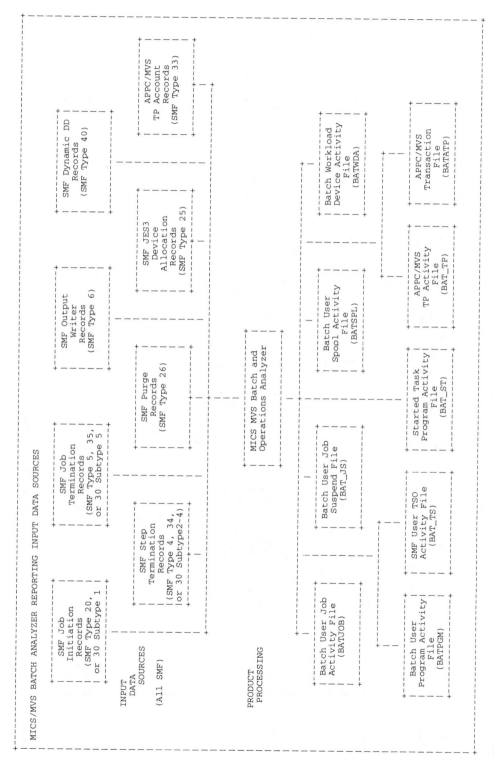

Figure 1-8a MVS Batch Programs SMF Input to MICS Performance Database

WHAT IS SMF DATA?

IBM's System Management Facilities (SMF) is an integral part of the MVS operating system. Its primary function in the operating system is to collect and record information about the activities, events, and resource utilizations that occur throughout the data center. SMF writes this information, as SMF data records, in system data sets. SMF also performs a secondary function in that it provides macros that can be used to write customer-developed or vendor product records to the SMF data sets.

SMF data is the collection of records written to the SMF data sets by the System Management Facilities or by an external system using SMF write macros. The data is written to the SYS1.MANx data sets (where x can be the letters A-Z and the numbers 0-9). These data sets act as a temporary repository for the data and they are periodically (usually daily) unloaded to permanent SMF data sets (usually tape).

SMF records are identified by a number from 0 to 255, which is referred to as the SMF record type. Record types 0 through 127 (standard records) are reserved for use by IBM. Record types 128 through 255 (non-standard records) are set aside for vendor products and user routines that are used to create their own SMF records. SMF provides two micros that are used to write standard or non-standard records to the SYS1.MANx data sets. Non-standard SMF records are typically generated by vendor products such as TSOMON or ACF2. Much in the same way that MVS uses SMF to track and record systemwide resource consumption and activities, these vendor-generated SMF records show the resource consumption and activities of the users of their product in more detail than is available from the MVS standard record types 0-127.

Some record types, such as the SMF type 30 Common Address Space Work Record, have record subtypes that dictate how the contents of the various record fields should be interpreted. Certain SMF records are fixed length, while others are variable.

SMF records are written to the SYS1.MANx data sets in response to certain events. For example, the IPL of the system, the end of a TSO session, or the closing of a data set all constitute events that can trigger the writing of a standard SMF record. Interval records are also written in response to an event -- the expiration of a timer.

The writing of an SMF record to the SYS1.MANx data sets is usually the culmination of a process that started sometime earlier. For example, the writing of a type 30 subtype 4 (step end) record occurs after a series of events that began with the initiation of the job step. When the step was first initiated, control blocks within the step's address space were set to zeros and blanks. As the step performed I/Os, used TCB and SRB time, etc., counts of each utilization were added to the appropriate control blocks. As events occurred within the step, time stamps were created and stored. Finally, at step end, SMF gathered all the relevant control block values and formatted them into a type 30 subtype 4 record. The formatted record was then written to the SYS1.MANx data set.

NEW TECHNOLOGY VERSUS OLD

SMF records have been around a long time. IBM operating systems such as VS1 and MVT produced SMF record types similar to those being produced by the MVS operating systems today. In 1979, the MVS/SE2 enhancement made available a new Common Address Space Work Record, the SMF type 30 record. Type 30 subtypes 1, 2, 3, 4, and 5 records completely replace the information found in the obsolete SMF type 4, 5, 20, 34, 35, and 40 records. Those record types represent old technology. IBM no longer enhances its old technology record types --it appears to be keeping them solely for compatibility reasons. By comparison, the type 30 records represent the current level of technology and provide more information. In addition, interval record generation is possible with the type 30 records.

A comparison of the new technology records and their old counterparts are shown below. The old technology provides no means of interval recording, so the SMF type 30 subtypes 2 and 3 have no match in the old technology column.

New Technology Record Type	Event	Old Technology Record Type
30-1	Initiation	20
30-2	Interval End	-
30-3	Last Interval	
30-4	Step End	(4 or 34) and 40
30-5	Job End	(5 or 35) and 40

MICS decides which SMF record types to process, based upon parameters specified in product installation tables. Either the old or new SMF record type technologies can be supported.

Figure 1-8b Summary of SMF System Log Inputs to MICS Performance Database

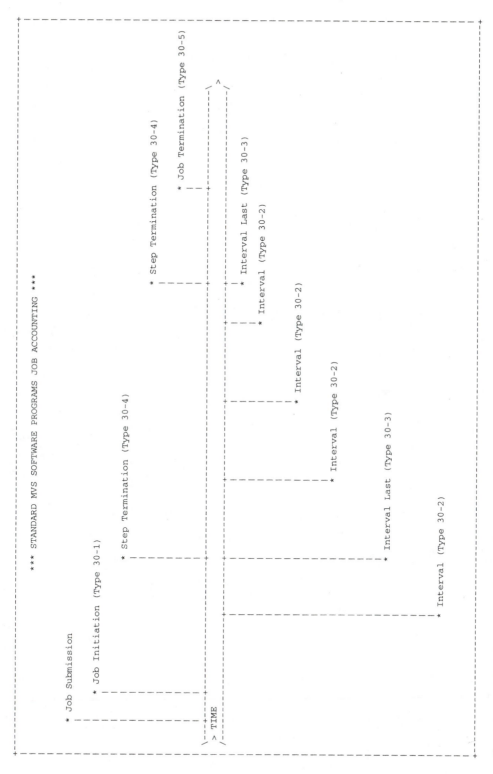

Figure 1-8c MICS Performance Database Summary for Type 30 SMF Records

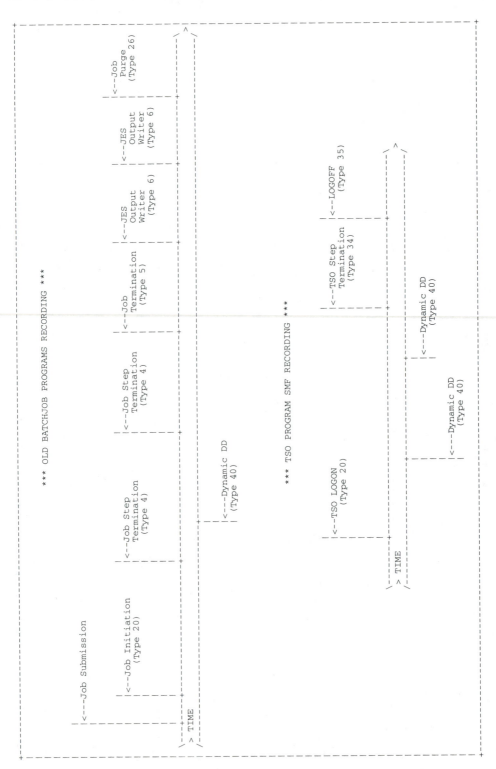

Figure 1-8d   MICS Performance Database Summary Using SMF Pre-Type 30 Records

NEW SYSTEM LOG TECHNOLOGY SMF JOB ACCOUNTING RECORDS

The first group of Batch SMF record types are the execution type records. These record types contain measurement data from the reader start time stamp up to the termination of the job. MVS/SE2 and later versions of MVS should produce and use the current technology SMF type 30 records. Pre-MVS/SE2 versions of MVS must use the old technology SMF types 4, 5, 20, 34, 35, and 40 records.

SMF TYPE 30 RECORD

The SMF type 30 record, or Common Address Space Work Record, has six subtypes, the first five of which are used by MICS. This record type completely replaces the old technology SMF types 4, 5, 20, 34, 35, and 40.

o SMF Type 30 Subtype 1 - Initiation Record

The SMF type 30 subtype 1 record is written when an initiator selects a batch job, a started task begins, a TSO user logs on, and an APPC/MVS ASCH scheduled TP is selected by an APPC initiator. It contains user identification, programmer's name, accounting information from the JOB statement, and RACF and ACF2 related information.

o SMF Type 30 Subtype 2 - Interval Record

If interval SMF recording is active (see Section 6.2.1.3) and a step has not completed within the interval time period (normally 15, 30, or 60 minutes), an SMF type 30 subtype 2 record is written showing resources consumed over the interval. This SMF record contains all of the same resource measurements as the SMF type 30 subtype 4 step end record, except for the initiator CPU time measures, the amount of SYSIN card images read by the reader, and data space storage, found only in the step end record.

o SMF Type 30 Subtype 3 - Interval End Record

If interval SMF recording is active (see Section 6.2.1.3) and a step ends, a SMF type 30 subtype 3 interval record is written. It contains measures of resource consumption since either the start of the step or start of the last interval. If a step ends before the specified interval duration has elapsed, no SMF type 30 subtype 2 records are produced, just a single SMF type 30 subtype 3 interval end record. It contains all of the same resource measurements as the SMF type 30 subtype 4 step end record, except for the initiator CPU time measures.

o SMF Type 30 Subtype 4 - Step End Record

The SMF type 30 subtype 4 record is written at the end of each job step, TSO session, and started task to record such resource-related data as elapsed time, CPU time, main storage allocated and used, EXCP count by device address, and paging activity for that program. It is written at normal or abnormal termination of the job step or system task.

o SMF Type 30 Subtype 5 - Job Termination Record

The SMF type 30 subtype 5 record is written at the end of each job execution to summarize its resource usage. This record includes the start and stop time for processing of the job by the Reader/Interpreter, the job initiation time and date, the number of steps in the job, accounting information, and the completion code of the last step of the job. It is written at the normal termination of the job.

o SMF Type 33 - APPC/MVS TP Accounting Record

The SMF type 33 record is produced once for each APPC/MVS ASCH standard scheduled TP and represents the complete resource utilization for the TP. For multi-trans TPs, the TP remains in execution between conversation requests from partner TPs. This type of TP is composed of two parts, the TP portion and the multi-trans shell portion. An SMF type 33 record is produced at the completion of each conversation from a requesting partner TP. It is also produced at the completion of each execution of the multi-trans shell portion of the TP. Type 33 records produced for standard TPs and the TP portion of multi-trans TPs contain time stamp information for each event from the moment that APPC/MVS first became aware of the TP request through TP completion. Resource utilization information is limited, but complete accountability of the requesting partner TP is provided. This record is similar to the transaction records provided by applications such as CICS and IMS. The type 33 records produced for the shell portion of a multi-trans TP provide only generic accounting information and minimal time stamps since the shell execution is not related to any particular partner TP.

Figure 1-8e MICS Performance Database Input Based on New Type 30 Series Job Accounting SMF Records

OLD SYSTEM LOG TECHNOLOGY SMF JOB ACCOUNTING RECORDS

If the operating system is pre-MVS/SE2, then the old technology SMF record types must be used.

o SMF Type 20 - Initiation Record

The SMF type 20 record is written when an initiator selects a batch job, or when a started task begins or a TSO user logs on. It contains user identification, programmer's name, accounting information from the JOB statement, and RACF and ACF2 related information.

o SMF Type 4 - Step End Record

The SMF type 4 record is written at the end of each job step and started task to record such resource-related data as elapsed time, CPU time, main storage allocated and used, EXCP count by device address, and paging activity for that program. It is written at normal or abnormal termination of the job step or system task.

o SMF Type 34 - Tso Step Termination

The SMF type 34 record is written when the TSO logoff function processes a job step termination. This record contains operation information such as number of TPUTs issued, number of TGETs satisfied, termination status, TSO session start time, step CPU time, step service, and device allocation start time. It contains the paging information about the VIO data sets. It also has an entry for each non-spooled data set containing the EXCP count and the device address.

o SMF Type 5 - Job Termination

The SMF type 5 record is written at the end of each job execution to summarize its resource usage. This record includes the start and stop time for processing of the job by the Reader/Interpreter, the job initiation time and date, the number of steps in the job, accounting information, and the completion code of the last step of the job. It is written at the normal termination of the job.

o SMF Type 35 - TSO Session Termination

The SMF type 35 record is written at the termination of a TSO session to summarize its resource usage. This record contains execution information such as number of TPUTs issued, number of TGETs satisfied, termination status, TSO session start time, step CPU time, step service, and device allocation start time. It contains the paging information about the VIO data sets. It also has an entry for each non-spooled data set containing the EXCP count and the device address. In addition, it has the session initiation time and date, and accounting information. It is written at the normal or abnormal termination of the session.

o SMF Type 40 - Dynamic DD

The SMF type 40 record is written for each unallocation, concatenation, or deconcatenation request for a data set. This record contains step number, channel address, unit address, and EXCP count for the data set. This can be a high volume record. The second set of SMF record types are the JES type records, the SMF record types 6, 25 (for JES3 only) and 26.

o SMF Type 6 - Output Writer

The SMF type 6 record is written when a writer has finished processing a SYSOUT class or a form within a class. It includes the date and time the writer began processing this job, the number of records written per form number and class, an I/O error flag, and the total number of data sets processed by the writer for this job. MICS currently reads JES2, JES3, External Writer, and PSF generated SMF type 6 records.

o SMF Type 25 - JES3 Device Allocation

The SMF type 25 record is written for each job processed by JES3 main device scheduling and is written after JES3 has scheduled devices for this job. One type 25 record is written for all device allocations required through the user's DD statements for the job. This record contains allocation-related information such as the number of tape and disk volumes fetched and mounted, and the time and date of JES3 device verification.

o SMF Type 26 - Job Purge

The SMF type 26 record is written at job purge time after all SYSOUT for the job is processed. This record may be written much later than the other SMF records on the job because it is not written until all the SYSOUT is processed, including held SYSOUT. This record is critical because it indicates the end of a job and it contains time stamp and network information about the entire job that is not available elsewhere. This record contains operation information such as JES job class, and the start and stop times and dates for the reader, the converter, the execution processor, and the output processor.

Figure 1-8f MICS Performance Database Input Based on Pre-Type 30 Series (Old) Job Accounting SMF Records

OPERATIONS PROCESS ANALYSIS RECORDS

The operations SMF records contain information about IPLs, outages, hardware software, and system configurations. These SMF records are generated as particular system events occur.

o SMF Type 7 - SMF Data Lost

The SMF type 7 record is the first record built when no SMF data sets are available. Data existing in the SMF buffer is written to the newly available SMF data set before record type 7 is built in the buffer. This record contains a count of the SMF records that were not written, and the start and end times of the period during which no records were written.

o SMF Type 8 - I/O Configuration

The SMF type 8 record is written after the IPL of the system is completed and the SET DATE operator command is issued. This record identifies each device that is online at IPL by device class, unit type, channel address, and unit address.

o SMF Type 9 - Vary Online

The SMF type 9 record is written when a VARY ONLINE command is processed. This record identifies the device being added to the configuration by device class, unit type, channel address, and unit address. With ESCON support, the reason for the VARY command is given.

o SMF Type 10 - Allocation Recovery

The SMF type 10 record is written after a successful device allocation recovery. This record identifies the device that is made available by device class, unit type, channel address, and unit address.

o SMF Type 11 - Vary Offline

The SMF type 11 record is written when a VARY OFFLINE command is processed. This record identifies the device being removed from the configuration by device class, unit type, channel address, and unit address. With ESCON support, the reason for the VARY command is given.

o SMF Type 22 - Configuration

The SMF type 22 record is written after every IPL of the system when a VARY CPU or VARY CH operator command is processed, when a VARY STOR operator command is processed, and when a VARY ONLINE,S or VARY OFFLINE,S operator command is processed. This record describes the CPU, channel, storage range, or mass storage device that is varied. It also describes the MSS units online at IPL.

o SMF Type 31 - TIOC Initialization

The SMF type 31 record is written when a MODIFY TCAM operation command is issued. This record contains the number of time-sharing buffers, buffer size, maximum number of output and input buffers allowed per terminal before wait thresholds, and number of buffers reserved on the free queue.

o SMF Type 43 - JES Start

The SMF type 43 record is written during JES initialization. This record contains an indicator for the type JES start, JES initialization deck origin type and contents, and JES procedure name.

o SMF Type 45 - JES Stop

The SMF type 45 record is written during JES termination. This record contains an indicator for the type of JES stop and JES completion code.

o SMF Type 90 - System Status

The SMF type 90 record is written whenever certain operator commands are issued. The record is created for operation and reporting of reliability data and allows the installation to establish availability statistics. MICS uses record subtypes 1 through 18, which are summarized below:

```
SMF  Type 90  Subtype  1 - SET TIME
SMF  Type 90  Subtype  2 - SET DATE
SMF  Type 90  Subtype  3 - SETDMN
SMF  Type 90  Subtype  4 - SET IPS
SMF  Type 90  Subtype  5 - SET SMF
SMF  Type 90  Subtype  6 - SWITCH SMF
SMF  Type 90  Subtype  7 - HALT EOD
SMF  Type 90  Subtype  8 - IPL PROMPT
SMF  Type 90  Subtype  9 - IPL SMF
SMF  Type 90  Subtype 10 - IPL SRM
SMF  Type 90  Subtype 11 - SET OPT
SMF  Type 90  Subtype 12 - SET ICS
SMF  Type 90  Subtype 13 - SET SMF
SMF  Type 90  Subtype 14 - SET MPF
SMF  Type 90  Subtype 15 - SET SMF (Restart)
SMF  Type 90  Subtype 16 - SET DAE
SMF  Type 90  Subtype 17 - SET PFK
SMF  Type 90  Subtype 18 - SET GRSRNL
```

Figure 1-8g   MICS Performance Database Input Based on Operational Process Audit Series SMF Records

RESOURCE MEASUREMENT FACILITY (RMF) SMF RECORDS (TYPE 70-74)

The RMF record types 70 through 79 are used by the MICS MVS Hardware and SCP Analyzer. Following are brief descriptions of these records:

TYPE 70

The type 70 record contains CPU measurement data. It contains CPU wait time and the serial and version numbers for each processor. It indicates the number of jobs and the percentage of jobs in the following states:

o IN - Tasks in real memory on the SRM IN queue.
o IN-READY - Tasks in real memory and ready to execute.
o OUT-WAIT - Tasks not in real memory that are waiting before they will be ready to execute.
o LOGICAL-OUT-READY - Tasks logically swapped out but not yet physically swapped out that are now ready to execute.
o LOGICAL-OUT-WAIT - Tasks logically swapped out but not yet physically swapped out that are waiting.

Type 70 records recognize three different types of jobs - batch, TSO, and started task. For each type the minimum, average, and maximum number of users in the recording interval is captured.

For MVS/XA and MVS/ESA the type 70 record contains the number of I/O interrupts and the number of interrupts for each processor.

TYPE 71

The type 71 record contains Paging and Swapping measurement data. Swapping is the primary way the MVS SRM deals with resource shortages or overutilization.

The type 71 record contains information regarding CSA, LPA, SQA, LSQA, and Private areas. This information includes the minimum, average, and maximum frames used in these areas for both fixed and pageable frames.

Type 71 records also contain paging information. For CSA, LPA, Private VIO, and Private non-VIO areas, RMF records the number of pages read in, the number of pages written out, and the number of pages reclaimed. From this information and the duration of the recording interval, a number of different paging rates are calculated.

TYPE 72

The type 72 record contains Workload measurement data. The overall system workload is divided into groups called Control Performance Groups. These can be subdivided into Performance Periods. The service priorities for each performance group and each performance period can be specified individually by the installation if desired. For each period of each group the type 72 record contains the resources used during the RMF recording interval.

RMF also provides Report Performance Groups. It should be noted that the information captured for Control Performance Groups is also counted in Report Performance Groups. This "multiple-counting" can make the analysis of workload data difficult.

CPU data contained in the type 72 records is in CPU service units, not CPU seconds. This data can be converted to CPU seconds by multiplying by the coefficient appropriate for model and type of CPU. I/O and Memory utilization information is also captured in this record. The number of ended transactions and the total elapsed time of these transactions is also recorded.

TYPE 73

The type 73 record contains Physical and Logical Channel Activity measurement data. The data contains information for each channel path indicating the type of channel and channel busy time. For MVS/370 systems, the data also contains information for each channel concerning the channel busy time, the average queue length, the number of successful requests, and the number of queued requests by category.

TYPE 74

The type 74 record contains Device Activity measurement data. The data contains information for each device about the number of Start Subchannels (SSCHs) or Start I/Os (SIOs) for the device, the number of I/O requests deferred, the device active time, connect time, disconnect time, pending time, and the number of allocations in effect on the device.

Figure 1-8h MICS Performance Database Input Based on Resource Measure Facility Series SMF Records (Type 71-74)

RESOURCE MEASUREMENT FACILITY (RMF) SMF RECORDS (TYPE 75-79)

TYPE 75

The type 75 record contains Page/Swap Data Set Activity measurement data. The data contains information for each page or swap data set. Information captured includes the number of pages transferred, the number of I/O requests, and number of slots available and used for each dataset.

TYPE 76

The type 76 record contains Trace measurement data. The data contains information for each field traced. Information captured includes the field name and its last value.

TYPE 77

The type 77 record contains Enqueue measurement data. The data contains information for each device that was enqueued during the RMF recording interval. Information captured includes the current owner, the waiting users, and the queue length for each enqueue event.

TYPE 78

The type 78 record is called the RMF Monitor I Activity record. The type 78 subtype records are the I/O Queuing Activity record for 308x, 908x, and 4381 processors (subtype 1, the Virtual Storage Activity record (subtype 2), and the I/O Queuing Activity record for ES/3090 and ES/9000 processors (subtype 3).

The I/O Queuing Activity record for 308x, 908x, and 4381 processors (subtype 1) contains information on the I/O configuration, I/O activity rates, and queue lengths recorded for logical control units (LCUs) for 308x, 908x, and 4381 processors.

The Virtual Storage Activity record (subtype 2) contains information concerning the amount of virtual storage reserved for the CSA, MLPA, FLPA, PLPA, SQA, and nucleus, both below and above the 16 megabyte line. The amount of storage allocated for SQA is recorded by subpool and, for CSA, by subpool and storage key. SQA expansion into CSA is also recorded. Private virtual storage usage information is recorded for jobs specified with the RMF Monitor I VSTOR option.

The I/O Queuing Activity record for ES/3090 and ES/9000 processors (subtype 3) contains information on the I/O configuration, I/O activity rates, and queue lengths recorded for logical control units (LCUs) for ES/3090 and ES/9000 processors. This record also contains measurements pertaining to the IOPs (I/O processors) for these processors.

TYPE 79

The type 79 record contains RMF Monitor II measurement data. RMF Monitor II is often run to diagnose a specific problem or to gather more detailed data. Type 79 records are only generated when RMF Monitor II is run as a background session. The type 79 subtype records processed by MICS are Address Space Resource (subtype 2), Real Storage/Processor/SRM (subtype 3), Reserve (subtype 6), and Domain Activity (subtype 10).

The Address Space Resource record (subtype 2) records measurements on CPU time, EXCP count, paging statistics, fixed frames used, and hiperspace pages used for given address spaces.

The Real Storage/Processor/SRM record (subtype 3) records measurements on real storage and expanded storage usage for some storage categories, UIC count, processor utilization, and some of the SRM queues on a system-wide basis.

The Reserve Activity record (subtype 6) records the RESERVE macros that were issued. This can be very useful in a shared DASD environment. Included in the information recorded is the volume serial number, the job that issued the reserve, major and minor resource names, and the status of the reserve.

The Domain Activity record (subtype 10) records information pertaining to SRM domains such as multiprogramming levels, SRM queue lengths, domain contention index, and domain average service rate.

Figure 1-8i   MICS Performance Database Input Based on Resource Measure Facility Series SMF Records (Type 75-79)

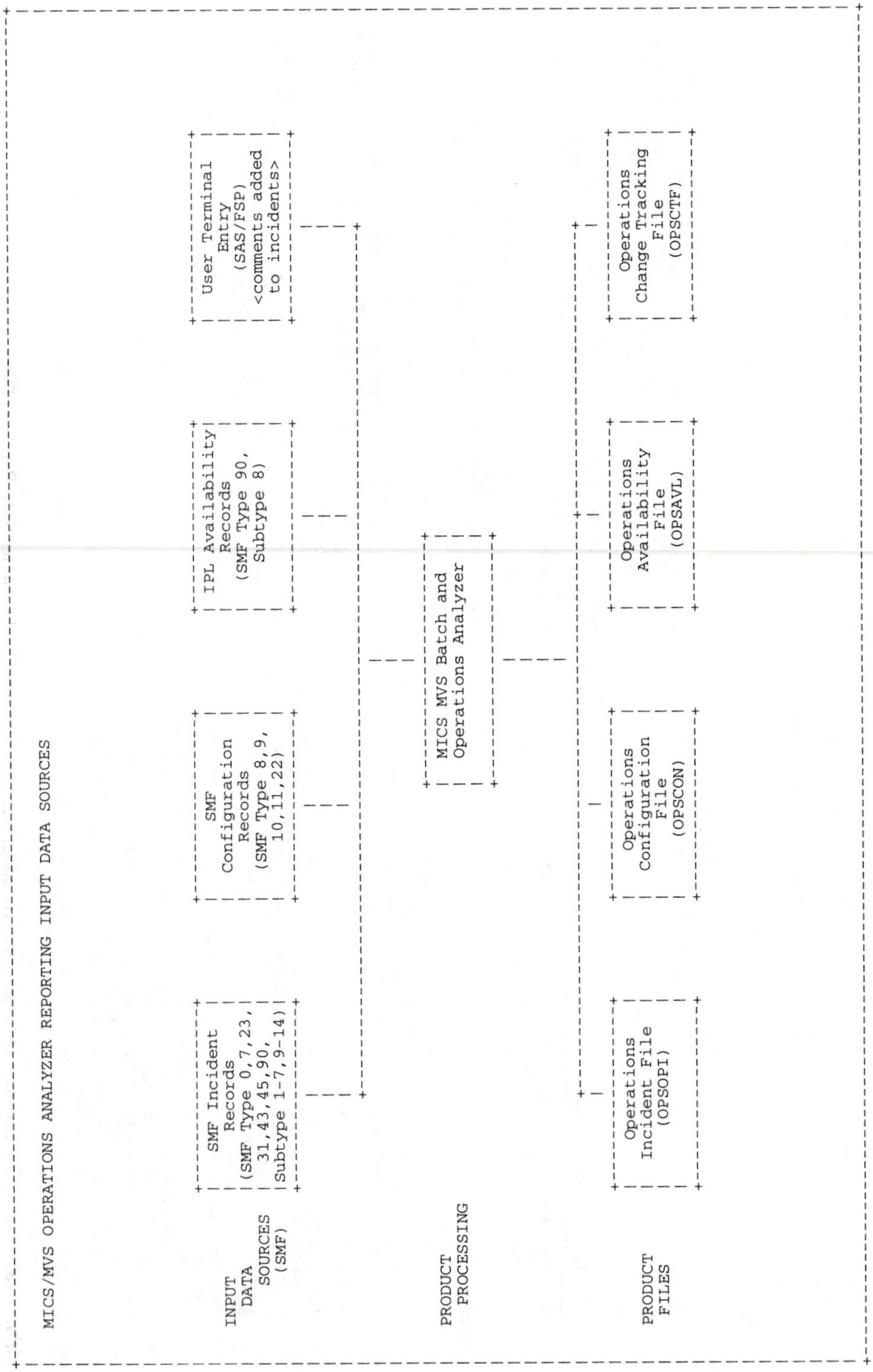

```
MICS/MVS OPERATIONS ANALYZER REPORTING INPUT DATA SOURCES

                       +-------------+         +-------------+         +-------------+         +-------------+
                       | SMF Incident|         |     SMF     |         |     IPL     |         |    User     |
                       |   Records   |         |Configuration|         |Availability |         |  Terminal   |
INPUT                  |(SMF Type 0,7,23,|     |   Records   |         |   Records   |         |    Entry    |
DATA                   | 31,43,45,90,|         |(SMF Type 8,9,|        |(SMF Type 90,|         |  (SAS/FSP)  |
SOURCES                |Subtype 1-7,9-14)|     | 10,11,22)   |         | Subtype 8)  |         |<comments added|
(SMF)                  +-------------+         +-------------+         +-------------+         | to incidents>|
                                                                                              +-------------+


                                                  +--------------------+
                                                  |   MICS MVS Batch and|
PRODUCT                                           | Operations Analyzer |
PROCESSING                                        +--------------------+


                       +-------------+         +-------------+         +-------------+         +-------------+
                       | Operations  |         | Operations  |         | Operations  |         | Operations  |
PRODUCT                |Incident File|         |Configuration|         |Availability |         |Change Tracking|
FILES                  |  (OPSOPI)   |         |    File     |         |    File     |         |    File     |
                       +-------------+         |  (OPSCON)   |         |  (OPSAVL)   |         |  (OPSCTF)   |
                                               +-------------+         +-------------+         +-------------+
```

Figure 1-9a   MVS Operational Program Process SMF Input to MICS Performance Database

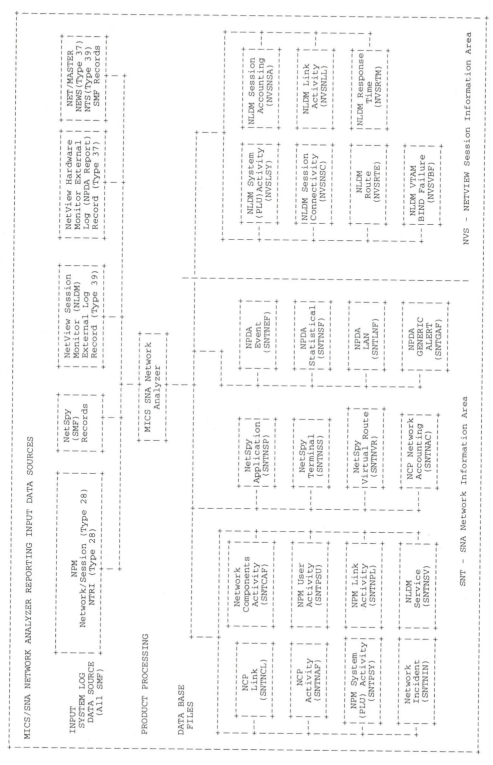

Figure 1-9b SNA System Network Processing SMF Input to MICS Performance Database

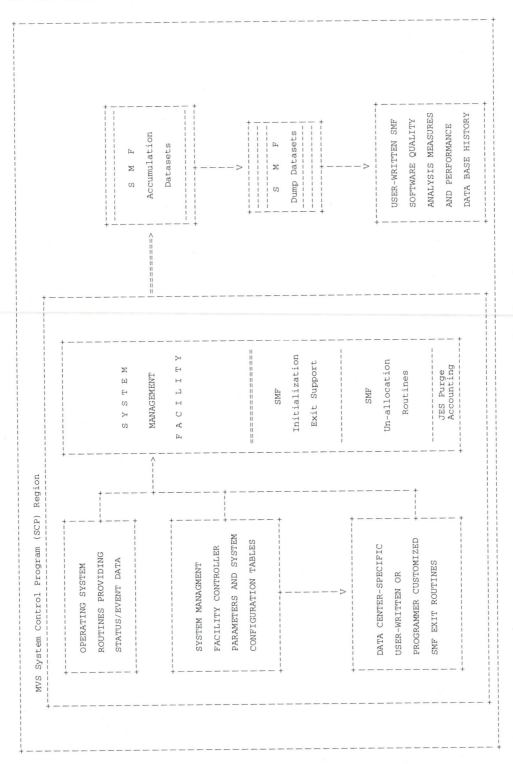

Figure 1-10   General Overview of IBM System Management System (SMF) Operational Processing

incomplete, interrupted, duplicated, or spanned across multiple records. It is the assumption of operating system designers that the application programmers who read system log data will be capable of developing validation edits and coding schemes which can detect all of the common types of problems occurring in system logs and can massage the data to a highly refined state of precision and accuracy.

Although some of the types of problems that occur in system logs can be extremely complicated and cumbersome to detect, such as millisecond phase irregularities or irregular parity problems in bit masks assigned to particular devices, these problems are important in very specialized usages of system logs. This is particularly so with respect to hardware diagnostics and does not normally affect the basic analysis of application software program quality. Basically, the most frequently occurring problems involved in the use of system logs to analyze program quality are related to null data records, which have program identifiers but no data. This is most often the result of a cancelled program or a program that was terminated immediately after it started. The simple response to reading this type of record is to drop or delete it as soon as it is detected. Another type of problem, which occurs much less often, is a duplicate system log record; the simple solution to this type of problem is to sort the records by timestamp, and to then delete records which have identical timestamps and other unique identifiers. To be really safe, delete the exact same data.

All of these complications can be avoided and the process of capturing system log data can be greatly reduced depending on the selection of the programming language. If a system log manager product is used, it becomes a simple matter of specifying the logical category of system log data, and the programming can be done automatically according to the sophistication of vendor products involved. If it is desirable or necessary to develop application programs in-house without the benefit of a system log management facility purchased from one of the many reputable vendors that offer such products, it is critical to have both the system programmer manuals and a complete set of specification manuals for the operating system as well as operating system logs. A more critical matter is that all programs which reference system log data elements must be analyzed and modified according to the specifications of the vendor before each new release of the operating system can be applied. Fortunately, if a vendor's system log management product has been purchased, these changes will be supplied in the form of new versions of their programs. These can simply be loaded to the current installation, and the cost of this update service is no more than any normal maintenance fee charged for any vendor software on the commercial mainframe market.

Regardless of whether the system log load and format management programs are purchased or developed in-house, language and design are both critically important. In the early days of system log management software, programs were written in high-level languages such as COBOL and PL/1. Because of the high volume and condition of the data, these languages resulted in programs that were cumbersome and slower than desirable. Most system log management programs written today are coded in either Basic Assembly Language (BAL), to get the greatest speed, or Statistical Analysis System (SAS) language. The latter is an interpreter language that has slightly slower machine translation than Assembler's facilities but has much more efficient and more precise number crunching than is usually available with high-level languages such as COBOL or PL/1.

If a vendor's system log management product is selected, there will be only a nominal need for application program coding. In most cases, this will take the form of one-statement "exit" programs, or macro code that specifies a single command or condition controlling the processing at the particular decision points where an installation control parameter is specified by a systems analyst. If the product is written in SAS, as most system log management products are, any proficient COBOL, PL/1, or FORTRAN applications programmer will have little difficulty coding these exits, since SAS is very similar to the simple "pseudo-code" used by many structured programming environments to document program design specifications.

SYSTEM ACCOUNTING STANDARDS NEEDED FOR SOFTWARE METRIC AUTOMATION

In most cases, the largest task associated with the administration of a system log management product is the maintenance of cross-referenced tables or files, used by the system log management product to perform system job accounting. The term "job accounting" originated with a method devised by IBM to account for chargeback billing of batch OS job submissions, but has now evolved to refer to online system resource billing as well.

The establishment of the internal standards and naming conventions required in order to classify and track system resources is a major function of job accounting. The effectiveness of this activity can have a critical impact on the level of effort required in order to automate the collection and summarization of system log data. If the names and methods used to assign and assure conformity to internal standards are not consistently applied, the automated software quality measurement process will necessarily be followed by time-consuming and labor-intensive manual audit procedures—in order to resolve and reassign system resource usage that cannot be automatically assigned by the system audit log management programs. If the names or naming conventions overlap or are not unique, there could be a misassignment of resources to summary resource groupings or workloads, without any audit trail data to reassign the resources to the right place. Therefore, the standards that are defined for *tagging* or identifying the source of all system resource usage requests must be applied consistently and, if at all possible, in a totally automated manner. This enforcement of data center standards has in the past been a labor-intensive manual quality assurance function. However, an increasing number of vendor products are released each year that serve to automate most of the tasks related to developing: resource naming convention schemes, cross-referencing of resources, change control, data security, and administration of access to system resources. Most of these new tools are related to the system logs and system log management products, and make use of user-defined system log exits such as those described earlier in order to automatically control operating system self-check functions.

Job accounting involves the specification of account codes, based upon the internal standard names and naming conventions. They are then put into special files or tables required by each operating system before it will release resources to begin any processing activity in any multiprogramming environment. In the case of MVS, these job accounts are entered into a parameter field which is required in the first job card of the JCL in order to submit any batch job or initiate any TSO online session. The general form of the MVS job card is basically according to the following format:

```
//JOBNAME1  JOB   (ACCT1,ACCT2..ACCT9),(other JCL parameters)
```

Up to nine job accounting category codes are available under MVS and supported by most major system log management vendors. As few as one, or all nine accounting codes, can be defined by the system programmers to the system exit modules that manage SMF.

Although there is no industrywide standard for job accounting code categories, the most common include the specification of the customer who will be billed for the system resources used by a job. If the resource usage is internal, then *who*, *what*, or *where* the resource usage can be accumulated to for future reporting purposes. Some of the many possible account code categories include:

- Application System Name or Subsystem Name
- Customer Department or Billable Business Area
- Programming Group or Vendor Responsible for Maintenance
- Operational Type (Production, Test, *Ad Hoc* Reporting, etc.)
- Business Priority (Revenue, Administrative, Legal, etc.)
- Disposition Type (Hardcopy, Database, Transmit, Tape, etc.)

Many other job account categories are possible, including coding categories indicating a special status. These include a new program that should be watched closely because it has been abending frequently, or that the submitter is a new employee, or the job is being submitted by a customer according to a special contractual arrangement with the data center. As for the accounting code tags, they can be any number, name, or combination of both names and numbers.

The important point to remember in assigning these categories is that they are meant for the grouping of summary levels for offline batch analysis of log records. They are also used for real-time SMF exit handling to cancel unauthorized system requests or enforce standards as described earlier. If the purpose is unique to workloads or production process categories, the use of MVS exits related to the CLASS parameter of the job card would probably be more appropriate (and would not overburden SMF exits).

The key point in defining job accounting codes, and the assignment of specific codes under each account, is that an account category should correspond to each business organization or functional area that will ever desire reporting of a unique "cut" or "cross-section" across the entire system resource usage. Each account code within that category should correspond to the lowest level of detail that might ever be needed or requested for "breakout" within that category.

As the system log data is used by more and more areas for more and more diverse functions, an accounting code category will probably have to be added for each function. It is wise not to assign them all before the entire business organization is aware of the potential benefits of system log data to their operations.

It is also important to remember that each time an accounting code category is added, at least one additional performance database, and maybe more, may be added; and each time a new accounting code is added, it is likely that at the very least a new detail line will be added to each report and possibly a new page break for multiple levels that may be assumed within "intelligent" account codes. This may result in multiple "redundant" databases, which involve a different "cut" at the same data, or it may involve a "multiplier effect" in the summary levels within a single system performance database, in which each new accounting code category and all the possible job account code values defined under each category create a single record or observation equal to:

```
ACCT1(x#CODES)xACCT2(x#CODES)...xACCTn(x#CODES)=NUMBER OF RECORDS
```

Each of these two arrangements has its benefits and its drawbacks. The deciding factor should be based on the desire is to keep the data together or separate based upon whether it is *owned* by one area or multiple areas, since both arrangements have tradeoffs with regard to storage costs versus CPU costs to access and process.

2

VENDOR PRODUCTS THAT MANAGE SOFTWARE QUALITY MEASUREMENT DATA

Whatever the arrangement selected for job accounting and system performance databases, the system costs and the time needed to administer the system log data can be greatly reduced by a system log management product purchased from a reputable vendor. The impact of the procedures for administering the system log data upon the all-important costs of technical manpower labor can be greatly influenced in a positive way by the appropriate selection of vendor products supporting those automated software quality measurement functions that are most useful to your individual data center and business organization.

There are four basic categories of system log management products that are currently offered by commercial software vendors. These four basic categories include:

- System Log Data Administration Products
- System Performance Database Management Products
- System Capacity Planning and System Modeling Products
- Application Software Performance Analysis Products

These categories do not include all of the many application areas which make use of system logs to support automated software quality measurement. These and other specialized products will be covered throughout upcoming chapters.

One example from each of the first two categories is presented in this chapter. These are not by any means the only commercially available vendor products in each of these categories. (In fact, in at least one of these categories, over a dozen vendors currently offer products.) However, in each case the product that is being highlighted here, at the time of this writing, is the most commonly licensed product with the greatest market share for its category (according to analysis performed by a leading computer measurement group).

VENDOR SYSTEM LOG PERFORMANCE DATA ADMINISTRATION PRODUCT: MXG

The MXG product is both the most affordable and flexible way to automatically capture and format system log data for all major vendor operating systems. However, although it also handles over 100 other system logs, it was originally developed for SMF and is best known for its robust handling of the MVS operating system.

The MXG vendor-supported SAS code library handles SMF for batch processing, as well as such important IBM facilities as CICS, IMS, TSO, CMS, and POWER. Additional system logs and related system data records are also handled by MXG, including CICS Journal records, VM Accounting records, VM-Monitor records, DOS/VSE, ROSCOE, Netspy, NetView, ORACLE, and VTOC's as well as DB2 database access and audit logs. The MXG vendor strives to handle "every raw record on the face of the earth" and is constantly in the process of adding new system logs continuously as they are announced by all major operating system vendors. Notably, MXG has always been the first to decode every major system log.

MXG was developed entirely by one extremely talented, and boundlessly energetic, legendary operating systems programmer: Dr. Barry Merrill of Merrill Consultants in Dallas, Texas. The MXG product was developed over the course of a decade, between 1972 and 1980. MXG product development is closely linked with both the evolution and IBM's refinement of the SMF system log and the growth of the SAS Institute from an academic project on a North Carolina university campus to the major worldwide commercial software vendor organization that it is today.

The origins of MXG are the result of an unprecedented level of professional cooperation and technical information sharing between such world-class business data processing operations as State Farm, Computer Language Research, Sun Oil, and Texas Instruments, as well as a major commitment by IBM to address the needs and concerns of its customers through the auspices of its two mainframe user groups, GUIDE and SHARE. What began as the nation's first computer measurement project at State Farm in 1972, eventually led to the creation of a new special interest group, known as the Computer Measurement Group (CMG). This group has been instrumental in defining customer requests for the enhancement of SMF system log measurements, as well as the enhancement of IBM's performance monitoring capabilities for the past two decades.

As a systems programmer at State Farm in 1972, Barry Merrill noticed a four-line classified advertisement in the back of a DATAMATION magazine that described a new number crunching and reporting language named the *Statistical Analysis System* (SAS). SAS was the result of a North Carolina State University research project. After sending away for literature, Merrill was able to immediately recognize the power and potential of the new language in order to more efficiently read and process IBM System Management Facility (SMF) system logs.

State Farm, and all other IBM customers, had been struggling with both BAL and high-level compiled procedural languages as source for the programs to read SMF. This required extensive and complicated input data structure housekeeping in order to manipulate and handle the cumbersome file structure of SMF—which was of variable length with complex positional alignment changes in some data variables depending on other variables that had to be referred to individually for each record processed. The SAS language, on the other hand, afforded the significant benefit of doing all of the housekeeping for the programmer by making implicit calls to external compiled FORTRAN, BAL, and PL/1 routines based on the interpretation of a small set of parameters passed from simple SAS data steps or procedures call *statements.*

Merrill convinced State Farm to purchase the SAS package—which at that time cost little more than what a single day of programmer labor costs today—and was quickly able to develop a small library of SAS programs that could read every SMF record type and measure needed in order to solve all of State Farm's current and future software performance problems. Merrill thus became "the first customer of SAS and the first SAS programmer" (a fact that is recognized by SAS Institute as part of their new employee orientation exam even today). Merrill quickly spread the word of the many benefits of SAS when he attended an early IBM SHARE user group meeting and made a presentation on the use of SAS to read SMF system logs. Immediately after an IBM representative presented a report about a very complex system that he had been working on to reliably extract just a few measurments from just six basic record types, Merrill presented a report that showed how State Farm could reliably extract hundreds of measurements from dozens of SMF record types using just a few dozen lines of SAS programming language code. Since IBM itself was not able to duplicate this feat with several thousand lines of code, the IBM user community—as well as IBM—immediately took notice.

To make a long story short, SHARE and IBM established a new, special interest user group within SHARE just to address computer performance metrics and measurement issues related to the enhancement of SMF. This was done in order to give MVS customers an opportunity to help determine the ongoing strategic directions of IBM mainframe architectures and to give IBM customers the opportunity to get the best performance possible out of their IBM hardware and software. The response by IBM to address the satisfaction of their customers in this way is one reason why IBM came to be known as one of the best service organizations in the world during the 1970s. It is also the reason why the SMF system log for MVS is the most extensive and meaningful system measurement log of any operating system. This richness of detail in the SMF system log, and the willingness of IBM to satisfy its MVS customer requests for this level of detail, is probably the main reason why MVS has been one of the most successful operating systems ever marketed. It is also important to note that SMF was primarily designed to satisfy IBM customer requests for more data about what was happening in the system, rather than withholding information as most other vendors had done.

As SMF system log measurements were refined and expanded based on the requests by IBM customers, Merrill continued to be the first to code SAS programs to manage each new SMF measure. During this same time period, the SAS Institute was growing into one of the largest commercial mainframe software vendors in the United States. During the late 1970s, Merrill received his doctorate from Purdue and chose "Use of SAS Language to Analyze Computer Performance" as his doctoral thesis topic. At about that same time, SAS Institute requested that Merrill write a book based on his doctoral thesis. This book was sold by the SAS Institute beginning in 1980, along with a growing number of sample SAS programs for Computer Performance Evaluation (which was named MXG), marketed by the SAS Institute until 1990. Since 1990, both MXG and the book are marketed by Merrill Consultants.

Since it was first introduced, the purchase price of MXG has never exceeded $1,200 per site license, and annual maintenance fees ($500) are so low that industry analysts have observed it is barely enough money to cover a vendor's normal paperwork costs. The MXG product is currently marketed exclusively by the CPE consulting firm Merrill established in the early 1980s. Merrill has often stated that he has no intention of ever raising the price of MXG. Merrill's vision has been to price MXG low enough to elevate the product to being the national standard for SMF system log data collection. He strives to be the first to support every other system log in the world as well.

Over 4,500 commercial and academic sites have purchased MXG for use in their mainframe computer centers, and any site that does not have it should certainly get it. It is not only an outstanding software bargain, but it is also important for all American data processing installations to be using the same system log data structures and system measurement formulas. There are currently over 40,000 software performance measurements defined in the MXG product to support the major system logs in use today—which should give an indication of the serious need for standardization of the input record formats and methods of calculating system log measurements. The potential number of opportunities for an inaccurate system log record format alignment or miscalculation if each data center develops and maintains their own programs to read system log inputs is phenomenal.

MXG aims to assure that all comparisons between different data centers will always be a matter of comparing "apples to apples," and there will be no need to convert and recalibrate benchmarks—or conduct extensive EDP audits to confirm that two performance data sources are both reading data from the same position in the system logs or using the same methods to calculate system measurements.

The MXG system log management product arrives as a tape Partitioned Data Set (or CMS MACLIB) library with over 1,400 SAS programs, amounting to over 450,000 lines of sourcecode. The tremendous value of this product can easily be determined by applying the Function Point productivity factor for statistical languages to this volume of sourcecode, which yields an estimate of equivalent manpower to produce this volume of programs at somewhere over 150 man-years of effort and a commercial product value easily over 1,000 times greater than the purchase price.

The practical, let alone potential, benefits of MXG to a data center are so great that they are almost impossible to quantify. The savings from standardization and elimination of system log decoding analysis, documentation, and load program maintenance of a single SMF record type more than justifies the expenditure for MXG, which is continually updated and expanded as new system log records and measurements are added every year. Costs of software development for the Merrill organization are acknowledged as the lowest of any major worldwide vendor, due to the low overhead and high productivity that goes into the support of MXG. There is no corporate bureaucracy at Merrill Consultants, so new MXG products can be fully developed and documented in less time than it takes for a large vendor to write and approve design specifications.

Although MXG can be used with the SAS Display Manager in an online TSO session, it is primarily a batch product with limited online capabilities. For the most part, however, this is not a problem, since all of the extensive SAS reporting and graphing capabilities are processed in batch mode, and most types of basic analysis of software quality must be distributed and communicated in a hardcopy form. Although the MXG product is primarily a tool that is designed for system log data adminstration rather than in-depth performance analysis, it nonetheless comes with a wide variety of demonstration performance analysis programs providing reports on basic Computer Performance Evaluation functions.

MXG can be used in combination with a corporate transfer pricing and cost allocation or chargeback billing system in order to provide data that is extremely valuable to the business organization as a whole. MXG can also be used to develop a comprehensive *Performance Database* (PDB) to serve complex cross-vendor configurations. One of the strongest selling points of MXG is that a data center can selectively load only the system log measurement variables that the data center technical staff decides to install. This is notably not the case with any other system log management or performance database product. Merrill's recommendations for essential performance data detail level for most data centers results in a five-year trending database that can be stored on less than five cylinders of DASD. Competing products often will not allow the data center to drop any measurements, which can result in up to 350 cylinders of DASD (or more) to support another PDB product.

Examples of the types of SAS reporting programs that are provided by MXG are shown in Figures 2-1a to 2-1l. Although these are very basic software quality measurement reports, the MXG product libraries include hundreds of programs which in turn produce several hundred sophisticated software performance analysis and system trending reports that may require some specialized CPE training in

M X G

Environmental Subsystem	Computer Performance Software Quality Measure	Service-Level Objective Goal
BATCH	Percentage of batch job program executions meeting requested IWT (Initiation Wait Times) measured by SMF jobclasses of 15 min., 30 min., 1 hour, 2 hours or 4 hours	94 %
TSO	Trivial transactions meeting 4-second internal response as measured by SMF (TSO/MON name table defines trivial limit	92 %
IMS	IMS queue met expected response time according to customer-required service level objective measured by IMS system log	95 %
IMS	IMS transaction service time met customer defined service agreement measured by CONTROL/IMS log	98 %
CICS	FAST transactions met 4-second response measured by PAII system log, with class FAST assigned if AMCT I/O is less than 5	92 %

Figure 2-1a   General MXG Computer Performance Evaluation Workload Environment Service Objective Reports

M X G

Weekly MVS Batch Program Process Workloads Software Quality Performance Report for All Application Groups

WORKLOADS	15 Minutes		1 Hour		4 Hours		Overnight	
	Jobs met service goal (%)	Jobs at this priority (%)	Jobs met service goal (%)	Jobs at this priority (%)	Jobs met service goal (%)	Jobs at this priority (%)	Jobs met service goal (%)	Jobs at this priority (%)
All Groups	96 %	7 %	94 %	31 %	93 %	42 %	99 %	20 %
Group A	92 %	11 %	91 %	26 %	91 %	40 %	100 %	23 %
Group B	99 %	4 %	95 %	35 %	90 %	43 %	99 %	18 %
Group C	100 %	6 %	94 %	32 %	96 %	41 %	99 %	21 %

Objectives:

* 90 % of programs must meet service time objective as assigned or requested
* 10 % or less of a group's programs can be submitted for execution in the 15-minute category

Figure 2-1b   General MXG Computer Performance Evaluation Service Objective Reporting for Batch Programs

M X G

TSO Workload Group Response Time Performance Report

WORKLOADS	% in 2 Sec	% in 4 Sec	% in 8 Sec	% in 30 Sec	Count of Trans	Avg Resp Sec	% of Trans
All Groups							
Trivial	69	80	88	97	206,364	9.6	100
	82	88	92	97	105,624	6.2	51
Nontrivial	55	72	85	96	100,740	13.2	49
Group A							
Trivial	66	80	91	98	52,670	6.7	100
	86	93	97	99	17,403	5.7	33
Nontrivial	51	71	87	98	35,267	7.1	67
Group B							
Trivial	70	80	87	97	153,694	12.5	100
	81	87	91	97	88,221	6.7	57
Nontrivial	57	73	84	96	65,473	19.3	43

Number of Sessions   3384

Average Users Logged On   63

Maximum Users Logged On   101

Average Session Duration   54   minutes

Figure 2-1c   General MXG Computer Performance Evaluation Service Objective Reporting for TSO Programs

M X G

Daily Computer Center IMS Performance Measurement Report

August 15, 1992

Service Time

APPLICATION CATEGORY	Volume (%)	Goal	Half Goal	The Goal	Twice Goal
Credit Card	19826 (47.4%)	1.0	83.9%	95.9%	99.1%
Accounts Payable	5825 (13.9%)	1.0	93.4%	99.0%	99.8%
Collections	10639 (25.4%)	1.5	90.0%	98.9%	99.8%
Purchasing	2651 (6.3%)	4.0	88.4%	98.1%	99.6%
Inventory	1774 (4.2%)	6.5	85.9%	96.7%	99.2%
Insurance	336 (0.8%)	12.0	84.5%	96.6%	98.4%
Payroll	768 (1.8%)	6.5	85.7%	96.8%	98.3%
Total	41819 (100.0%)				

Input Queue Time

APPLICATION CLASS	Volume (%)	Goal	Half Goal	The Goal	Twice Goal
001	2240 (5.4%)	0.5	95.8%	98.2%	99.6%
002	9773 (23.4%)	1.0	98.7%	99.7%	99.9%
003	6845 (16.4%)	4.0	87.2%	91.9%	96.0%
004	314 (0.8%)				
005	2822 (6.7%)	4.0	82.2%	88.1%	94.2%
006	19825 (47.4%)	1.0	95.4%	98.0%	99.3%
Total	41819 (100.0%)	.	93.9%	96.7%	98.5%

Figure 2-1d   General MXG Computer Performance Measurement Reporting for IMS Service Objectives

M X G

PDB Analysis - HIUSEAGE Report - High Resource Program Usage

All Programs Ranked in Highest 50 on Any Resource

Performance Factors

APPLICATION PROGRAM NAME	TCB Ranks	SRB Ranks	EXCP Rank	Page Rank	Elapsed Rank	Total Times
EASYTREVR	1	1	1	1	1	4931
SORT	5	2	6	2	2	1023
IEWL	14	11	14	3	10	1011
XREF	11	5	5	4	8	352
ADRLIBR	12	9	9	5	5	1603
CPLAGON	3	6	15	6	7	219
IEBGENER	13	7	10	7	3	1155
IKFCBLOO	4	12	7	8	9	522
PGM=*.DD	7	4	8	9	4	256
DBULTRG	8	23	25	10	16	21
IERRCOOO	17	19	22	11	14	486
DBMALTGG	21	18	19	12	18	31
EAMATOLU	20	21	11	13	20	44
DPROOFU	2	15	17	14	12	38
ETBILDUG	10	17	13	15	15	22
DTAB49	9	8	12	16	6	44
WYLISTR	25	25	21	17	24	346
DSDUMP	16	10	3	18	13	227
IEHLIST	18	13	16	19	17	196
PCSTRUN	15	14	4	20	19	21
GGAL3164	6	3	2	21	11	23
DGPROBM	19	16	18	22	21	34
DATTESTR	24	24	20	23	25	333
IEHPROGM	23	20	23	24	22	33
IEFBR14	22	22	24	25	23	174

Figure 2-1e   MXG Computer Performance Measurement Reporting of High Resource Consuming Programs

M X G

Monthly Application Program Process Abend Analysis

Process Quality Factors

Message Return Codes:	Group A	Group B	Group C	Group D	TOTAL
JCL ERRORS:	357	109	446	204	1116
S00	888	206	1090	501	2685
04	371	85	428	136	1020
08	290	22	118	127	557
12	119	25	266	207	617
16	83	11	203	26	323
Other	25	63	75	5	168

SYSTEM Abend Codes:	Group A	Group B	Group C	Group D	TOTAL
x01	18	6	30	6	60
x06	9	4	17	4	33
x0A	1	-	2	6	9
x13	65	11	106	29	211
x37	20	4	49	13	86
x3B	9	-	6	-	15
x3D	3	-	-	-	3
0C1	12	2	9	2	25
0C2	5	1	4	-	10
0C3	15	-	-	-	15
0C4	8	2	21	1	32
0C5	44	-	13	-	57
0C6	2	4	30	6	42
0C7	-	3	8	-	11

USERS Abend Codes:	Group A	Group B	Group C	Group D	TOTAL
Total	28	15	39	50	132
TOTAL	4491	2147	7225	3179	17042

Figure 2-1f MXG Computer Performance Measurement Report of Monthly Accumulated Program Abends

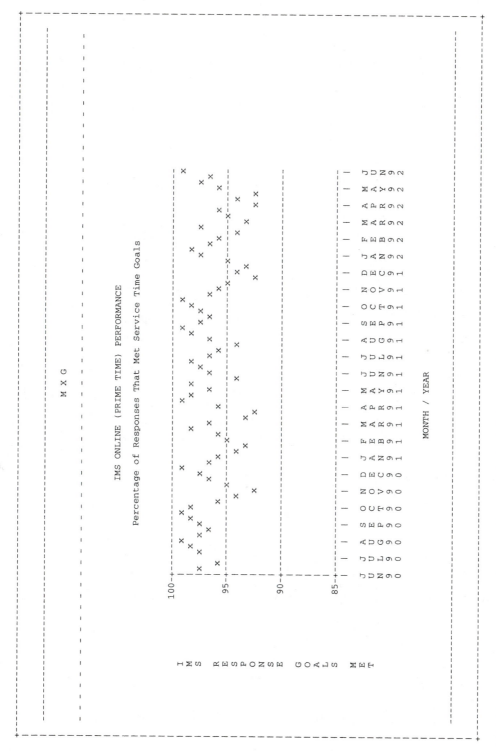

Figure 2-1g   MXG Computer Performance Measurement Plot of IMS Service Response Time Meeting Goals

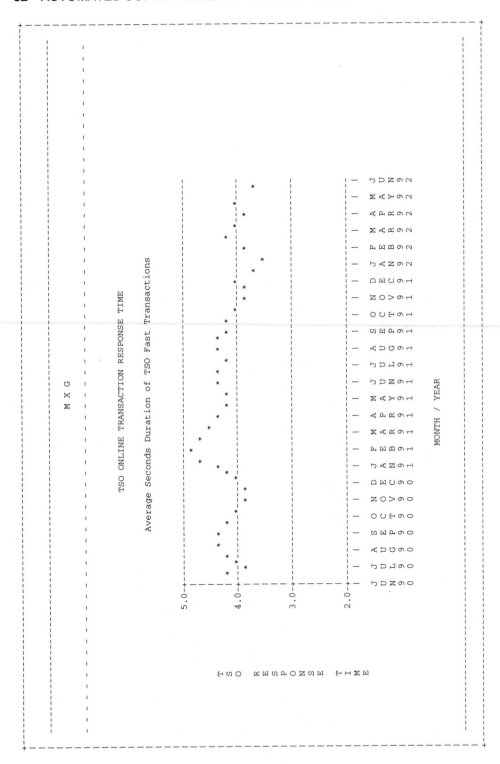

Figure 2-1h   MXG Computer Performance Measurement Plot of TSO Fast Class Transaction Response Time

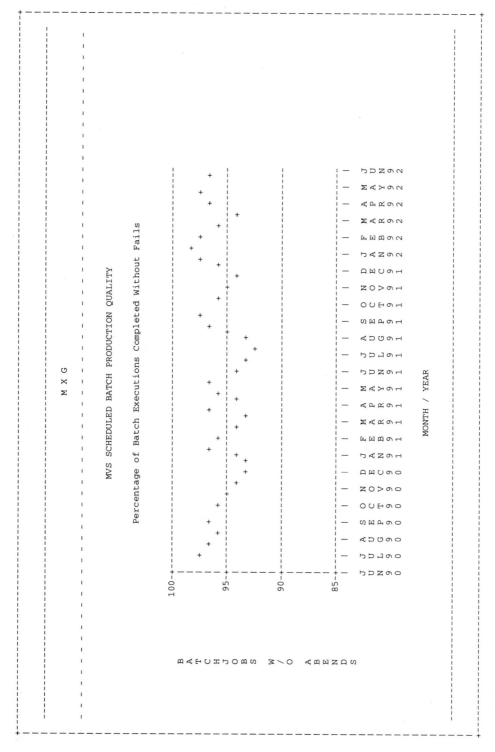

Figure 2-1i   MXG Computer Performance Measurement Plot of Scheduled Production Batch Process Quality

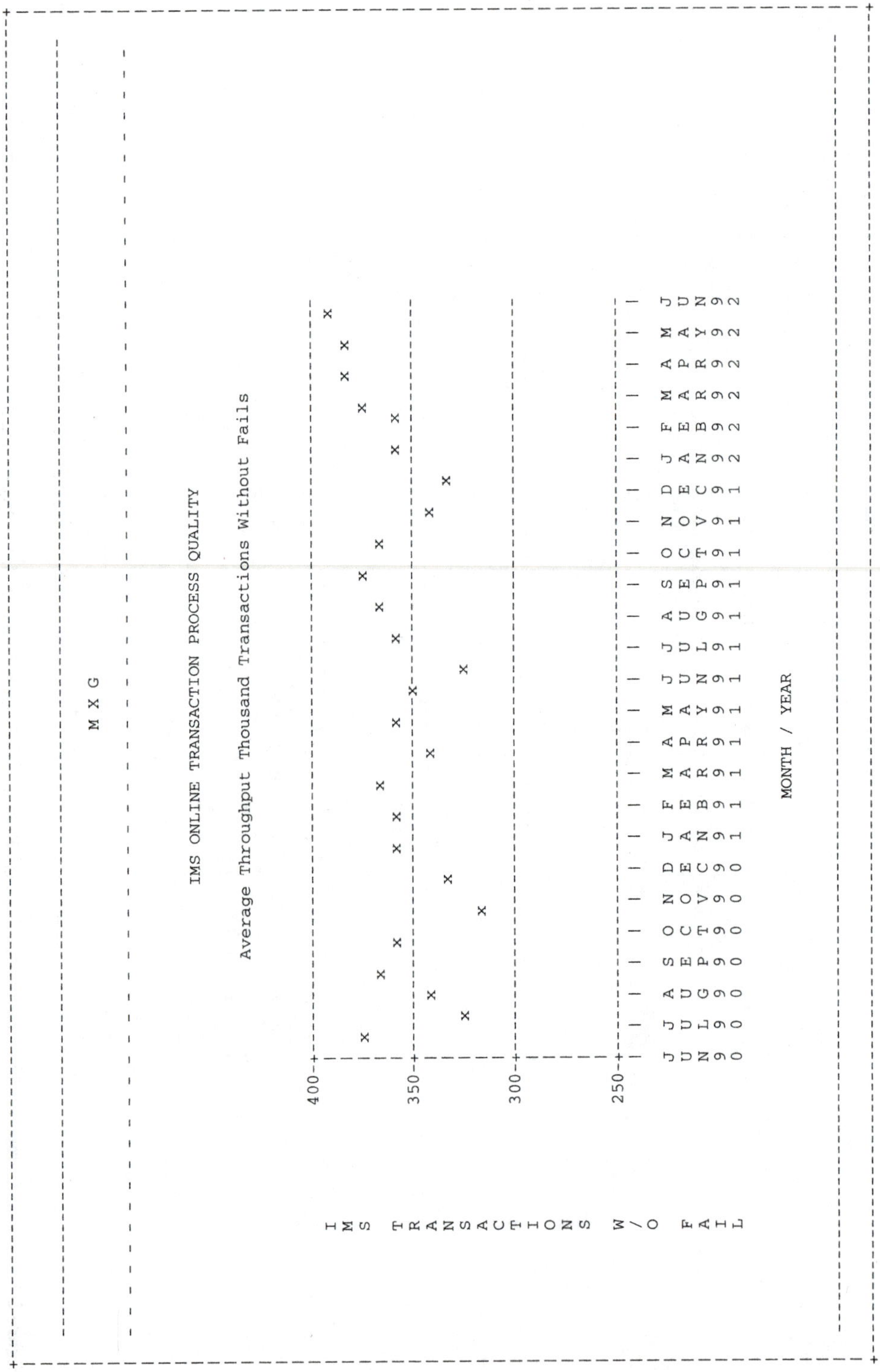

Figure 2-1j MXG Computer Performance Measurement Plot of IMS Transactions between Online Fails

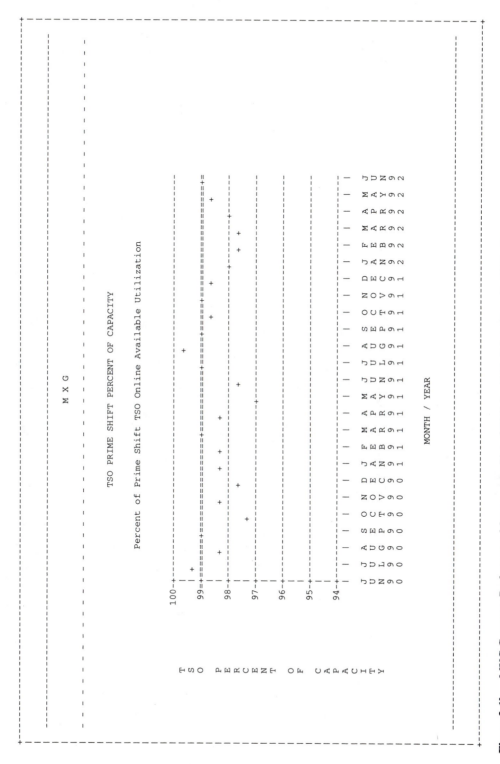

Figure 2-1k   MXG Computer Performance Measurement Plot of TSO Available Prime Capacity Utilization

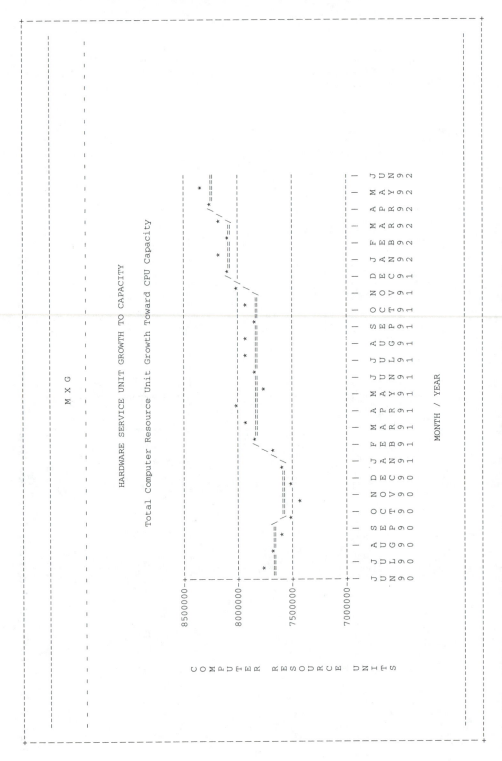

Figure 2-11   MXG Computer Performance Measurement Plot of Total Computer Resource Units Growth

order to realize their full benefits. Merrill Consultants and the SAS Institute work together to offer CPE training throughout the year, both in Dallas and Cary, North Carolina.

VENDOR SYSTEM PERFORMANCE DATABASE MANAGEMENT PRODUCT: MICS

The *MVS Integrated Control System* (MICS) product was developed shortly after MXG by another renowned leader in the computer performance evaluation field, Dr. Mario Marino of Marino Associates in Vienna, Virginia. Marino Associates has since merged with Duquesne Associates of Pittsburgh, Pennsylvania, to form a new company named Legent. Legent has enhanced MICS and developed a wide range of additional MICS-integrated system performance database component products. Like MXG, BEST/1, and most other major system log retrieval and management products, MICS is written in SAS language and uses the full complement of SAS formats and advanced statistical facilities for generation of its reports.

The major difference between MICS and MXG, is that MICS has a more extensive online database update and management capability, provides in-depth standard performance analysis reporting, and provides the basis for an integrated performance database environment that supports real-time monitoring and analysis of the ongoing operations of multiple operating system environments. Whereas MXG provides raw data formatting for every system log in the known world, MICS has concentrated on the top dozen or so system logs most often interconnected to IBM's MVS host mainframes. These are the most common central processors for large-scale, business data processing in the world today.

This narrower focus has enabled the MICS Legent vendor to develop an unparalleled dominance of MVS-centralized data center performance reporting. MICS continues to stay ahead of all competition, even as the world of IBM host mainframe technology becomes ever more complex. Despite the added complexity of SAA strategies and extended features for both SNA network and MVS processor technology, MICS continues to provide superior capability for standardized reporting. It is precisely this depth and variety of reporting (several thousand standard performance reporting formats are currently supported), that is consistently cited by data center management customers of MICS as the primary reason for purchasing MICS products. They want to be certain their technical staff has the opportunity to see the same performance reporting tools as other data centers, especially if there is any competition between them.

However, this considerable capability has a much higher price tag than MXG. MICS is not the outcome of a user group committee's specifications or a product developed with the support of public funding. MICS was developed privately for proprietary commercial marketing, and the costs are much more similar to other OEM and IBM value-added, vendor pricing arrangements.

Depending on the hardware configuration that is supported and the number of add-on products that are licensed, the cost of MICS currently ranges from $10,000 to $100,000 (or even more) per year, making it the most expensive system log management product on the market. MICS may be too costly for many small IBM mainframe data centers, but for those that can afford it, MICS is widely recognized and well worth the price.

MICS is regarded by most system performance analysts as the state-of-the-art in performance database management. It generally provides a much greater level of detail *granularity* than has been normally possible with MXG. MICS data is summarized to individual events occurring within individual hours of the day by customer zones or conditional categories of usage. It allows selection of very specific events or activities that are monitored either separately or within other workloads or zones. This capability makes MICS the ideal product if precision audit functionality is desired, or if the data center is a multiprocessing environment that requires a lot of cross-checking of resource impact across functional areas. However, this level of precision and sophisticated functionality requires substantially more system resources to process. Plus, the costs of storing the average MICS performance database details are all but beyond the budgets of only the largest corporate business or government data centers in the United States.

One of the most popular aspects of the Base MICS product is the online MICS Information Center Facility, which is a TSO/ISPF, menu-driven workstation. This online facility can be used to conduct inquiries against the MICS databases, or to conduct real-time analysis of ongoing operational environments.

Though the MICS online facility is normally processed under MVS, it can also be linked to VM, CMS, VAX, and SNA network environments. Each of these add-on environments must be licensed in addition to MICS Base product. However, this can raise yearly MICS product costs even higher.

For the data centers that can afford it, MICS performance database products have easily paid for themselves within reasonable ROI periods for financing and full recovery of costs. Legent offers several impressive examples of how effective the MICS system log management product can be at improving quality and cutting costs.

In one example, Legent cites a large national retail business that was able to improve the efficiency of their operations and reduce costs by 30 percent per year, with over $35 million in savings over a four-year period. In another example, MICS helped trim capital spending of a leading U.S. steel manufacturer by over $32 million over a two-year period, which resulted in reducing operating expenses by over $25 million per year. These are impressive statistics, but even more impressive is the fact that MICS customers have consistently achieved savings of 20 percent or more when standardized threshold management reports are used.

The MICS product requires a less sophisticated understanding of the SAS programming language than MXG. MICS was designed to be more of a turnkey system than the MXG system log administration toolkit libraries. MICS can also provide more powerful leverage capabilities to advanced performance analysts already proficient in the SAS language and advanced computer performance evaluation techniques.

The standard reports that are available from Legent make precise recommendations for the improvement of data center operations without the need for sophisticated system performance analysis skills. Yet some of the more complicated MICS reports can certainly benefit from the expertise of a trained computer performance analyst or certified quality analyst professional.

The Base MICS product currently consists of over 1.5 million lines of SAS sourcecode. When considering the cost of every MICS add-on component, the MICS product has a productivity value factor over 200 times better than the cost. MICS products have consistently demonstrated at least a four times greater, value-added benefit to business organizations that the data center operation serves.

Examples of the MICS online workstation facility menu screens and standard threshold management reports are shown in Figures 2-2a to 2-2x. Reports can be accessed in online sessions via the MICS online workstation facility on MVS/TSO using ISPF. They can also be combined with other SAS Graph functions and routinely produced on demand. There are currently several hundred MICS datasets summarizing critical performance data from the system logs, and a typical MICS configuration has several thousand individual SAS variables that can be automatically collected on a daily basis.

It is probably worth noting that the Legent Corporation has been repeatedly identified as a potential target for takeover by investment groups who have noticed the substantial value of the MICS product line. Legent has also been involved in two mergers with other commercial IBM-host mainframe, value-added software vendors within the last decade: Duquesne Systems, the developer of the SAS

```
/-------------------- ISPF/PDF PRIMARY OPTION MENU --------------------\
|OPTION ===> MWF                                                        |
|                                                       USERID - yourid |
|   0   ISPF PARMS  - Specify terminal and user parameters  TIME   - 10:19 |
|   1   BROWSE      - Display source data or output listings TERMINAL - 3278 |
|   2   EDIT        - Create or change source data      PF KEYS - 24   |
|   3   UTILITIES   - Perform utility functions                         |
|   4   FOREGROUND  - Invoke language processors in foreground          |
|   5   BATCH       - Submit job for language processing                |
|   6   COMMAND     - Enter TSO command or CLIST                        |
|   7   DIALOG TEST - Perform dialog testing                            |
|   8   LM UTILITIES- Perform library management utility functions      |
|   C   CHANGES     - Display summary of changes for this release       |
| MWF   MICS        - MICS Workstation Facility (MWF)                   |
|   T   TUTORIAL    - Display information about ISPF/PDF                |
|   X   EXIT        - Terminate ISPF using log and list defaults        |
|                                                                       |
|Enter END command to terminate ISPF.                                   |
|                                                                       |
|                                                                       |
|                                                                       |
|                                                                       |
\----------------------------------------------------------------------/
```

Figure 2-2a Selecting MICS from TSO ISPF/PDF Primary Option Menu

Billing Database Facility (also known as BDBF), and the Goal Systems Corporation, which is most widely known for its automated data center operational support products. In both cases, Legent has accomodated their products into the Legent-Marino product line, with support for the customers of the merged product continuing for a reasonable period of time. Legent customers continue to be among the

```
/-------------------- MICS Workstation Facility (MWF) --------------------\
|Option ===>                                                              |
|                                                                         |
|                                                                         |
|      1 - Documentation Access (DOC)                                     |
|          Browse, print, and/or cross reference MICS Documentation.      |
|      2 - MICS Information Center Facility (MICF)                         |
|          Compose and/or replay MICS Data Base inquiries.                |
|      3 - SAS With MICS Libraries (MSAS)                                  |
|          Use interactive SAS with MICS libraries and macros.            |
|      4 - Management Support Applications (APPL)                          |
|          IS Management Alert, Accounting and Chargeback, Capacity Planner, |
|          MVS Performance Manager, StorageMate, and Network Service       |
|          Reporter.                                                      |
|      5 - System Administrator Functions (MAF)                           |
|          Status and tracking, operation, installation, modification,    |
|          maintenance, and authorization.                                |
|      T - Tutorial                                                       |
|      X - Exit                                                           |
|                                                                         |
|                                                                         |
\------------------------------------------------------------------------/
```

Figure 2-2b Online Host MICS Workstation Facility (MWF) Panel

```
/-------------------- Management Support Applications  --------------------\
|Option ===>                                                               |
|                                                                          |
|                                                                          |
|      1 - I/S Management Alert (IMA)                                       |
|          Define and modify parameters, or online data entry.             |
|      2 - Accounting and Chargeback                                        |
|          Modify parameters, execute operational jobs, run reports,       |
|          and enter application files data.                               |
|      3 - Capacity Planner                                                 |
|          Define and update capacity planning data base files and perform |
|          forecasting analysis.                                           |
|      4 - MVS Performance Manager                                          |
|          Analyze performance of MVS systems.                             |
|      5 - StorageMate                                                      |
|          Report and analyze storage resources.                           |
|      6 - Network Service Reporter Administration                          |
|          Maintain Network Service Reporter options and outage schedule.   |
|      7 - MVS Model Generation                                             |
|          Define parameters used to generate analytic queueing models.    |
|                                                                          |
\--------------------------------------------------------------------------/
```

Figure 2-2c　MICS/MWF Management Support Applications Menu

most satisfied in independent nationwide DP-industry service ratings. Therefore, regardless of future changes in the business organization marketing MICS, little change can be expected in the level of service that supports the MICS product.

```
/ ---------------------------- MICF Options  ---------------------------\
| Option ===>                                                           |
|                                                                       |
|                                                                       |
|      0 - ISPF Parameters                                              |
|            Specify ISPF parameters for the MICF environment.          |
|      1 - User Profile Parameters                                      |
|            Specify defaults for general MICF parameters.              |
|      2 - Foreground Execution Parameters                              |
|            Specify defaults for foreground MICF inquiry execution.    |
|      3 - Batch Execution Parameters                                   |
|            Specify defaults for batch MICF inquiry execution.         |
|      4 - Printer Format Parameters                                    |
|            Specify defaults for printed report and printer graphics formats.|
|      5 - Color Graphics Format Parameters                             |
|            Specify defaults for color graphic outputs.                |
|      6 - Data Set Allocation Parameters                               |
|            Specify parameters for MICF data set allocation.           |
|                                                                       |
|                                                                       |
|                                                                       |
\-----------------------------------------------------------------------/
```

Figure 2-2d　MICS Information Center Facility Options Menu

```
/----------------------------  SAS Statements  ------------------------------\
|Command ===>                                               Scroll ===> CSR  |
|                                                                            |
|Inquiry Step:  File & Data Element Sel.: PCS - PHYSICAL CHANNEL ACTIVITY FILE |
|Line Cmds: I Insert  D Delete  R Repeat  M Move  C Copy                     |
|                                                                            |
|Cmd  SAS Statements for:  Deriving new data elements and transposing the file |
| -   ------------------------------------------------------------------     |
| _ - %MACRO CAPSMRY;                                                        |
| _   IF CHANNEL = '1' THEN CHAN1BS + PCAPCBSY;                              |
| _   IF CHANCNT = '1' THEN CHAN1CNT + PCASIO;                              |
| _   IF CHANNEL = '2' THEN CHAN2BS + PCAPCBSY;                              |
| _   IF CHANCNT = '2' THEN CHAN2CNT + PCASIO;                              |
| _   IF CHANNEL = '3' THEN CHAN3BS + PCAPCBSY;                              |
| _   IF CHANCNT = '3' THEN CHAN3CNT + PCASIO;                              |
| _   IF CHANNEL = '4' THEN CHAN4BS + PCAPCBSY;                              |
| _   IF CHANCNT = '4' THEN CHAN4CNT + PCASIO;                              |
| _ - %MEND CAPSMRY;                                                         |
|*************************** BOTTOM OF DATA  *******************************|
|                                                                            |
\----------------------------------------------------------------------------/
```

Figure 2-2e   Example of SAS Display Manager Exit Coding Session

```
/-------------------------  MICF Execution  --------------------------------\
|Command ===>                                                                |
|                                                                            |
|Executing MICS Inquiry:  XXC     - CPU Standard Application                 |
|                                                                            |
|Inquiry Execution Mode     ===> BATCH      (BATCH/FOREGROUND)               |
|Override Execution Options ===> N          (Y/N)                            |
|SAS/DMS Options:  Resume   ===> Y          (Y/N)     Output Replay ===> Y (Y/N) |
|                                                                            |
|Press ENTER to execute the inquiry, or press END to cancel execution.       |
|                                                                            |
|--------------------- Batch Job Submission Parameters ---------------------|
|Edit Generated Jobstream%===> Y (Y/N)  Hold Inq. Output for Replay ===> N (Y/N)|
|                                                                            |
|SYSOUT Class  ===> A                     SYSOUT Form  %===> ____            |
|Destination  %===> ____                  SYSOUT Writer%===> _____        |
|SYSOUT Parms.%===> _____   |
|                                                                            |
|Job Card Information:                                                       |
|   ===> //jobname  JOB (accounting information),                            |
|   ===> // MSGLEVEL=(1,1),MSGCLASS=A,PRTY=5                                 |
|   ===> //*                                                                 |
|   ===> //*                                                                 |
\----------------------------------------------------------------------------/
```

Figure 2-2f   MICS Performance Database Inquiry Execution Panel

```
/-------------------- MICS File and Data Element Selection --------------------\
|Command ===>                                              Scroll ===> CSR |
|Enter a ? in any data entry field for more information on valid values.     |
|Composing CAP DB File def.:  WKL - System Workload Example                   |
|                                                                            |
|MICS file ===> CPU (fff) -  CPU PROCESSOR ACTIVITY FILE                      |
|Data base ===> P (Primary)  _          _            _            _          |
|                                                                            |
|Include application unit ===> N (Y/N)     Summarize work file by ===> _____|
|                                                                            |
|Specify MICS file processing exits ===> N (Y/N)                             |
|                                                                            |
|Line Cmds: I Insert  D Delete  R Repeat  M Move  C Copy                      |
|                                                                            |
|Cmd   Name       Data Element Label (long name)      D Tp Len  Output Format |
| -   --------  ------------------------------------- - -- --- -------------- |
| _   CPUMPBS  Average Pct Busy for CPU0 and CPU1     _ N  7    PERCENT.      |
| _   CPUMXT   Max TSO Users                          _ N  7                  |
| _   CPUPC0BS Pct Busy for CPU 0                     D N  7    PERCENT.      |
| _   CPUPC1BS Pct Busy for CPU 1                     D N  7    PERCENT.      |
| _   SYSID    System Identifier                      _ A  4    _____  |
\----------------------------------------------------------------------------/
```

Figure 2-2g   MICS File and Data Element Selection Variable Definition Panel

```
/-------------------- MICS File and Data Element Selection --------------------\
|Command ===>                                              Scroll ===> CSR |
|Enter a ? in any data entry field for more information on valid values.     |
|Composing CAP DB File def.:  WKL - System Workload Example                   |
|                                                                            |
|MICS file ===> CPU (fff) -  CPU PROCESSOR ACTIVITY FILE                      |
|Data base ===> P (Primary)  _          _            _            _          |
|                                                                            |
|Include application unit ===> N (Y/N)     Summarize work file by ===> _____|
|                                                                            |
|Specify MICS file processing exits ===> N (Y/N)                             |
|                                                                            |
|Line Cmds: I Insert  D Delete  R Repeat  M Move  C Copy                      |
|                                                                            |
|Cmd   Name       Data Element Label (long name)      D Tp Len  Output Format |
| -   --------  ------------------------------------- - -- --- -------------- |
| _   MONTH    Month of Year                          _ N  2    _____  |
| _   ZONE     Time Zone (Shift)                      _ A  1    _____  |
|**************************** BOTTOM OF DATA ****************************|
|                                                                            |
|                                                                            |
\----------------------------------------------------------------------------/
```

Figure 2-2h   MICS File and Data Element Edit Validations Panel

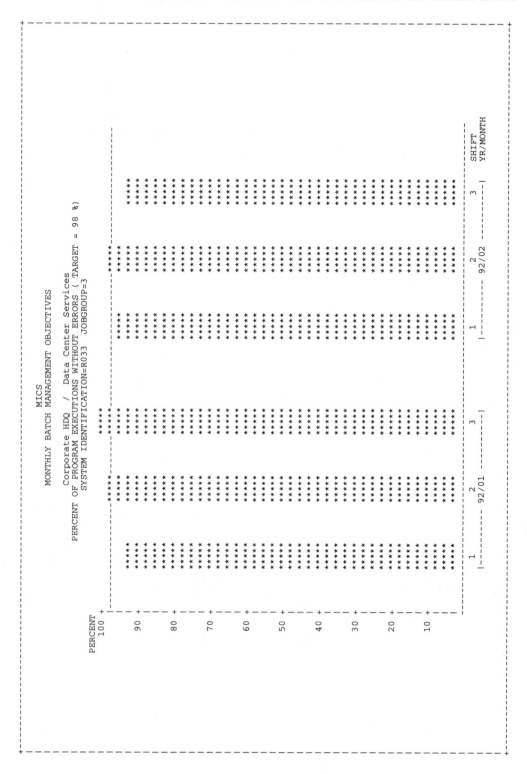

Figure 2-2i   MICS Monthly Batch Program Process Reliability Objective

MICS
Corporate HDQ / Data Center Services
MONTHLY BAT PROGRAM PRODUCT USAGE FINANCIAL ANALYSIS
CHARGING ALGORITHM OF $0.06 PER CPU SECOND, $3.60 PER 1000/EXCPS AND $0.50 PER PROGRAM EXECUTION

PROGRAM	DOLLAR COST	FREQ	BATCOST SUM
IDMSK	**	169	$14085.40
S2000	***	3	$14055.40
INQUIRE	**************************************	3	$10449.70
TSOPRMPT	************************************	53	$9818.11
PROMPTX	************************************	85	$7309.09
RETRIEVE	**********************	122	$4193.99
UNKNOWN	*********************	215	$3935.83
EASYTREV	*******************	47	$3525.92
SMFLOOK	******************	49	$3456.57
AUDIT	*****************	14	$3027.24
VTOCLIST	****************	8	$2692.31
TERMCHK	***************	13	$2193.23
P55G60	**************	65	$2141.29
SAS	**************	86	$2110.91
SAS79	*************	12	$1918.11
PROD4	************	3	$1856.94
OMEGAMON	**********	19	$1789.30
MONITOR	**********	45	$1715.24
PAN#1	********	13	$1443.14
PASSWD	********	32	$1399.11
PRINTER	********	139	$1138.01
PRECOMP	********	4	$1326.49
INTRDR	*******	50	$1324.83
EXIT78	*******	3	$1255.31
IEBCOPY	*******	128	$1179.78
TEMPNAME	****	62	$869.34
IKKA0034	****	14	$827.68
IEBGENER	****	48	$727.58
CALLS	****	181	$726.20
IEFBR14	***	6	$639.83
AXGLIST	***	27	$629.65
PASSER	**	15	$588.71
PROCALL	**	6	$493.78
XYU020AC	**	14	$488.45
IFOX00	**	49	$477.05
TRACK	**	60	$454.21
TSOQBE	**	3	$413.28
DUPLEX	**	22	$383.18
PROJECT2	**	12	$382.16
SPSS	**	16	$354.27
MYOWN	**	1	$345.28
TMS	**	9	$336.87
LOADMTCH	**	5	$324.67
TSMDRVR	**	5	$324.50

```
        2000.00   4000.00   6000.00   8000.00   10000.00   12000.00   14000.00
```

Figure 2-2j   MICS Monthly Batch Program Process Execution Cost Pareto Rank

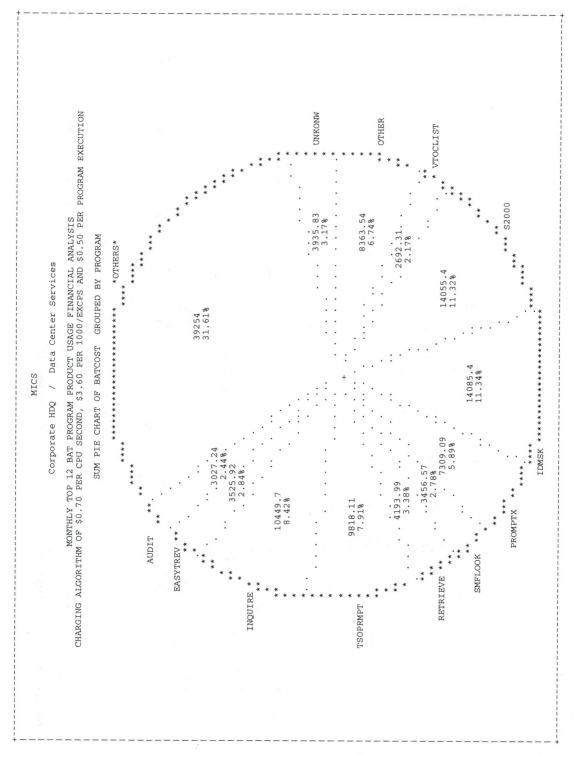

Figure 2-2k   MICS Monthly TOP-10 Batch Program Process Execution Cost Share

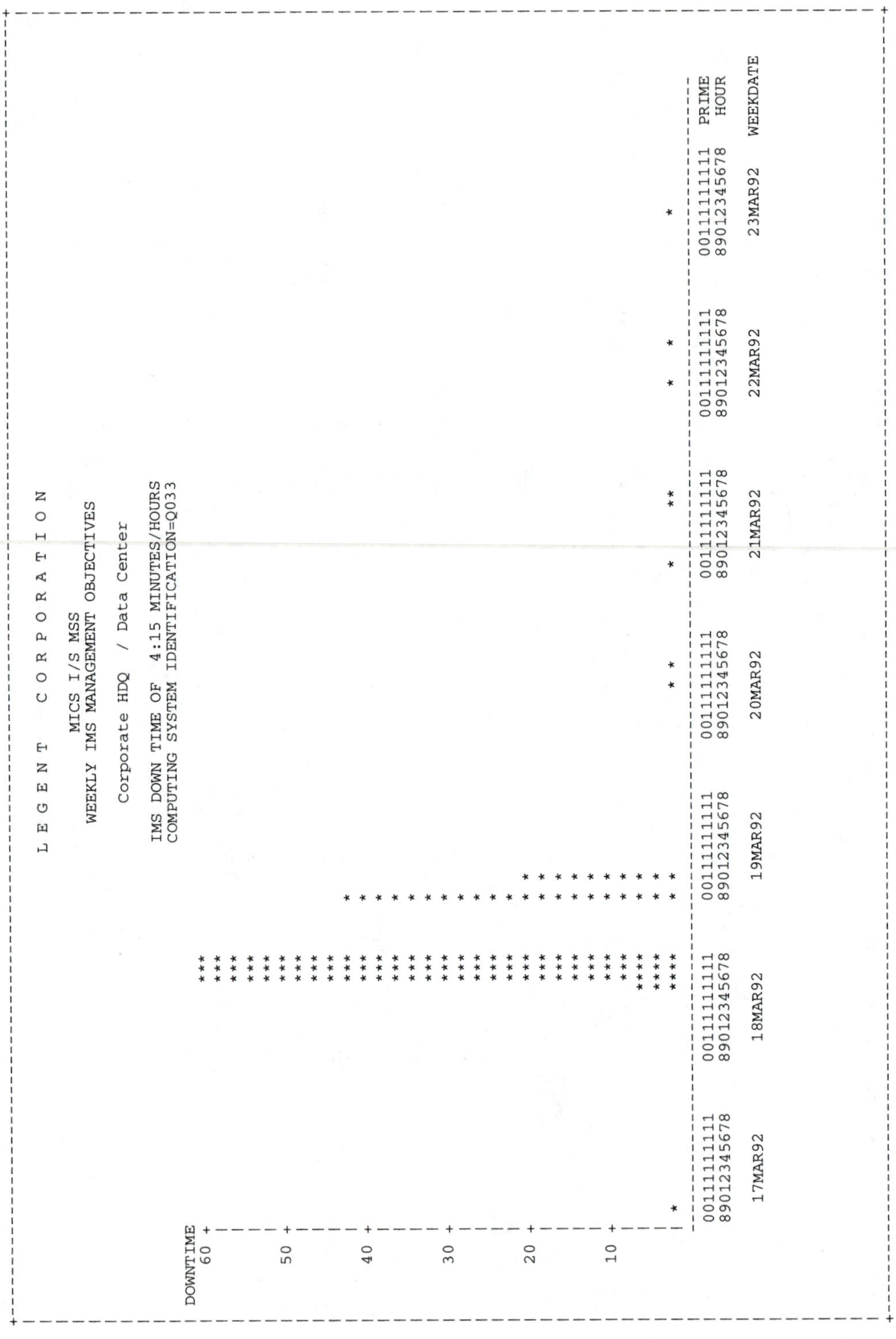

Figure 2-2I　MICS Weekly IMS Online System Downtime Availability Impact

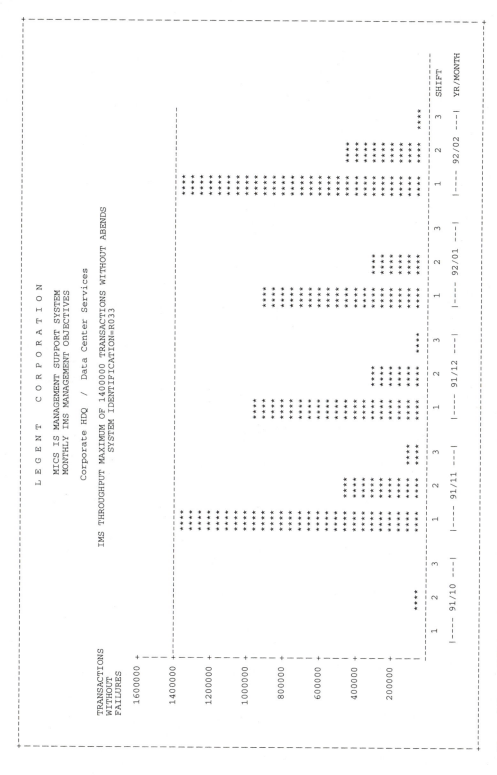

Figure 2-2m   MICS Weekly IMS Online System Throughput Reliability Impact

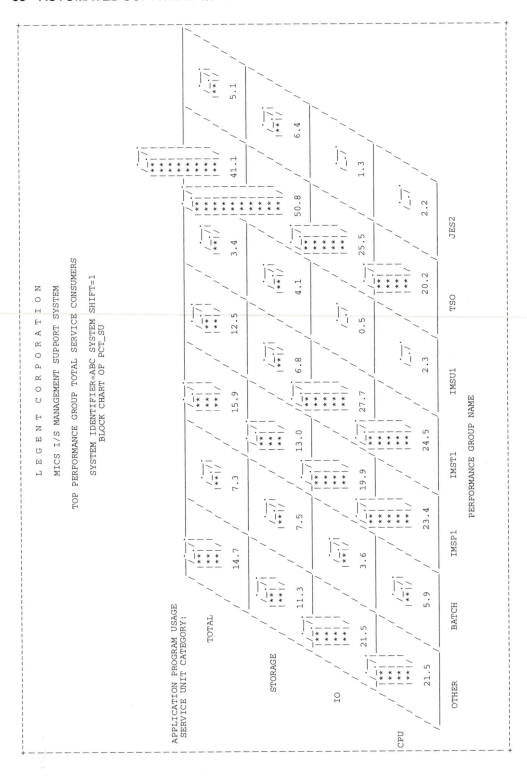

Figure 2-2n   MICS Application Software Program Resource Usage Profile

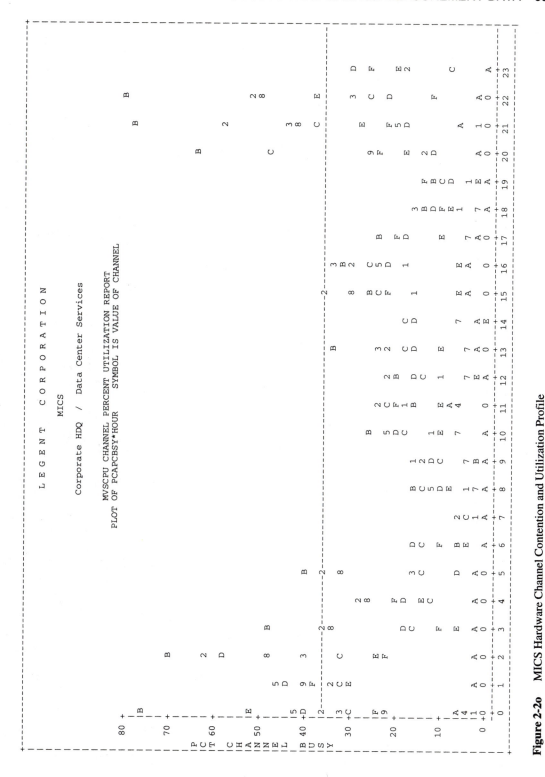

Figure 2-2o   MICS Hardware Channel Contention and Utilization Profile

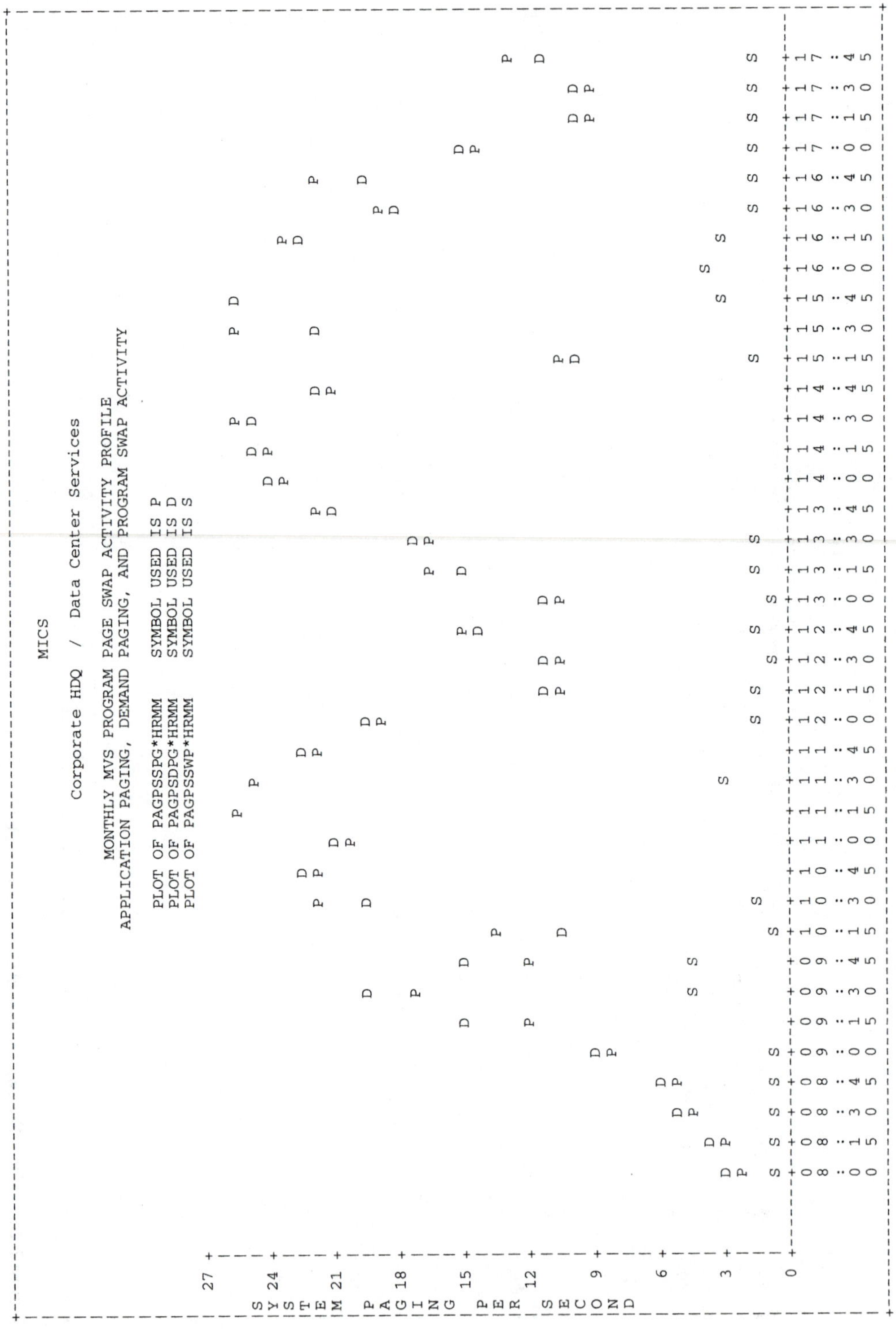

Figure 2-2p MICS Operating System Control Program Swap Activity Profile

MICS SNA NETWORK COMPONENT

(SNT1nn) NLDM SERVICE BY PERFORMANCE GROUP CLASS: TSO PROD
NETWORK: NETWORK1   SYSTEM: 3084
ZONE: PRIME TIME
PRODUCED: OCTOBER 20, 1992

ACTIVITY INDICATORS	09/16/92	09/15/92	09/14/92	CHG SINCE 3/92	CHG SINCE 9/91	CHG SINCE 9/90
TOTAL SERVICE						
TOTAL SERVICE OBJECTIVE 90%< 3						
% MET OVERALL	89.34	89.63	89.34	0.00	0.00	0.00
% MET BY SAMPLED INTERVALS	35.90	36.39	35.90	0.00	0.00	0.00
AVERAGE TOTAL RESPONSE TIME	0:01.95	0:01.90	0:01.95	0:00.00	0.00	0.00
% OF TOTAL RESPONSES < 1 SEC	47.42	48.92	47.42	0.00	0.00	0.00
% OF TOTAL RESPONSES < 3 SEC	89.34	89.63	89.34	0.00	0.00	0.00
% OF TOTAL RESPONSES < 5 SEC	95.69	95.79	95.69	0.00	0.00	0.00
% OF TOTAL RESPONSES < 10 SEC	98.33	98.36	98.33	0.00	0.00	0.00
TOTAL NO. OF RESPONSE EVENTS	21,682	22,601	21,682	0	0.00	0.00
TOTAL NO. OF SAMPLED INTERVALS	390	393	390	0	0.00	0.00

(SNTmnn) NPM SERVICE BY APPLICATION WORKLOAD: IMSPROD1
NETWORK: NETWORK1   SYSTEM: 3084
ZONE: PRIME TIME
PRODUCED: OCTOBER 20, 1992

ACTIVITY INDICATORS	10/18/92	10/17/92	10/16/92	CHG SINCE 3/92	CHG SINCE 9/91	CHG SINCE 9/90
HOST SERVICE						
AVERAGE HOST RESPONSE TIME	0:00.51	0:00.66	0:00.66	-0:00.15	-0.08	-22.93
MAXIMUM HOST RESPONSE TIME	0:12.19	0:07.02	0:05.83	0:06.36	3.18	109.09
NO. OF HOST RESPONSES	1,494	1,622	1,228	266	133.00	21.66
HOST RESPONSES NOT IN RANGE 0 - 1 SECS	178	316	252	-74	-37.00	-29.37
NETWORK SERVICE						
AVERAGE NETWORK RESPONSE TIME	0:01.47	0:01.61	0:01.56	-0:00.09	-0.05	-6.08
MAXIMUM NETWORK RESPONSE TIME	0:06.13	0:08.76	0:05.38	0:00.75	0.38	13.94
NO. OF NETWORK RESPONSES	1,437	1,573	1,198	239	119.50	19.95
NETWRK RESPONSES NOT IN RANGE 0 - 4 SECS	6	33	9	-3	-1.50	-33.33
TOTAL SERVICE						
AVERAGE TOTAL RESPONSE TIME	0:01.97	0:02.25	0:02.20	-0:00.23	-0.11	-10.40
PERCENT WITHIN 1 SECS	14.26	11.96	9.20	5.05	2.53	54.93
PERCENT WITHIN 2 SECS	59.37	52.09	53.18	6.19	3.10	11.64
PERCENT WITHIN 3 SECS	88.02	77.19	79.48	8.54	4.27	10.74
PERCENT WITHIN 4 SECS	97.79	90.93	93.48	4.30	2.15	4.60
MAXIMUM TOTAL RESPONSE TIME	0:13.37	0:08.89	0:07.90	0:05.47	2.74	69.24
TOTAL NO. OF RESPONSES	1,494	1,622	1,228	266	133.00	21.66
TOTAL RESPONSES NOT IN RANGE 0 - 6 SECS	2	23	6	-4	-2.00	-66.67
PCT RESPONSES WITH NO NET RESP	3.82	3.02	2.44	1.37	0.69	56.17

Figure 2-2q   MICS SNA Network Performance by Application and Workload Class

MICS SNA NETWORK COMPONENT
(SNT201) NPM WORKLOAD BY APPLICATION: IEMATRIX
NETWORK: NETWORK1 SYSTEM: 3084
PRODUCED: OCTOBER 20, 1992   ZONE: PRIME TIME

ACTIVITY INDICATORS	08/08/92	08/07/92	08/06/92	AMOUNT OF CHANGE SINCE 08/06/92	PER-PERIOD RATE OF CHANGE SINCE 08/06/92	PERCENTAGE CHANGE SINCE 08/06/92
THROUGHPUT DATA						
TOTAL CONTROL BYTES / MIN	25.47	35.69	20.80	4.67	2.34	22.47
CTRL BYTES SENT / MIN	16.65	24.35	13.78	2.87	1.43	20.83
CTRL BYTES RECEIVED / MIN	8.82	11.33	7.02	1.80	0.90	25.70
TOTAL DATA BYTES / MIN	47704.17	55749.70	40053.24	7650.93	3825.47	19.10
DATA BYTES SENT / MIN	42385.56	48636.54	35285.18	7100.38	3550.19	20.12
DATA BYTES RECEIVED / MIN	5318.61	7113.15	4768.06	550.55	275.28	11.55
TOTAL BYTES / MIN	47729.65	55785.38	40074.04	7655.61	3827.80	19.10
TOTAL BYTES SENT / MIN	42402.21	48660.90	35298.96	7103.25	3551.62	20.12
TOTAL BYTES RECEIVED / MIN	5327.43	7124.49	4775.08	552.36	276.18	11.57
TOTAL CTRL PIUS / MIN	4.29	5.44	3.39	0.90	0.45	26.64
CTRL PIUS SENT / MIN	2.13	2.69	1.68	0.45	0.23	26.90
CTRL PIUS RECEIVED / MIN	2.16	2.75	1.71	0.45	0.23	26.39
TOTAL DATA PIUS / MIN	145.94	165.83	119.70	26.25	13.12	21.93
DATA PIUS SENT / MIN	69.13	77.07	56.03	13.10	6.55	23.39
DATA PIUS RECEIVED / MIN	76.81	88.76	63.67	13.14	6.57	20.64
TOTAL PIUS / MIN	150.23	171.27	123.08	27.15	13.57	22.06
TOTAL PIUS SENT / MIN	71.26	79.76	57.70	13.55	6.78	23.49
TOTAL PIUS RECEIVED / MIN	78.97	91.50	65.38	13.60	6.80	20.79
NUMBER OF RESPONSES / MIN	66.36	73.40	53.94	12.42	6.21	23.02
WORKLOAD STATISTICS						
TOTAL BYTES TRANSMITTED	14,604,476	17,069,398	12,261,988	2,342,488	1171244.00	19.10
CTRL BYTES TRANSMITTED	7,794	10,920	6,364	1,430	715.00	22.47
DATA BYTES TRANSMITTED	14,596,682	17,058,478	12,255,624	2,341,058	1170529.00	19.10
TOTAL PIUS TRANSMITTED	45,968	52,405	37,661	8,307	4153.50	22.06
CTRL PIUS TRANSMITTED	1,312	1,664	1,036	276	138.00	26.64
DATA PIUS TRANSMITTED	44,656	50,741	36,625	8,031	4015.50	21.93
TOTAL RESPONSES	20,304	22,458	16,504	3,800	1900.00	23.02
AVG BYTES PER CNTL PIU SENT	7.82	9.05	8.22	-0.39	-0.20	-4.79
AVG BYTES PER CNTL PIU REC'D	4.08	4.12	4.11	-0.02	-0.01	-0.54
AVG BYTES PER DATA PIU SENT	613.15	631.05	629.80	-16.65	-8.33	-2.64
AVG BYTES PER DATA PIU REC'D	69.24	80.14	74.89	-5.65	-2.82	-7.54
AVG BYTES PER RESPONSE	719.29	760.06	742.97	-23.68	-11.84	-3.19
AVG PIUS PER RESPONSE	2.26	2.33	2.28	-0.02	-0.01	-0.79

Figure 2-2r   MICS SNA Network Performance by Individual Application Software Product

```
                                     MICS

                          Corporate HDQ  / Data Center

                   TSO APPL(IEMATRIX) SUMMARY FOR USER (Z9999   )

CURRENT DATE/TIME:    OCT 17 1992 (92.290)/ 8:59
```

PERFORMANCE QUALITY CATEGORIES	SEPTEMBER 1992 SUMMARY	AUGUST 1992 SUMMARY	JULY 1992 SUMMARY	JUNE 1992 SUMMARY	PERCENT CHANGE FROM JUNE 1992
SERVICE FACTORS					
AVG RESPONSE TIME (ALL FUNCTIONS)	1.01	0.71	1.25	1.38	26.8-
WITHIN 2.00 SECONDS	89.4%	92.1%	90.2%	91.6%	2.2-
WITHIN 3.00 SECONDS	93.2%	95.0%	93.9%	94.2%	1.0-
AVG RESPONSE TIME (SHORT)	1.00	0.56	1.53	0.69	44.9
WITHIN 2.00 SECONDS	89.5%	94.1%	90.0%	94.0%	4.5-
WITHIN 3.00 SECONDS	93.4%	96.4%	93.8%	97.0%	3.6-
AVG RESPONSE TIME (MEDIUM)	0.93	0.72	1.17	1.33	30.0-
WITHIN 2.00 SECONDS	90.1%	91.9%	90.5%	91.5%	1.4-
WITHIN 3.00 SECONDS	93.9%	91.8%	94.1%	94.0%	0.1-
AVG RESPONSE TIME (LONG)	2.98	1.46	1.69	7.34	59.4-
WITHIN 2.00 SECONDS	71.5%	83.3%	87.6%	78.9%	7.4-
WITHIN 3.00 SECONDS	77.1%	88.7%	91.5%	84.8%	7.7-
SYSTEM LOAD					
NUMBER OF DIALOG MANAGER PANELS	1508	2009	1536	1093	37.9
NUMBER OF SHORT RESPONSES	1524	2104	1594	1172	30.0
NUMBER OF MEDIUM RESPONSES	10987	11794	8393	6560	67.4
NUMBER OF LONG RESPONSES	464	222	566	185	150.8
TCB CPU TIME (HH:MM)	0:15	5:09	3:42	0:09	65.5
SRB CPU TIME (HH:MM)	0:01	0:01	0:01	0:01	74.9
RESIDENCY TIME (HH:MM)	4:24	3:24	4:30	3:09	39.4
NON-TERMINAL I/O (EXCPS)	197271	178336	166304	112704	75.0
TERMINAL I/O (TGET/TPUT)	48348	56590	40903	28344	70.5
SERVICE UNITS	8193495	7594146	7509271	4876965	68.0
NUMBER OF ENDED SRM TRANSACTIONS	16188	16506	12676	9549	69.5
INVOCATIONS PER HOUR	28	21	19	29	3.4-
ENDED SRM TRANSACTIONS PER HOUR	109	113	87	83	31.3
SERVICE UNITS PER HOUR	55327	52304	52107	42784	29.3
NON-TERMINAL I/O PER HOUR	1332	1228	1154	988	34.8
CPUTIME PER HOUR (TCB+SRB) (MM:SS)	0:07	2:08	1:52	0:05	27.9
SYSTEM AVAILABILITY					
NUMBER OF INVOCATIONS	50	42	38	30	60.0
APPLICATION ELAPSED HOURS (HH:MM)	148:05	145:11	144:06	113:59	29.9

Figure 2-2s   MICS TSO Application Software Performance by Individual Product User

```
                                    MICS
                          Corporate HDQ / Data Center
                       TOP 3 PROGRAMS USAGE BY TOTAL RESPONSE
                                System = TSOP

INQUIRY:  TSOLXQ                                            RUN DATE:  12JUN92
```

/TOP LINE IS QUANTITY / BOTTOM LINE IS PCT OF TIME PERIOD TOTAL.

TIME	PROGRAM	PGN	RESP EVENT	RESPONSE AVERAGE / DISTRIBUTION TOTAL	SHORT	MEDIUM	LONG	CPUTIME	EXCPS	TERMIO	SWAPS	CMDS	SERVICE	TRANS
8:00- 9:00 59 USERS IN INTERVAL	ABCX51	2	2	0:11.46 0.0%	0:00.00 0.0%	0:11.46 0.0%	0:00.00 0.0%	0:01.9 0.0%	518 0.0%	26 0.0%	2 0.0%	20 0.1%	16252 0.0%	18 0.0%
	ABCX67	2	3	0:10.80 66.7%	0:00.75 50.0%	0:00.00 0.0%	0:30.90 0.0%	0:03.1 0.4%	901 1.1%	8 0.1%	2 0.3%	35 1.7%	22622 0.3%	36 0.9%
	ABCY20	2	66	0:10.38 90.9%	0:00.35 91.2%	0:02.53 58.6%	3:19.83 0.0%	0:13.5 1.9%	4268 5.0%	132 2.0%	26 4.5%	19 0.9%	160113 2.1%	68 1.7%
9:00-10:00 79 USERS IN INTERVAL	ABCX35	2	66	0:17.71 87.9%	0:00.42 94.1%	0:03.54 43.3%	8:44.11 0.0%	0:33.0 3.5%	33875 17.3%	140 1.2%	11 0.8%	41 0.8%	364885 4.1%	94 1.4%
	ABCY22	2	4	0:12.96 25.0%	0:00.01 100.0%	0:14.20 0.0%	0:23.45 0.0%	0:04.1 0.4%	1185 0.6%	18 0.2%	7 0.5%	30 0.6%	35185 0.4%	34 0.5%
	ABCY79	2	199	0:08.28 94.0%	0:00.26 93.7%	0:04.22 29.4%	3:38.79 0.0%	2:44.2 17.5%	38814 19.9%	414 3.5%	15 1.2%	102 1.9%	1704513 19.1%	256 3.9%
10:00-11:00 81 USERS IN INTERVAL	ABCX57	2	40	0:09.70 67.5%	0:00.55 77.8%	0:02.80 46.7%	0:21.33 37.5%	1:46.3 9.6%	2024 1.3%	86 0.7%	21 1.7%	7 0.2%	1123294 10.3%	44 0.7%
	ABCY06	2	76	0:08.18 72.4%	0:00.31 88.9%	0:02.52 60.7%	0:18.18 46.7%	2:17.3 12.4%	4549 3.0%	176 1.5%	18 1.4%	21 0.6%	1526078 14.0%	90 1.5%
	ABCX47	2	102	0:05.17 84.3%	0:00.54 76.4%	0:01.00 80.0%	0:17.67 40.7%	2:31.4 13.7%	3766 2.5%	226 1.9%	45 3.6%	14 0.4%	1640028 15.1%	113 1.9%

DATES=NONE,TIME=(08:00-17:00),INCREMENT=60,TOTAL=5.00,SHORT=1.00,MEDIUM=2.00,LONG=5.00

Figure 2-2t   MICS TSO Application Software Performance Detail by Executed Program Usage

```
                        L E G E N T   C O R P O R A T I O N

                                      MICS

                            TSO Program Activity Report
                            Corporate HDQ / Data Center

                                 System = TSOP

INQUIRY: TSOLX5                                              RUN DATE:  2JUN92
```

Program Name	User ID Number	Pgm Exec Count	Response Avg. 0.5S Y/ 1.0S P/ T/ X/	Storage Residency	TCB CPU Time SRB CPU Time	Excp Counts	TermIO TGET TPUT	Swapping Count Avg Max	SRM Values Ended Trans Service Unit
ABCX03	Z9099	1	1.10 45.9 X / 67.6	0:00:59.9	0:00:04.8 / 0:00:00.4	650	39 / 47	26 364 / 1104	72 / 48221
ABCX04	Z7890	2	1.40 42.9 X / 61.9	0:01:32.3	0:00:06.4 / 0:00:00.7	2825	22 / 33	7 823 / 1204	22 / 73514
ABCX08	Z2085	1	1.62 37.5 X / 37.5	0:00:56.4	0:00:02.4 / 0:00:00.2	93	25 / 25	7 158 / 272	30 / 14575
ABCX10	Z9534	10	1.48 48.2 X / 59.1	0:07:13.5	0:00:38.6 / 0:00:03.5	8287	268 / 271	112 733 / 1564	299 / 437746
ABCX25	Z2344	4	0.93 60.4 X / 80.5	0:09:14.9	0:00:56.9 / 0:00:05.1	8544	552 / 597	97 706 / 1388	561 / 597520
ABCX26	Z8732	2	0.86 47.1 X / 76.5	0:00:42.6	0:00:02.7 / 0:00:00.3	586	19 / 19	24 522 / 1260	31 / 29153
ABCX28	Z9884	9	1.39 24.1 X / 38.9	0:01:12.5	0:00:03.1 / 0:00:00.6	675	59 / 75	5 235 / 368	64 / 24516
ABCX29	Z3487	2	1.51 55.2 X / 68.3	0:11:57.0	0:01:04.3 / 0:00:05.3	12368	424 / 448	166 724 / 1020	509 / 724140
ABCX30	Z2948	5	1.17 50.0 X / 50.0	0:00:56.7	0:00:04.3 / 0:00:00.5	810	40 / 42	15 402 / 1124	49 / 41935
ABCX31	Z2849	7	1.62 35.0 X / 40.0	0:03:35.2	0:00:15.3 / 0:00:01.2	1833	106 / 107	32 553 / 1256	119 / 144016
ABCX41	Z2823	2	1.27 55.6 X / 64.7	0:03:13.5	0:00:15.6 / 0:00:01.6	3430	144 / 146	70 624 / 952	225 / 174001

Data Level: 51   Option: USER,DATES=NONE,TIME=(00:00-24:00),DISTRIBUTION=(0.5,1.0)

Figure 2-2u   MICS TSO Application Software Performance Detail by Executed Program and User

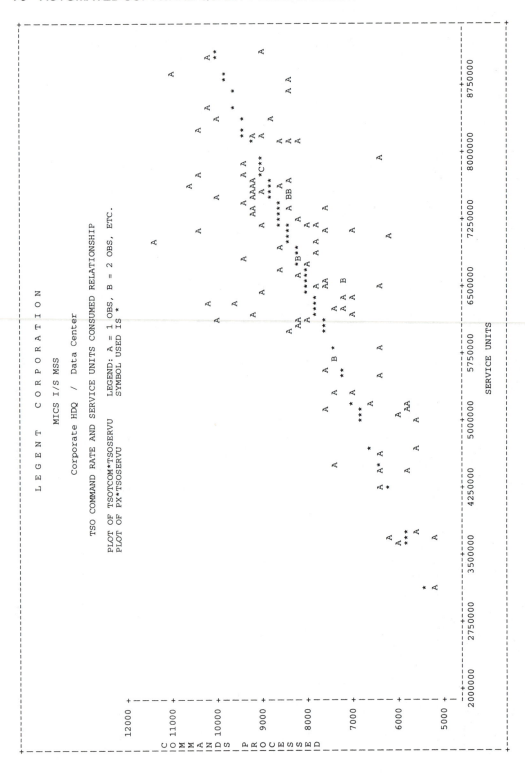

Figure 2-2v   MICS TSO Application Software Command Execution Rate and Processor Service Units Used

```
                    L E G E N T   C O R P O R A T I O N

                              MICS I/S MSS

                          Corporate HDQ / Data Center

         PROFILE STATISTICAL ANALYSIS OF TSO INTERACTIVE SERVICE UNIT CONSUMPTION

                                 UNIVARIATE

VARIABLE TSUSERVU    SERVICE UNITS

       MOMENTS                              QUANTILES                    EXTREMES

N          11753    SUM WGTS    11753    100% MAX   290693   99%  61408.3        LOWEST    HIGHEST
MEAN       6727.82  SUM       79072084    75% Q3      7153.5  95%  23820.4        0         222153
STD DEV    14354.7  VARIANCE 206056956    50% MED     2952    90%  15273.4        0         229069
SKEWNESS   8.11851  KURTOSIS    98.189    25% Q1      845.25  10%  197            0         274194
SS         2.954E+12 CSS      2.422E+12    0% MIN      109     5%  109            0         290097
CV         213.363  STD MEAN    132.41                        1%  0              0         290693
T:MEAN=0   50.8107  PROB>|T|    0.0001   RANGE      290693
                                         Q3-Q1      6308.25
                                         MODE       0

     BAR CHART                             #   BOXPLOT           NORMAL PROBABILITY PLOT
280000+*                                   2     *
      .*                                   1     *
      .*                                   2           *
      .*                                   4           *
      .*                                   3           *
      .*                                   8           *
140000+*                                  13           *
      .*                                  10           *
      .*                                  16           *
      .*                                  22           *
      .*                                  48           *
      .***                               109           *
     0+************************************ 559      *--*--*
      +---+---+---+---+---+---+---+---+    10956  *--*--*
   * MAY REPRESENT UP TO 228 COUNTS

                                        280000+

                                        140000+

                                             0+
```

Figure 2-2w   MICS TSO Application Software Interactive Process Service Unit Statistical Profile

L E G E N T   C O R P O R A T I O N

MICS I/S MSS

Corporate HDQ / Data Center

TSO USER PRIMARY COMMAND PROGRAM USAGE ANALYSIS

ANALYSIS IS FOR APPLICATION PROGRAM GROUP = ABCNNN

TABLE OF COMMANDS BY PROGRAM

TSO COMMAND FREQUENCY	APPLICATION SOFTWARE PROGRAM NAME				GROUP TOTAL
	ABC001	ABC002	ABC003	ABC004	
ALLOCATE	15	3	39	67	124
ASK	0	0	0	26	26
ATTRIB	0	0	14	2	16
BACKLOG	3	0	0	5	8
CALL	2	2	22	31	57
CANCEL	4	1	2	3	10
COPY	1	0	0	8	9
DELETE	0	0	4	5	9
EDIT	4	4	18	35	61
END	1	0	18	3	22
ENQUE	1	0	1	1	3
EVALUATE	0	0	1	0	1
EXECUTE	21	7	50	68	146
FREE	7	3	31	61	102
FREEALL	6	2	31	57	96
TOTAL	251	55	454	941	1701

(CONTINUED)

Figure 2-2x MICS TSO Application Software Interactive Command Usage Frequency

3

TURNING SOFTWARE FAILURES INTO SYSTEMATIC SUCCESS

In every successful business operation, as in most human endeavors, the single most critical survival skill is the ability to learn from your mistakes. The data processing industry is no exception to this rule. In fact, it is probably even more important since a single, computer-generated error can be multiplied many times before it can be corrected.

Computers can magnify even the smallest human errors to catastrophic proportions. This is why all operating systems are designed to quickly detect and isolate most common errors. Operating systems have a multitude of separate programs to handle all of the possible errors that were documented to occur on hardware devices or in the high-level languages that they support. These special error-handling programs either force the system to stop processing before more serious damage can be done, or else attempt automatic, *fault-tolerant* override procedures to correct or bypass operations sensitive to a particular type of error.

Regardless of whether it requests all processing to terminate or attempts to override the error, the operating system always writes a large amount of detail to the system log storage area. Even if a catastrophic error occurs which has no program for special error handling or if there is a full system outage, detail is always written to the system logs. This chapter will explain types of computer software failures and how logs can be automatically analyzed to reduce human errors and improve system quality.

HOW COMPUTERS KNOW WHEN SOMETHING HAS GONE WRONG

Computers are machines designed to perform thousands, or even millions, of discretely controlled electronic actions every second. Each and every individual physical and electronic event is requested by a logical instruction that has been coded into the computer's operating system—in a manner that both depends on and builds upon the physical characteristics of the system hardware's architecture. The operating system provides templates of electronic activity which continuously take in and respond to external electronic patterns. This is done according to hard-coded internal patterns of electronic activity selectively induced in a direct relationship matching electronic patterns against templates of anticipated external activity.

Each individual step in this continuous process is known as a *logical instruction*, that is, the aggregate of a series of physical electronic actions that either take in external electronic patterns, attempt to match the patterns against internal templates of electrical activity, or activate a continuous series of electrical actions according to other internal patterns. Each of these types of instructions may be prescribed in order to define a process, or a hierarchy of processes, known as *tasks*. Tasks are requests for coordinated work processes, by which operating systems control all of the functions possible based on mechanical characteristics of the system architecture and the set of logical instruction patterns built upon it.

Tasks are imprinted into special units of instruction patterns known as *control blocks*. These control blocks are the parts of the operating system that manage the introduction of electronic input patterns, match against intrinsic patterns, and control the desired patterns of electronic response. These three functions of operating system activity are manifested in the MVS operating system as three types of task control blocks:

- Virtual Storage Control (subpool queue and descriptor queue)
- Load Modules (content directory, load list, or job pack area)
- Input/Output (task I/O, data extent, and job file control)

Each of these types of task control blocks is constantly in the process of taking in, matching up, and responding to the electronic patterns that the system architecture is designed to accommodate. Each of the three general types of control blocks is made up of, and can selectively interact with, other specialized task control blocks within the operating system. An example of how these general task control blocks relate in an MVS operating system is shown in Figure 3-1.

The IBM MVS architecture provides two categories of control blocks: the general *Task Control Blocks* (TCBs) and more specialized *Service Request Blocks* (SRBs). The SRBs are involved any time that task activities must span other control block area address space. Some special MVS control block queues, or process linkage patterns, allow task work units to communicate with other MVS control blocks, in order to request special processing when unusual electronic patterns or conditions are detected. Among these special control blocks are:

- Console Command Control (from operator console or a program)
- Cross-Memory Services (program register mode addressability)
- Linkage Stack Services (request for call to another program)
- Task Dispatcher (request for uninterrupted series of tasks)
- Recovery Termination Manager (program check control routine)

Each of these special types of control blocks includes *interrupts* or branch instructions that involve electronic pattern matching, followed immediately by a specific electronic response. In each of these cases, a special circumstance requires that a normal series of instructions is either temporarily or permanently stopped in order to redirect the process to an alternative task linkage path.

In some cases, a special override process has been requested outside of the normal parameters or conditions of processing. In all cases, these special routines are the result of either the computer operator

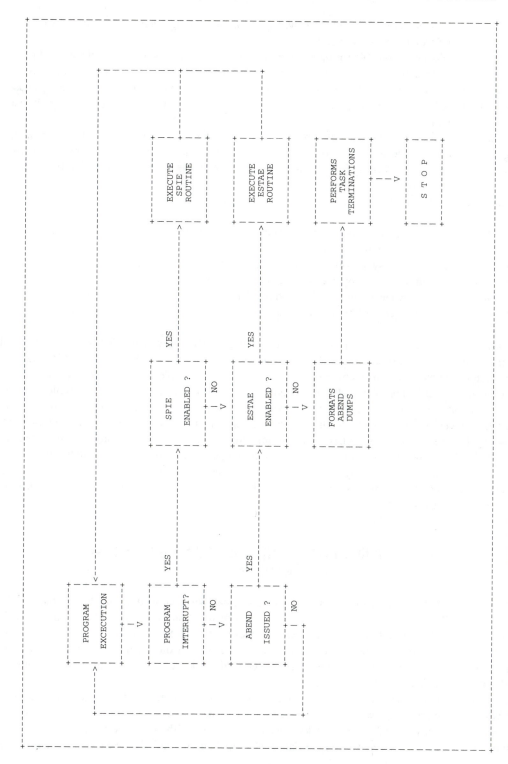

Figure 3-1   MVS Operating System ESTAE (Extended Specify Task Abnormal Abend Exit) and SPIE (Specify Program Interrupt Exit)

or the computer detecting that something is wrong or that something undesirable will likely go wrong if an alternative special process is not invoked.

The control blocks responsible for interrupt processing do not always imply that the normal process flow has been permanently interrupted. In almost all circumstances, the interrupt control task is more like stopping at a traffic intersection. Most often, these processes are invoked because something unusual has been detected, either about the pattern of electronic activity taken in or the pattern taking place as a response to that input.

Interrupts can be the result of detecting something wrong that may have either an external or an internal origin. Most interrupts, however, are not even associated with something being wrong, but may involve precautions ensuring that a complicated task is processed with special precision or help from another specialized control block.

Among the most important specialized control interrupt routines are:

- Program Check (when an operating system instruction fails)
- I/O Interrupt (to signify the beginning and end of an I/O)
- External Interrupt (to synchronize with an external device)
- Supervisor Call (to receive operating system control tasks)
- Machine Check (when a failure is detected in the hardware)
- Restart (to clear all control block linkage and start again)

Each of these special interrupts results in a lock being placed on the process that is underway. A task is either removed from the control block process linkage queue area or an attempt is made to place the critical information needed to recover the task in special register holding areas, while the problem is checked against critical problem patterns that have a specified response. If a task control block known as a *Functional Recovery Routine* is found to exist for that specific pattern of problem, control is given over the recovery routine in order to automatically fix or accommodate whatever it has determined to be wrong. If no recovery routine exists, the task is immediately terminated and control returns to a higher level. Even if a recovery routine does indeed exist, it may not be able to accommodate the problem; at any time a second interrupt may terminate the automated functional recovery effort and another functional recovery routine may take over. It will either succeed or else ultimately result in the eventual termination of the task.

WHAT KINDS OF PROBLEMS CAN OPERATING SYSTEMS DETECT?

If the task is terminated, an "SVC-13" supervisor service call will be issued by an ABEND macro. This coordinates all of the process locks and special shut-down actions necessary when a task must be abnormally ended. The shut-down actions may include attempts to cleanly disconnect devices or close file resources in a manner that prevents more serious damage from occurring. Another important shut-down action is to *dump* the contents of critical control block areas and spool as streamed output to a file or printer dedicated to this purpose.

This dump can be used later for diagnostic troubleshooting to determine the cause of the problem. However, the dump is not always able to preserve data, since the severity of the problem may have caused the necessary critical control blocks to be impeded. Even if there was nothing wrong to prevent printing the dump, it may be desirable for data centers to "dummy out" the SYSUDUMP 'DD' in the

JCL of batch jobs or sessions that are likely to terminate often for trivial reasons—the reason being that the ABEND dump process locks out all other resources and can consume substantial core storage or waste considerable paper printing if the problem is repetitive.

In the case of a catastrophic failure or systemwide outage, there may be no control blocks to dump or salvage—it may be unreadable garbage. Even if the critical data is captured, the volume of machine code that must be searched to find the essential bit of data where normal processing terminated may not be worth the trouble. Often, data center operations analysts elect to simply restart a process and just hope it doesn't happen again.

The tedious and time-consuming process of analyzing program abend dump reports is very costly in terms of technical staff labor and the operational delays that occur while problems are diagnosed. Abend dump analysis involves extremely complex procedures, which can be seen in the high-level flowchart shown in Figure 3-2.

MEASURING AND CONTROLLING CATASTROPHIC SYSTEM FAILURES

Fortunately, there is another option to troubleshooting system failures and attempted recovery actions based on *core* dumps. Since the SMF system logs were designed by IBM with their own special hierarchy of separate cross-memory control blocks, critical status information is always logged to SMF when the system issues a critical interrupt, attempts a recovery action, or begins the execution of the ABEND macro.

This data is recorded in a wide variety of specialized SMF record types, for recording and measuring all categories of system failures and program terminations. SMF Types 2 and 3 record various dump actions. Types 4 and 5 record job and program step termination status. Type 7 helps to recreate lost or damaged SMF data by collecting suspense information. Type 10 records device allocation recovery data. Type 22 records how devices were varied online and offline, before and after the interrupt and restart attempts. Type 26 records JES output purge activity. In fact, these are only a few of the many record types used to recreate and analyze the series of events that took place before a system failure or program termination occurred.

The procedure for analyzing SMF data to determine the cause of system failure, without the need to correlate to core dump data, is fairly straightforward. The basic method is to use a general lookup table of IBM abend codes, as shown in Appendix D. More detailed troubleshooting requires referring to system messages.

Although the SMF is primarily used to assist in reducing abend terminations by means of a *post-mortem* process, the SMF can also be used to create customized error-handling controls that provide additional automated real-time recovery management. This capability can be based on the customized SMF exits which were described in Chapter 1. Especially if a particular type of system problem has been occurring repeatedly and cannot be handled simply by standards enforcement alone, an SMF exit can be written which will respond to a particular abend code or series of system status messages and invoke an automated procedure to recover the problem. These SMF exits then become a permanent part of the operating system for that particular data center and can easily result in substantial savings due to the avoidance of system downtime. Although it is not a trivial task to write and test the impact of a new SMF exit on the operating environment, this is always an option that should be explored as part of any TQM program that is intended to reduce the impact of critical repeated system problems.

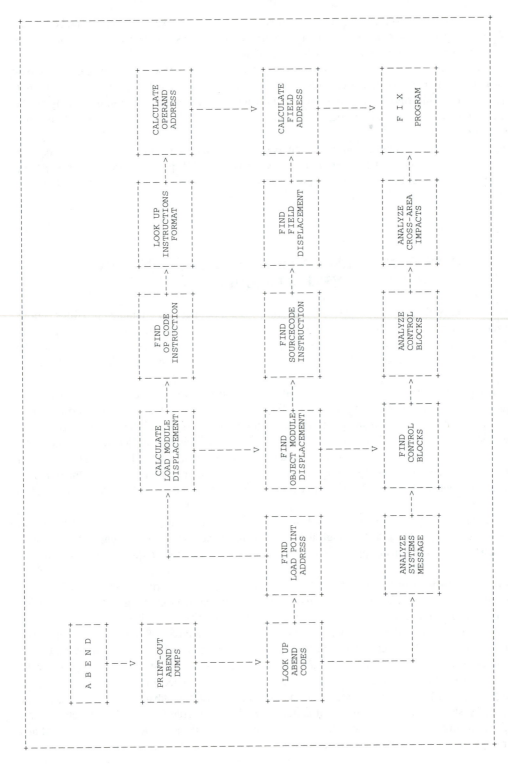

Figure 3-2 Example of a Typical Manual Abend Dump Analysis and Diagnostic Troubleshooting Procedure

MEASURING LEVELS OF SYSTEM FAULT TOLERANCE

Among the most critical functions of automated software quality measurement is the routine accumulation of data. Thus, the historical performance of the operating system is recorded, as well as the failure history of every application system and program routinely processed in the production operating environment. This historical data is an essential part of any effective data center problem management program and is also one of the most important sources of data that can be used in a productive TQM program.

First of all, it is necessary to automatically log the sequence of system failures, including hardware and operating system failures, every abnormal program termination, all data available concerning the nature of the abend, and the status of the system within several minutes on either side of the abend event. This includes a running log of critical system events and status for several minutes leading up to the time of the abend, as well as all the abend codes and system status messages that preceded it.

It is also very important to cross-reference abend events occurring within the same time period, including a cross reference of all abend events across processors if the data center is a multiprocessor or parallel-processed environment. An example of this type of cross-reference and a related time plot report are shown in Figures 3-3, 3-4, and 3-5. Examples of the SAS language program code used to produce related application reports based on SMF system log data is in Appendix C.

It is important to provide a profile of the utilization data at the time of the abend event. This profile should include any indication that the system CPU was overutilized or stressed, or that any attached system device was backed up or experiencing hardware problems within the recent past. It is important to be able to relate the type of abend to the amount of CPU region, as well as to the I/O buffers being used by the program that abended. Additionally, some indication of the availability of additional region or buffer area in the pools should be conveyed.

Every abend code should be classed according to the diagnostic resolution categories in the system messages and troubleshooting manuals. It is also desirable to have the related system messages along with the abend code, since the abend code may be general and require the system message code to fully resolve the cause of the problem. In reality, however, cross-referencing may be more important than the detail (since the abend codes are necessarily general, and every problem investigation is more likely to depend on what else was happening in the system environment at the time of the abend, than merely the abend code alone).

Examples of the general nomenclature IBM designed to report all of its abends are shown in Figure 3-6. Even though the number of abend codes grows with each new IBM control program release, this coding matrix continues to be the basis to assign all codes.

Actually, there are over 2,000 specific IBM system and user abend codes, as well as an equal number of messages. A table for grouping and general diagnostics of the most critical IBM abend codes automatically logged to SMF is in Appendix D. This table has demonstrated some correspondence to the relative amount of technical labor required to fix the problem, which also corresponds to costs incurred by system downtime and related business costs. These costs can be quantified and analyzed as part of a TQM effort to prioritize problems and develop standardized procedures for reducing their level of impact.

These levels of system failure impact are one of the most useful areas where automated software quality measurement data can be applied. The cost benefits will depend on how diligently the data center problem management process makes use of this analysis data.

DAILY COMMERCIAL BATCH << PROD JOBS >> AUTOMATED AUDIT OF SMF JOB-LEVEL APPLICATION < DUMP ACTIVITY BY TIMESTAMP >

** SORT ALL PRODUCTION BATCH JOB ABENDS AND IBM STANDARD ERROR CODES BY MVS/SMF SYSTEM LOG INCIDENT TIME SEQUENCE **

OBS	RUN DATE	PGMDUMP TIMESTAMP	CPU ID X	JOB EXEC RUNTIME	PRODUCT OR LOGON	ABENDED JOBNAME	JOBSTEP NAMES	CPU X S370	ABEND CODE	IBM STD ERROR DESCRIPTION	RAW INCID	IBM STD ERR CAUSETYPE
1	10/22/92	0:54:55	Z	0:00:10	ABCAPP	ABC002	ABC00235	*09.86	U3001	PGM FORCED SYS CALL	1	PGM DEFECT
2	10/22/92	2:51:48	K	0:00:36	CANDX	CX014	CX014005	*06.78	U0016	DCB/DSCB CONFLICTS	1	INPUT DATA
3	10/22/92	9:36:00	K	0:00:12	PAYROLL	PAY001	PAY00168	*06.78	U3001	PGM FORCED SYS CALL	1	PGM DEFECT
4	10/22/92	10:39:27	X	0:00:00	DOXSX	DOX005	DOX00570	*03.10	S714	TAPE LABEL/DS ERROR	1	INPUT DATA
5	10/22/92	10:29:00	Z	0:00:07	DXCS	DXC001	DXC00120	*09.86	U4044	UNEXPECTED DS LRECL	1	INPUT DATA
6	10/22/92	21:06:02	K	0:00:30	RDRX	RDR004	RDR00466	*06.78	U3002	FAILED PL1 EDITCODE	1	PGM DEFECT
7	10/22/92	21:07:33	K	0:00:45	RDRX	RDR004	RDR00466	*06.78	U3001	PGM FORCED SYS CALL	1	PGM DEFECT
8	10/22/92	21:16:22	K	0:00:16	RDRX	RDR004	RDR00466	*06.78	S714	TAPE LABEL/DS ERROR	1	INPUT DATA
9	10/22/92	22:02:04	K	0:00:02	FASTRX	FTX003	FTX00234	*09.86	S0C7	DATA EXCEPTION	1	PGM DEFECT
10	10/22/92	22:23:56	K	0:00:01	DXCS	DXC002	DXC00567	*06.78	U4044	UNEXPECTED DS LRECL	1	INPUT DATA

** SEPARATE PRODUCTION BATCH JOB ABENDS AND IBM STANDARD ERROR CODES BY CPU IDENTIFIER AND MIPS PROCESSOR MULTIPLE XS370 **

OBS	RUN DATE	PGMDUMP TIMESTAMP	JOB EXEC RUNTIME	TIME FROM LAST FAIL	PRODUCT OR APRNO	ABENDED JOBNAME	JOBSTEP NAMES	CPU ID X S370	ABEND CODE	IBM STD ERROR DESCRIPTION	RAW INCID	IBM STD ERR CAUSETYPE
								CPU ID X S370=K*06.78				
1	10/22/92	2:51:48	0:00:36	2:51:48	CANDX	CX014	ABC00235	K*06.78	U0016	DCB/DSCB CONFLICTS	1	INPUT DATA
2	10/22/92	9:36:00	0:00:12	6:44:11	PAYROLL	PAY001	PAY00168	K*09.86	U3001	PGM FORCED SYS CALL	1	PGM DEFECT
3	10/22/92	21:06:02	0:00:30	11:40:58	RDRX	RDR004	RTS00466	K*06.78	U3002	FAILED PL1 EDITCODE	1	PGM DEFECT
4	10/22/92	21:07:33	0:00:45	0:01:29	RDRX	RDR004	RTS00466	K*06.78	U3001	PGM FORCED SYS CALL	1	PGM DEFECT
5	10/22/92	21:16:22	0:00:16	0:05:50	RDRX	RDR004	RTS00466	K*06.78	S714	TAPE LABEL/DS ERROR	1	INPUT DATA
6	10/22/92	22:02:04	0:00:02	0:44:48	FASTRX	FTX003	RTS00234	K*06.78	S0C7	DATA EXCEPTION	1	PGM DEFECT
7	10/22/92	22:23:56	0:00:01	0:21:51	DXCS	DXC002	RTS00567	K*06.78	U4044	UNEXPECTED DS LRECL	1	INPUT DATA
								CPU ID X S370=X*03.10				
8	10/22/92	10:39:27	0:00:00	10:39:27	DOXSX	DOX005	DOX00570	X*03.10	S714	TAPE LABEL/DS ERROR	1	INPUT DATA
								CPU ID X S370=Z*09.86				
9	10/22/92	0:54:55	0:00:10	0:54:55	ABCAPP	ABC002	ABC00235	Z*09.86	U3001	PGM FORCED SYS CALL	1	PGM DEFECT
10	10/22/92	20:29:00	0:00:07	19:34:05	DXCS	DXC001	DXC00120	Z*09.86	U4044	UNEXPECTED DS LRECL	1	INPUT DATA

Figure 3-3   Sample SMF Software Prod Job Failure Abend System Cross-Reference Report Based upon MXG Performance Quality Data

DAILY COMMERCIAL BATCH << PROD JOBS >> AUTOMATED AUDIT OF SMF JOB-LEVEL APPLICATION < DUMP ACTIVITY BY TIMESTAMP >

** SORT ALL PRODUCTION BATCH PGM ABENDS AND IBM STANDARD ERROR CODES BY MVS/SMF SYSTEM LOG INCIDENT TIME SEQUENCE **

OBS	RUN DATE	PGMDUMP TIMESTAMP	CPU ID XS370	JOB EXEC RUNTIME	ABENDED PROGRAMS	PRODUCT ACCOUNT	PRODJOB ACCOUNT	JOBSTEP NAMES	RAW INCID	ABEND CODE	ABEND DESCRIPTION	IBM STD ERR CAUSETYPE
1	10/23/92	0:54:55	Z*09.86	0:00:10	ABC0021	BACSX1	BAC002	AAD00235	1	U3001	PGM FORCED SYS CALL	PGM DEFECT
2	10/23/92	2:03:13	Z*09.86	0:00:34	PAY0234	PAYR1	PAY142	PAY142G2	1	S0C7	DATA EXCEPTION	PGM DEFECT
3	10/23/92	2:14:21	U*13.76	0:00:42	DSNUTIL	BACSX2	BAC027	BAC02730	1	S0C7	DATA EXCEPTION	PGM DEFECT
4	10/23/92	2:20:26	U*13.76	0:00:06	CAN228	CANX1	CN027	CN027037	1	S0C7	DATA EXCEPTION	PGM DEFECT
5	10/23/92	2:31:48	K*06.78	0:00:36	CAN234	CANX1	CN014	CN014005	1	U0016	DCB/DSCB CONFLICTS	INPUT DATA
6	10/23/92	5:44:03	Z*09.86	0:00:06	PAY020	PAYR1	PAY086	PAY08698	1	S0C7	DATA EXCEPTION	PGM DEFECT
7	10/23/92	7:28:21	Z*09.86	0:03:27	ABC829	BACSX1	BAC429	BAC42955	1	S0C7	DATA EXCEPTION	PGM DEFECT
8	10/23/92	9:03:36	Z*09.86	0:00:49	FAX488	FAX1	FAX360	FAX358A5	1	S0C7	DATA EXCEPTION	PGM DEFECT
9	10/23/92	10:03:42	K*06.78	0:01:24	ABCGENR	BACSX1	BAC243	BAC24340	1	S0C7	DATA EXCEPTION	PGM DEFECT
10	10/23/92	11:04:10	Z*09.86	0:48:48	FAX488	FAX1	FAX074	FAX01995	1	S0C7	DATA EXCEPTION	PGM DEFECT
11	10/23/92	14:05:11	Z*09.86	0:00:46	FARTAPE	FAX1	FAR014	FAR02275	1	S0C7	DATA EXCEPTION	PGM DEFECT
12	10/23/92	19:36:00	K*06.78	0:00:12	MAXTAPE	MAX1	MAX101	MAXI0168	1	U3001	PGM FORCED SYS CALL	PGM DEFECT
13	10/23/92	20:39:27	X*03.10	0:00:00	DOXGENR	DOX1	DOX005	DOX00570	1	S714	TAPE LABEL/DS ERROR	INPUT DATA
14	10/23/92	21:12:31	Z*09.86	0:00:12	CAN345	CANX1	CAN004	CAN00466	1	S0C7	DATA EXCEPTION	PGM DEFECT

** SEPARATE PRODUCTION BATCH PGM ABENDS AND IBM STANDARD ABEND CODES BY APPLICATION SYSTEM PRODUCT AND OCCURS FOR MTD **

ABEND CODE/DESCRIPTION	PRODUCT NAME	OCT 9	OCT 10	OCT 12	OCT 13	OCT 14	OCT 15	OCT 16	OCT 17	OCT 18	OCT 19	OCT 20	OCT 21	OCT 22	OCT 23
SOC7-/DATA-DEF-EXCEPTIONS	BACSX1		2				1	2						1	2
	BACSX2					1							1		1
	CANX1	3		2		1	2		1	2	1	2	1	2	3
	FAX1					1		1		1	1		1	1	2
	PAYR1			1		1	3	1	1	3	1	1	1	1	2

Figure 3-4   Sample SMF Software Program Failure Abend System Cross-Reference Report with History of Selected Abend Type MTD

```
       DAILY COMMERCIAL BATCH  << PROD JOBS >>  AUTOMATED PROCESS QUALITY TIMELINE AUDIT OF ABEND DUMP ACTIVITY BY PROCESSOR

                                                           MIN                                                          MAX
CPU_X   JOBNAME    DATE    STARTED    ENDED             0:00:01                                                      23:59:01
                                                         *                                                             *
CPU_Z   ABC002    22OCT   0:53:59    0:54:55             X
CPU_K   PAY014    22OCT   2:00:30    2:51:48             |   S-E                                         S-E
CPU_K   MAX001    22OCT   8:54:37    9:36:00             |                                                 X
CPU_X   DOX005    22OCT  10:39:27   10:39:27             |                                                         SE
CPU_Z   DOX001    22OCT  20:01:12   20:29:00             |                                                            X
CPU_K   RDR004    22OCT  22:16:02   22:16:02             *                                                             *


       DAILY COMMERCIAL BATCH  << PROD PGMS >>  AUTOMATED PROCESS QUALITY TIMELINE AUDIT OF ABEND DUMP ACTIVITY BY PROCESSOR

                                                           MIN                                                          MAX
CPU_X   JOBSTEP    PROGRAM    DATE    STARTED    ENDED   0:00:01                                                      23:59:01
                                                         *                                                             *
CPU_Z   ABC00235   ABC0293   22OCT   0:53:59   0:54:55   X
CPU_Z   PAY142G2   PAYTAPE   22OCT   1:20:22   2:13:13     S-E
CPU_U   CAN02730   CANTAPE   22OCT   1:55:46   2:18:21      SE
CPU_U   CAN27037   CAN228    22OCT   0:06:51   2:50:26   S---E
CPU_K   PAY01405   PAY0934   22OCT   2:00:30   2:51:48      S-E
CPU_K   PAY08698   PAY020    22OCT   4:10:29   4:14:03
CPU_Z   ABC42955   ABC829    22OCT   8:02:50   8:18:21                    X
CPU_Z   FAX358A5   FAX488    22OCT   8:16:11   9:03:36                       SE
CPU_K   ABC24340   ABCGENR   22OCT   8:32:20   9:03:42                       SE
CPU_Z   FAX01995   FAX488    22OCT   8:13:04   9:04:10                       S-E
CPU_Z   FAR02275   FAX234    22OCT   7:00:05   9:05:11                     S---E
CPU_K   MAX00168   MAXGENR   22OCT   8:54:37   9:36:00                          S-E  X
CPU_X   DOX00570   DOXTAPE   22OCT  10:39:27  10:39:27                                  X
                                                         *                                                             *

                                                                        (CONT.)
```

Figure 3-5   Sample SMF Software Program Failure Abend System Log Sequence Time Plots Based upon MXG Performance Quality Data

System Completion Code (SCC) Cross-Reference

SCC Group	MVS Function	MACRO Name	Related SCC Codes
00x	Data Management	CHECK, PUT, GET	001, 002
01x	Data Management	OPEN, CLOSE	x13, x14
03x	Data Management/ISAM	OPEN, CLOSE	03x
08x	Virtual Storage Management	OPEN, CLOSE	x04, x0A
0Cx	Program Interrupt Handler	OPEN, CLOSE	0Cx
x00	Data Management	EXCP	400
x01	Data Management	WAIT	301
x02	Data Management	POST	102
x03	Task Termination	EXIT	C03
x04	Virtual Storage Management	GETMAIN	x04, x0A
x05	Virtual Storage Management	FREEMAIN	x04, x0A
x06	Program Management	LINK, LOAD, ATTACH	x04, x0A
x0A	Virtual Storage Management	DELETE, XCTL	x06
x0E	Interrupt Handler	GETMAIN (RTYPE)	x0A, x04
x12	Data Management	GETMAIN	x0A
x13	Data Management	SPIE	0Cx
x14	Data Management	BLDL/FIND	x06, B14
x15	Data Management	OPEN	x13, x14, x37
x16	Data Management	CLOSE	x13, x14, x37
x22	Task Management	CLOSE (TTYPE)	214, 714, B14
x37	Data Management	MGCR/QEDIT	x22
x40	Data Management	EOV	x37, x14, x13
x44	Data Management	RDJFCB	x37, x14, x13
x6B	Data Management	SYNADAF	001, x37
x78	Virtual Storage Management	MODESET	Fxx
x79	I/O Supervisor	GETMAIN/FREEMAIN	x04, x0A
x7D	Task Management	GETMAIN/FREEMAIN	102, 301
xFC	Supervisor	GETMAIN/FREEMAIN	Fxx

Figure 3-6 MVS Operating System Completion Coding Conventions and System Abend Diagnostic Cross-Reference Nomenclatures

MEASURING THE IMPACT OF HUMAN ERRORS

One of the first steps in the analysis of historical system failure data is to create profiles of the condition codes, time period, utilization patterns, and other characteristics existing at the time when each abend occurred. It is also important to build profiles of the types of failures that occur most often in each application system, vendor product, and customer area.

It is important to group the abends and failures according to the type of problem that caused the failure. In most cases, system failures will be related to the following basic causes:

- System Errors (including all hardware or media failures)
- Transmit Errors (including parity errors or line failures)
- JCL Errors (including invalid parameters and coding errors)
- DCB Errors (including inconsistent record length or BLKSIZE)
- Data Exceptions (such as incompatible program input types)
- I/O Exceptions (such as improper use of a service or device)

Out of these six common types of failures, only the first two—system errors and transmit errors—are due to hardware problems, the rest are due to human errors. Just as it is necessary to monitor and maintain records as to the reliability of the system hardware, it is also necessary to monitor the incidence with which common human errors cause problems resulting in system failure. Just as it is necessary to use system failure data to identify devices that may need maintenance or replacement, it is also necessary to identify software programs or products in need of maintenance or modification and to identify the technical staff or customer areas that might benefit from additional training in the proper use of the system.

The most common way to measure the impact of human errors is to keep historical performance data in at least one of two possible failure measurement forms. The first form, which emphasizes volume, is to calculate the *effective throughput*. This is done by dividing the total number of failures that occur in a given time period by the total number of work units (such as batch jobs or transactions) that were processed successfully during that same period. The second form, which emphasizes *effective reliability*, is calculated by measuring the duration of time between each successive failure, then averaging the *Mean Time Between Failures* (MTBF) over a suitably long period of time, such as a month or a year.

Generally, it is necessary to maintain a performance history of at least one, preferably both, of these software quality data measurements for every application system, vendor product, in-house program, online access pathway, and customer area. This will ensure the systematic and continuous improvement in the overall system environment. Each of these areas can be analyzed either individually or together, in order to identify procedures, processes, or functional areas whose quality can be improved.

This data is particularly important with respect to the introduction of programs, or program changes, into the production systems environment before the new software has been fully tested. This matter has always been particularly controversial because of the wide variety of testing methods and philosophies of systems management. In reality, the most important consideration in program testing and validation is that sufficient coverage has been achieved. This relates to the number of possible program process paths that have been tested and the number of possible inputs and outputs that have been demonstrated.

In practice, it is rarely possible to be able to completely test all of the alternate process paths, inputs, and outputs. So, it is more important to test a random sample of possible process paths, inputs, and outputs, up to a level that is indicated as sufficient by the results of testing over a period of time. This method helps minimize errors, achieving quality without incurring unreasonable costs.

How much testing is enough? This is a matter of judgment for each data center, which should largely be determined by how much cost and delay the data center is willing to incur in order to achieve zero defects. In applications that involve human safety, it is often essential to achieve zero defects at any cost. However, most common applications can afford to forego some of the testing and fix the errors when they surface, after the programs have been released for implementation. Yet, there is a proven method which has been demonstrated to help assign a cutoff of testing and achieve optimum reliability within the limits of the resources that are available and reasonable.

This method simply involves tracking the number of errors encountered during steady, repetitive testing using similarly sized volume test data beds. Also used are automated system log tracking of the average number of test software failures that occur within similar periods of time, as well as the severity level and type of failures that occur. The number and functional type of failures occurring within a given time period, expressed in either one of the two forms of failure measurement, can determine whether or not the testing can be ended and when the program can be approved for release.

This may seem like another judgment call. However, there is substantial research demonstrating that 99 percent of all programs written by reasonably competent programmers can be fully rid of 99 percent of the bugs within a relatively short period of well-designed, well-planned testing effort. Each program bug that is identified and removed will result in greater throughput, and a greater MTBF, until the failure curve flattens, indicating that the program probably cannot be improved any further and can be released to production. This flat failure curve, which is characterized by extremely high throughput and long time between failures, should remain more or less constant throughout the normal life cycle of the program— unless something in the system environment or the nature of the input data dramatically changes without notice.

Eventually, however, the entropy of discrete changes in operating systems, new technology, or introducing new customers to the data center, will result in a destablization of the failure curve. The number of errors will increase, as the effective throughput and MTBF drops off. This pattern relates to the beginning and end of the application system life cycle, which also has been characterized as the *bathtub* curve. Some examples of bathtub curves are shown in Figure 3-7, including examples of normal and unusual *Software Development Life Cycle* (SDLC) error detection patterns.

CUSTOMIZING ERROR CODES TO LOG SPECIAL PROGRAM ACTIONS

In addition to the system abend and operational condition codes automatically collected by the system logs, it is also possible to create *user-defined* failure codes, which appear on system logs whenever any such errors that are of special interest may occur. Most programmers are aware that such vendor products as CICS, IMS, DB2, or a utility product such as SYNCSORT can issue *user* abend codes to the system log when a product-specific error is encountered.

However, IBM has designed the operating system in a manner that allows each application programmer to call the ABEND macro and recovery management control blocks in order to force an interrupt that terminates the program if a particular type of undesirable condition or error is detected by the application program. This is a relatively advanced procedure that is documented in the IBM system programmers manual, as well as the special procedures manual for each supported compiler and high-level language.

This procedure involves specifying a unique error code (other than the codes reserved by the vendor's own products) and coding special error-handling instructions in the program according to the vendor

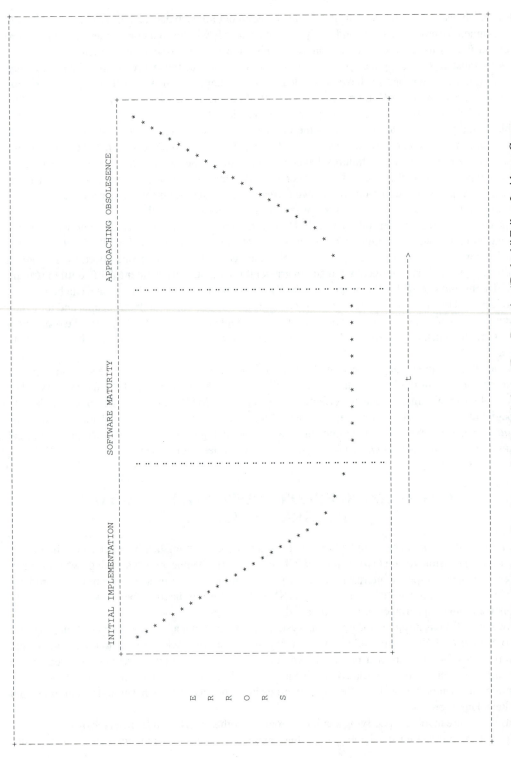

Figure 3-7 Example of a Typical System Development Life Cycle Software Error Detection "Bathtub" Failure Incidence Curve

manual's instructions. This procedure also makes use of operating system control blocks and special task services.

These user-defined error codes are preceded by a "U," in the form "U*nnnn*," which is expanded from a numeric hex value coded according to vendor instructions. Comparable system abend codes in IBM systems are preceded by an "S," in the form "S*nnnn*," so there is never any possibility that they will get confused. This method allows for the errors to be automatically captured on SMF. They are then sorted so that they are easily grouped according to whether they are caused by the system or by an application program.

There are some special requirements for each language and version of the operating system, but the process of implementing such user-defined abend codes is fairly straightforward. The more difficult process usually relates to the administration of the codes by the system configuration management function. It must be certain that two programs do not use the same code in signifying substantially different types of errors.

It is a good idea to use the same general coding convention that IBM uses to group and classify its system error codes. Yet, it is also important to avoid potential overlap of future codes.

DETERMINING THE COST OF SOFTWARE ERRORS

There are two common methods for determining costs related to software errors, both of which have applications to planning support to the life cycle of application software systems in a manner that optimizes the highest quality at the lowest possible cost. Both methods can be based directly upon automated software metrics and performance history data collected from SMF system logs and can then be supplemented by chargeback billing or system transfer-priced cost allocation data—if the data center is so equipped.

The first method involves determining the average cost to fix each particular type of problem that either causes, or is closely related to, each category of application program abend or system failure captured by the SMF system log. This method can be used along with effective throughput calculations and MTBF data to estimate the technical support required to fix an estimated number of failures and program abend incidents. Errors can then be forecast based on past performance history for each system, product, program, and customer pathway that is supported. Estimates of the labor costs can be used to justify and plan for software quality improvement efforts. These can result in direct savings due to the reduction in data center operational costs.

The second method involves determining the estimated business impact of system failures and program abends, in terms of revenue losses from computer downtime or delayed processing. This method involves using the same techniques that are used in underwriting and risk management. Basically, the damages involved in each potential type of failure must be estimated within a range of probable events over a given period of time. These are then based on the number of similar events which can be found within a given time period on failure performance databases derived from system logs.

The costs of these events can be calculated as real losses sustained over a period of time, and forecast over longer periods into the future. Estimates as to the potential costs of each particular type of system failure and abend can be determined. This data can then be used in order to cost-justify prospective remedies for each category of software error, up to the time when the costs of quality approach a breakeven point determined by the probability that a given number of failure-related losses will occur. This is basically self-insurance by the data center. But, if the data indicates the likelihood that a number of specific errors will occur or not occur within a particular time period, it is reasonably possible to purchase insurance from an underwriter using the data to support a fair premium.

Examples of the types of errors that can be prevented by specific strategies are shown in Figure 3-8, along with the types of system log data that are involved. In all cases, this failure performance history data can be used to predict relative probability that particular types of errors will occur and to devise quality improvement procedures as a result.

PREDICTING SOFTWARE FAILURE RATES FOR MANAGING IMPACT OF ERRORS

The basic methodology of probability calculus involves the determination of all the possible events or outcomes that can result from a particular set of assumed circumstances or conditions. This is done in order to estimate the chance that one out of all the many possible outcomes will occur with a given level of frequency during a given period of time. In reality, some events are more likely to happen than others. This is based on the strength of certain criteria which can be measured in order to determine if the strength of that influence is either increasing or decreasing

The volume of software quality measurement history data captured from system logs can be used to determine the number of possible outcomes and the strength of the trends that impact outcomes. The variety of data can lead to an extensive, statistically sophisticated analysis of any number of possible system-related errors, as well as human factors which can increase or decrease the number and timing of system failures and program abend events. However, this analysis is dependent upon the basic determination of the trend in number and types of system failures. These can then be forecast in order to predict future failure rates, as well as seasonal periods when particular types of failure are most likely to occur.

The two most basic failure prediction measurements relate to the effective throughput and effective reliability data that routinely accumulated to a historical performance database. These measurements are probably the highest priority to improve the quality of the application programming environment and are also probably the easiest to learn.

The first measurement is a simple calculation of the effective number of batch jobs or online transactions that were processed. This is expressed as the percentage of successfully processed batch jobs or transactions out of the total number attempted. In stabilized batch processing environments, the effective workloads processed can approach 99.9 percent, or one failure out of 1,000 programs executed. In stabilized online processing environments, the effective workloads can surpass 99.9999 percent, or less than one failure out of 1,000,000 real-time transactions. This metric should be calculated for every production application system, batch job, program, and customer area, or any resource user that has an extremely low or erratic success rate. This is automatically indicated by red flag threshold management reports based on range exceptions or extreme standard deviations, and it should be plotted and its abend codes analyzed in order to determine why failures occurred.

The second measurement can take two forms: either the raw number of failures that occurred for a common standardized time unit measure or the average amount of either elapsed clock time or normalized CPU time expended in successful program execution between failures. This type of measurement can be automatically collected from the system logs and accumulated to a performance history database. It is then plotted to show either the average number of particular types of errors that occurred every past month, quarter, or year, or the average clock time or CPU time between system failure or program errors using a comparable historical timeline. This data can be forecast using general,

SMF SYSTEM LOG RECORDS AND FAIL DATA TYPE	SMF MEASUREMENT PROCESS
S M F TYPE 2, 3 : Dump Program Header/Trailer ===============>	DUMP EVENT W/TIMESTAMP
S M F TYPE 4, 30_4: TSO/JOB Program Step Abends ===============>	PROGRAM ABEND W/TIMESTAMP
S M F TYPE 5, 30_5: TSO Session/Batch Job Abends ===============>	JOB/SESSION ABEND W/TIMESTAMP
S M F TYPE 7, 10: SMF Dump and Event Errors ===============>	DUMP EVENT W/TIMESTAMP
S M F TYPE 14,15, 61,65,66: DASD Catalog Failures ===============>	FAILURE EVENT W/TIMESTAMP
S M F TYPE 21, 22: Tape and I/O Device Errors ===============>	FAILURE EVENT W/TIMESTAMP
S M F TYPE 26: Program Interrupts or Cancels ===============>	INTERRUPT EVENT W/TIMESTAMP
S M F TYPE 38: Network Failure Events ===============>	FAILURE EVENT W/TIMESTAMP
S M F TYPE 71,72,75,76 CPU Process Exception Events ===============>	FAILURE EVENT W/TIMESTAMP
S M F TYPE 82,90: Security and Operator Fails ===============>	FAILURE EVENT W/TIMESTAMP

Figure 3-8 Types of Software Program Quality and Process Fail Events Captured by SMF

linear modeling methods normally used to predict the number of system outages and their impact during given future time periods.

Examples of some of the kinds of data that can be accumulated and plotted in order to predict software failure rates are shown in Figure 3-9. Also shown are examples of common TQM metrics and ratios that are used to monitor software quality.

ISOLATING THE IMPACT OF SOFTWARE FAILURES

Once historical data on the software errors is collected, it is possible to further analyze the impact of these errors by comparing two or more related factors to a type of error or the area where it most often occurs. This method involves basic *hypothesis testing* to confirm or disprove possible conclusions as to why particular errors are happening or to evaluate potential solutions to substantially reduce or prevent particular types of errors.

This is often one of the most critical data applications in a TQM program. It is the basis for most of the control limit analysis used in statistical process control methods.

These methods are largely based on elementary statistics and probability theory, which relate to the bell curve distributions and the assumption that as the number of observations of a randomized event is increased, the distribution of values associated with it approaches the normal bell curve. But if the values do not normalize, then the data is dependent on some outside influence that tends to skew the distribution, and most of the values tend to accumulate in either the high or low range, as opposed to the midrange of normally distributed values. This high or low *loading* of distribution demonstrates that conclusions can be drawn as to whether or not a particular factor was critical to the outcome and whether control of that factor can result in control over the critical software quality problem being analyzed.

One of the simplest methods is known as the *t-Test*, which gets its name from the "t" used to designate the "tail," or most extreme ends of the normal bell distribution curve. This test uses tables of probability values associated with the likelihood that a normal distribution will be achieved due to randomized influences as the number of observations increases. It can be used in order to determine if the difference between two groups is likely to be due to coincidence or if specific factors contributed to a difference between the two groups. The t-Test method is found in almost any statistics textbook, as it is a fundamental method.

An example of the use of a t-Test to demonstrate that a standardized test documentation form was more effective at speeding up the process of removing defects from a new system, as opposed to a free-form, nonstandardized test documentation, is shown in Figures 3-10a and 3-10b. Examples of the SAS code used to produce similar t-Test analysis are found in Appendix C.

CATEGORIES OF SOFTWARE QUALITY PROBLEMS AND AVAILABLE SMF SYSTEM LOG RECORDS SOURCE	SOFTWARE MEASUREMENTS FAILURE DATA TYPE
SOFTWARE PROGRAM FAILURES	
S M F TYPE 2, 3 : Dump Program Header/Trailer	-----------> DUMP EVENT W/TIMESTAMP
S M F TYPE 4, 30_4: TSO/JOB Program Step Abends	-----------> PROGRAM ABEND W/TIMESTAMP
S M F TYPE 5, 30_5: TSO Session/Batch Job Abends	-----------> JOB/SESSION ABEND W/TIMESTAMP
S M F TYPE 7: SMF Program Error Dump Event	-----------> DUMP EVENT W/TIMESTAMP
S M F TYPE 71,72,75,76 CPU Process Exception Events	-----------> FAILURE EVENT W/TIMESTAMP
DATA I/O PROCESS FAILURES	
S M F TYPE 10: I/O Resource Allocation Fail	-----------> DUMP EVENT W/TIMESTAMP
S M F TYPE 14,15 Non-VSAM Dataset Access Error	-----------> FAILURE EVENT W/TIMESTAMP
S M F TYPE 61,65,66 VSAM Catalog Failures	-----------> FAILURE EVENT W/TIMESTAMP
S M F TYPE 21: Tape and Magnetic Media Error	-----------> FAILURE EVENT W/TIMESTAMP
S M F TYPE 22: I/O Device Activity Failures	-----------> FAILURE EVENT W/TIMESTAMP
S M F TYPE 75: CPU I/O Paging Event Errors	-----------> FAILURE EVENT W/TIMESTAMP
S M F TYPE 76: CPU I/O Trace Event Failures	-----------> FAILURE EVENT W/TIMESTAMP
DATA SECURITY EXCEPTIONS	
S M F TYPE 82: Security Access Failure Audit	-----------> FAILURE EVENT W/TIMESTAMP
OPERATIONAL PROCESS FAILS	
S M F TYPE 26: Program Interrupts or Cancels	-----------> INTERRUPT EVENT W/TIMESTAMP
S M F TYPE 90: System Crash or Operator Fail	-----------> FAILURE EVENT W/TIMESTAMP
NETWORK OPERATIONAL ERROR	
S M F TYPE 38: Network Failure Events	-----------> FAILURE EVENT W/TIMESTAMP

Figure 3-9   Categories of Software Quality Failure Measurements and SMF Source Record Type

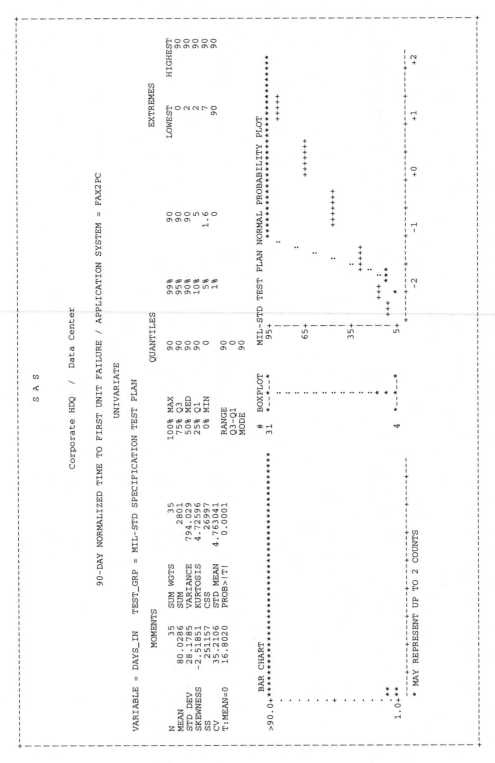

Figure 3-10a   SAS Univariate Plot of Implemented Software Program Time to First Failure with MIL-STD Testing Plan

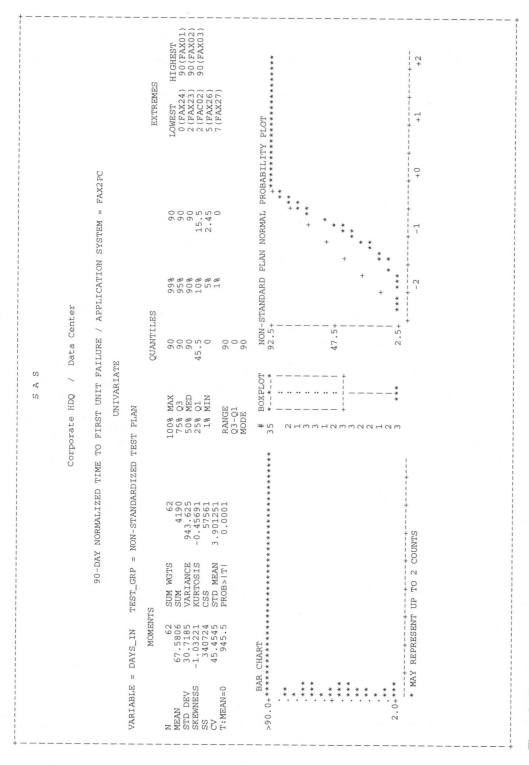

Figure 3-10b   SAS Univariate Plot of Implemented Software Program Time to First Failure without Standardized Testing

4

VENDOR PRODUCTS THAT HELP MANAGE SOFTWARE ERRORS

There are numerous products on the market that assist in tracing program control block linkages and procedural flow involved in executing application programs having repeated abends or performance problems. These include special add-on facilities offered by the operating systems vendor. There are also a number of products which assist in testing and debugging program abend dumps. However, there are only a limited number of products which use SMF system logs as automated input for the analysis of program failures, in spite of the fact that SMF system logs were originally designed as a program diagnostic analysis tool. This is a reflection of a traditional view of program debugging and dump analysis as an art more than a science and has been reflected in the cumbersome nature of many painstaking manual procedures. However, there is considerable interest in use of artificial intelligence and expert systems to assist in this procedure, and it is likely that a considerable number of vendors will apply these new technologies to assist in automated analysis of system logs in the not too distant future.

VENDOR APPLICATION PROGRAM FAILURE ANALYSIS PRODUCT: ABEND-AID

By far the most widely known and widely used application program failure analysis tool is ABEND-AID, which is developed and marketed by Compuware, Inc., of Farmington Hills, Michigan. Although ABEND-AID does not make direct use of SMF system logs, it uses the same control regions and methods as SMF in order to partition itself away from the recovery management process when a problem is detected and the ABEND macro is initiated.

ABEND-AID has its own control blocks and supersedes some of the standard control functions of the IBM host operating systems. ABEND-AID is constantly sampling task status and condition codes in order to provide its own real-time monitoring of all supervisory processes controlled by the operating system. It is parallel to the monitoring of the SMF control blocks, except that the ABEND-AID product collects much more extensive information about the addresses and tasks requested by the program load module and its related program control blocks. In the event that the program is interrupted for recovery management tasks due to the detection of a possible error condition, the ABEND-AID product immediately begins to capture and format only the most critical diagnostic portions of the massive volume of data that would normally be unloaded in the event of a core program dump. ABEND-AID is able to accomplish this by using the critical program address data that it has been closely monitoring in order to jump to the beginning of the control blocks most important to diagnostic troubleshooting. Only the critical data from each control section is copied to an ABEND-AID output writer file, so that all of the most important data are captured before a potential loss occurs. It also serves to greatly reduce the incredible volume of trivial or damaged data that would otherwise require many hours to painstakingly search for the abend's cause.

In addition, the ABEND-AID product provides troubleshooting hints in the form of simple descriptive textual documentation summarizing individual abend code and associated system messages which could be found buried in the overwhelming detail of IBM diagnostic manuals. ABEND-AID also provides instructions for further analysis and recommended procedures for fixing the problem indicated by system error codes. These two characteristics allow users of ABEND-AID to dramatically reduce wasted system resources when a recovery management control action is initiated to dump an abending program from processor memory. It will also reduce the level of advanced diagnostic skill required to quickly fix a program error and to ensure that the error is fixed with minimum time and cost.

Examples of some of these ABEND-AID reports are shown in Figures 4-1a to 4-1h. Although these reports are not based on SMF system log data, they can be used in combination with automated quality measurements and the performance database history accumulated from SMF data to cross-reference multiple ABEND-AID reports of individual abend events, thus providing a comprehensive analysis of why the abends actually occurred, as well as the cost of eliminating software errors.

```
/------------------------------------------------------------------\
| COMPUWARE/SPF---- 'TSO.AA.F600.REPORT.FILE' TSN050TS    JOB09691--- |
|                                                                  |
|                     OUTPUT SELECTION MENU                        |
| SELECT OPTION ===>                                               |
|                                                                  |
|  1 or HEADER  - Top of output (header and help if present)       |
|  2 or NSI     - Next Sequential Instruction (location of abend)  |
|  3 or REGS    - Register contents and PSW's                      |
|  4 or DIAGS   - Diagnostic Information                           |
|  5 or TRACE   - Trace of flow from program to program            |
|  6 or PROG    - Program Storage                                  |
|  7 or PLIST   - Program Listing (from Procedure Div-(PAR, ALL or nn) |
|  8 or FILES   - Data Management Control Blocks                   |
|  9 or IMS     - IMS diagnostic and status information            |
| 10 or IDMS    - CA-IDMS diagnostic and status information        |
| 11 or DB2     - DB2 diagnostic and status information            |
| 12 or SORT    - Current sort record                              |
| 13 or EPILOG  - Abend-AID termination information                |
|                                                                  |
|           Key option number and press ENTER.  Or                 |
|           press ENTER to start at top of output and view         |
|           options 1 through 5.                                   |
|                                                                  |
\------------------------------------------------------------------/
```

Figure 4-1a   Compuware/SPF ABEND-AID Error Control Center Main Menu

```
/------------------------------------------------------------------\
| COMPUWARE/SPF --- 'TSO.AA.R600.RPTFILE' -------------- ROW 1 OF 52 |
| COMMAND INPUT ===>                                                |
|                  ABEND-AID DATASET DIRECTORY                      |
| JOBNAME  RPT NUMBER  JESID   ABEND    DATE      TIME   PGMR   SIZE|
| TSS070CS       71  JOB08223  S0C7   12 APR 91  17.23.20 CLAYTON,D 31K|
| TSS070CS (L)   70  JOB07462  U1035  12 APR 91   9.16.47 DONNA,C  15K|
| TSH050CS       69  JOB09637  U0240  12 APR 91   7.42.23 WOODS,D  15K|
| TSH0750S       68  JOB06383  S0C2   11 APR 91  22.46,39 TWEED,S  15K|
| TSH025CS       67  JOB08792  SNAP   11 APR 91  21.39.53 SMITH,T  15K|
| TSH020CS       66  JOB07303  S0C1   11 APR 91  17.56.15 GARY,K   15K|
| TSH030CS       65  JOB07725  U1020  11 APR 91   3.05.08 WOODS,D  31K|
| TSH030CS (L)   64  JOB06559  S0C7   10 APR 91  22.17.42 TAYLOR,G 31K|
| TSH025CS       63  JOB08860  S0CB   10 APR 91  21.55.23 WOODS,D  15K|
| TSH025CS (L)   62  JOB08953  S0C7   10 APR 91  19.44.37 SMITH,T  31K|
| TSS070CS       61  JOB09371  S213   10 APR 91  18.19.51 WOODS,D  64K|
| TSS060CS       60  JOB06556  SD37   10 APR 91   9.47.07 DONNA,C  31K|
| TSA065CS       59  JOB07632  S0C7   10 APR 91   7.16.24 RANDAL,L 31K|
| TSA065CS (L)   58  JOB05861  S0CF   10 APR 91   4.25.43 SMITH,R  15K|
| TSA080CS       57  JOB08490  S2222  10 APR 91   3.43.13 HEED,E   15K|
| TSH070CS       56  JOB09313  S0C7    9 APR 91  18.38.57 FRANKEN,S 31K|
| TSF020CS       55  JOB06736  SD37    9 APR 91  17.50.18 FRANKEN,S 31K|
| TSD020CS (L)   54  JOB05312  S0CB    9 APR 91  16.22.24 CLAYTON,D 15K|
|                                                                  |
\------------------------------------------------------------------/
```

Figure 4-1b   Compuware/SPF ABEND-AID Problem Manager File Selection

The ABEND-AID/CWSMF product is also developed by Compuware. In fact, it is designed to be used as a summary reporting product to evaluate the effectiveness of ABEND-AID in the ongoing diagnosis and elimination of program failure events. The Compuware-SMF product reads large volumes of archived SMF system log data, usually spanning a period from one month to one year. It prepares a

```
/------------------------------------------------------------------\
|                                                                  |
|                                                                  |
|          *****************************************               |
|          *  Next Sequential Instruction Section  *               |
|          *****************************************               |
|                                                                  |
|                                                                  |
|   The next sequential instruction to be extracted in program     |
|          SUBPGM1 was at displacement  0002DB.                    |
|                                                                  |
| The program was compiled on 17 MAY 91 and is 002036 bytes long.  |
|                                                                  |
|          It is part of load module MAIN2PGM.                     |
|                                                                  |
|    The module was loaded from STEPLIB library TSO000.AA.LOAD;     |
|    It was link edited on 17 MAY 91 and is 0064B8 bytes long.     |
|                                                                  |
|   The last known I/O operation or call was issued from program   |
|          SUBPGM1 at displacement  000294.                        |
|                                                                  |
\------------------------------------------------------------------/
```

Figure 4-1c   Compuware ABEND-AID Next Sequential Instruction Section

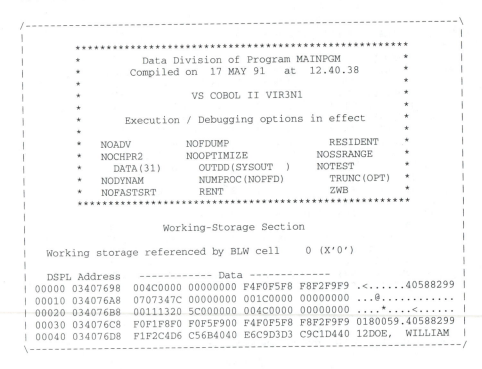

```
/-------------------------------------------------------------------\
|                                                                   |
|       *********************************************************   |
|       *            Data Division of Program MAINPGM          *   |
|       *          Compiled on  17 MAY 91   at  12.40.38       *   |
|       *                                                      *   |
|       *                VS COBOL II VIR3N1                    *   |
|       *                                                      *   |
|       *         Execution / Debugging options in effect      *   |
|       *                                                      *   |
|       *    NOADV         NOFDUMP               RESIDENT       *   |
|       *    NOCHPR2       NOOPTIMIZE            NOSSRANGE       *   |
|       *     DATA(31)      OUTDD(SYSOUT  )      NOTEST          *   |
|       *    NODYNAM       NUMPROC(NOPFD)        TRUNC(OPT)      *   |
|       *    NOFASTSRT     RENT                  ZWB             *   |
|       *********************************************************   |
|                                                                   |
|                     Working-Storage Section                      |
|                                                                   |
|   Working storage referenced by BLW cell     0 (X'0')            |
|                                                                   |
|    DSPL Address   ------------ Data -------------                 |
|  00000 03407698  004C0000 00000000 F4F0F5F8 F8F2F9F9 .<......40588299 |
|  00010 034076A8  0707347C 00000000 001C0000 00000000 ...@........... |
|  00020 034076B8  00111320 5C000000 004C0000 00000000 ....*....<...... |
|  00030 034076C8  F0F1F8F0 F0F5F900 F4F0F5F8 F8F2F9F9 0180059.40588299 |
|  00040 034076D8  F1F2C4D6 C56B4040 E6C9D3D3 C9C1D440 12DOE,  WILLIAM |
\-------------------------------------------------------------------/
```

Figure 4-1d   Compuware ABEND-AID Problem Program Storage Section

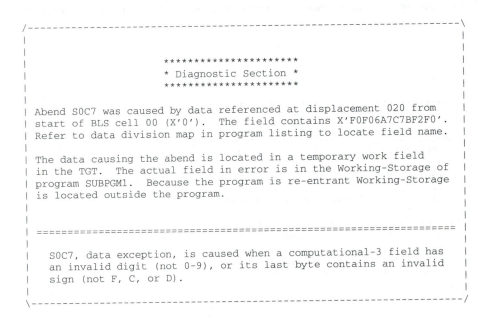

```
/-------------------------------------------------------------------\
|                                                                   |
|                                                                   |
|                                                                   |
|                  ***********************                          |
|                  * Diagnostic Section *                          |
|                  ***********************                          |
|                                                                   |
| Abend S0C7 was caused by data referenced at displacement 020 from |
| start of BLS cell 00 (X'0').  The field contains X'F0F06A7C7BF2F0'.|
| Refer to data division map in program listing to locate field name.|
|                                                                   |
| The data causing the abend is located in a temporary work field   |
| in the TGT.  The actual field in error is in the Working-Storage of|
| program SUBPGM1.  Because the program is re-entrant Working-Storage|
| is located outside the program.                                   |
|                                                                   |
|                                                                   |
| ================================================================= |
|                                                                   |
|   S0C7, data exception, is caused when a computational-3 field has |
|   an invalid digit (not 0-9), or its last byte contains an invalid |
|   sign (not F, C, or D).                                          |
|                                                                   |
\-------------------------------------------------------------------/
```

Figure 4-1e   Compuware ABEND-AID Problem Program Diagnostic Section

```
/------------------------------------------------------------------\
|                   * * * * * * * * * * * * * * * * * * * * *        |
|                   * Call Trace Summary *                          |
|                   * * * * * * * * * * * * * * * * * * * * *        |
|                                                                   |
| ******Calling******   ***Return***           ******Called******  |
| Load-Mod   Program    Type  Value            Program   Load-Mod   |
|                                                                   |
| *SYSTEM                               Calls  MAINPGM   MAIN2PGM   |
| MAIN2PGM  MAINPGM     DISP  000784    Calls  SUBPGM1   MAIN2PGM * |
| MAIN2PGM  SUBPGM1     DISP  0003D6    Calls  IGZETRN   IGZCPCO    |
|                                                                   |
|                                              Abending Program *   |
|                                                                   |
| **************************************************************    |
| *                Application Program Attributes              *    |
| **************************************************************    |
|                                                                   |
| Load-Mod   Program    Compile Date   Length   Language            |
|                                                                   |
| MAIN2PGM  MAINPGM      17 MAY 91      00405E   VS COBOL II V1R3M1  |
| MAIN2PGM  SUBPGM1      17 MAY 91      002036   VS COBOL II V1R3M1  |
|                                                                   |
\------------------------------------------------------------------/
```

Figure 4-1f   Compuware ABEND-AID Problem Program Attributes Section

series of summary reports that can be used in combination with the ABEND-AID product to identify the errors that occur most often, as well as the number of executions of each specific program by language and IBM system facility. This can then be cross-referenced to calculate measurements of effective

```
/------------------------------------------------------------------\
|  **************************************************************    |
|  *                  Program Listing Section               *       |
|  **************************************************************    |
|  000035           CALC-SAVINGS.                                   |
|  000037               MOVE GROSS-PAY       TO WS-GROSS-PAY.       |
|  000038               MOVE SAVINGS-FACTOR TO WS-SAVINGS-FACTOR.   |
|  000039               MOVE ZEROS           TO WS-SAVINGS-AMT.     |
|  000040               MOVE SPACES          TO MIN-MAX-PRT.        |
|  ABND STMT ==>        MULTIPLY WS-SAVINGS-FACTOR BY WS-GROSS-PAY  |
|  000042                 GIVING WS-SAVINGS-AMT.                    |
|  000043               MOVE WS-SAVINGS-AMT TO SAVINGS-AMT.         |
|  000044           *                                               |
|  000045           *  VALIDATE SAVINGS FACTOR--IF INVALID,         |
|  000046           *    SET SAVINGS AMOUNT TO ZERO AND PRINT MSG.  |
|  000047           *                                               |
|  000048               IF WS-SAVINGS-FACTOR > MAX-FACTOR THEN      |
|  000049                 MOVE 'MAXIMUM' TO MIN-MAX-PRT             |
|  000050               ELSE                                        |
|  000051               IF WS-SAVINGS-FACTOR < MIN-FACTOR THEN      |
|  000052                 MOVE 'MINIMUM' TO MIN-MAX-PRT             |
|  000053               ELSE NEXT SENTENCE.                         |
\------------------------------------------------------------------/
```

Figure 4-1g   Compuware ABEND-AID Program Sourcecode Listing Section

```
/------------------------------------------------------------------\
|           Data Management Control Blocks for DDNAME - TIMECARD    |
|                                                                  |
|          DSNAME=CWV.TSO000.AA.TIMECARD                           |
|                                               ACC METH=VSAM      |
|   File Excp Count=1                                              |
|   File Summary:                                                  |
|     Access type.......BASE CLUSTER                              |
|     Dataset type.......ESDS                                     |
|     Processing type....ADR,AMODE31,NFX,DDN,NDF,SEQ,NCI,IN,NIS,NRM,NRS |
|   File errors.........None                                      |
|                                                                  |
|   Current record:                                               |
|   00044F70    CHAR  4058829912DOE,  WILLIAM   T.      00|@#200   |
|               ZONE  FFFFFFFFFFCDC644ECDDCCD44E44444444444FF677FFF |
|               DIGIT 4058829912465B006933914003B000000000000ACB200 |
|                     1...5...10....*...20....*...30....*...40....* |
|   Previous record:                                              |
|   0340E8A0    CHAR  4014003912JOHNSTONE, REGINALD     12003983   |
|               ZONE  FFFFFFFFFFDDCDEEDDC64DCCCDCDC44444444FFFFFFFF |
|               DIGIT 4014003912158523655B095795134000000000012003983 |
|                     1...5...10....*...20....*...30....*...40....* |
|   Last request:                                                 |
|      ID...............GET              Mode.........MOVE         |
|      Request ECB.......completed       Access........SEQ        |
|   Misc:                                                         |
|      *Locate record at specified RBA*   Current RBA........000000F0 |
\------------------------------------------------------------------/
```

Figure 4-1h   Compuware ABEND-AID Problem Program File Area Section

throughput, as well as incidence of each functional category of error by abend code type, which can be useful as a TQM process analysis tool.

CWSMF can also be used to estimate the cost savings incurred by using ABEND-AID in the diagnosis and prevention of particular types of program abends. This forms a powerful basis for a TQM program for the continuous improvement of the data center's operational environments. In addition, CWSMF provides a series of customizable tables which relate each abend code and each type of system failure to an average cost and time to fix. These baseline problem management tables can be updated according to the experience and performance history data of the individual data center and can provide the basis for powerful estimating tools that aid in the planning delivery of technical support services. It can also predict the impact of ongoing trends in the predominant types of errors upon the availability of technical manpower as well as uninterrupted system resources.

The CWSMF product was originally provided at no cost to the prospective Compuware customers of the ABEND-AID line of products. A demonstration version of this impressive tool may still be available from a Compuware vendor for those data centers considering the purchase of ABEND-AID. It is highly recommended for data centers considering the use of SMF as an automated software quality measurement tool. The CWSMF reports can be used to quickly identify a wide range of potential cost savings from the elimination of program errors, as well as increasing the efficiency of each individual data center environment based upon expert systems analysis of the SMF system log data.

Examples of the CWSMF reports can be seen in Figures 4-2a to 4-2e.

```
****************************************************************************
*                                                                          *
*            C O M P U W A R E    S O F T W A R E    S M F                  *
*                         ABEND ANALYSIS                                    *
*                                                                          *
*     ABEND-AID COPYRIGHT (C) COMPUWARE CORPORATION 1983, 1990,             *
*                     ALL RIGHTS RESERVED.                                  *
*                                                                          *
****************************************************************************


****************************************************************************
*            SMF BASED ABEND ANALYSIS              REL 5.4  05/18/90   *
****************************************************************************
```

COMPUWARE CORPORATION IS PLEASED TO PROVIDE YOU WITH THIS ANALYSIS OF YOUR
ABEND ACTIVITY. IN ORDER FOR THIS REPORT TO BE MEANINGFUL THE PROGRAM
SHOULD HAVE BEEN PROVIDED WITH 28 TO 60 DAYS OF DATA.
     THE DATA SUPPLIED CAME FROM DATASET SMF.SYSTEM.LOG.DAYS.G0888V00.
THIS REPRESENTS 32 DAYS OF ACTIVITY BETWEEN APRIL 19, 1991
AND MAY 20, 1991. THERE WERE 32 DAYS IN THIS INTERVAL. THE ANALYSIS
SHOWS THAT ABEND-AID HAD A POTENTIAL COST SAVING OF $999,999 FOR THIS
PERIOD AND THE POTENTIAL FOR INCREASED PROGRAMMER PRODUCTIVITY BY A TIME
SAVING OF 9,999 HOURS 15 MINUTES.
     YOUR INSTALLATION HAD A TOTAL OF 99,999 ABENDS OR AN AVERAGE
OF 9999 PER DAY. THIS AVERAGE IS BASED ON DAYS ACTUALLY WORKED. THE
ABEND COUNT INCLUDES SYSTEM AS WELL AS USER ABENDS. ABEND-AID SUPPORTS
ALL SYSTEM ABENDS AND A HIGH PERCENTAGE OF THE IMS USER ABENDS. WE
RECOMMEND THAT YOU SUPPRESS ALL USER DUMPS UNLESS SPECIFICALLY REQUESTED.
ABEND-AID WOULD HAVE SUPPRESSED THE DUMP FOR 99,999 ABENDS WHICH IS
APPROXIMATELY 99 PERCENT OF THE ABENDS THAT YOU HAD.
     THE PROGRAMMER SAVINGS ARE DEVELOPED TWO WAYS. ONE AS A TOTAL NUMBER
OF HOURS SAVED AND THE OTHER AS THE ECONOMIC VALUE OF THESE HOURS AT
YOUR OWN HOURLY RATE SHOWN ABOVE. IN ORDER TO ESTIMATE THE TIME
SAVINGS WE HAVE WEIGHTED EACH ABEND CODE WITH THE NUMBER OF MINUTES
WE FEEL THAT ABEND-AID CAN CUT OFF THE TIME IT TAKES THE PROGRAMMER
TO SOLVE A PARTICULAR ABEND. THESE FACTORS ARE, OF COURSE, BASED ON
AVERAGES. A GIVEN ABEND CODE MAY VARY FROM 2 MINUTES TO 2 DAYS BASED
ON THE PARTICULAR PROBLEM AND THE PROGRAMMER INVOLVED. WE FEEL THAT
OUR NUMBERS ARE CONSERVATIVE AND THAT THE SAVINGS PROJECTED ARE
EASILY ATTAINABLE. PLEASE REMEMBER THAT THE PROGRAMMER SAVINGS ARE
BASED ON APPLICATION PROGRAMMERS -- NOT SYSTEMS PROGRAMMERS.

```
****************************************************************************
*                  PROGRAMMER TIME FACTORS                            *
****************************************************************************
```

ONE OF THE FOLLOWING TIME FACTORS HAS BEEN ASSIGNED TO EACH ABEND CODE. THIS
IS BASED ON THE DIFFICULTY OF THE ABEND AND THE INFORMATION AND ANALYSIS WE CAN
PROVIDE FOR YOU. THE ABEND-AID OUTPUT MAY RANGE FROM PROVIDING THE CORRECT
LOCATION AND BRIEF EXPLANATION, WITH SOLUTION, OF THE ERROR TO CASES WHERE WE
HAVE DONE SIGNIFICANT ANALYSIS OF THE PROBLEM AND PROVIDED INFORMATION THAT IS
NOT READILY FOUND IN THE STANDARD IBM DUMP.

            1.   5 MINUTES SAVED.
            2.   10 MINUTES SAVED.
            3.   15 MINUTES SAVED.
            4.   60 MINUTES SAVED.

WE BELIEVE THESE VALUES ARE QUITE CONSERVATIVE. HOWEVER, THEY MAY BE INCREASED
IF DESIRED. ANY ABEND CODE THAT YOU STRONGLY BELIEVE SHOULD NOT BE USED IN
THIS REPORT CAN BE MARKED NON-APPLICABLE, THEREBY NULLIFYING THE PROGRAMMER
TIME FACTOR FOR THAT ABEND.

Figure 4-2a   Compuware ABEND-AID / CWSMF Analyzer Report

```
*************************************************************************
*                      OPERATIONAL SAVINGS                             *
*************************************************************************
```

THE NUMBERS BELOW WILL GIVE YOU AN IDEA OF THE SAVINGS IN THE OPERATIONS
AREA THAT CAN BE ATTAINED WITH ABEND-AID.   THESE FIGURES DO NOT INCLUDE
THE SAVINGS DUE TO COSTS SUCH AS REDUCED OPERATOR SET UP AND TRANSPORTATION OF
PAPER AND LISTINGS TO AND FROM PROGRAMMERS.

```
                        PERIOD - 32 DAYS

                  *************************
                  *   WITHOUT ABEND-AID   *
                  *************************

      TOTAL DUMPS                                99,999
      AVERAGE MEMORY USED PER DUMP                1,024K
      TOTAL PRINT LINES OF DUMP              999,999,999
      TOTAL PAGES OF DUMP OUTPUT               9,999,999

      PRINT TIME:
                    @ 900 LPM           99999 HRS.    47 MIN.
                    @ 600 LPM           99999 HRS.    41 MIN.
```

THE TOTAL LINES PRINTED CALCULATIONS ARE BASED ON 1.8 K PER PAGE OF
DUMP OUTPUT.

```
                  *********************
                  *   WITH ABEND-AID   *
                  *********************

      TOTAL DUMPS SUPPRESSED BY ABEND-AID        99,999
      PERCENTAGE OF DUMPS SUPPRESSED                 99%
      AVERAGE MEMORY USED PER SUPPRESSED DUMP     1,263K
      TOTAL PRINT LINES OF DUMP SUPPRESSED   999,999,999
      TOTAL PAGES OF DUMP OUTPUT SUPPRESSED    9,999,999

      PRINT TIME SAVED:
                    @ 900 LPM        ***** HRS. 19 MIN.
                    @ 600 LPM        ***** HRS. 59 MIN.

*************************************************************************
*                 OPERATIONAL COST SAVINGS SUMMARY                     *
*************************************************************************
      COST SAVINGS PAPER                       $ 99,999
      COST SAVINGS ADDITIONAL PRINT SUPPLIES   $ 99,999
      COST SAVINGS PRINTER                     $ 99,999


*************************************************************************
*                      PROGRAMMER SAVINGS                              *
*************************************************************************
```

THESE SAVINGS ARE BASED ON AN HOURLY RATE OF $99.99 AND THE WEIGHTING
SCHEME DISCUSSED ABOVE AND DOCUMENTED IN THE TABLES AT THE END OF THE
REPORT.   AGAIN, WE DO NOT THINK THAT THESE NUMBERS, ON THE AVERAGE, ARE
OUT OF LINE.   IN FACT, WE BELIEVE THAT IN MANY ENVIRONMENTS WE CAN HAVE
AN EVEN LARGER IMPACT.   HOWEVER, WE RECOGNIZE THAT THIS IS A VERY SUBJECTIVE
AREA SO WE WANT YOU TO TRY THE PRODUCT TO SEE WHAT BENEFITS YOU BELIEVE WE
WILL HAVE.   EVEN IF YOU DISCOUNT OUR FIGURES SUBSTANTIALLY YOU WILL
FIND THAT ABEND-AID WILL BE OF SIGNIFICANT HELP TO YOUR COMPANY AND WILL
MORE THAN PAY FOR ITSELF IN THE FIRST YEAR.

Figure 4-2b   Compuware ABEND-AID / CWSMF Analyzer Report (*continued*)

```
****************************************************************************
*                                                                          *
*                        SMF ANALYSIS SUMMARY                              *
*                                                                          *
****************************************************************************

          PARAMETER VALUES:
              - PAPER COST                      $ 9.99
              - PAGES PER BOX                    9,999
              - ADDITIONAL PRINT SUPPLIES       $99.99
              - LINES PER PRINT SUPPLIES       999,999
              - PRINTER LOW RATE                   999
              - PRINTER HIGH RATE                9,999
              - PROGRAMMER COST                 $99.99

              - PRINTER TIME PER HOUR           $9.99
              - AVERAGE MEMORY PARAMETER            0

          TOTAL DUMPS SUPPRESSED BY ABEND-AID        99,999
          PERCENTAGE OF DUMPS SUPPRESSED                99%
          AVERAGE MEMORY USED PER SUPPRESSED DUMP    1,028K
          TOTAL PRINT LINES OF DUMP SUPPRESSED   999,999,999
          TOTAL PAGES OF DUMP OUTPUT SUPPRESSED     9,999,999
          PRINT TIME SAVED:   @ 900 LPM         9,999 HRS. 19 MIN.
                              @ 600 LPM         9,999 HRS. 59 MIN.

THE NUMBERS BELOW ARE RECAPPED FOR YOUR BENEFIT AND WILL BE USED TO PROJECT
THE FIRST YEAR SAVINGS POSSIBLE WITH THE PRODUCT.

SAVINGS FOR THIS PERIOD  (32 DAYS)
              - PAPER                           $ 99,999
              - ADDITIONAL PRINT SUPPLIES       $ 99,999
              - PRINTER TIME                    $ 99,999
              - VALUE OF PROGRAMMER TIME        $ 99,999
                  TOTAL SAVINGS         $  999,999
              -PROGRAMMER TIME SAVED        9,999 HOURS 15 MINUTES

BELOW WE HAVE PROJECTED THE FIRST YEAR'S SAVINGS POSSIBLE WITH OUR PRODUCT.
WE HAVE BASED THIS ANALYSIS ON THE DATA YOU HAVE SUPPLIED US AND EXPANDED
IT TO A ONE YEAR PERIOD WITH 295 WORK DAYS.  FROM THIS YOU WILL BE
ABLE TO MAKE AN INTELLIGENT DECISION ON THE VALUE OF OUR PRODUCT.

PROJECTED YEARLY SAVINGS  (295 DAYS)
              - PAPER                           $  999,999
              - ADDITIONAL PRINT SUPPLIES       $  999,999
              - PRINTER TIME                    $  999,999
              - VALUE OF PROGRAMMER TIME        $  999,999
                  TOTAL SAVINGS        $ 9,999,999
              -PROGRAMMER TIME SAVED       99,999 HOURS 10 MINUTES

      TOTAL YEARLY SAVINGS                     $99,999,999
```

Figure 4-2c   Compuware ABEND-AID / CWSMF Analyzer Report (*continued*)

```
**************************************************************************
*            OPERATIONAL SAVINGS - DASD STORAGE (ALTERNATIVE)            *
**************************************************************************
```

THIS PAGE REPRESENTS AN ALTERNATE METHOD OF PROJECTING OPERATIONAL SAVINGS
BASED ON DASD STORAGE RATHER THAN PRINTING THE DUMPS. THE DEFAULT ASSUMPTION
IS THAT DUMPS ARE STORED ON A 3380-BE4 MODEL DEVICE FOR AN AVERAGE OF THREE
DAYS EACH. FOLLOWING IS A LIST OF ALTERNATIVE DEVICES THAT COULD BE USED,
AND THE CORRESPONDING COST PER DAY. THIS COST REPRESENTS RENT PLUS MAINTENANCE
FOR THE DEVICE. THE DEFAULT COST AND TIME INTERVAL COULD BE ALTERED TO WHATEVER
IS APPROPRIATE FOR YOUR INSTALLATION, IF REQUIRED.

```
            DEVICE              COST (PER DAY)
            3380-BD4            $ 99            (SINGLE DENSITY)
            3380-BE4            $ 99            (DOUBLE DENSITY)
            3380-BK4            $ 99            (TRIPLE DENSITY)
```

THE SAVINGS REPRESENTED BY THIS PAGE ARE NOT INCLUDED IN THE OVERALL TOTALS,
SINCE THEY ARE AN ALTERNATIVE, NOT AN ADDITION, TO THE PRINTER COSTS ILLUS-
TRATED ELSEWHERE.

```
                    PERIOD - 32 DAYS

                **************************
                *    WITHOUT ABEND-AID   *
                **************************
    TOTAL DUMPS                                        99,999
    AVERAGE MEMORY USED PER DUMP                        1,028K
    TOTAL BYTES OF DASD USED TO STORE DUMPS    999,999,999,999
    NUMBER OF CYLINDERS USED TO STORE DUMPS            99,999
    PERCENT OF DEVICE USED TO STORE DUMPS              9.999%

                *********************
                *   WITH ABEND-AID   *
                *********************

    TOTAL DUMPS SUPPRESSED BY ABEND-AID               99,999
    PERCENTAGE OF DUMPS SUPPRESSED                        99%
    AVERAGE MEMORY USED PER SUPPRESSED DUMP            1,028K
    TOTAL BYTES OF DASD SAVED                 399,999,999,999
    NUMBER OF CYLINDERS SAVED                          79,999
    PERCENT OF DEVICE SAVED                            8.999%
```

```
**************************************************************************
*                   DASD STORAGE SAVINGS SUMMARY                         *
**************************************************************************

       TOTAL COST SAVINGS                     $   999,999

**************************************************************************
*            DASD STORAGE - PROJECTED YEARLY COST SAVINGS                *
**************************************************************************

       TOTAL YEARLY SAVINGS                   $ 9,999,999
```

Figure 4-2d   Compuware ABEND-AID / CWSMF Analyzer Report (*continued*)

```
**************************************************************************
*                 PROGRAM ABEND DUMP CORRECTION LABOR COST IMPACT        *
**************************************************************************
```

SYSTEM ABEND COUNTS BY ABEND CODE

ABEND CODE	DESCRIPTION	PROGRAMMER TIME EACH	ANALYZED NO DUMP	ANALYZED WITH DUMP
S 001	INPUT/OUTPUT ERROR	120	311	
S 002	FILE ERROR	120	50	12
S 013	OPEN ERROR	20	588	
S 03D	OPEN ERROR - BAD DD	30	6	
S 047	UNAUTHORIZED SVC REQUEST	10	5	
S 0C1	OPERATION EXCEPTION	30	81	81
S 0C2	PRIVILEGED-OPERATION EXCEPTION	30	1	1
S 0C4	PROTECTION EXCEPTION	30	272	117
S 0C6	SPECIFICATION EXCEPTION	30	3	4
S 0C7	DATA EXCEPTION	30	208	
S 0C9	FIXED-POINT-DIVIDE EXCEPTION	30	3	4
S 0CA	DECIMAL-OVERFLOW EXCEPTION	10	1	1
S 0CB	DECIMAL-DIVIDE EXCEPTION	30	11	
S 106	LINK,LOAD,ATTACH,OR XCTL ERROR	10	96	
S 113	TYPE=J OPEN ERROR	20	1	
S 117	TYPE=T BASM CLOSE ERROR	10	1	
S 122	OPERATOR CANCEL WITH DUMP	10		40
S 130	DEQ MACRO INSTRUCTION ERROR	10		3
S 137	END-OF-VOLUME TAPE ERROR	20	2	
S 13E	SUBTASK DETACHED BEFORE ENDED	10	1	
S 200	EXCP PROCESSING ERROR	10		1
S 213	OPEN ERROR	20	16	
S 214	CLOSE ERROR	20	4	
S 222	OPERATOR CANCEL WITHOUT DUMP	0	(3,291)	
S 228	EXTRACT EXECUTION ERROR	10		183
S 237	END-OF-VOLUME ERROR	20	10	
S 23E	DETACH MACRO INSTRUCION	10		1
S 306	LINK,XCTL,ATTACH,OR LOAD ERROR	10	7	
S 314	CLOSE EXECUTION ERROR	20	2	
S 322	TIME LIMIT EXCEEDED	30	2,370	
S 328	EXTRACT EXECUTION ERROR	10		13
S 400	EXCP PROCESSING ERROR	10		3
S 413	OPEN EXECUTION ERROR	20	13	
S 522	WAIT STATE TIME LIMIT EXCEEDED	10	50,431	
S 613	OPEN EXECUTION ERROR	20	2	
S 614	CLOSE EXECUTION ERROR	20	2	
S 622	TSO TERMINAL TASK INIT. ERROR	10	10,846	
S 637	END-OF-VOLUME ERROR	20	3	
S 706	LINK,ATTACH,XCTL OR LOAD ERROR	10	41	
S 714	CLOSE EXECUTION ERROR	20	6	
S 722	OUTPUT LIMIT EXCEEDED	10	1,079	
S 737	END-OF-VOLUME ERROR	20	45	
S 806	LINK, ATTACH, OR XCTL ERROR	10	279	
S 80A	GETMAIN/FREEMAIN ERROR	20	96	
S 813	OPEN EXECUTION ERROR	30	72	
S 837	END-OF-VOLUME ERROR	20	10	
S 878	GETMAIN/FREEMAIN ERROR	10		24
X XXX	XXXXXXXXXXXXXXXXXXXXXX	..	..	..

Figure 4-2e   Compuware ABEND-AID / CWSMF Analyzer Report (*continued*)

VENDOR APPLICATION PROGRAM EFFICIENCY OPTIMIZER PRODUCT: STROBE

The STROBE product is developed and marketed by Programart, of Cambridge, Massachusetts. Like BEST/1, it has undoubtedly received many benefits from its close proximity to the campus of M.I.T. However, unlike BEST/1, it does not seem to have any significant competition in its own market area. When it comes to the automated diagnosis of mainframe application program and database problems, there is nothing else that comes close to STROBE. It is commonly used in combination with system log exception reporting to follow up on programs which have symptoms of potential problems. It is in many ways similar to viewing MICS or MXG as a routine family physician checkup, while STROBE is the full workup of diagnostic tests prescribed by a specialist.

STROBE is essentially a batch product. Although it does have some TSO/ISPF menu-driven as well as command-driven facilities, it does not seem to have been intended as competition for OMEGAMON or related products used by operators for real-time monitoring.

The real strength of STROBE is as an attached software monitor which collects and accumulates trace information over the entire course of the processing of a batch job. This includes every program task execution, every device request and dataset I/O operation, as well as each operating system event requested to process a program. STROBE does not use SMF system logs; however, it operates as its own *virtual system log* during the execution of the attached program.

The output from STROBE consists of a series of histograms, which show where the bulk of the resources were used. This includes which line or statement in the program was getting executed the most times. This is extremely useful in finding program loops and can also be used to focus on statements that should not have been executed under particular conditions. When used with system logs, the effective rate of isolating and solving program coding problems is unsurpassed.

The STROBE manuals and training courses give the application programmers all they need to convert the histograms into estimates of how much resources they should be able to save by making very discrete changes in the program. The STROBE product is famous for being able to immediately flag the "5 percent of the program that can be changed in order to achieve 95 percent improvement in its efficiency." This is not just an idle claim. Demonstration projects using STROBE have been able to recover the purchase price of the product in less than one month of use.

Permanent production resource recovery projects, which use SMF to identify "heavy hitters" and routinely assign for STROBE analysis, have had between 5 percent to 20 percent decrease in recurring operating expense of most of the data centers that have purchased STROBE. Actual results may depend on how good the in-house programming standards have been with regard to preventing inefficient programs from getting into production prior to purchasing STROBE.

Application programmers seem to enjoy using STROBE and have a high level of intuitive understanding of the reports because they can relate them to their compile listings. This makes STROBE a painless way for capacity planners and operations analysts to assign application programmers to take apart their own programs if the baseline resource statistics indicate a particular program may be the source of performance problems. In addition, there is probably no better way to help educate applications programmers to the problems faced by systems programmers and to help systems programmers understand the problems facing applications programmers. In this context alone, the STROBE product is a wise purchase by any data center. Examples of STROBE screens and sample program diagnostic reports can be found in Figures 4-3a to 4-3v.

```
/---------------------------- STROBE OPTIONS ---------------------- REL  8.6\
|OPTION  ===>                                                                |
|                                                                            |
|                                                                            |
|                                                                            |
|   0   USER DEFAULTS - STROBE/ISPF user default options                     |
|   1   ADD ACTIVE   - Add a measurement request for an executing job        |
|   2   ADD QUEUED   - Add a measurement request for a job not yet executing |
|   3   STATUS       - Monitor/change measurement requests and create profiles|
|   4   PROFILE      - Create a Profile of a STROBE measurement session       |
|   5   INDEX        - Create a map data set                                  |
|   6   CROSS-SYSTEM - Submit/control requests on another system in the complex|
|   M   MESSAGES     - Display information about a STROBE message             |
|   L   BROWSE LOG   - Display the STROBE system log                          |
|   T   TUTORIAL     - Display information about STROBE                       |
|   C   CHANGES      - Display summary of changes in this release             |
|                                                                            |
|                                                                            |
|                                                                            |
|                                                                            |
|STROBE is a registered trademark of PROGRAMART CORPORATION                  |
|                                                                            |
\----------------------------------------------------------------------------/
```

Figure 4-3a   Programart STROBE Main Menu Selection Screen

```
/-------------------- STROBE - ADD ACTIVE REQUEST ------------------------\
|COMMAND ===>                                                             |
|                                                                         |
|JOBNAME ===>                 Clear to list active jobs   LIST TYPE ===>  |
|                             Qualified by type:  (J)obs, (T)SO sessions, (S)tarted|
|                                                 tasks, or Blank for all types |
|                                                                         |
|MEASUREMENT SESSION INFORMATION:                                         |
|   SESSION DURATION      ===> 1                  (Estimated time in minutes) |
|   TARGET SAMPLE SIZE    ===> 10000              (Target number of samples) |
|                                                                         |
|TSO USERID TO NOTIFY   ===> Z2823                (Notify when session completes|
|                                                                         |
|SAMPLE DATA SET INFORMATION:                                             |
|   DATA SET NAME PREFIX ===> PP.A.STROBE                                 |
|   UNIT NAME   ===> SYSDA    VOLUME ===>         DISP ===> CATLG (CATLG/KEEP) |
|                                                                         |
|SELECT ADDITIONAL PARAMETERS: (Y or N; Use Y only when overriding defaults) |
|   DATA COLLECTORS      ===> N     MODULE MAPPING DATA         ===> N    |
|   SESSION MANAGEMENT   ===> N     OTHER PARAMETERS            ===> N    |
|                                                                         |
\-------------------------------------------------------------------------/
```

Figure 4-3b   Programart STROBE Performance Analysis Request Menu

```
/--------------------- STROBE - ADD QUEUED REQUEST  ------------------------\
|COMMAND ===>                                                               |
|                                                                           |
|JOBNAME   ===>                                                             |
|  PROGRAM ===>              or  STEP SPECIFICATION ===>                     |
|                              (A stepname or stepnumber or procstepname.stepname|
|                                                                           |
|MEASUREMENT SESSION INFORMATION:                                           |
|  SESSION DURATION      ===> 1              (Estimated time in minutes)     |
|  TARGET SAMPLE SIZE    ===> 10000          (Target number of samples)      |
|                                                                           |
|TSO USERID TO NOTIFY    ===> Z2823          (Notify when session complete)  |
|                                                                           |
|SAMPLE DATA SET INFORMATION:                                               |
|  DATA SET NAME PREFIX ===> PP.A.STROBE                                     |
|  UNIT NAME   ===> SYSDA    VOLUME ===>         DISP ===> CATLG (CATLG/KEEP) |
|                                                                           |
|SELECT ADDITIONAL PARAMETERS: (Y or N; Use Y only when overriding defaults) |
|  DATA COLLECTORS       ===> N    MODULE MAPPING DATA        ===> N         |
|  SESSION MANAGEMENT    ===> N    OTHER PARAMETERS           ===> N         |
|                                                                           |
|                                                                           |
|                                                                           |
\---------------------------------------------------------------------------/
```

Figure 4-3c   Programart STROBE Execution Parameter Selection Screen

```
/------------ STROBE  - PRODUCE A PERFORMANCE PROFILE  ----------------------\
|OPTION ===>                                                                |
|                                                                           |
|           B  - Background processing                                      |
|           F  - Foreground processing                                      |
|                                                                           |
|                                                                           |
|ENTER BLANKS TO VIEW A DATASET SELECTION LIST                              |
|SAMPLE DATA SET NAME ===>                                                  |
|             UNIT ===>              VOLUME ===>                            |
|                                                                           |
|                                                                           |
|SPECIFY REPORT PARAMETERS: (Y or N)                                        |
|  Detail Reports?     ===> N                                               |
|  Tailor Reports?     ===> N                                               |
|  Indexing?           ===> N                                               |
|                                                                           |
|                                                                           |
|Optionally specify a data set name to save a copy of the STROBE Profile:    |
|DATA SET NAME ===>                                                         |
|        UNIT ===> SYSDA    VOLUME ===>                                     |
\---------------------------------------------------------------------------/
```

Figure 4-3d   Programart STROBE Performance Profile Execution Controls

```
/------------   STROBE - INDEX TO CREATE A MAP DATA SET  ----------------------\
|OPTION ===>                                                                   |
|          B  - Background processing   F  - Foreground processing             |
|                                                                              |
|PROGRAM LANGUAGE: (Specify Y -- select one language)                          |
| ASSEMBLER        ===>      COBOL          ===>     DB2 DBRM        ===>       |
| FORTRAN G         ===>      FORTRAN VS OR H ===>     PL/I          ===>       |
|                                                                              |
|                                                                              |
|                                                                              |
|OUTPUT: MAP DATA SET                                                          |
|      ===>                                                                    |
|  UNIT ===> SYSDA       VOLUME ===>                                           |
|                                                                              |
|INPUT: COMPILER SYSPRINT DATA SETS                                            |
|      ===>                                                                    |
|      ===>                                                                    |
|      ===>                                                                    |
|      ===>                                                                    |
|      ===>                                                                    |
|      ===>                                                                    |
\------------------------------------------------------------------------------/
```

Figure 4-3e   Programart STROBE Index to Create a Map Dataset

```
/------------------   STROBE  -  CROSS-SYSTEM OPTIONS  ------------------------\
|OPTION  ===>                                                                  |
|                                                                              |
|                                                                              |
|                                                                              |
|    1  ADD ACTIVE      - Add a measurement request for an executing job       |
|    2  ADD QUEUED      - Add a measurement request for a job not yet executing|
|    3  CHANGE ACTIVE   - Send a sampling control command to an active request |
|    4  CHANGE QUEUED   - Change a queued measurement request                  |
|    5  LIST/DELETE     - Display/delete measurement requests                  |
|    6  JOB STREAM MENU - Process the generated job stream                     |
|                                                                              |
|  END  CANCEL          - Exit without submitting the generated job stream     |
|                                                                              |
|                                                                              |
|                                                                              |
|                                                                              |
|                                                                              |
|                                                                              |
|                                                                              |
\------------------------------------------------------------------------------/
```

Figure 4-3f   Programart STROBE Cross-System Options Selection Menu

```
/--------- STROBE - CROSS-SYSTEM CHANGE ACTIVE REQUEST ---------------------\
|OPTION  ===>                                                               |
|                                                                           |
|REQUEST NUMBER ===>        or  JOBNAME ===>                                 |
|                                                                           |
|                                                                           |
|  1  - Terminate the request                                               |
|                                                                           |
|  2  - Begin a new measurement session changing the following parameters:  |
|                                                                           |
|       SESSION DURATION     ===>           (Estimated time in minutes)      |
|       TARGET SAMPLE SIZE   ===>           (Target number of samples)       |
|       FINAL SESSION ACTION ===>           (Q)uit, (S)top, or (C)ontinue    |
|                                                                           |
|  3  - Suspend sampling in the current measurement session                 |
|                                                                           |
|  4  - Restart sampling in the current measurement session                 |
|                                                                           |
|  5  - End the measurement session, but do not terminate the request       |
|                                                                           |
\---------------------------------------------------------------------------/
```

Figure 4-3g   Programart STROBE Cross-System Change Action Request Menu

```
/---------------- STROBE - BROWSE THE STROBE/CV LOG ------------------------\
|COMMAND ===>                                                               |
|                                                                           |
|                                                                           |
|Limit the display by specifying criteria below                             |
|or leave all fields BLANK for the entire log.                              |
|                                                                           |
|                                                                           |
|REQUEST NUMBER ===>               (Limit display by request number)        |
|                                                                           |
|OWNERID        ===>               (Limit display by ownerid)               |
|                                                                           |
|JOBNAME        ===>               (Limit display by jobname)               |
|                                                                           |
|STARTING DATE  ===>    /    /     (Display messages from this date to       |
|                                   present. Format is mm/dd/yy.)            |
|                                                                           |
|                                                                           |
|Press ENTER to browse the log.                                             |
|                                                                           |
\---------------------------------------------------------------------------/
```

Figure 4-3h   Programart STROBE Performance Profile Log Browse Menu

```
/TUTORIAL --------- STROBE  -  REPORTS PRODUCED BY STROBE --------- Panel 1 of 4\
|OPTION ===>                                                                   |
|                                                                              |
|The STROBE Performance Profile is a set of reports detailing the use of system |
|resources by both user programs and system service routines.  These reports  |
|contain the following information (a more detailed description of the reports |
|is in the STROBE Concepts and Facilities manual).                            |
|                                                                              |
|     The Measurement Session Data report presents a description of the job    |
|     environment, measurement parameters, measurement statistics, and report  |
|     parameters.                                                              |
|                                                                              |
|     The Time Distribution of Activity Level report displays a chronological   |
|     record of the level of task execution and data set access activities     |
|     throughout the measurement session.                                      |
|                                                                              |
|     The Resource Demand Distribution report summarizes the usage of CPU and   |
|     I/O facilities by programs executing in the measured job step.          |
|                                                                              |
|     The Working Set Size Through Time report displays a chronological record  |
|     of the variations in active working set size within the address space    |
|     throughout the measurement session.                                      |
\------------------------------------------------------------------------------/
```

Figure 4-3i   Programart STROBE Performance Reports Summary (Part 1)

```
/TUTORIAL -------- STROBE - REPORTS BY THE STROBE FEATURES -------- Panel 1 of 3\
|OPTION ===>                                                                   |
|                                                                              |
|Reports Produced by the STROBE Features                                       |
|                                                                              |
|If your installation uses the STROBE DB2, CICS, Adabas/Natural, or IDMS       |
|Features, then additional reports will appear in the Performance Profile.  For |
|a complete description of these reports, see the appropriate STROBE Feature    |
|manual.                                                                       |
|                                                                              |
|STROBE DB2 Feature Reports                                                    |
|                                                                              |
|     The DBRM CPU Usage Summary report shows the distribution of CPU          |
|     activityamong the DBRMs that invoked system service routines during      |
|     themeasurement session.                                                  |
|                                                                              |
|     The CPU Usage by SQL Statement report shows the distribution of          |
|     CPU activity among SQL statements within a DBRM.  The DBRM name is        |
|     displayed in the header line, and sites of invocation are identified by   |
|     their precompiled statement number.                                      |
|                                                                              |
\------------------------------------------------------------------------------/
```

Figure 4-3j   Programart STROBE Performance Reports Summary (Part 2)

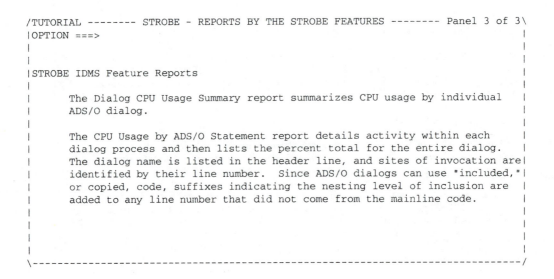

```
/TUTORIAL -------- STROBE - REPORTS BY THE STROBE FEATURES -------- Panel 2 of 3\
|OPTION ===>                                                                    |
|                                                                               |
|STROBE CICS Feature Reports                                                    |
|                                                                               |
|     The CICS Performance Supplement provides CICS-specific reports showing    |
|     time distribution of transaction activity, transaction activity, network  |
|     activity, I/O activity, and configuration parameters and system-wide      |
|     statistics.                                                               |
|                                                                               |
|STROBE Adabas/Natural Feature Reports                                          |
|                                                                               |
|     The Callers' DB Usage Summary report shows the percentage of total CPU    |
|     activity consumed by each caller of Adabas services.  Callers are         |
|     identified by job name (for a batch job), TSO userid (for a TSO region),  |
|     or logical terminal name (for a CICS region).                             |
|                                                                               |
|     The Callers' DB Usage by Control Section report is produced for each of   |
|     the database users identified in the Callers' DB Usage Summary report.    |
|     The report header line identifies the calling region, and each detail     |
|     line shows solo and total CPU time spent on behalf of the caller in       |
|     either an Adabas or IBM system module or in a user-written control        |
|     section.                                                                  |
\-------------------------------------------------------------------------------/
```

Figure 4-3k   Programart STROBE Performance Reports Summary (Part 3)

```
/TUTORIAL -------- STROBE - REPORTS BY THE STROBE FEATURES -------- Panel 3 of 3\
|OPTION ===>                                                                    |
|                                                                               |
|                                                                               |
|STROBE IDMS Feature Reports                                                    |
|                                                                               |
|     The Dialog CPU Usage Summary report summarizes CPU usage by individual    |
|     ADS/O dialog.                                                             |
|                                                                               |
|     The CPU Usage by ADS/O Statement report details activity within each     |
|     dialog process and then lists the percent total for the entire dialog.    |
|     The dialog name is listed in the header line, and sites of invocation are|
|     identified by their line number.  Since ADS/O dialogs can use "included,"|
|     or copied, code, suffixes indicating the nesting level of inclusion are   |
|     added to any line number that did not come from the mainline code.        |
|                                                                               |
|                                                                               |
|                                                                               |
|                                                                               |
\-------------------------------------------------------------------------------/
```

Figure 4-3l   Programart STROBE Performance Reports Summary (Part 4)

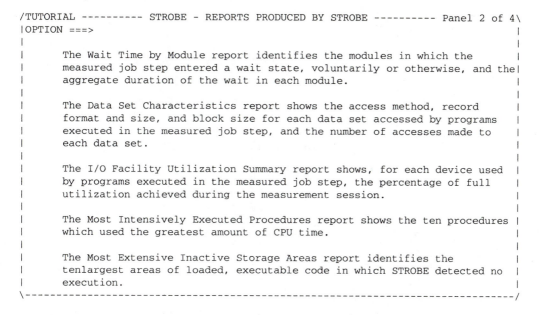

```
/TUTORIAL ---------- STROBE - REPORTS PRODUCED BY STROBE ---------- Panel 2 of 4\
|OPTION ===>                                                                    |
|                                                                               |
|       The Wait Time by Module report identifies the modules in which the      |
|       measured job step entered a wait state, voluntarily or otherwise, and the|
|       aggregate duration of the wait in each module.                          |
|                                                                               |
|       The Data Set Characteristics report shows the access method, record     |
|       format and size, and block size for each data set accessed by programs  |
|       executed in the measured job step, and the number of accesses made to   |
|       each data set.                                                          |
|                                                                               |
|       The I/O Facility Utilization Summary report shows, for each device used |
|       by programs executed in the measured job step, the percentage of full   |
|       utilization achieved during the measurement session.                    |
|                                                                               |
|       The Most Intensively Executed Procedures report shows the ten procedures |
|       which used the greatest amount of CPU time.                             |
|                                                                               |
|       The Most Extensive Inactive Storage Areas report identifies the         |
|       tenlargest areas of loaded, executable code in which STROBE detected no  |
|       execution.                                                              |
\-------------------------------------------------------------------------------/
```

Figure 4-3m   Programart STROBE Performance Reports Summary (Part 5)

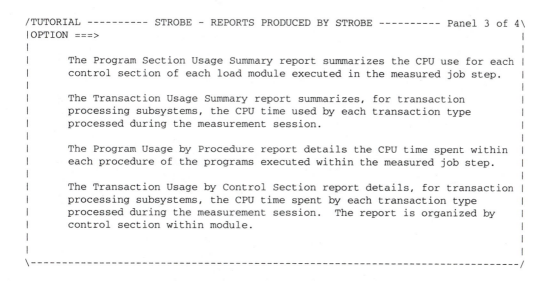

```
/TUTORIAL ---------- STROBE - REPORTS PRODUCED BY STROBE ---------- Panel 3 of 4\
|OPTION ===>                                                                    |
|                                                                               |
|       The Program Section Usage Summary report summarizes the CPU use for each |
|       control section of each load module executed in the measured job step.  |
|                                                                               |
|       The Transaction Usage Summary report summarizes, for transaction        |
|       processing subsystems, the CPU time used by each transaction type       |
|       processed during the measurement session.                              |
|                                                                               |
|       The Program Usage by Procedure report details the CPU time spent within |
|       each procedure of the programs executed within the measured job step.   |
|                                                                               |
|       The Transaction Usage by Control Section report details, for transaction |
|       processing subsystems, the CPU time spent by each transaction type      |
|       processed during the measurement session.  The report is organized by   |
|       control section within module.                                          |
|                                                                               |
|                                                                               |
\-------------------------------------------------------------------------------/
```

Figure 4-3n   Programart STROBE Performance Reports Summary (Part 6)

```
$$$$$$$$$$$  $$$$$$$$$$$  $$$$$$$$$$$
$$$$$$$$$$$  $$$$$$$$$$$  $$$$$$$$$$$
  $$$$$        $$$$$        $$$$$
  $$$$$        $$$$$        $$$$$
  $$$$$        $$$$$        $$$$$
  $$$$$        $$$$$        $$$$$
  $$$$$        $$$$$        $$$$$
  $$$$$        $$$$$        $$$$$
  $$$$$        $$$$$        $$$$$
$$$$$$$$$$$  $$$$$$$$$$$  $$$$$$$$$$$
$$$$$$$$$$$  $$$$$$$$$$$  $$$$$$$$$$$
```

** MEASUREMENT SESSION DATA **

```
------ JOB ENVIRONMENT ------
PROGRAM MEASURED      - ABCXX001
JOB NAME              - ABC009
JOB NUMBER            - JOB03889
STEP NAME             - ABC009.ABC00920

DATE OF SESSION       - 11/14/92
TIME OF SESSION       - 08.49.46

SYSTEM -                ESA SP3.1.3
CPU MODEL             - 5990
SYSTEM ID             - MU14
REGION SIZE BELOW 16M - 7,680K
REGION SIZE ABOVE     - 32,768K

STROBE PTF LEVEL      - 8.6.670/622
STROBE TAPE NUMBER    - 000-S86531

SAMPLE DATA SET  - ABCXX.ABC009.S001D001
```

```
------- MEASUREMENT SESSION PARAMETERS -------
ESTIMATED SESSION TIME  - 10 MIN
TARGET SAMPLE SIZE      - 10,000
REQUEST NUMBER          - 18
FINAL SESSION ACTION    - QUIT

SUBSYSTEM  -              IMS DB 3.1

OPTIONS -                 IMS
ATTRIBUTORS  -            ATTRSVC

-------- REPORT PARAMETERS --------
REPORT RESOLUTION   -     64 BYTES
LINES/PAGE          -     60
NODASD
```

```
----- MEASUREMENT STATISTICS -----
CPS TIME PERCENT        - 48.88
WAIT TIME PERCENT       - 51.12
MARGIN OF ERROR PERCENT - .98

TOTAL SAMPLES TAKEN     - 10,000
TOTAL SAMPLES PROCESSED - 10,000
INITIAL SAMPLING RATE   - 16.67/SEC
FINAL SAMPLING RATE     - 16.67/SEC

SESSION TIME  - 10 MIN 59.20 SEC
CPU TIME      -  4 MIN 49.84 SEC
WAIT TIME     -  5 MIN  1.43 SEC
STRETCH TIME  -  1 MIN  7.93 SEC

PAGES IN-    0    OUT-         0
PAGING RATE  -         0.00/SEC
EXCPS -        23,805  36.11/SEC
```

Figure 4-3o Programart STROBE Measurement Session Summary

ABCXX001

** TIME DISTRIBUTION OF ACTIVITY LEVEL **   * IS GREATER THAN 95%   - IS LESS THAN 5%

```
-TASK OR
 DDNAME    RESOURCE   N X 10 PLUS OR MINUS 5 IS PERCENT OF FULL UTILIZATION
ABCXX001   CPU        --           5788**9*9988**8598541697899*99****7*88**9697878?*****6891
OFDITMP1   3380       2332- ---    1122-1241261-1-321 11 --- 3-21--14231213-- -421
.FILEMGT               2  2*7
OFCS0141   3480       64           2335444744454244343428*6445345456634334633435454653441
JOBLIB     3390       .2-36
IFCS0141   3480                    36444364544454324422-3334354447655423555755556553461
RECON1     3480       -1
RECON2     3380       -1
DFSRESLB   3380        1  -1
DFSVSAMP   3380       -1
IMS        3380       -

START RUN  0---0---1---1---2---2---3---3---4---4---5---5---6---6---7---7---8---8---9---9---*  END RUN
           0---5---0---5---0---5---0---5---0---5---0---5---0---5---0---5---0---5---0---5---*
                          PERCENT OF ALLOCATED RUN TIME
```

** RESOURCE DEMAND DISTRIBUTION **

TASK OR DDNAME	RESOURCE	PERCENT OF RUN TIME			PERCENT OF RUN TIME SPENT				CUMULATIVE PERCENTAGES	
		SERVICED BY CPU	SERVICED BY I/O	SERVICED BY EITHER	SOLO IN CPU	SOLO IN I/O	SOLO IN EITHER	SOLO CAUSING CPU WAIT	SOLO TIME	CAUSING CPU WAIT
ABCXX001	CPU	48.78	.00	48.78	13.82	.00	13.82	.88	13.82	.88
OFDITMP1	3380	.00	7.37	7.37	.00	6.10	6.10	7.36	19.92	8.24
.FILEMGT		.04	3.21	3.25	.04	3.20	3.24	39.27	23.16	47.51
OFCS0141	3480	.04	24.55	24.58	.00	2.01	2.01	2.03	25.17	49.54
JOBLIB	3390	.00	1.13	1.13	.00	1.13	1.13	.83	26.30	50.37
IFCS0141	3480	.02	25.29	25.31	.00	.36	.36	.31	26.66	50.68
RECON1	3480	.00	.15	.15	.00	.15	.15	.16	26.81	50.84
RECON2	3380	.00	.11	.11	.00	.11	.11	.11	26.92	50.95
DFSRESLB	3380	.00	.09	.09	.00	.09	.09	.07	27.01	51.02
DFSVSAMP	3380	.00	.07	.07	.00	.07	.07	.08	27.08	51.10
IMS	3380	.00	.03	.03	.00	.03	.03	.02	27.11	51.12

Figure 4-3p   Programart STROBE Time and Resource Distribution

ABCXX001

** WORKING SET SIZE THROUGH TIME **

AVERAGE PAGE FRAME COUNT

```
1200 .
 600 .
   0 0---0---1---1---2---2---3---3---4---4---5---5---6---6---7---7---8---8---9---9---*
     0---5---0---5---0---5---0---5---0---5---0---5---0---5---0---5---0---5---0---5---*
     START RUN                                                               END RUN
```

PERCENT OF ALLOCATED RUN TIME

RUN TIME HISTOGRAM   MARGIN OF ERROR: .98%
.00   6.00   12.00   18.00   24.00

MODULE NAME	SECTION NAME	FUNCTION	PAGE	TOTAL
.IMS	DFSKBDP0	DB-IMS BATCH DISPATCHING	.00	7.65
.IOCS	IGG019AQ	QSAM GET, NEXT BUFFER	.00	.32
.IOCS	IGG019AR	QSAM PUT, NEXT BUFFER	.00	2.03
.IOCS	TOTALS	DATA MANAGEMENT SERVICES	.00	2.35
.LKD/LDR	IEWFETCH	PROGRAM FETCH	.00	.02
.SVC	SVC 006	PROGRAM MANAGER/LINK	.00	.04
.SVC	SVC 008	PROGRAM MANAGER/LOAD	.00	.14
.SVC	SVC 018	BLDL/FIND	.00	1.03
.SVC	SVC 019	OPEN	.00	13.21
.SVC	SVC 020	CLOSE	.00	.04
.SVC	SVC 022	OPEN (TYPE = J)	.00	.02
.SVC	SVC 026	CATALOG MANAGEMENT	.00	.17
.SVC	SVC 027	DA SPACE MGR/OBTAIN	.00	.11
.SVC	SVC 055	END OF VOLUME	.00	23.83
.SVC	SVC 056	RESOURCE MANAGER/ENQUEUE	.00	1.89
.SVC	SVC 076	SYSTEM ERROR RECORDING	.00	.02
.SVC	SVC 109	EXT. SVC ROUTER-TYPE 4	.00	.02
.SVC	SVC 130	RACHECK	.00	.04
.SVC	SVC 231	USER SVC	.00	.18
.SVC	SVC 242	USER SVC	.00	.09
.SVC	TOTALS	SUPERVISOR CONTROL	.00	40.83

Figure 4-3q   Programart STROBE Working Set Size and Module Waits

```
                                    ABCXX001

                        ** DATA SET CHARACTERISTICS **

          ACCESS      -RECORD-  BLK/CI   BUF    RPL - SPLITS-    EXCP    DATA SET NAME
DDNAME    METHOD      FMT SIZE   SIZE   NO STRINGS  CI   CA     COUNTS

DFSRESLB  BPAM        U         23552                              49    ABCSYP1.RESLIB
DFSVSAMP                                                            3
IFCS0141  QSAM        FB   89   32752     20                   12,130    AB.AB706M01.G0460V00
IFCS0141  QSAM        FB   89   32752     20                           ABCX.AB138.M01.G0005V00
IMS       BPAM                  32760                              13    ABCSYP1.DBDLIB
IMS                   F         23476                               3    ABCSYP1.PSBLIB
JOBLIB    BPAM        F                                                  AB.IJOBLIB
JOBLIB                                                              6    AB.PJOBLIB
JOBLIB                                                            181    ABCSYP1.RESLIB
                                                                        AB.MJOBLIB
OFCS0141  QSAM        FB   83   32702      5                   10,051    ABCXX.ABC009.B01
OFDITMP1  OSAM        8192      8192                            1,299    AB.ABCXTMP1
RECON1    VSAM KSDS   62144    22528      25     1                 27    RECONP1.RECON1
RECON1    VSAM INDEX  2041      2048       5     1                 16    RECONP1.RECON1
RECON2    VSAM KSDS   LSR 62144 22528     12     5                 20    RECONP2.RECON2
RECON2    VSAM INDEX  LSR 2041  2048       6     5                  7    RECONP2.RECON2
```

Figure 4-3r   Programart STROBE Working Dataset File Statistics

ABCXX001

** I/O FACILITY UTILIZATION SUMMARY **

MARGIN OF ERROR: .98%

RUN TIME HISTOGRAM scale: .00   6.50   13.00   19.50   26.00

UNIT NO	DEVICE TYPE	VOLUME ID	DDNAME	RUN TIME PERCENT SOLO	RUN TIME PERCENT TOTAL
A53	DA 3390	D40010	JOBLIB	.01	.01
BCB	TAPE 3480/3490	360818	.FILEMGT	.32	.32
BCB	TAPE 3480/3490		.FILEMGT	.60	.60
UNIT BCB TOTALS				.92	.92
B25	TAPE 3480/3490	521880	.FILEMGT	.23	.23
B25	TAPE 3480/3490		IFCS0141	.36	25.29
UNIT B25 TOTALS				.59	25.52
B9D	TAPE 3480/3490	321121	.FILEMGT	1.30	1.30
B9D	TAPE 3480/3490		.FILEMGT	.61	.61
B9D	TAPE 3480/3490	321121	OFCS0141	2.01	24.55
UNIT B9D TOTALS				3.92	26.46
D32	DA 3380	D30099	DFSVSAMP	.07	.07
238	DA 3380	DD8003	JOBLIB	.04	.04
45A	DA 3380	IMSP01	.FILEMGT	.03	.03
45A	DA 3380	IMSP01	DFSRESLB	.09	.09
45A	DA 3380	IMSP01	JOBLIB	1.07	1.07
UNIT 45A TOTALS				1.19	1.19
66D	DA 3380	DD8014	JOBLIB	.01	.01
8D5	DA 3380	DB8033	.FILEMGT	.00	.01
8D5	DA 3380	DB8033	OFDITMP1	6.10	7.37
UNIT 8D5 TOTALS				6.10	7.38
826	DA 3380	IMS806	.FILEMGT	.03	.03
826	DA 3380	IMS806	RECON1	.15	.15
UNIT 826 TOTALS				.18	.18
860	DA 3380	IMS801	.FILEMGT	.01	.01
860	DA 3380	IMS801	IMS	.02	.02
UNIT 860 TOTALS				.03	.03

Figure 4-3s   Programart STROBE I/O Device Utilization Summary

ABCXX001

** MOST INTENSIVELY EXECUTED PROCEDURES **

MODULE NAME	SECTION NAME	LINE NUMBER	PROCEDURE/FUNCTION NAME	STARTING LOCATION	PROCEDURE LENGTH	CPU TIME SOLO	PERCENT TOTAL	CUMULATIVE SOLO	PERCENT TOTAL
.IMS	DFSDLR00		DFSDLR00 DB-LOGICAL RETRIEVE			6.75	25.49	6.75	25.49
.IMS	DFSDLA00		DFSDLA00 DB-CALL ANALYZER			4.56	16.43	11.31	41.92
.IMS	DFSPR000		DFSPR000 DB-CTL, BATCH PROG REQ			2.00	7.41	13.31	49.33
.IMS	DFSDLAS0		DFSDLAS0 DB-ANALYZE/PROCESS SSA			1.90	6.87	15.21	56.20
.IMS	DFSDBH00		DFSDBH10 DB-ISAM/OSAM BUFFER			1.62	5.14	16.83	61.34
.IMS	DFSDVBH0		DFSDVBH0 DB-BUFFER HANDLER ROUTER			1.15	4.05	17.98	65.39
.PL/ILIB	IBMBRQAA		IBMBRQA1 QSAM/VSAM NON-SPAN			1.02	3.36	19.00	68.75
ABC014	.PL/ILIB		IBMBDLI1 PL/I LIBRARY SUBROUTINES	000000	176	.72	2.50	19.72	71.25
.PL/ILIB	IBMBPSMA					.76	2.50	20.48	73.75
ABC014	*ABC0141		IBMBRIO1 RECORD I/O INTERFACE	000E80	64	.51	1.92	20.99	75.67

** MOST EXTENSIVE INACTIVE STORAGE AREAS **

MODULE NAME	SECTION NAME	FROM LINE	THRU LINE	WITHIN PROCEDURE	FROM LOCATION	THRU LOCATION	AREA LENGTH	CUMULATIVE LENGTH
DSPCINT0					000040	03F957	260376	260376
ABC014	*ABC0142				000000	000BCB	3020	263396
ABC014	*ABC0141				0001C0	00083F	1664	265060
ABC014	.PL/ILIB			IBMBEEF1	000000	0002B6	695	265755
ABC014	*ABC0141				000000	00013F	320	266075
ABC014	.PL/ILIB			IBMBPIR1	000000	00012B	300	266375
ABC014	IMSEXIT				000000	0000AF	176	266551
ABC014	PLISTART				000000	00007F	128	266679
ABC014	*ABC0141				000F40	000FBF	128	266807
ABC014	.PL/ILIB			IBMBEER1	000000	000077	120	266927

Figure 4-3t   Programart STROBE Program Procedure Utilizations

```
                                    ABCXX001

                        ** PROGRAM SECTION USAGE SUMMARY **

MODULE    SECTION   SECTION                            CPU TIME PERCENT   CPU TIME HISTOGRAM  MARGIN OF ERROR:   1.40%
NAME      NAME      SIZE    FUNCTION                   SOLO    TOTAL      .00    17.00    34.00    51.00    68.00

.SYSTEM   .IMS              IMS SYSTEM SERVICES        18.39   66.65      .*********+++++++++++++++++++++++++++++++++
.SYSTEM   .IOCS             DATA MANAGEMENT SERVICES    .00     .12       .
.SYSTEM   .PL/ILIB          PL/I LIBRARY SUBROUTINES   1.78    5.85       .*++
.SYSTEM   .SVC              SUPERVISOR CONTROL          .18     .18       .
.SYSTEM   .VSAM             VIRTUAL STORAGE ACC METH    .02     .02       .
                                                       ------  ------
.SYSTEM   TOTALS            SYSTEM SERVICES            20.37   72.82

DSPCINT0            260440                              .02     .02       .

ABC014    .IMS       232    IMS SYSTEM SERVICES         .10     .25       .
ABC014    .PL/ILIB  4933    PL/I LIBRARY SUBROUTINES    .80    2.74       .+
ABC014   *ABC0141   4064                               7.06   24.16       .****+++++++++
                                                       ------  ------
FCS014    TOTALS    9229                               7.96   27.15
                                                       ------  ------
PROGRAM ABCXX001 TOTALS                               28.36   100.00


TRANSACTION                                            CPU TIME PERCENT   CPU TIME HISTOGRAM  MARGIN OF ERROR:   1.40%
NAME          FUNCTION                                 SOLO    TOTAL      .00    25.00    50.00    75.00    100.00

.IMS          IMS SYSTEM SERVICES                     28.36   100.00      .*********+++++++++++++++++++++++++++++++++
                                                       ------  ------
PROGRAM ABCXX001 TOTALS                               28.36   100.00
```

Figure 4-3u   Programart STROBE Program Functional Usage Data

```
                                   ABCXX001

                        ** PROGRAM USAGE BY PROCEDURE **
```

.IMS IMS SYSTEM SERVICES

MODULE NAME	.SYSTEM SECTION NAME	SYSTEM SERVICES FUNCTION	INTERVAL LENGTH	.IMS CPU TIME SOLO	IMS PERCENT TOTAL	IMS SYSTEM SERVICES CPU TIME HISTOGRAM
DFSBNUCO		BATCH NUCLEUS	1120	.37	1.21	.+
DFSDBH10	DFSDBH00	DB-ISAM/OSAM BUFFER	9058	1.62	5.14	.*++++++
DFSDLAS0	DFSDLAS0	DB-ANALYZE/PROCESS SSA	5872	1.90	6.87	.**++++++++
DFSDLA00	DFSDLA00	DB-CALL ANALYZER	17796	4.56	16.43	.*******+++++++++++++
DFSDLR00	DFSDLR00	DB-LOGICAL RETRIEVE	43808	6.75	25.49	.**********++++++++++++++++++++++++++
DFSDVBH0	DFSDVBH0	DB-BUFFER HANDLER ROUTER	7738	1.15	4.05	.*++++++
DFSHDC40		DB-GENERAL HDAM RANDOMIZ	64	2.02	7.02	.
DFSPR000	DFSPR000	DB-CTL, BATCH PROG REQ	2628	2.00	7.41	.***++++++++
DFSSBIL0			3176	.02	.04	.
.IMS TOTALS				18.39	66.66	

```
MARGIN OF ERROR:  1.40%
                  26.00
HISTOGRAM SCALE:  .00   6.50   13.00   19.50   26.00
```

.IOCS DATA MANAGEMENT SERVICES

OMODULE NAME	.SYSTEM SECTION NAME	SYSTEM SERVICES FUNCTION	INTERVAL LENGTH	.IOCS CPU TIME SOLO	PERCENT TOTAL	CPU TIME HISTOGRAM
IGG019AA		QSAM SMPL GET LOCATE F/U	296	.00	.04	.
IGG019AI		QSAM SMPL PUT LOCATE F/U	144	.00	.02	.
IGG019AR		QSAM PUT, NEXT BUFFER	304	.00	.02	.
IGG019CW		SAM EOB CHAIN.CHAN DA	680	.00	.04	.
.IOCS TOTALS				.00	.12	

```
MARGIN OF ERROR:  1.40%
                  2.00
HISTOGRAM SCALE:  .00   .50   1.00   1.50   2.00
```

.PL/ILIB PL/I LIBRARY SUBROUTINES

MODULE NAME	.SYSTEM SECTION NAME	SYSTEM SERVICES FUNCTION	INTERVAL LENGTH	.PL/ILIB PL/I CPU TIME SOLO	PERCENT TOTAL	CPU TIME HISTOGRAM
IBMBPSMA	IBMBRIO1	RECORD I/O INTERFACE	246	.76	2.50	.*******++++++++++++
IBMBRQAA	IBMBRQA1	QSAM/VSAM NON-SPAN	1232	1.02	3.36	.**********++++++++++++++++
.PL/ILIB TOTALS				1.78	5.86	

```
MARGIN OF ERROR:  1.40%
                  4.00
HISTOGRAM SCALE:  .00   1.00   2.00   3.00   4.00
```

Figure 4-3v   Programart STROBE Program Usage by System Procedure

5

GETTING TO THE SOURCE
OF YOUR SOFTWARE QUALITY

The beginning and end of software quality can be found in individual program source modules. The craft and care that went into a program's development is clearly evident in its size and structure, which are both measurable.

These measures include program file size and density, as well as complexity and logical flow of source statements—which can be easily automated from system logs and program file directories. Several measures indicate the effort required to code the program and the relative productivity that was achieved.

Other measures indicate the proportion of the program that was based on *reusable* subprogram module components, and the proportion of the program structure which it was possible to *generate* or *clone* by automated or semi-automated methods.

Still other measures indicate stability of a program and *turnover* in terms of the proportion of a program that has been changed by application maintenance programmers.

The most widely accepted measure of software programs, *function points*, is a multipurpose indicator combining various characteristics of all these factors. However, it involves a set of complicated scales that can be interpreted and scored in a wide variety of ways. Normally, it is collected manually by trained analysts in order to obtain function point counts comparable to the accepted industry standards.

Fortunately, research has shown statement counts yielding function point estimates with under 15 percent error when counts are calibrated to established benchmarks for each language. This chapter will explain various types of metrics that can be automated to analyze programmer productivity and base system performance factors for improving software quality.

HOW PROGRAMS GET EXECUTED BY COMPUTER
OPERATING SYSTEMS

Software programs are generally executed in one of two ways: either as compiled *load* modules or as *interpreter* modules. Both can be brought into the system's internal reader as a file referenced by a SYSIN

DD or as card images in in-stream JCL. Either way, the programs originate as high-level language source code component modules, which must conform to syntax and coding conventions according to the specifications of a given language.

The high-level language module consists of a series of program statements which are individually read and converted into a series of machine language statements in the internal operating system's instruction code. They are then *link edited* to define a logical process path by a special operating system program known as a compiler. The object code module is *relocatable*, which means that it contains symbolic addresses allowing it to be loaded anywhere in computer memory. There it is eligible to reside, and can even be partially resident in the host memory, with a part of the program object load module *paged* in and out by the operating system's supervisor services.

The interpreter module also consists of a series of special high-level program statements. These statements are not converted into an object load module machine language, but are instead translated or interpreted at *run time*. The interpreter process usually involves cross-memory services and load service calls to subprograms or subroutines. These are normally compiled object load modules originally written in a high-level sourcecode language, as is the case with SAS statistical function libraries.

The compiled module achieves substantially greater efficiency since it is written in a highly compressed form and is often procedurally streamlined by compiler optimizing algorithms. The interpreter language module also uses object load modules, but the process path is not compressed or optimized.

Each sourcecode statement in an interpreter language creates a separate call to a compiled interpreter subprogram or macro routine, which must process as a separate program execution and return control after each statement is individually interpreted and processed. The interpreter program processing method can take considerably longer to execute and use greater system resources, if the program has idle waits in order to reload any subprograms which have been *swapped out*.

The compiled object load module normally has all special program tasks and system services link edited within the load module itself. It is always loaded with all the special functions that have been defined as essential to its normal procedural processing. This method involves cross-linking *control blocks* of operating system machine instruction code, within a range of address space. This space can be relocated as needed to achieve optimum efficiency for the entire operating system environment, as well as the individual functional program module.

The program management and object load services are a special type of operating system control block supervisory service unique to every operating system. In an MVS operating environment, the program object load module is executed according to a process that is a specialized extension of the architecture and operational system infrastructure described in Chapter 3. These program control block services involve *Task Control Block* (TCB) as well as *Service Request Block* (SRB) cross-memory services and controls. The process flow of a typical application program-requested system task is shown in Figure 5-1.

HIGH-LEVEL LANGUAGE CODING INTERPRETATION BY OPERATING SYSTEMS

Compiled load modules, also known as object modules or target modules, are *Partitioned Data Set* (PDS) library files containing machine code instructions in the host resident architectural language. This language is unique to each operating system, yet conforms to a set of universal machine code standards allowing load modules a degree of transportability across various classes of machines and various operating environments. The compiled load modules begin as another PDS library member file, which contains a sequential series of high-level language statements defining the logical procedural steps the

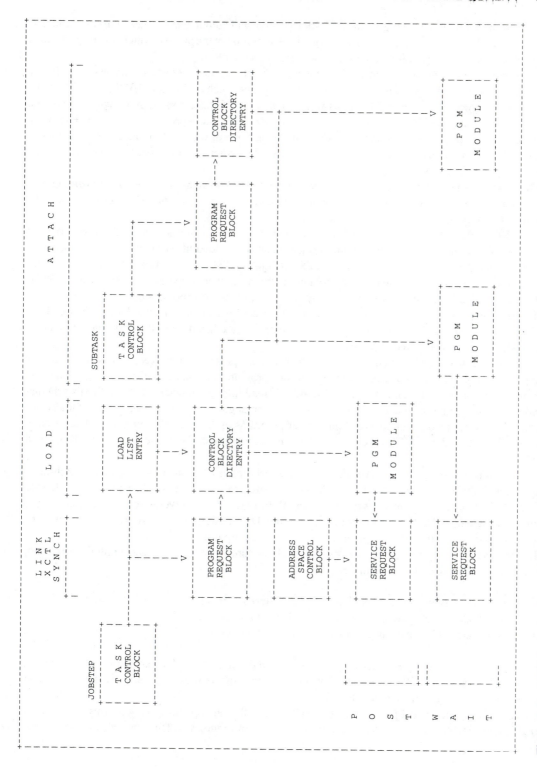

Figure 5-1 MVS Operating System Program Management MACRO Instruction System Resource and Task Control Blocks

program should follow. This includes the definition of input and output data formats, working variables, algorithms, and data item interrelationships, as well the definition of the process which is to be performed on the data according to conditional edits and selective process rules.

The source program module, from which the load or object module is compiled, can be written in any one of a wide variety of popular high-level computer languages such as: PL/1, COBOL, FORTRAN, C, Ada, ALGOL, APL, PROLOG, or LISP, as well as a number of Basic Assembly Languages (BALs). The sourcecode module file is compiled by a special operating system program which translates each statement in the program into a machine code instruction. Each of the resulting machine code control blocks, which are organized in pages or blocks of relocatable memory address space, must be link-edited into a compiled object code load module.

This module is then added as a member file to a special PDS known as an *object load library*. Object load library PDSs are located within common address areas by the system *Initial Program Load* (IPL) and are referenced by JCL in a JOBLIB statement.

The PROCs (or program step procedure process flow), which is defined in the JCL, will request execution of a program object load module resident in an object load library dataset. This dataset was referenced in a JOBLIB statement when an MVS batch job or TSO session was initiated. A procedure step can reference an override object library containing the program to be executed by way of a STEPLIB statement that loads an object library for only a single procedure process step. Both JOBLIB and STEPLIB statements in JCL can concatenate or stack a series of object load library dataset Data Definition (DD) names. These are searched in the order they are listed, until the first object module is found with the requested program name.

This method of requesting and processing load module programs for execution is the same for interpreter language modules, except that the requested program is the name of the interpreter language translator program module. The interpreter program is read into the translator from a SYSIN DD that references a PDS dataset member containing the interpreter language sourcecode statements. Otherwise, the SYSIN internal reader can also read interpreter programs in the form of sourcecode statements in card images stacked into JCL. Examples of common interpreter languages are SAS, RPG, and MARK-IV.

The compile process itself involves the use of a special program translator that reads a high-level language module from a sourcecode library PDS—or in stream card images stacked into JCL and loaded into the SYSIN symbolic internal system reader. Both may involve several special versions of the translator program, and both can have symbolic output DD definitions used as working storage areas or as final disposition for formatted, converted, or interpreted output files.

In the case of compilers, there are usually at least three versions of each compiler program, corresponding to three common compile levels:

- Checkout Compile (syntax checking and cross-reference only)
- Compile and Go (execute program sourcecode without link edit)
- Compile and Link (create an executable object load module)

Each compile level involves requesting execution of a different compiler translation program name, all of which usually have the same letters at the beginning of the program name. This has a special purpose, which will become apparent later in this chapter.

An example of the logical procedure flow and the JCL that the operating system uses to execute a COBOL language compiler translation program is shown in Figure 5-2. This example also shows the

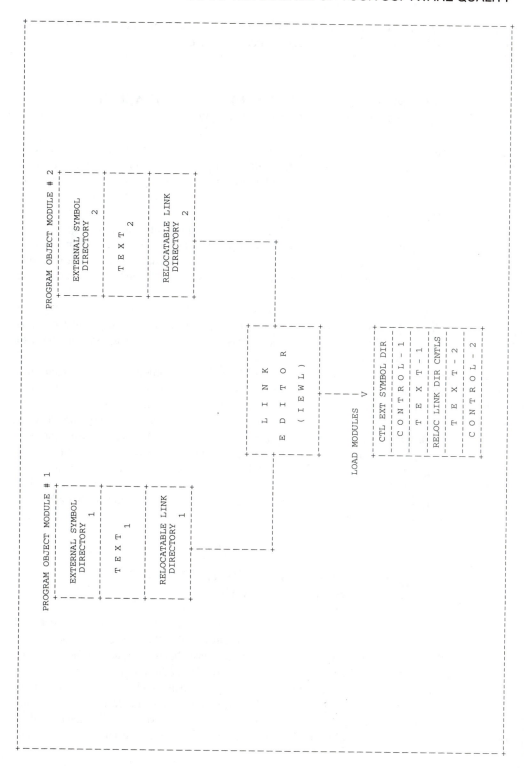

Figure 5-2   MVS Operating System Program Management Object Load Module Link Edit Processing and Sourcecode Regions

logical procedural flow and JCL skeleton required to execute an interpreter program written in the SAS language via the SYSIN internal system card image sourcecode reader.

HOW COMPILERS AND INTERPRETERS MEASURE PROGRAM CHARACTERISTICS

The control block addresses and relocates displacements of symbolic and physical system devices. Requests for special task services may be related to positional displacement from an ascending address that is recorded in the cross-reference at the end of most compiler listing printouts or files. This cross-reference relates back to the movement of control blocks recorded as events in the SMF system log and can be traced back to SMF with millisecond precision.

This kind of system log data can be critical in the evaluation of program testing or diagnostics to analyze the events leading up to a critical system failure or program abend. The most common use of this kind of system log data is in evaluating the procedural flow in the execution of logical instructions within a program and relating them back to the program's sourcecode statements that generated those compiled instructions.

This method is at least functionally similar to the process used by a large variety of IBM online program trace facilities which associate system resource usage to program control blocks. However, it is dependent on the availability of the original compiler's cross-reference in order to associate back to related application software program sourcecode statements.

This technique requires that program compile listings be archived as hardcopy, or as complete files on magnetic media, in order to relate the compiled addresses back to the system trace data. This has traditionally been an even more cumbersome process than debugging program dumps.

There is substantially greater productivity associated with automated software monitors such as OMEGAMON or TSOMON, since they do not require continual cross-referencing. Also, since the control block addresses are transparently resolved, all that the analyst must work with is the linkage between system resource usage or events and the original sourcecode statements that requested it.

The control block cross-reference listing is normally output at the end of each COBOL or PL/1 high-level program object module compile listing. The compiler execution options also allow for selecting cross-references of data names and trace addresses.

HOW SYSTEM LOGS MEASURE EXECUTION OF PROGRAM MODULES

As each JCL procedure-requested object load module program, or interpreter-requested object load subprogram, is requested, program control blocks are either referenced within the address space or else loaded from an external storage space into the memory area. Each task that is requested, and each service that may be requested across memory areas, will generate system log audit trail measurements used to monitor the progress of processing the program task requests. It is also available as a permanent history of the activity of the program as it was executed. This information is available in two forms: job accounting and paging. Job accounting occurs at the jobstream or session level, as well as the procedure step or program level. This includes all of the CPU and device allocations, timestamps, total systems resource usage, and control block linkage activity, indicating the addresses, number, and time of program control block loading. Paging or partial loading and unloading of reentrant as well as nonreentrant relocatable object code control block tasks is another form.

The main difference between interpreters and compiler language modules as they are measured by system logs is that interpreter modules do not have absolute or relative addresses that are defined as they are in compile program object load module cross-reference listings. Since the interpreter program can execute with any number of address positions depending on how the macro subprogram calls are loaded into memory, unloaded, or remain resident in memory, they can be different each time an interpreter program is executed. Thus, the only useful information that can be obtained about interpreter programs from the system logs is in job account and CPU utilization data indicating the resources used and not used. This is actually more important, since the main concern with quality of interpreter language programs is wasted CPU time. A software performance monitor such as Candle's OMEGAMON can provide much more detailed information about interpreter programs than SMF system logs alone. However, the interpretation of OMEGAMON data is more complicated than analysis of object load program modules and can require special training.

In both cases, system logs can provide substantial information about the efficiency of system resource usage by the translator program. In the case of interpreter language programs, the information about the efficiency of the translator program will directly relate to the quality of the interpreter language application program module. This includes data used for prioritizing production interpreter modules for maintenance or possible conversion to a compiler language, as well as information that can be used in tuning the CPU region size or the data buffers required by its input and output dataset files. In the case of compiler languages, the same benefits can be obtained by analyzing the system logs. Additional benefits can be realized by collecting performance statistics about the compiler execution of individual program sourcecode modules, which give automated system log data measurements of the actual functional complexity and size of the compiled application program. This data can be accumulated in a performance database and correlated to future resource usage data or used in system resource usage forecasting.

Examples of the program measurements available in SMF system logs and summaries of the differences between measurements of compiled object programs and interpreter programs are shown in Figures 5-3, 5-4, 5-5, and 5-6.

MEASURING THE SIZE OF HIGH-LEVEL PROGRAM MODULES

Since the high-level program modules that are used to generate compiled object load modules, as well as interpreter language program modules, are both normally stored in PDS sourcecode libraries, one of the simplest ways to measure the program's sourcecode size is to access the data in PDS directory records stored with each PDS. These records are stored in a PDS member, which can be unloaded using IBM utilities, as well as an SAS language procedure, which automatically extracts PDS directory records and calculates applied descriptive statistics for each member.

These directory records contain information about the identification of the programmer or other system user who first added the program to the sourcecode library data set, as well as the date and time the program was first added and most recently updated or changed. The PDS directory also keeps track of the original size in terms of number of lines of code, the most current number of lines, and a running count of the total number of times a program has been changed.

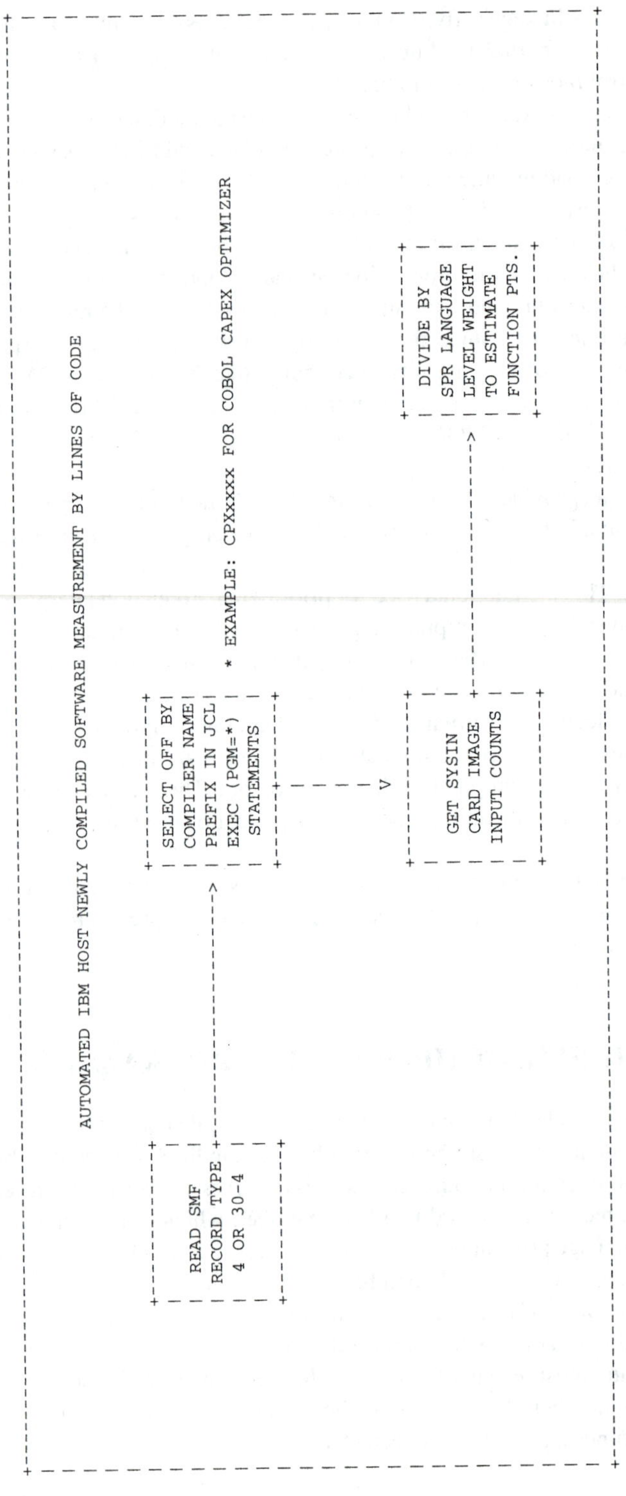

```
AUTOMATED IBM HOST NEWLY COMPILED SOFTWARE MEASUREMENT BY LINES OF CODE

                        + - - - - - - - +
                        | SELECT OFF BY |
                        | COMPILER NAME |
                        | PREFIX IN JCL |    * EXAMPLE: CPXxxxx FOR COBOL CAPEX OPTIMIZER
                        | EXEC (PGM=*)  |
                        | STATEMENTS    |
                        + - - - - - - - +
                            |
                            |
                            v
   + - - - - - - - +    + - - - - - - - +         + - - - - - - - +
   | READ SMF      |    | GET SYSIN     |         | DIVIDE BY     |
   | RECORD TYPE   +--->| CARD IMAGE    +-------->| SPR LANGUAGE  |
   | 4 OR 30-4     |    | INPUT COUNTS  |         | LEVEL WEIGHT  |
   + - - - - - - - +    + - - - - - - - +         | TO ESTIMATE   |
                                                  | FUNCTION PTS. |
                                                  + - - - - - - - +
```

Figure 5-3   Automated Process for SMF-Based Software Function Point Estimation for Compiler Programs by SPR Backfire Method

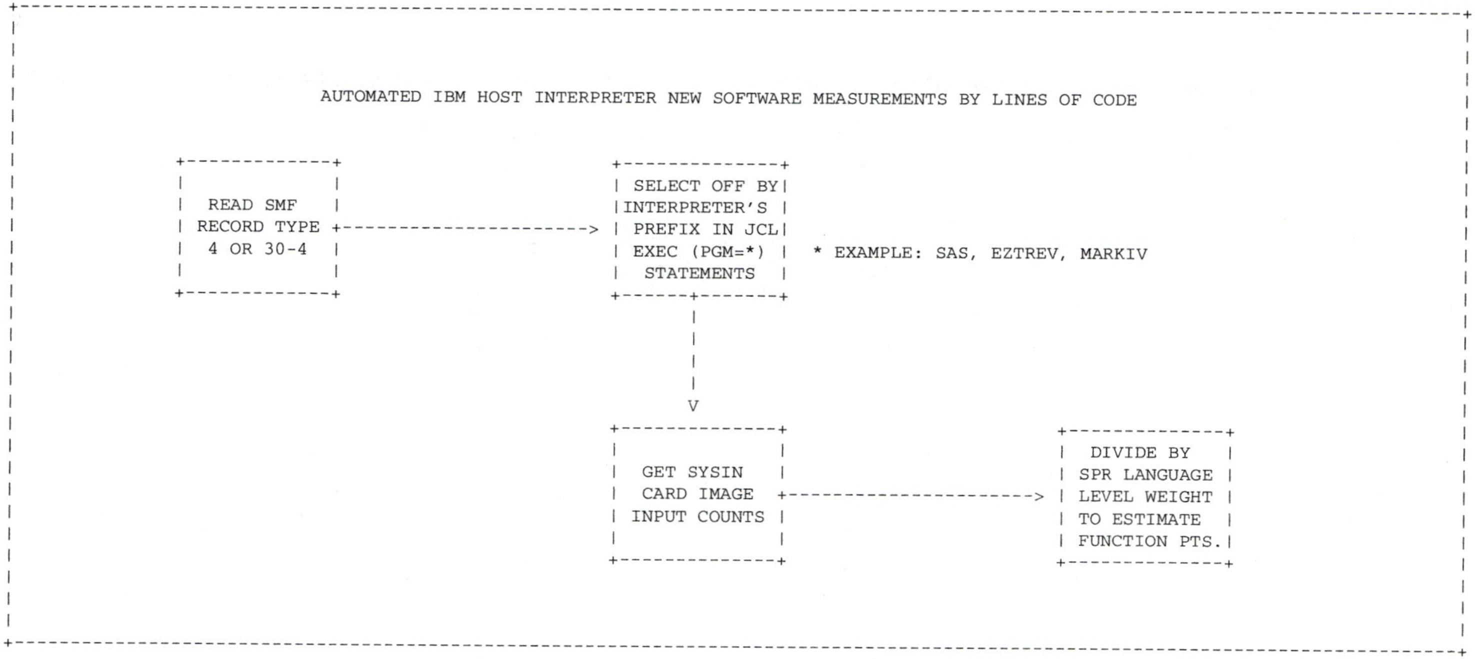

AUTOMATED IBM HOST INTERPRETER NEW SOFTWARE MEASUREMENTS BY LINES OF CODE

```
+---------------+                    +---------------+
| READ SMF      |                    | SELECT OFF BY |
| RECORD TYPE  +--------------------->| INTERPRETER'S |
| 4 OR 30-4     |                    | PREFIX IN JCL |
+---------------+                    | EXEC (PGM=*)  | * EXAMPLE: SAS, EZTREV, MARKIV
                                     | STATEMENTS    |
                                     +---------------+
                                            |
                                          --+--
                                            V
                                     +---------------+
                                     | GET SYSIN     |              +---------------+
                                     | CARD IMAGE    |              | DIVIDE BY     |
                                     | INPUT COUNTS +--------------->| SPR LANGUAGE  |
                                     |               |              | LEVEL WEIGHT  |
                                     +---------------+              | TO ESTIMATE   |
                                                                    | FUNCTION PTS. |
                                                                    +---------------+
```

Figure 5-4   Automated Process for SMF-Based Software Function Point Estimate for Interpreter Program by SPR Backfire Method

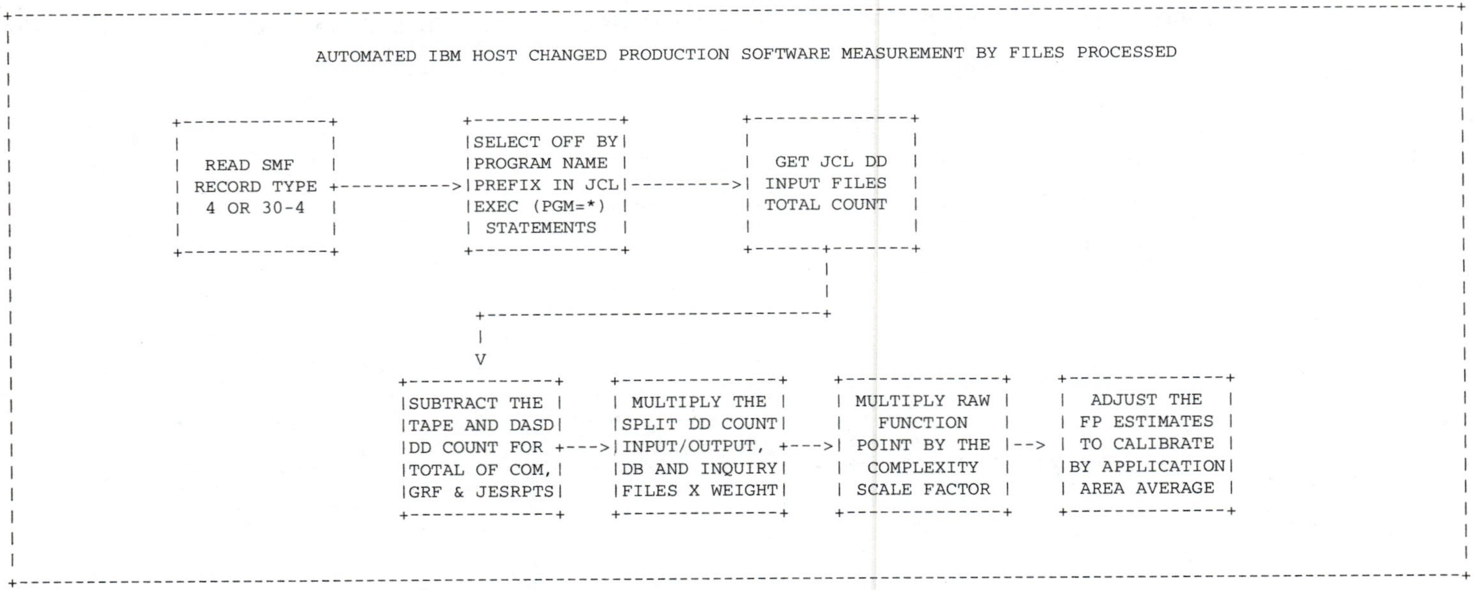

```
            AUTOMATED IBM HOST CHANGED PRODUCTION SOFTWARE MEASUREMENT BY FILES PROCESSED

                                        +-------------+   +-------------+
                                        |SELECT OFF BY|   | GET JCL DD  |
                                        |PROGRAM NAME |   | INPUT FILES |
 +-------------+                    +-->|PREFIX IN JCL|-->| TOTAL COUNT |
 | READ SMF    |                    |   |EXEC (PGM=*) |   +-------------+
 | RECORD TYPE +--------------------+   | STATEMENTS  |
 | 4 OR 30-4   |                        +-------------+
 +-------------+
                                             |
                                             V

                            +-------------+   +-------------+   +-------------+   +-------------+
                            |SUBTRACT THE |   | MULTIPLY THE|   |MULTIPLY RAW |   | ADJUST THE  |
                            |TAPE AND DASD|   |SPLIT DD COUNT|  | FUNCTION    |   | FP ESTIMATES|
                            |DD COUNT FOR +-->|INPUT/OUTPUT,+-->|POINT BY THE |-->| TO CALIBRATE|
                            |TOTAL OF COM,|   |DB AND INQUIRY|  | COMPLEXITY  |   |BY APPLICATION|
                            |GRF & JESRPTS|   |FILES X WEIGHT|  | SCALE FACTOR|   | AREA AVERAGE|
                            +-------------+   +-------------+   +-------------+   +-------------+
```

Figure 5-5   Automated Process for SMF-Based Software Function Point Estimation for Compiler Programs Using Basic IBM Method

```
AUTOMATED IBM HOST CHANGED INTERPRETER SOFTWARE MEASUREMENTS BY FILES PROCESSED

  +--------------+        +--------------+        +--------------+
  | READ SMF     |        |SELECT OFF BY |        | GET JCL DD   |
  | RECORD TYPE  |------->|PRODUCT NAME  |        | INPUT FILES  |
  | 4 OR 30-4    |  +-----|PREFIX IN JCL+|------->| TOTAL COUNT  |
  +--------------+  |     |EXEC (PGM=*)  |        +--------------+
       +------------+     | STATEMENTS   |
       |                  +--------------+
  +--------------+
  |MERGE AGAINST |          * EXAMPLE: SAS, etc.
  | SMF TYPE 14  |
  |TO GET MEMBER |                +-----+
  |NAME OR SYSIN |                  V
  |INPUT AS DD=*|
  +--------------+

  +--------------+        +--------------+        +--------------+
  |SUBTRACT THE  |        | MULTIPLY THE |        | MULTIPLY RAW |
  |TAPE AND DASD |        | SPLIT DD COUNT|       | FUNCTION     |
  |DD COUNT FOR +------->|INPUT/OUTPUT, +------->| POINT BY THE |--->
  |TOTAL OF COM, |        |DB AND INQUIRY|        | COMPLEXITY   |
  |GRF & JESRPTS|         |FILES X WEIGHT|        | SCALE FACTOR |
  +--------------+        +--------------+        +--------------+

                                                 +--------------+
                                                 | ADJUST THE   |
                                                 | FP ESTIMATES |
                                                 | TO CALIBRATE |
                                                 |BY APPLICATION|
                                                 | AREA AVERAGE |
                                                 +--------------+
```

Figure 5-6   Automated Process for SMF-Based Software Function Point Estimate for Interpreter Program Using Basic IBM Method

The importance of this PDS information to automated software quality measurement lies primarily in two areas:

- Routine automated monitoring of new programs, as well as change in size, can provide important information to confirm whether system development projects delivered program sourcecode on schedule and within size range estimated from original design specifications.

- If sufficient in-house program standards and naming conventions are implemented and enforced, application systems growth can be measured over time by grouping program modules with the same system prefix; this data can be used to forecast basic resource requirements.

The number of lines in a program can also be determined by system logs. This is done by monitoring the number of EXCPs that are issued by the MVS operating system when application program modules in a PDS library are read into a compiler program via the internal system reader. EXCPs are special I/O requests which correspond to one block of logical records for fixed blocked datasets, such as PDS files, or individual records in the case of VSAM or *direct access* (DA) files. Since it is possible to extract the logical record length, storage, access method, block size, and number of EXCPs from SMF Type 14 and 15 system log records, it is feasible to routinely extract program size measurements from SMF system logs in support of automated software inventory reporting.

Extraction from SMF Type 14 records can be merged with the Type 30, Subtype 5 Job step Accounting records in order to link the session name, number, and timestamps on each record type. This is done to build a new record, which contains the compiler program's name that accessed the sourcecode in the PDS source library. This method is based on dropping all records that do not have a name contained in a table of possible compiler program names. Most have a prefix than can be used in order to determine the language that the program was written and compiled in. This information can be stored in the automated software inventory performance database along with the estimated number of *Lines of Code* (LOCs) for the program. It can be used to estimate program functionality and complexity, based on established benchmarks for LOCs by language.

It is also necessary to have in-house standards and program naming conventions which assign individual programs to application software system groupings based on a prefix within the maximum eight characters allowed. Since it is often desirable to leave the last character of the name as a qualifier to indicate the type of program or software entity, this results in seven positions for assignment of names.

If the system name equates to a two-character prefix, unique system names can be supported, and up to 99,999 unique sequence numbers, or up to 67,599,324 unique program names, can be supported. And so on for a three-character and four-character prefix. The most common arrangement is the three-character prefix with three numeric sequence numbers, leaving two sequence numbers as qualifiers for special characteristics such as program type or version. This arrangement supports 10,520,365 unique program names and is probably the most useful convention for most DP shops.

Automated measurements can easily be programmed and processed as scheduled production batch jobs on a routine basis. This is achieved by either using IBM utilities to unload PDS directories for standardized sourcecode library data sets, or by using SMF Type 14, 15, and 30-5 records to automatically capture and measure every compiler execution regardless of where the program sourcecode originated. Both methods yield accurate program size data.

The basic record format for unloaded PDS directories, as well as the JCL for an IBM utility program to unload such directory records, is shown in Figures 5-7, 5-8, 5-9, and 5-10. Some of the IBM compiler program names used to search SMF Type 30-5 records and utilize the batch job name, job number, and

```
EXAMPLE OF BASIC SAS/SOURCE PROCEDURE PROGRAM TO UNLOAD LIBRARY PDS

PROC SOURCE NOPRINT  INDD=SRCLIB1   OUTDD=SRCDIR1 NOALIAS;
PROC SOURCE NOPRINT  INDD=SRCLIB2   OUTDD=SRCDIR2 NOALIAS;
PROC SOURCE NOPRINT  INDD=SRCLIB3   OUTDD=SRCDIR3 NOALIAS;

DATA SCANDIR1;
   INFILE SRCDIR1;
   INPUT @1  PROGRAM    $CHAR8.      /* SOURCE PROGRAM MODULE NAME */
         @18 CREATEDT   PD3.         /* MODULE DATE FIRST CREATED  */
         @22 UPDATEDT   PD3.         /* MODULE DATE LAST CHANGED   */
         @27 LINESOCD   IB2.         /* RAW MODULE LINES OF CODE   */
         @34 PGMR_ID    $CHAR4.;     /* USERID CODE OF PROGRAMMER  */
   IF SUBSTR(PROGRAM,1,3) NE 'ABC' THEN DELETE;  /* ABC SYSTEM ONLY   */
                                                 /* FROM THIS SRCLIB  */

DATA SCANDIR2;
   INFILE SRCDIR2;
   INPUT @1  PROGRAM    $CHAR8.      /* SOURCE PROGRAM MODULE NAME */
         @18 CREATEDT   PD3.         /* MODULE DATE FIRST CREATED  */
         @22 UPDATEDT   PD3.         /* MODULE DATE LAST CHANGED   */
         @27 LINESOCD   IB2.         /* RAW MODULE LINES OF CODE   */
         @34 PGMR_ID    $CHAR4.;     /* USERID CODE OF PROGRAMMER  */
   IF PGMR_ID NE '9999' THEN DELETE; /* ONLY WANT LIB TOTALS-TO-DATE */
                                     /* FROM PROGRAMMER ID NO. Z9999 */

DATA SCANDIR3;
   INFILE SRCDIR3;
   INPUT @1  PROGRAM    $CHAR8.      /* SOURCE PROGRAM MODULE NAME */
         @18 CREATEDT   PD3.         /* MODULE DATE FIRST CREATED  */
         @22 UPDATEDT   PD3.         /* MODULE DATE LAST CHANGED   */
         @27 LINESOCD   IB2.         /* RAW MODULE LINES OF CODE   */
         @34 PGMR_ID    $CHAR4.;     /* USERID CODE OF PROGRAMMER  */
   IF CREATDT < '01JAN91'D OR        /* ONLY WANT SOURCE LIB TOTALS */
      CREATDT > '31DEC91'D OR        /* FROM PROGRAMMER ID NO. Z9999 */
      PGMR_ID NE '9999' THEN DELETE; /* FOR THE YEAR 1991 ONLY      */
```

Figure 5-7   Example of an SAS/SOURCE and Data Procedure for Unloading a PDS Directory for Use in Function Point Estimation

```
      EXAMPLE OF A TYPICAL IBM HOST MVS SOFTWARE LANGUAGE PHASED COMPILER PROCESS

//PHASE1 EXEC..   ..SYSIN DD *       //PHASE2 EXEC..   ..SYSIN DD *       //PHASE 3         ..SYSIN DD *
+-------------+   +-------------+    +-------------+   +-------------+                       +-------------+
|COBOL COMPILE|   |COBOL PROGRAM|    |IBM BASIC    |   |IBM BASIC    |    |PREVIOUSLY   |
|JCL PROCEDURE|   |SOURCECODE   |    |ASSEMBLER    |   |ASSEMBLER    |    |EXISTING     |
|REQUESTS EXEC+---->|LIBRARY PDS |    |LANGUAGE    +---->|PROGRAM MODULE|  |PROGRAM LOAD |<......+
|OF A STANDARD|   |IS REFERENCED|    |(BAL) COMPILED|   |SEGMENT REFS |    |MODULE CALL  |  :
| PGM=IKFCBL00|   | IN JCL DD * |    |AS PGM=IEV90 |   |IN JCL AS DD *|    |SUBROUTINE   |  :
+-------------+   +-------------+    +-------------+   +-------------+                       +-------------+

          ..SYSOUT | DD *                    ..SYSOUT | DD *                      ..EXEC..
                   V                                  V                                V
          +-------------+                    +-------------+                    +-------------+
          |CREATES THE  |                    |CREATES A    |                    |IBM STANDARD |
          |   FIRST     |                    |SECOND       |                    |LINK EDITOR  |
          |PHASE COMPILED|                    |PHASE COMPILED+--+---->|COMBINES THE |
          |OBJECT PROGRAM|                    |OBJECT PROGRAM|                    |MACHINE OBJECT|
          |MODULE AS DD *|                    |MODULE AS DD *|                    |VIA PGM=IEWL |
          +-------------+                    +-------------+                    +-------------+

                                                                                     V
                                                                               +-------------+
                                                                               |EXECUTABLE   |
                                                                               |PROGRAM LOAD +......+
                                                                               |MODULE       |
                                                                               +-------------+

                                                                               RE-USE LIB
```

Figure 5-8 Operational Three-Phase IBM Standard Software Program Compiler Execution Process Involving Card Image Source Input

```
         AUTOMATED IBM HOST CURRENT SOURCECODE LINES AND CHANGES BY PDS DIRECTORY SCAN

+--------------+    +--------------+    +----------------+    +----------------+    +----------------+
| ESTABLISH &  |    | USE IBM UTILS|    | SEPARATE BY     |    | DIVIDE BY      |    | ADJUST THE     |
| MAINTAIN SITE|    | OR SAS/SOURCE|    | LANGUAGE TYPES |    | SPR LANGUAGE   |    | FP ESTIMATES   |
| STANDARDIZED +--->| PROCEDURE TO +--->| AND TALLY UP   +--->| LEVEL WEIGHT   +--->| TO CALIBRATE   |
| SOURCE PDS   |    | UNLOAD PDS   |    | LINES OF CODE  |    | TO ESTIMATE    |    | BY APPLICATION |
| PROGRAM LIBS |    | DIRECTORIES  |    | BY MODULE      |    | FUNCTION PTS.  |    | AREA AVERAGE   |
+--------------+    +--------------+    +----------------+    +----------------+    +----------------+
```

Figure 5-9   Automated Process for PDS Directory-Based Software Program Sourcecode Module Estimation by SPR Backfire Method

```
         AUTOMATED IBM HOST COMPILE PROCESS LOG AND COMPILE OBJECT DELIVERY AUDIT PROCESS

+--------------+    +--------------+    +----------------+    +----------------+    +----------------+
|              |    | SELECT OFF BY|    | SEPARATE BY     |    | DIVIDE BY      |    | SORT AND ADD   |
| READ SMF     |    | PROGRAM NAME |    | LANGUAGE TYPES |    | SPR LANGUAGE   |    | TO SOFTWARE    |
| RECORD TYPE  +--->| PREFIX IN JCL+--->| AND TALLY UP   +--->| LEVEL WEIGHT   +--->| INVENTORY DB   |
| 4 OR 30-4    |    | (SAMPLE CODE |    | LINES OF CODE  |    | TO ESTIMATE    |    | BY APPLICATION |
|              |    | SHOWN BELOW) |    | BY MODULE      |    | FUNCTION PTS.  |    | TIME & PROJECT |
+--------------+    +--------------+    +----------------+    +----------------+    +----------------+

<SAS DATA STEP>
  IF SUBSTR(PROGRAM,1,3) = 'CPX' THEN COMPILER='COBOL CAPEX OPTIMIZER  '; ELSE
  IF SUBSTR(PROGRAM,1,3) = 'IEL' THEN COMPILER='PL1 CHECKOUT COMPILER '; ELSE
  IF SUBSTR(PROGRAM,1,3) = 'IEN' THEN COMPILER='PL1 OPTIMIZING COMPILER'; ELSE
  IF SUBSTR(PROGRAM,1,3) = 'IEU' THEN COMPILER='ASSEMBLER VERSION F   '; ELSE
  IF SUBSTR(PROGRAM,1,3) = 'IEV' THEN COMPILER='ASSEMBLER VERSION H   '; ELSE
  IF SUBSTR(PROGRAM,1,3) = 'IGY' THEN COMPILER='COBOL II COMPILER     '; ELSE
  IF SUBSTR(PROGRAM,1,3) = 'IKF' THEN COMPILER='COBOL OPTIMIZER COMPILE';    < ETC. >
```

Figure 5-10   Automated Process for Audit of Software Development Project Module Compile Process Delivery and Inventory Update

timestamps to locate the corresponding SMF Type 14 PDS sourcecode library dataset are shown in Figures 5-8 and 5-10.

Examples of SAS language sourcecode used for merging SMF with external data, such as PDS directories, are shown in Appendix C.

HIGH-LEVEL PROGRAM LIBRARY ARCHIVAL AND SOURCECODE STORAGE

The most significant problem with using PDS directories, as well as raw measures of program size using SMF system logs, is that the LOC counted for different programs may have different densities. In other words, some lines may have only a few words, or a small part of a program statement, whereas other lines may actually contain several statements on a single line. Since each program statement corresponds to one or more compiled machine code instructions, the density of statements per line of code can be a very important measurement to provide a valid size metric.

If the raw measurement of PDS directories or compiled program EXCPs is the primary method of program module inventory and sizing, it is periodically necessary to calibrate size metrics by routine audits. This is done to determine the average density of statements per LOC for each individual system, language type, and time period. These numbers will vary for each of these categories at each individual data center environment and must be determined by a random sample to estimate the average number of statements per line (or more often, the number of lines per statement). These averages should also *break out* the average number of comment lines per program. Relative averages should be used in order to calibrate or adjust the LOC numbers to a common standard.

There are a large number of vendor products that support the management of PDS sourcecode libraries and provide more detailed statistics than is possible by PDS directory statistic reporting, SMF Type 14, or Type 30-5 record scans alone. Some of the most well known are PDSMAN, Pansophic Systems Panvalet, and ADR's Librarian. These sourcecode library products provide significant benefits in managing the backup, archival, and optimization of program source library datasets to protect program sourcecode from damage, loss, or fragmentation.

In addition, these management products provide substantially more audit trails than the PDS directory alone. Several of these products actually provide an expanded sourcecode library directory that can be used to automatically calibrate the LOC measurements when they are routinely updated to an automated software inventory database. Among the directory statistics in one typical archival management product are both the average number of characters per line, as well as the average number of words per line. In addition, these products will typically include status flags used to mark modules with the same member name as being in production as opposed to test, active, or obsolete data.

These statistics can be extracted for each program module and automatically grouped by system, language, and time period when they were originally developed. This information is then automatically analyzed by exception report programs and correlated against system development project schedules. It is then analyzed for size and quality variations using TQM and Statistical Process Control methods. It is also possible to use library directories or expanded module statistics to automatically prepare and update software program inventories. Software inventories or portfolios commonly track the number of each program category by such critical groups as system, customer, language, and relative size.

MEASURING FUNCTIONAL COMPLEXITY OF
APPLICATION PROGRAM MODULES

Measurement of the functional complexity of a program is much more complicated than the straightforward measurement of the program LOC. However, depending on the descriptive data available, the LOCs can normally be used to provide a relatively accurate estimation of a program's complexity. The most important estimators of program complexity have been determined to be the high-level programming language and the functional type of software application.

In the early days of mainframe technology, the complexity of a program was directly associated with the size of the compiled program module. The size of the module was especially important in the days before virtual storage and multiprocessing, since the object load control blocks were not relocatable and could not be split into pages to be swapped in and out of main memory. If a program was too complex, it could not be processed. Once the program was compiled, it was a simple process to relate the size of the module to the complexity of the program and assess the relative demands that it would place upon the system. However, with early compilers, if a program surpassed certain levels of size and complexity, it normally could not be compiled and resulted in failure if some level of compilation was achieved.

Raw measurements of the size of the program's sourcecode, in terms of LOC, could be used as a rough estimator. Yet, the complexity of the instructions generated by the compiler are more dependent on the individual commands or data process requests in the statements than on the number of LOCs or statements. The number of LOCs can be estimated based on measures of the average density of characters or words per line. One method developed during this period was based on research that determined that the most important factor in establishing the size and complexity of system task requests was the total number of input and output datasets, as well as the number of edits or validation case statements and the data format conversions that are performed.

This method of estimating functional program complexity based on inputs, outputs, inquiries and interfaces, was refined by A. J. Albrecht of IBM and became known as function points. The practice of counting function points as an estimate of software complexity has become the most common method of measuring application software in the United States today. Additionally, ever since IBM first introduced function points in 1979, there have been over a dozen different versions of the function point measurement methodology published by independent researchers.

Although there are differences with respect to the weights and adjustment factors that are applied based on the nature of the application development support environment, the basic calculation of all the function point methodologies is founded upon a simple tally of the number of inputs, outputs, inquiries, data files, and interfaces. Each count is adjusted by standard weight factors, and then the total raw function point count may be adjusted by complexity factor coefficients. These can be calibrated based upon local research to determine the relative importance of each complexity factor on an individual data center environment. The administrative procedures related to the manual collection of data and the calibration of complexity factors have largely dominated, and in many cases even monopolized, the resources of many software quality management organizations in the past.

However, more recent developments with regard to vendor products that automate the reporting of measurements based on system logs, and techniques such as the Capers Jones "backfire" methods (which apply formulas for estimating function points of existing software inventories in program sourcecode library archives), have greatly reduced the amount of the data center budget devoted to supporting software quality. These techniques have demonstrated substantial return on investment by relying on automated methods to measure quality.

The backfire process for estimation of function points was developed in 1986 by Capers Jones of Software Productivity Research, Inc. in Burlington, Massachusetts. This method uses "language level and expansion factors" in order to directly convert LOC into a function point equivalent value. It is based on a simple procedure which involves dividing the number of program LOCs by the average number of LOCs per function point for the high-level language in which the program is coded. This method has been demonstrated to be consistently within 15 percent of the value assigned and at less than 15 percent of the cost and time required by more cumbersome and time-consuming manual function point calculation methods.

When combined with automated methods of monitoring updates to program sourcecode libraries, the backfire method can provide substantial benefits at minimal cost. This data can provide rapid return on investment that can quickly pay for expanded software quality management activities, thus resulting in better system development management and on-time delivery of software products and services, at lower cost with higher quality.

Examples of the basic function point calculation method and worksheets for assigning weights and complexity factors are shown in Figures 5-11, 5-12, and 5-13. Examples of backfire method language-level conversion factors and variability related to alternative methods to count program LOCs are shown in Figure 5-14.

STANDARDIZING PROGRAM SOURCECODE FOR MAXIMUM EFFICIENCY

One of the most significant advances in high-level application language program development is *structured programming*, which is the use of the internal, logically structured design of a program's procedural flow to increase the understandability, maintainability, and the ease of compiler optimization of the object code generated from the sourcecode. Although there are a variety of different schools of structured programming, the most basic characteristic of structured programs is *modularity*. Defined, it is the level of program code that passes control in a sequential manner and has limited internal cycles or logic loops.

In addition to modularity, most structured programming is characterized by formatting standards for data structure declarations and indenting of the logical levels within each process step or procedure. To some extent, there are general standards and conventions associated with each high-level program language, but there are also in-house standards which should be recommended and enforced as well. The *cleanness of* structured code is one of the most important factors associated with software quality. Both the elimination of defects through desk-checking or by automated program scans, as well as ease of program diagnostic troubleshooting or maintenance required for discrete enhancements, enhance the code.

Another important characteristic is the establishment of in-house standards for internal program documentation and comments. This can be as important to the maintainability of the program as are structured coding methods. Although these characteristics cannot be measured by system logs, comparative testing of the efficiency and reliability of structured program sourcecode can be based on system log data. Such analysis of the benefits of structured methods has been repeatedly demonstrated by system log benchmarks of coding conventions to make a world of difference in both the execution time and resources used by a program.

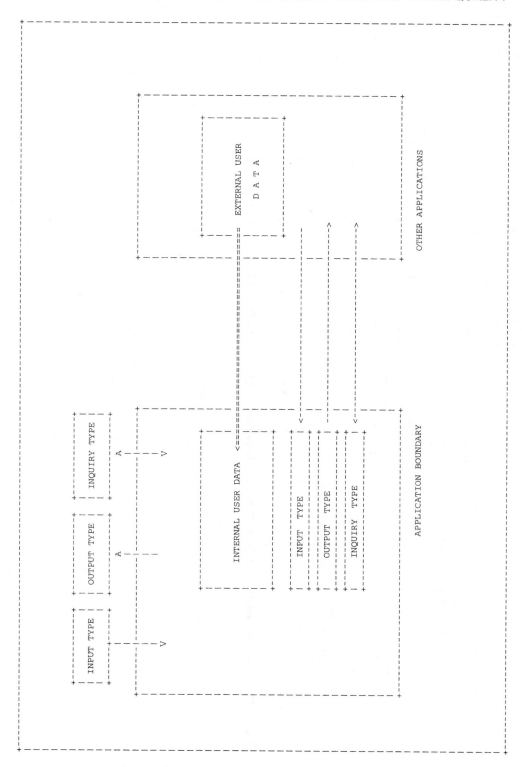

Figure 5-11   Basic Function Point Software Sourcecode Measurement Process as Defined by IBM and A. J. Albrecht (1979)

1979 FUNCTION POINT CALCULATOR

APPLICATION SOFTWARE PROGRAM NAME _____   SYSTEM NAME _____

FUNCTION POINT FACTORS	RAW COUNT	EMPIRICAL WEIGHT		UNADJUSTED TOTALS
NUMBER OF INPUTS	_____	X 4	=	_____
NUMBER OF OUTPUTS	_____	X 5	=	_____
NUMBER OF INQUIRIES	_____	X 4	=	_____
NUMBER OF MASTER FILES	_____	X 10	=	_____

UNADJUSTED TOTAL

COMPLEXITY ADJUSTMENT: HIGHLY COMPLEX= +25%; LOW COMPLEXITY = (-25%)

ADJUSTED TOTAL FUNCTION POINTS

Figure 5-12   Basic Function Point Calculation Worksheet for the Original IBM 4-Factor Weight Estimating Method (1979)

1984   FUNCTION   POINT   CALCULATOR

APPLICATION SOFTWARE PROGRAM NAME _____   SYSTEM NAME _____

FUNCTION POINT FACTORS	RAW COUNT	EMPIRICAL WEIGHT	UNADJUSTED TOTALS
LOW COMPLEXITY APPLICATION			
EXTERNAL INPUTS	_____	X 3 =	_____
EXTERNAL OUTPUTS	_____	X 4 =	_____
LOGICAL FILES	_____	X 7 =	_____
INTERFACES FILES	_____	X 5 =	_____
INQUIRIES	_____	X 3 =	_____
MEDIUM COMPLEXITY APPLICATION			
EXTERNAL INPUTS	_____	X 4 =	_____
EXTERNAL OUTPUTS	_____	X 5 =	_____
LOGICAL FILES	_____	X 10 =	_____
INTERFACES FILES	_____	X 7 =	_____
INQUIRIES	_____	X 4 =	_____
HIGH COMPLEXITY APPLICATION			
EXTERNAL INPUTS	_____	X 6 =	_____
EXTERNAL OUTPUTS	_____	X 7 =	_____
LOGICAL FILES	_____	X 15 =	_____
INTERFACES FILES	_____	X 10 =	_____
INQUIRIES	_____	X 6 =	_____

UNADJUSTED TOTAL
SCALED INPUT FOR 14 INFLUENCE FACTORS
ADJUSTED TOTAL FUNCTION POINTS

Figure 5-13   Basic Function Point Calculation Worksheet for the Revised IBM 5-Factor/3-Tier Estimating Method (1984)

SPR "BACKFIRE METHOD" PROGRAM LANGUAGE MULTIPLIERS

Language	Assembler Calibration Equivalents	LOC per Function Point
Basic Assembly Language (BAL)	1.0	320
Macro Assembly Language (MASM)	1.5	213
C and C++	2.5	128
Interpreter BASIC	2.5	128
FORTRAN 77	3.0	105
ALGOL	3.0	105
ANSI COBOL 74	3.0	105
PASCAL	3.5	91
Compiled BASIC	3.5	91
RPG-II	4.0	80
PL/I	4.0	80
Modula	4.0	80
Ada	4.5	71
Prolog	5.0	64
LISP	5.0	64
FORTH	5.0	64
Turbo BASIC	5.0	64
DLI or other database language	8.0	40
SAS or other statistical language	10.0	32
SMALLTALK or other object-oriented language	12.0	26
TELON or other program generator language	20.0	16
DB2/QMF or other database language query	25.0	13
Spreadsheet macro language script	50.0	6
Graphical user interface objects	75.0	4

Figure 5-14   SPR Function Point Estimation Language-Level Multipliers and Equivalent Source Statement Lines per FP

BENCHMARKING AND BASELINE COMPARISON OF APPLICATION SOFTWARE

The establishment and enforcement of application programming standards are dependent upon activities which take examples of two alternative methods of program coding and compare them statistically to show performance differences resulting from each of the two programming methods. In most cases this involves writing a simple program to perform a basic process function that is common to a large number of programs of a particular type or using a common benchmark process formula or algorithm that can be compared to a vendor process standard. This is done by making two versions of the program, in which the only difference is one statement or procedure which is coded two different ways. The two programs are then run together or under the same workload conditions, and the results are statistically compared. In order to assure that all other factors other than the amount of system resources used or the execution time is fully equivalent between the two programs, full SMF system log profile statistics are accumulated and reported alongside the resource usage and benchmark numbers.

It is also common to accumulate standardized baseline data to analyze comparative quality and efficiency of equivalent system products or application software based on the SMF system log data. This method uses program LOC sizing data and backfire function point estimates to group programs into equivalent workloads or classes of programs based on functional type and resource demand characteristics. It should be understood that it is essential to compare programs that share common class characteristics in order to get a true picture of the quality within the constraints of each class. Such constraints determine what qualities the customer regards as most important for a given category of programs and also determine the reasonable changes that can be made to improve quality.

There are apparent divisions that should be made in classifying application software programs for analysis of baseline average resource usage, turnaround, throughput, responsiveness, and other indicators of software quality. These distinctions require both an accumulation of automated software quality measurements into a system performance history database, as well as descriptive sizing and complexity statistics on the sourcecode used to generate the application software.

6

VENDOR PRODUCTS THAT HELP MEASURE PROGRAM SOURCECODE

There are several available vendor products that help manage program sourcecode libraries and support sourcecode backup and archival. These include such renowned packages as ADR's Librarian, Pansophic's Panvalet, and Legent's Endevor. However, there are thus far only a limited number of automated sourcecode sizing and quality measurement products on the market. Program quality metric products that do exist, however, are extremely powerful and can be used in combination with other automated measurement application product tools.

VENDOR PRODUCT TO MEASURE PROGRAM SOURCECODE QUALITY: Q/AUDITOR

Q/AUDITOR-COBOL is developed and marketed by Eden Systems Corporation of Carmel, Indiana. Q/AUDITOR is another one of those special automated measurement products that have no major competition. Although there are a number of pre-testing tools and pre-compile program scanning tools that basically give the same error messages and warnings that the program compiler gives, Q/AUDITOR goes several steps beyond the language error messages. It scans for several hundred types of program coding styles which have been identified as causing potential program inefficiency or difficulty of program maintenance. In the process, Q/AUDITOR also collects statistics on a number of program sourcecode sizing, complexity, and functionality measurements that are automatically updated to a program profile's database record and output to a quality audit report each time that the sourcecode is scanned for the program.

Q/AUDITOR provides a tally of several hundred program coding characteristics for each source module. This includes number of procedural levels, nested if statements, case statements, undeclared or unresolved references, and external fetch or dependent program calls. It also measures characteristics which raise the risk of implementing the program to production. These characteristics are generally regarded as poor programming practices according to statements and findings issued by the IBM vendor and IBM Guide user groups. Each individual data center that installs Q/AUDITOR can specify machine request table file entries to activate or deactivate each of the available Q/AUDITOR measurements, according to whether or not that item is prescribed by in-house programming standards.

Based upon these tables, each program that is updated to production program sourcecode library archives, as well as each program that is checked out from the library and changed, can be measured according to its level of compliance to in-house standards and risk factors. It can then be graded according to relative quality classes. Statistics about the number of programs that meet each quality level can be reported as individual program profiles. Summary data from the in-house software inventory database can be used to compare quality of particular systems, all systems supporting a particular customer area, or all systems in a data center inventory. This data supports a TQM program to continuously improve the efficiency and effectiveness of data center products and services.

In addition, Q/AUDITOR provides an automated calculation of the function points for each program based on the backfire method. The precision of Q/AUDITOR calculations reflect not only the ability to count the exact number of logical statements, but also the ability to detect machine macro-code, or even COBOL copy members, and comments which should not be counted as statements under most of the function point counting methods. Q/AUDITOR is also able to get a more precise function point count because it scans the logic flow of the program, allowing it to obtain more precise counts of the number of inputs and outputs, inquiries, interfaces, and individual data elements. It can also be adjusted by Q/AUDITOR user exit logic statements to duplicate any one of the major function point counting methods that might be counted manually by a data center.

Q/AUDITOR also provides a series of Halstead complexity metrics and some McCabe-related complexity measures such as the cyclomatic complexity. These are used to determine the relative risk of making changes or not making changes to any program that is introduced into a real-time, multiprocessing, or online teleprocessing networking environment. These software metrics can be used to locate the most dangerous sections of a program requiring additional care and analysis before modification, and can also automatically calculate the number of possible process paths that must be accounted for to fully test the program or to even consider returning a program for redesign.

One of the most popular capabilities of Q/AUDITOR is that it provides standardized *cost-quality statements* used to estimate value as well as Return on Investment resulting from making changes to a group of programs or redesigning new programs to replace the old. These reports are similar to the reports used by CPAs and are easily understood by management.

Q/AUDITOR provides a powerful basis for automated software quality measurement programs. It can quickly achieve high levels of programming excellence and approach the highest standards possible with the most current level of application language standards and optimizing compiler technology. Q/AUDITOR's companion product, Q/ARTISAN, can automatically reformat the sourcecode for a COBOL program that has been identified as having quality or performance problems by automated Q/AUDITOR scans.

This Q/ARTISAN product, which uses a new technology known as *reengineering*, can help create a highly efficient software manufacturing environment that can be monitored, measured, and optimized just as any other manufacturing environment, thus providing a significant edge over competitive data centers using manual quality assurance procedures. Although there are several products involving this technology that have become available during the past decade, only Q/ARTISAN is designed for the engineering of existing program sourcecode in a manner that is based upon continuous quality improvement of human programming skills or services.

The Q/AUDITOR and Q/ARTISAN products are currently available separately or together and support COBOL and other high-level language sourcecode, as well as the TELON automated program generator sourcecode. Additional languages such a PL/1, Assembler, and C may be supported in the future. It is available in both a host mainframe sourcecode library inventory support version and a PC workstation version. The cost varies depending on the environment. Examples of Q/AUDITOR reports and screens can be seen in Figures 6-1a to 6-1i.

```
/----------------------------------------------------------------------\
|                                                                      |
| QXP0001    Q/AUDITOR SOURCE CODE ANALYSIS (1.0.0) 89/12/20 14:24      |
| OPTION ===>                                                          |
|                                                                      |
| STANDARD SOURCE LIBRARY:    NEW                                      |
|         Library Type  ===> PDS      (PDS, PANvalet, or LIBrarian)    |
|         Project       ===> USERID                                   |
|         Group         ===> TEST                                     |
|         Type          ===> PLI                                      |
|         Member        ===> MEMBER    (Also, *, ?)                   |
| Password/Access code  ===>                                          |
|                                                                      |
| NON-STANDARD SOURCE LIBRARY:                                        |
|    Library Name   ===>                                              |
|                                                                      |
| Specify:       SYSOUT Class ===> *       Report to file ===> N (Y,N) |
|                                          Report member name ===>     |
|                                                       (1-5 CHAR)     |
| Reports requested:  Audit ===> Y (Y,N)      Diagnostic ===> Y (Y,N)  |
|                                                                      |
| Specify Analysis option   ===> 1 (1,2,3)                            |
|    1    SAMPLE LOWEST GRADING STANDARDS                              |
|    2    SAMPLE PERCENT GRADING STANDARDS                             |
|    3    SAMPLE RE-ENGINEERING STANDARDS                              |
\----------------------------------------------------------------------/
```

Figure 6-1a   Eden Q/AUDITOR Program Sourcecode Analysis Main Menu

```
/----------------------------------------------------------------------\
| QXP0002 Q/AUDITOR DELTA AUDIT REPORT CREATION (1.0.0) 89/12/20 14:24| |
| OPTION ===>                                                          |
|                                                                      |
| STANDARD SOURCE LIBRARY:    ORIGINAL       REVISED                   |
|         Library Type  ===> PDS       ===> PDS     (PDS, PAN or LIB)  |
|         Project       ===> USERID    ===> USERID                     |
|         Group         ===> PROD      ===> TEST                       |
|         Type          ===> PLI       ===> PLI                        |
|         Member        ===> TESTSK    ===> TESTSK                      |
| Password/Access code  ===>           ===>                            |
|                                                                      |
| NON-STANDARD SOURCE LIBRARY:                                        |
|    Library Name   ===>                                              |
|                                                                      |
| Specify:       SYSOUT Class ===> *       Report to file ===> N (Y,N) |
|                                          Report member name ===>     |
|                                                       (1-5 CHAR)     |
| Reports requested:  Audit ===> Y (Y,N)      Diagnostic ===> Y (Y,N)  |
|                                                                      |
| Specify Analysis option   ===> 1 (1,2,3)                            |
|    1    SAMPLE LOWEST GRADING STANDARDS                              |
|    2    SAMPLE PERCENT GRADING STANDARDS                             |
|    3    SAMPLE RE-ENGINEERING STANDARDS                             |
\----------------------------------------------------------------------/
```

Figure 6-1b   Eden Q/AUDITOR Sourcecode Change Impact Analysis Menu

```
----- QPSTD3 Standards File -----
**********************************************************
* (c) COPYRIGHT EDEN SYSTEMS 1989.  ALL RIGHTS RESERVED. *
**********************************************************
*                  STANDARDS CHANGE LOG                  *
*   DATE       PROGRAMMER      DESCRIPTION OF CHANGE      *
* 12/20/89   A.B. PROGRAMMER   NEW EDITS TO VALIDATE ENTRY GRADE *
**********************************************************
STANDARD=SAMPLE PL/I RE-ENGINEERING STANDARDS (LOWEST GRADING)
VERB COUNTS
FLOW          A 000  B N/A  C N/A  D N/A  F FLOW'S FOUND
GET           A 000  B N/A  C N/A  D N/A  F GET'S FOUND
NOFLOW        A 000  B 002  C N/A  D N/A  F NOFLOW'S FOUND
PUT           A 000  B N/A  C N/A  D N/A  F PUT'S FOUND

VERB STATISTICS
LIT%PROC      A 005  B N/A  C N/A  D N/A  F PROCS WITH > 5 LITERALS
OPEN%FILE     A 001  B 002  C N/A  D N/A  F MAXIMUM OPENS PER FILE
CLOSE%FILE    A 001  B 002  C N/A  D N/A  F MAXIMUM CLOSES PER FILE
READ%FILE     A 001  B 002  C N/A  D N/A  F MAXIMUM READS PER FILE
WRITE%FILE    A 001  B 002  C N/A  D N/A  F MAXIMUM WRITES PER FILE

SIZE ANALYSIS
MAINSTMTS     A 050  B N/A  C N/A  D N/A  F MAINLINE STATEMENTS
PROCSTMT      A N/A  B N/A  C N/A  D N/A  F PROCEDURE STATEMENTS  (100S)
NCMMTCODE     A N/A  B N/A  C N/A  D N/A  F EXECUTABLE LINES      (100S)
TOTALSTATE    A N/A  B N/A  C N/A  D N/A  F TOTAL STATEMENTS      (100S)
STMT%PROC     A 000  B N/A  C N/A  D N/A  F # OF PROC'S OVER 15 STMTS
TOTALLINE     A N/A  B N/A  C N/A  D N/A  F TOTAL LINES OF CODE   (100S)
HALSTEAD      A N/A  B N/A  C N/A  D N/A  F HALSTEAD'S VOLUME METRIC

STANDARDS ANALYSIS
DCLENTRY      A N/A  B N/A  C N/A  D N/A  F # EXTERNAL ENTRY DECLARES
REQPROCS      A N/A  B N/A  C N/A  D N/A  F REQUIRED PROCS NOT FOUND
ONGROUP       A 000  B N/A  C N/A  D N/A  F ON CONDITIONS NOT TOGETHER
NULLELSE      A 000  B N/A  C N/A  D N/A  F NULL ELSE'S (ELSE;) FOUND
NULLTHEN      A 000  B N/A  C N/A  D N/A  F NULL THEN'S (THEN;) FOUND
COMPLEXIF     A 000  B 005  C 010  D 020  F EXCESSIVELY COMPLEX IF'S
COMPLEXDO     A 000  B 005  C 010  D 020  F EXCESSIVELY COMPLEX DO'S
COMPLEXSEL    A 000  B 005  C 010  D 020  F EXCESSIVELY COMPLEX SELECT'S

STRUCTURE ANALYSIS
PGMEXIT       A 001  B N/A  C N/A  D N/A  F NUMBER OF PROGRAM EXITS
PGMENTRY      A 001  B N/A  C N/A  D N/A  F NUMBER OF PROGRAM ENTRIES
HIDNMAIN      A 000  B 000  C 005  D 005  F HIDDEN MAINLINE STATEMENTS
UNREFPROC     A 000  B 000  C 000  D 000  F UNREFERENCED PROCEDURES
MCCABE01      A N/A  B N/A  C N/A  D N/A  F CYCLOMATIC COMPLEXITY
MCCABE1MAX    A 002  B N/A  C N/A  D N/A  F PROC'S > 5 TEST CASES
MCCABE02      A 010  B 010  C 012  D 012  F ESSENTIAL COMLEXITY
INVG01        A 000  B 000  C 015  D 015  F # OF INVALAID GO TO'S (#1)
```

Figure 6-1c   Eden Q/AUDITOR Sourcecode Standards Definition File

```
+----------------------------------------------------------------------+
|                                                                      |
| DATE: 07/28/89          Q/AUDITOR (R) QUALITY BALANCE SHEET           |
| TIME: 16:48:58    (C) COPYRIGHT EDEN SYSTEMS CORPORATION 1985-89      |
|                                                                      |
|                    AS OF 07/01/89 AT 00:00:00:00                     |
|                                                                      |
|       PROGRAM            NUMBER OF             PERCENTAGE OF          |
|        GRADE             PROGRAMS                PROGRAMS             |
|       =======           =========           ==============          |
|                                                                      |
|          A                 024                    16%                |
|                                                                      |
|          B                 045                    30%                |
|                                                                      |
|          C                 066                    44%                |
|                                                                      |
|          D                 012                    08%                |
|                                                                      |
|          F                 003                    02%                |
|       =======           =========           ==============          |
|                                                                      |
|        TOTAL               150                    100%               |
|                                                                      |
+----------------------------------------------------------------------+
```

Figure 6-1d   Eden Q/AUDITOR Sourcecode Inventory Quality Grading

```
+----------------------------------------------------------------------+
|                                                                      |
| DATE: 11/30/89          Q/AUDITOR (R) QUALITY GRADE LEVEL BALANCE     |
| TIME: 11:26:38    (C) COPYRIGHT EDEN SYSTEMS CORPORATION 1985-89      |
|                                                                      |
|                    AS OF 07/01/89 AT 00:00:00:00                     |
|                                                                      |
|        GRADE             NUMBER OF             PERCENTAGE OF          |
|        LEVEL             PROGRAMS                PROGRAMS             |
|       =======           =========           ==============          |
|                                                                      |
|        1 -  10             000                    00%                |
|       11 -  20             000                    00%                |
|       21 -  30             000                    00%                |
|       31 -  40             000                    00%                |
|       41 -  50             000                    00%                |
|       51 -  60             001                    20%                |
|       61 -  70             002                    40%                |
|       71 -  80             003                    40%                |
|       81 -  90             000                    00%                |
|       91 -100             000                    00%                 |
|       =======           =========           ==============          |
|                                                                      |
|        TOTAL               150                    100%               |
|                                                                      |
+----------------------------------------------------------------------+
```

Figure 6-1e   Eden Q/AUDITOR Sourcecode Inventory Grade-Level Balance

```
+------------------------------------------------------------------+
| DATE: 07/28/89  Q/AUDITOR (R) WEEKLY QUALITY POSITION CHANGE IMPACT |
| TIME: 16:49:43   (C) COPYRIGHT EDEN SYSTEMS CORPORATION 1985-89   |
|                                                                  |
|                                                                  |
|               FOR THE PERIOD STARTING: 07/21/89 AT 00:00:00:00   |
|                                ENDING: 07/28/89 AT 00:00:00:00   |
|                                                                  |
|                                                                  |
|                                                                  |
|                                                                  |
|                 P R E V I O U S   V E R S I O N                  |
|                                                                  |
|               _____   |
|                                                                  |
|       ]    ]   A          B          C          D          F     |
|               _____   |
|                                                                  |
|       ] A ]  000( 00%)   000( 00%)   000( 00%)   000( 00%)   000( 00%) |
| U V ]     ]          \\                                          |
| P E ] B ]  000( 00%)   000( 00%)   000( 00%)   000( 00%)   000( 00%) |
| D R ]     ]                    \\                                |
| A S ] C ]  000( 00%)   000( 00%)   000( 00%)   001( 33%)   000( 00%) |
| T I ]     ]                           \\                         |
| E O ] D ]  000( 00%)   000( 00%)   001( 33%)   001( 33%)   000( 00%) |
| D N ]     ]                                        \\            |
|       ] F ]  000( 00%)   000( 00%)   000( 00%)   000( 00%)   000( 00%) |
|               _____   |
|                                                                  |
|            000( 00%)   000( 00%)   001( 33%)   002( 66%)   000( 00%) |
|                                                                  |
|                                                                  |
|                                                                  |
|                                 NUMBER OF     PERCENTAGE OF      |
|                                 PROGRAMS       PROGRAMS          |
|                                 =========     ==============     |
|                                                                  |
|        PROGRAM QUALITY IMPROVED      001         ( 33%)          |
|        PROGRAM QUALITY MAINTAINED    001         ( 33%)          |
|        PROGRAM QUALITY DEGRADED      001         ( 33%)          |
|                                 =========     ==============     |
|                          TOTAL       003         (100%)          |
|                                                                  |
|                                                                  |
+------------------------------------------------------------------+
```

Figure 6-1f   Q/AUDITOR Program Weekly Inventory Quality Position Change

```
+-------------------------------------------------------------------+
| DATE: 07/01/89   Q/AUDITOR (R) MONTHLY QUALITY BALANCE STATEMENT   |
| TIME: 11:27:48    (C) COPYRIGHT EDEN SYSTEMS CORPORATION 1985-89   |
|                                                                   |
|                FOR THE PERIOD STARTING: 06/01/89 AT 00:00:00:00    |
|                              ENDING: 07/01/89 AT 00:00:00:00       |
|                                                                   |
|                                      CHANGES        CHANGES        |
|                                      ENHANCING      DECREASING     |
|                                      QUALITY        QUALITY        |
|                                      =======        ==========     |
|         NEW PROGRAMS DEVELOPED                                     |
|         ========================                                  |
| NEW PROGRAMS ENTERING AT TOP GRADE   022 ( 11%)     004 (  2%)     |
| NEW PROGRAMS NOT ENTERING AT TOP GRADE  0 (  0%)      0 (  0%)     |
|                                                                   |
|           OLD PROGRAMS CHANGED                                     |
|           =====================                                   |
| PROGRAMS WITH QUALITY IMPROVED        014 (  7%)                   |
| PROGRAMS WITH QUALITY MAINTAINED      058 ( 79%)                   |
| PROGRAMS WITH QUALITY DEGRADED                      002 (  1%)     |
| ==================================== === =======    === =======   |
|              TOTAL                    194 ( 97%)     006 (  3%)     |
|                                                                   |
+-------------------------------------------------------------------+
```

Figure 6-1g   Q/AUDITOR Program Inventory Monthly Quality Balance Sheet

```
+-------------------------------------------------------------------+
| DATE: 07/01/89   Q/AUDITOR (R) YEARLY QUALITY BALANCE STATEMENT    |
| TIME: 11:27:48    (C) COPYRIGHT EDEN SYSTEMS CORPORATION 1985-89   |
|                                                                   |
|                FOR THE PERIOD STARTING: 11/30/88 AT 00:00:00:00    |
|                              ENDING: 11/30/89 AT 00:00:00:00       |
|                                                                   |
|                                    IMPACT ON PORTFOLIO QUALITY     |
|                                    ==========================      |
|                                    CHANGES        CHANGES          |
|                                    ENHANCING      DECREASING       |
|                                    QUALITY        QUALITY          |
|                                    =======        ==========       |
|          NEW PROGRAMS: HURDLE GRADE 70                             |
|          =============                                            |
| NEW PROGRAMS ENTERING ABOVE HURDLE   000 ( 00%)                    |
| NEW PROGRAMS NOT ABOVE HURDLE GRADE                 008 ( 03%)     |
|                                                                   |
|           OLD PROGRAMS: HURDLE CHANGE 10                           |
|           =====================                                   |
| PROGRAMS WITH QUALITY IMPROVED        003 ( 01%)                   |
| PROGRAMS WITH QUALITY MAINTAINED      224 ( 94%)                   |
| PROGRAMS WITH QUALITY DEGRADED                      002 (  1%)     |
| ==================================== === =======    === =======   |
|              TOTAL                    227 ( 95%)     010 (  4%)     |
|                                                                   |
+-------------------------------------------------------------------+
```

Figure 6-1h   Q/AUDITOR Program Inventory Yearly Quality Income Value

```
          Q/AUDITOR (R) DELTA AUDIT REPORT
(C) COPYRIGHT EDEN SYSTEMS CORPORATION 1985-1989        12/21/89  12:00:34

PROGRAM: TESTPGM
ORIGINAL GRADE: F 1                                      NEW GRADE: D 1

                                                    GRADE
                                           -------------------------
    STANDARD                      #         A    B    C    D    F
                                  --        --   --   --   --   --
    VERB COUNTS
 1  ALLOCATE'S FOUND              0        000  N/A  N/A  N/A  N/A
 2  DISPLAY'S FOUND               7        000  N/A  N/A  N/A  N/A
 3  FLOW'S FOUND                  0        000  N/A  N/A  N/A  N/A
 4  GET'S FOUND                   0        000  N/A  N/A  N/A  N/A
 5  LOCATE'S FOUND                0        000  N/A  N/A  N/A  N/A
 6  NOFLOW'S FOUND                0        000  N/A  N/A  N/A  N/A
 7  PUT'S FOUND                   0        000  N/A  N/A  N/A  N/A
 8  WAIT'S FOUND                  0        000  N/A  N/A  N/A  N/A
    DECLARE ATTRIBUTES
 9  BACKWARD ATTRIBUTES           0        000  N/A  N/A  N/A  N/A
10  GENERIC ATTRIBUTES            0        000  N/A  N/A  N/A  N/A
11  LABEL ATTRIBUTES              0        000  N/A  N/A  N/A  N/A
    VERB STATISTICS
12  PROCS WITH > 5 LITERALS       0        005  N/A  N/A  N/A  N/A
13  MAXIMUM OPENS PER FILE        1        001  002  N/A  N/A  N/A
14  MAXIMUM CLOSES PER FILE       1        001  002  N/A  N/A  N/A
15  MAXIMUM READS PER FILE        0        001  002  N/A  N/A  N/A
16  MAXIMUM WRITES PER FILE       0        001  002  N/A  N/A  N/A
    COMMENT ANALYSIS
17  VALUABLE COMMENTS           + 10       030  020  010  N/A  N/A
18  PROC VALUE COMMENTS         + 10       020  010  005  N/A  N/A
19  PROCS W/HDR COMMENTS        + 10       N/A  N/A  N/A  N/A  N/A
    SIZE ANALYSIS
20  MAINLINE STATEMENTS           0        050  N/A  N/A  N/A  N/A
21  PROCEDURE STMTS    (100S)     0        033  N/A  N/A  N/A  N/A
22  EXECUTABLE STMTS   (100S)     0        047  N/A  N/A  N/A  N/A
23  TOTAL STATEMENTS   (100S)     0        066  N/A  N/A  N/A  N/A
24  # OF PROCS > 15  STMTS        0        000  N/A  N/A  N/A  N/A
25  # OF PROCS > 40  LINES        0        000  N/A  N/A  N/A  N/A
26  TOTAL LINES OF CODE(100S)     0        080  N/A  N/A  N/A  N/A
27  HALSTEADS VOLUME METRIC      15        N/A  N/A  N/A  N/A  N/A
98  IFPUG FUNCTION POINT EST     70        093  N/A  N/A  N/A  N/A
99  ......ETC.....               99        999  999  999  999  999
    DATA DIVISION ANALYSIS
    STANDARDS ANALYSIS
    FORMATTING ANALYSIS
    STRUCTURE ANALYSIS
    ......ETC.....               99        999  999  999  999  999

    TOTAL QUALITY SCORES         99        999  999  999  999  999
                                ====      ==== ==== ==== ==== ====
```

Figure 6-1i   Eden Q/AUDITOR Sample Program Quality Grading Profile

VENDOR PRODUCT TO HELP MEASURE PROGRAM
SOURCE OBJECTS: FILE-AID

The FILE-AID series of products is developed and marketed by Compuware, the same vendor who makes ABEND-AID. The FILE-AID products include online and batch foreground tools which are managed from a series of TSO/ISPF Dialog panels. The FILE-AID batch program can also be executed in a traditional batch background processing environment. FILE-AID is a tool that allows programmers to browse, edit, make global changes, scan and count for specific character or numeric data strings, or build customized audit log data sets supplementing the statistics in either PDS directories or the program source library directory datasets.

This capability has many value-added features, since FILE-AID can be used to develop an in-house automated quality measurement application somewhat comparable to Q/AUDITOR. The real benefit of FILE-AID is that it not only can open PDS members and sequential files, but it can also open and edit PDS directories, sequential datasets greater than 255 (or even 32,000) characters in logical record length, variable or undefined record formats, VSAM, Direct Access data formats (such as SASv datasets, DB2 table files, IMS databases), and even link-edited program object load modules. This is done in a manner that is familiar to programmers using the standard TSO/Edit or REXX/Xedit, full-screen, line editors on IBM's host mainframe systems.

The original purpose of FILE-AID was to provide programmers with a quick and handy method of opening all of the file types that could not be handled by the TSO/Edit facility to fix damaged database files or program load object modules without having to run dangerous *ZAP* programs. All of the changes applied by FILE-AID can be made on the literal level, which is to say that the data can be displayed in EBCDIC character and full numeric formats, even though entries or changes must be converted to a packed form before changes are saved to the file.

The importance of FILE-AID to automated quality measurement is a more recent development. A number of expanded facilities of FILE-AID products allow it to store automated data structure mapping modules for the critical datasets. This allows testing and analysis of all types of datasets in a split screen display mode alongside the data structure of the program copy member that created it. It also provides an extended capability to count strings of data and to extract records and strings of data within a specified number of characters from hit strings. An additional application of FILE-AID is that it provides JCL syntax checking and parameter scanning tools used to count string occurrences and build cross-references of the number of "DD" dataset and file definitions in production JCL procedures. This can be used in combination with statement counts to provide more reliable estimates of function point counts for each program application.

It is also possible to search program modules using complex "depending on" algorithms which allow some scanning for programming standard conventions, such as the number of "nested if" statements, program fetch calls, and other potential coding problems. Although developing such applications of FILE-AID would be a major in-house undertaking, the relatively low cost of FILE-AID and benefits of such a tool make an in-house software inventory application a reasonable option for many midsize and smaller data centers.

Examples of FILE-AID screens and reporting capabilities are shown in Figures 6-2a to 6-2j.

```
/------------------- ISPF/PDF PRIMARY OPTION MENU  --------------\
|OPTION  ===>                                                     |
|                                                                 |
|                                                                 |
|  0  SPF PARMS    - Specify Terminal and User Parameters         |
|  1  BROWSE       - Display Source Data or Output Listing        |
|  2  EDIT         - Create or Change Source Data                 |
|  3  UTILITIES    - Perform Utility Functions                    |
|  4  FOREGROUND   - Invoke Language Processors in Foreground     |
|  5  BATCH        - Submit Job for Language Processing           |
|  6  COMMAND      - Enter TSO Command or C-List                  |
|  7  DIALOG TEST  - Perform Dialog Testing                       |
|  A  ABEND-AID    - Abend-Aid Output Processor                   |
|  F  FILE-AID     - INTERACTIVE DATASET BROWSE AND EDIT UTILITIES |
|  T  TUTORIAL     - Display Information About ISPF               |
|  X  EXIT         - Terminate ISPF Using Log and List Defaults   |
|                                                                 |
|              ENTER END COMMAND TO TERMINATE ISPF.               |
|                                                                 |
|                                                                 |
\-----------------------------------------------------------------/
```

Figure 6-2a   TSO/ISPF Main Menu with COMPUWARE's File-AID Installed

```
/---------------- FILE-AID VL-6.2.0 - PRIMARY OPTION MENU -----------\
|SELECT OPTION ===>                                                  |
|                                                                    |
|        +---------------------------------------------------+       |
|        |                                                   |       |
|        |    0  -  FILE-AID DEFAULT OPTIONS                 |       |
|        |    1  -  FILE-AID BROWSE                          |       |
|        |    2  -  FILE-AID EDIT                            |       |
|        |                                                   |       |
|        |    3  -  FILE-AID UTILITIES                       |       |
|        |              3.1 - LIBRARY                        |       |
|        |              3.2 - DATASET                        |       |
|        |              3.3 - COPY                           |       |
|        |              3.4 - CATALOG                        |       |
|        |              3.5 - VSAM                           |       |
|        |              3.7 - VTOC                           |       |
|        |              3.8 - FORMAT                          |       |
|        |                                                   |       |
|        |    4  -  INTERACTIVE FILE-AID EXECUTION           |       |
|        |    5  -  BACKGROUND FILE-AID SUBMISSION           |       |
|        |    C  -  NEW FILE-AID RELEASE FEATURES            |       |
|        |                                                   |       |
|        +---------------------------------------------------+       |
|                                                                    |
|           USE END KEY TO END FILE-AID MODE                         |
|                                                                    |
\--------------------------------------------------------------------/
```

Figure 6-2b   Compuware FILE-AID Source Data Management Utility Menu

```
/----------------- FILE-AID VL-6.2.0 - DEFAULT PARAMETERS ------------\
| COMMAND ===>                                                        |
|                                                                     |
| FUNCTION DEFAULTS FOR: YOUR ID                                      |
|      INCLUDE RECORD INFORMATION  ===> N     (Y=YES, N=NO)           |
|      SEQ/VSAM PROCESS DIRECTION  ===> F     (F=FORWARD, B=BACKWARD) |
|      NUMBER OF RECORDS TO SEARCH ===> 0     (0 = ALL)               |
|      NUMBER OF RECORDS TO SELECT ===> 250   (0 = ALL)               |
|      NUMBER OF SELECTIONS        ===> 3     (3 - 999)               |
|                                                                     |
| SELECTION PARAMETER DEFAULTS:                                       |
|      LENGTH/OPERATOR ===> EQ   (EQ NE GT LT GE LE NO MX)            |
|      AND/OR          ===> AND  (AND OR)                             |
|                                                                     |
| INTERMEDIATE WORK FILE ALLOCATION DEFAULTS:                         |
|      ALLOCATION TYPE       ===> TRKS  (TRKS CYLS)                   |
|      PRIMARY ALLOCATION    ===> 10    (IN ABOVE UNITS)              |
|      SECONDARY ALLOCATION  ===> 5     (IN ABOVE UNITS)              |
|                                                                     |
| VSAM INTERMEDIATE NAME  ===> TSOID01                                |
|                                                                     |
\---------------------------------------------------------------------/
```

Figure 6-2c   Compuware FILE-AID Source Data Control Parameter Menu

```
/-------------------FILE-AID - SELECTIVE BROWSE/EDIT-----------------\
| SELECT OPTION ===>                                                 |
|                                                                    |
|  B - NON-SELECTIVE (USING OPTIONS BELOW)     F - NON-SELECTIVE /   |
|  M - SPECIFY MEMBER SELECTION                S - SELECTIVE / FORM  |
|  BLANK - SPECIFY RECORD SELECTION                                  |
|                                                                    |
| SPECIFY BROWSE DATASET:                                            |
|   DATASET NAME  ===>                                               |
|   VOLUME SERIAL ===>            (IF NOT CATALOGED)                 |
|   PASSWORD      ===>            (IF PASSWORD PROTECTED)            |
|                                                                    |
| SPECIFY RECORD LAYOUT DATASET:    (TO ALLOW RECORD MAPPING WITH F) |
|   DATASET NAME  ===>                                               |
|   MEMBER NAME   ===>            (BLANK FOR MEMBER SELECTION LIST)  |
|   VOLUME SERIAL ===>            (IF NOT CATALOGED)                 |
|   SELECTION     ===> N          (EXTRACT RECORD LAYOUT (Y OR N))   |
|                                                                    |
| ENTER/VERIFY PROCESSING OPTIONS BELOW:                             |
|   INCLUDE RECORD INFORMATION  ===> N     (Y=YES, N=NO)             |
|   SEQ/VSAM PROCESS DIRECTION  ===> F     (F=FORWARD, B=BACKWARD)   |
|   NUMBER OF RECORDS TO SELECT ===> 250   (0=ALL)                  |
|   STARTING RECORD KEY OR RBA  ===>                                |
|                                                                    |
|                                                                    |
\--------------------------------------------------------------------/
```

Figure 6-2d   Compuware FILE-AID Source Data Selective Browse Menu

```
/------------------------FILE-AID - FORMAT UTILITY------------------\
| SELECT OPTION ===>                                                |
|                                                                   |
|   C  -  COMPILE RECORD LAYOUT              B  -  BROWSE MAP        |
|   S  -  CREATE/MODIFY SELECTION TABLES     D  -  DELETE MAP        |
|   CVT - CONVERT OLD MAPS TO NEW FORMAT     P  -  PRINT MAP         |
|                                                                   |
| RECORD LAYOUT DATASET:                                            |
|   DATASET NAME    ===>                                            |
|   MEMBER NAME     ===>           (OR MEMBER MASK NAME)            |
|   VOLUME SERIAL   ===>           (IF NOT CATALOGED)               |
|   PASSWORD        ===>           (IF PASSWORD PROTECTED)          |
|   SOURCE OPTIONS ===> NO         Y = SPECIFY SOURCE COMPILE OPTION |
|                                                                   |
| MAP DATASET:                                                      |
|   DATASET NAME    ===> 'TSOD001.DEMO.MAPSLIB'                     |
|   MEMBER NAME     ===>                                            |
|   DESCRIPTION:    ===>                                            |
|   VOLUME SERIAL   ===>           (IF NOT CATALOGED)               |
|   REPLACE LIKE MEMBERS  ===> N     ( Y = YES, N = NO)            |
|                                                                   |
|                                                                   |
\------------------------------------------------------------------/
```

Figure 6-2e   Compuware FILE-AID Source Data Format Edit Layout Menu

```
/--- FILE-AID/XE - EXTENDED EDIT/SOURCE STATEMENT SELECTION PANEL ----\
| COMMAND ===>                                                        |
|                                                                     |
| "CURRENT" SOURCE DATASET: TSOD001.SEGTEST.COPYLIB(TWOREF)          |
|                                                                     |
|     PLEASE ENTER THE BEGINNING AND ENDING CHARACTER STRINGS OR      |
|     SOURCE STATEMENT LINE NUMBERS OR BLANK FOR ENTIRE MEMBER.       |
|                                                                     |
| RECORD LAYOUT SELECTION BY CHARACTER STRING:                        |
|     BEGINNING STRING    ===>                                        |
|     ENDING STRING       ===>                                        |
|                                                                     |
| RECORD LAYOUT SELECTION BY SOURCE STATEMENT NUMBER:                 |
|     BEGINNING NUMBER    ===> 1                                      |
|     ENDING NUMBER       ===> 7                                      |
|     NUMBER TYPE         ===> REL    (STANDARD, COBOL OR RELATIVE)   |
|                                                                     |
| COMPILER OPTIONS:                                                   |
|     LANGUAGE            ===> PL/1   (COBOL OR PL/1)                 |
|     STARTING LEVEL NBR  ===> 01                                     |
|     LITERAL DELINEATOR  ===> APOST  (QUOTE OR APOST; COBOL ONLY)    |
|                                                                     |
|                                                                     |
|                                                                     |
\--------------------------------------------------------------------/
```

Figure 6-2f   Compuware FILE-AID Source Data Format Edit Specs Menu

```
/--- FILE-AID MAP DISPLAY -------------------------------------------\
|                                                                    |
| COMMAND ===>                                                       |
|                                                                    |
| --------- FIELD LEVEL/NAME--FORMAT ----- FLD   START    END LENGTH |
| FILEAID                                          1     169    169  |
| 3 OCCURS-1                    99          1      1       2      2  |
| 3 OCCURS-2                    99          2      3       4      2  |
| 3 OCCURS-GROUP-1(1) OCCURS1 TO 15 TIMES  DEPENDING ON OCCURS-1     |
|                               GROUP       3      5      13      9  |
|   5 PIC-9(1)                  X(9)        4      5      13      9  |
| 3 OCCURS-GROUP-1(2)           GROUP       3     14      22      9  |
|   5 PIC-9(2)                  X(9)        4     14      22      9  |
| 3 OCCURS-GROUP-1(3)           GROUP       3     23      31      9  |
|   5 PIC-9(3)                  X(9)        4     23      31      9  |
| 3 OCCURS-GROUP-1(4)           GROUP       3     32      40      9  |
|   5 PIC-9(4)                  X(9)        4     32      40      9  |
| 3 OCCURS-GROUP-1(5)           GROUP       3     41      49      9  |
|   5 PIC-9(5)                  X(9)        4     41      49      9  |
| 3 OCCURS-GROUP-1(6)           GROUP       3     50      58      9  |
|   5 PIC-9(6)                  X(9)        4     50      58      9  |
|                                                                    |
\--------------------------------------------------------------------/
```

Figure 6-2g   Compuware FILE-AID Source Data Logical Field Map Display

```
/--- FILE-AID/XE - TEST.CLIENT.DATA ---------------------------------\
| COMMAND ===>                                                       |
|                                                                    |
| RECORD:     2                    CLIENT-MASTER                     |
|                                                                    |
| ---- FIELD LEVEL/NAME ------- COLUMNS- ----+----1----+----2----+----|
| ***************************** TOP OF DATA ***********************|
| 2 CL-DELETE-CODE               1     D                             |
| 2 CL-KEY                       2                                   |
|   3 CL-FULL-CLIENT             2                                   |
|     4 CL-CLIENT                4     1                             |
|     4 CL-SUB-CLIENT            6     AA                            |
|   3 FILLER                    10                                   |
| 2 CL-CLIENT-INFO              10                                   |
|   3 CL-NM                     10     BACH, JOHANN SEBASTIAN        |
|   3 CL-ADDR                   40     ADDRESS LINE TWO 01           |
|   3 CL-CITY                   70     PARK RIDGE                    |
|   3 CL-ST                     85     IL                           |
|   3 CL-ZIP                    87     60068                        |
|   3 CL-CONTACT                92     000001980080010110500101231  |
|   3 CL-PURGE-M               122     0                            |
|   3 CL-PURGE-D               124     0                            |
|   3 CL-PURGE-V               126     0                            |
|                                                                    |
\--------------------------------------------------------------------/
```

Figure 6-2h   Compuware FILE-AID Source Data Format Map Edit Display

```
/--- FILE-AID/XE - TEST.FILE ------------------------------------------\
|                                                                      |
| COMMAND ===>                                                         |
| RECORD:    2                         MASTER-RCD                      |
| ---- FIELD LEVEL/NAME ------- -FORMAT- ----+----1----+----2          |
| 3 OCCURS-OBJECT-ONE            2/NUM  2                              |
| 3 OCCURS-OBJECT-TWO            2/NUM  2                              |
| 3 OCCURS-OBJECT-THREE          2/NUM  2                              |
| 3 GROUP-ITEM-1                 6/GRP                                 |
|   5 PIC-V9-DISPLAY             1/NUM  0.1                            |
|   5 PIC-X3-DISPLAY             3/AN   ABC                            |
|   5 PIC-99-COMP                2/BI   3                              |
| 3 GROUP-ITEM-2(1) OCCURS 2 TIMES                                     |
|   5 PIC-S999999-COMP(1)        6/NUMS 1                              |
|   5 PIC-S9V9-COMP(1)           2/NUMS 2.0                            |
|  3 GROUP-ITEM-2(2)             8/GRP                                 |
|   5 PIC-S999999-COMP(2)        6/NUMS 1234                           |
|   5 PIC-S9V9-COMP(2)           2/NUMS 5.5                            |
| 3 PIC-SPLIT-COMP              17/GRP                                 |
|   5 PIC-COMP-1                 4/SPFP 1.9300E+02                     |
|   5 PIC-COMP-2                 8/DPFP 1.00000000000000E+01           |
\----------------------------------------------------------------------/
```

Figure 6-2i   Compuware FILE-AID Source Data Format Logical Map Edit

```
/--- FILE-AID/XE - TEST.INPUT.PHYSICAL.INPUT.FILE--------------------\
|                                                                    |
| COMMAND ===>                                                       |
| ****** **************************** TOP OF DATA ******************|
| =PROF> ....CAPS OFF....HEX OFF....AUTOSAVE ON....STATS OFF.........|
| =PROF> ....BOUNDS 1 4993....PAD X'00'..............................|
| =INFO> ....DSORG PS...RECFM VB...LRECL 4992...RKP 0...KEYLN 0......|
| =INFO> ....ERRORS 0...SEQ ERRORS 0...DUP KEYS 0...CHANGES 0........|
| 000002  01AA     BACH, JOHANN SEBASTIAN      ADDRESS LINE TWO 01  |
| 000003  02BB     BEETHOVEN, LUDWIG VAN       ADDRESS LINE TWO 02  |
| 000004  03CC     BRAHMS, JOHANNES            ADDRESS LINE TWO 03  |
| 000005  04DD     CHOPIN, FREDERIC            ADDRESS LINE TWO 04  |
| 000006  05EE     DEBUSSY, CLAUDE             ADDRESS LINE TWO 05  |
| 000007  06FF     DVORAK, ANTONIN             ADDRESS LINE TWO 06  |
| 000008  07GG     ELGAR, EDWARD               ADDRESS LINE TWO 07  |
| 000009  08HH     GERSHWIN, GEORGE            ADDRESS LINE TWO 08  |
| 000010  09II     HANDEL, GEORGE FRIDERIC     ADDRESS LINE TWO 09  |
| 000011  10JJ     HAYDN, (FRANZ) JOSEPH       ADDRESS LINE TWO 10  |
| 000012  11KK     HOLST, GUSTAV               ADDRESS LINE TWO 11  |
| 000013  12LL     LISZT, FRANZ                ADDRESS LINE TWO 12  |
| 000014  13MM     MAHLER, GUSTAV              ADDRESS LINE TWO 13  |
|                                                                    |
|                                                                    |
\--------------------------------------------------------------------/
```

Figure 6-2j   Compuware FILE-AID Source Data Format Physical Map Edit

7

SIZING UP YOUR SOFTWARE AGAINST THE COMPETITION

Although most organizations are reluctant to release their software quality measurements, there are several published research studies which survey data processing organizations on an anonymous basis. These studies are often segmented by categories such as the size of the computer center operations, the size of the application system or software development project, and the industrial business sector. Such studies provide answers to traditional questions asked by data center management:

- "How are we doing compared to the competition?"
- "What can we do to surpass the competition?"

There is no single standard for comparative quality analysis of software (other than "total sales," which might answer the first question, but cannot directly answer the second). Thus, it is important to maintain historical software performance data, including such measures as function points, logical statement counts per program, program fails per unit time, time between program defects, and resource usage measures.

Computer system logs provide machine-readable, easily automated sources of such historical data in a form that is statistically reliable and provides consistent units of measure. This chapter will discuss some of the strategies and standards involved in automating a software quality and system operational performance history database. The focus will be on industrial engineering methods which can improve the process of developing software products and the quality of software support services. Also, market research methods for comparing product and service quality to national leaders in data processing are discussed in terms of using system logs as benchmark data sources.

SOFTWARE INDUSTRY DATABASES AND COMPARATIVE INFORMATION SOURCES

The first step in determining how internal software products and services compare to their competitors is to define an internal procedure for the routine collection and analysis of software industry data. This should include the automated processes developed to support data entry and maintenance of comparative software quality measurements data, as well as the standards, guidelines, reporting formats, and business units that will be routinely compared.

The second step, which is traditionally much more difficult, is the identification of suitable sources of comparative data. These sources can range from inquiries against textual information data bank services to specialized databases that provide baseline average data. Both can be used to benchmark internal software product and service quality against external operations.

Once the sources of comparative data have been identified, and a routine procedure implemented supporting the accumulation of this data into a benchmarking database, it is possible to use SMF to automatically compare operations against external data centers. This automated analysis can take the form of the yearly—or even quarterly—comparison of financial ratios, operational process unit costs, customer satisfaction indicator levels, and critical processes which exceed the range of acceptable performance quality or cost objectives.

Because of the proprietary nature of cost and quality data, it is normally quite difficult to obtain precise and comparative data about another data center or business organization. If the nature of the supporting business organization is directly competitive with a company or companies in the same industrial sector, it may be possible to obtain specific business indicators through an internal business marketing research department. Key financial ratios can also be determined from annual stockholder reports or public financial database services. Examples of such services are NEXIS annual stockholder report and business databases managed by Mead Corporation and Dow Jones retrieval database of key corporate financial information.

This financial data can be weighted against data center operational statistics obtainable from database services specializing in information system technology and the data processing industry. These services include the Gartner Group online subscription services and Auerbach/DataPro reports. It is often possible to obtain key financial and operational data from published annual rankings and comparative key rating issues. These reports are often found in major information industry publications, such as *Computerworld* or *Info Week*.

An often overlooked source of up-to-date operational statistics—including size and number of staff, hardware and software used—can be obtained on a confidential basis from the subscription qualification department of industry trade magazines.

One of the most important sources of operational statistics and related information includes various types of online information services and databases. The DIALOG online bibliography and database service, developed by Lockheed Corporation, provides several hundred categories of technical publications and data. This data can be downloaded into local workstation data stores or spreadsheet reporting applications. Such services are also offered by Boeing Corporation. Boeing has accumulated Department of Defense (DoD) prime contractor and aerospace industry statistics used for various methods of "COmponent COst MOdeling" (COCOMO) software development project cost and scheduling.

A similar commercial operation, BRS/Search Service, is supported by the Maxwell Information Services subsidiary of the British-based worldwide communications organization. A related product,

BRS/After Dark, was developed with the cooperation of several American aerospace engineering research companies. It is used by many major industrial, political, and military intelligence-gathering organizations because it has the capability to make keyword-based searches of existing databases and request transmission of any new publication or online database information within twenty-four hours after it is published.

There are a multitude of local PC bulletin boards, as well as many nationwide online networks such as Prodigy or Compuserve, that can be a source of benchmark data-sharing contacts. In many cases, it is possible to solicit interest to exchange benchmark data, especially between organizations not in direct competition or who share a common basis for a strategic business alliance.

Another important source of statistics is the *Computer Industry Almanac*, which is updated and published each year by Brady Books (Simon & Schuster). This almanac summarizes industry information from dozens of trade publications and identifies sources which can provide more detailed data.

If the supported organization is a member of a government or trade industry sponsored data-sharing association, the best source of comparative data will probably be in the form of data processing industry baseline average data. Since critical statistics may be available in a form that is directly comparable, there is no need to calibrate or convert the data into in-house business units.

The most common arrangement for such data sharing includes payment of a preliminary subscription fee for the service. This fee can range from a nominal $100 corporate membership in a trade association to over $30,000 or more per year, depending on the level of detail and methods of certifying precision (or confidentiality) of the statistics.

Such data-sharing services also normally require that the subscriber answer a survey or provide a summary system log statistics tape or disk which can be added to the sponsoring organization's database. Examples of organizations that often support such data-sharing arrangements are: the Quality Assurance Institute of Orlando, Florida; Software Quality Engineering of Jacksonville, Florida; and the American Society for Quality Control of Milwaukee, Wisconsin. There are also several organizations for military and government prime contractors, including: DoD's DARPA, DAC, and the Rome Air Development Center (RADC), as well as the Software Engineering Institute of Pittsburgh, Pennsylvania. These often include specific operational statistics that are public and accessible as required by government regulations.

For the most part, however, software quality and system performance data-sharing arrangements are usually available only as baseline averages segmented by the industrial business sector, or as "anonymous" business units—which may be profiled by size, staff, or major source of business revenues, yet not directly identified by name. Such data-sharing arrangements normally will guarantee confidentiality in order to encourage accurate reporting of business statistics. However, it is worth pointing out that there is no guaranteeing the accuracy of the data submitted. There is even the possibility organizations may submit distorted data in order to avoid being easily identified.

There have been regulatory recommendations before the U.S. Department of Commerce for several decades which would require information industry reporting similar to the level of production data that is required for forecasts by the U.S. Department of Agriculture. There has been severe resistance to such reporting requirements by private corporations because of the potential impact on proprietary business processes. Until, and if, the U.S. Department of Commerce ever begins requiring the accurate regulatory reporting of such data, the best source of baselines will be data processing trade databases and related information services.

VENDOR SOFTWARE PERFORMANCE BENCHMARKS
AND CALIBRATION METHODS

Most hardware vendors provide software performance baseline and benchmarking tools as part of their standard maintenance licensing agreement. It is always in the best interest of the hardware vendor to make every reasonable effort to help data center customers optimize their operational environment. There is some belief among the data center industry that hardware vendors would prefer software environments to be so inefficient that they will sell more hardware, the fact is that there is enough competition that vendors know they will sell the most hardware to data centers whose customers are pleased with the quality of software and data processing services they currently receive.

It is also necessary for the vendor to provide benchmarking methods and system log measurement tools which assure precision comparison of the same and similar architectures and operating systems across data centers and product environments. This includes programs and program algorithms which are used to compare the relative efficiency of alternative software configurations or methods of application software service support. These benchmark tools must provide precise quantitative weights and ratios which can be applied to data according to a variety of environmental specifications. This is done to adjust or calibrate the data from similar and dissimilar system environments or data centers in a manner that results in fully comparable data.

IBM provides standard benchmarks and formulas for each of its hardware devices and support products in the form of several alternative units of measure. One of the most common is *Million Instructions Per Second* (MIPS). MIPS is also comparable across vendors, since every system architecture must process machine instructions. However, this rating is not always reliable, because of discrete differences in the size and complexity of equivalent machine instructions supported by different vendors, as well as system architectures supported by a large hardware vendor such as IBM.

A more common benchmark standard is the IBM 370 series CPU equivalent, which rates all advanced IBM mainframe CPU processors as unit multiples greater than the original IBM 370 machines. This benchmark standard is slowly being replaced by a new IBM machine instruction speed rating which is comparable across SAA universal platform architectures. However, IBM may not completely replace 370 ratings.

Some services are already beginning to compare host mainframe CPU ratings to 8086 microprocessor or Norton PC benchmarks. Additionally, as desktop mainframes become more prevalent and 486 or RISC architecture machines are used more commonly in local networks, many new benchmarks that compare hosts to PCs may be introduced.

Regardless of the nature of the hardware system and software benchmarks available, several alternative values should be calculated as a basis for converting and calibrating data. This assures the best comparability between data sources originating from different data centers, as well as system log data from CPU processors with different ratings in any multiprocessor environment. These benchmark ratings are required by some SMF control tables and must normally be defined to a control table for any of the automated measurement products that read and accumulate SMF system log audit trail data.

Another kind of benchmark, involving relative productivity and software support service labor conversion data, may also need to be defined for any product estimating software development factors. Such benchmarks are used in calibrating function point or statement estimates of software size to compare the quality and reliability of data centers.

PRODUCTIVITY INDEXES AND SOFTWARE INDUSTRY QUALITY BASELINES

The development of comparitive programmer productivity and software quality indexes has mostly been pioneered by IBM. Surprisingly, few have exploited IBM system logs.

Although IBM pioneered the development of function points, the first development in the measurement of software support service productivity was made by the U.S. Army more than a decade earlier. The original productivity studies were based upon *Source-statement Lines of Code* (SLOC), then validated using function points. Many such studies used IBM system log data.

One such leader in Army productivity research was Lawrence Putnam, who founded Quantitative Software Management, Inc. in 1978, and is still a leader in the area. Putnam originated the analogy of the software development process to a *Life Cycle*. He defined the first mathematical models of a system development project at about the same time the Raleigh curve was defined as the fundamental pattern for isolating software defects based on system log data.

The primary contribution of Putnam has involved the definition of two fundamental software measurement indexes:

- PI—the Productivity Index
- MBI—the Manpower Buildup Index

These two indexes have been a major influence upon the COCOMO cost models developed by Barry Boehm while he was with Boeing Corporation and later as part of Defense Advanced Research Projects Agency (DARPA).

The QSM organization offers consulting services, software estimating tools, comparative software quality, and productivity database access. The QSM productivity database is arguably the largest comparative software metrics database in existence. It is based on analysis of over 3,500 software development projects which have been meticulously measured using the same methods and instruments according to a wide variety of software development, process quality, schedule, size, and complexity factors.

The QSM productivity database can be accessed by online inquiry via dial-up. Data centers can also purchase subsets of the extensive QSM database in the form of average software quality and productivity measures for organizations and projects that are comparable in size, complexity, or application software type to the customer data center. This data can then be automatically compared to routine summary data accumulated in SMF system log performance history databases. This is done to determine how an in-house data center operation rates as compared to the baseline productivity averages for the most current comparable projects surveyed by QSM.

The only problem with the QSM data is that it is geared very heavily toward military and DoD prime contractor system development. Additionally, all of the index data must be rated against comparable military software applications, even if the project surveyed is from a nonmilitary business operation. This has not limited the usefulness of a QSM project database as a comparative, noncompetitive benchmark standard.

Precise coefficients of the difference between military and nonmilitary application software productivity have been determined within a normal range. In spite of all the progress made with the Ada object language and quality initiatives by DARPA and DAC, military software development is normally between 10 percent to 50 percent less than nonmilitary software development of the same application type, size, and complexity.

This difference can be used to easily calibrate QSM data from military to nonmilitary projects. The current number of nonmilitary projects surveyed by QSM has been increasing rapidly since the number of U.S. government–sponsored military projects began to drop off in the late 1980s and early 1990s.

The QSM database may become less oriented toward military projects in the future, especially since several of the large corporations associated with QSM, such as GTE, EDS, General Motors, General Electric, and Boeing, have all become less involved in government projects as prime contractors and more involved in private sector commercial projects. Such projects are not burdened by complex specifications and record keeping, as required by DoD MIL-stds and other complicated government contract paperwork.

There have been unprecedented opportunities to reevaluate and establish new internal standards. Many large corporations are using automated measurement products and system log-based performance history data to determine which of the military-compliant standards can comfortably be dropped to reduce costs without suffering a significant reduction in software quality. Presumably, some of this data will become available on QSM databases in the future. It is also likely that many of the methods and procedures used by military and government contractors may become commonly used to enforce quality as these personnel rejoin the civilian workforce.

Examples of Putnam productivity index and manpower buildup index plots typical of extracts from the QSM database are shown in Figures 7-1, 7-2, 7-3, and 7-4. More information on QSM is in Appendix B.

BUSINESS PROCESS BENCHMARKS AND BUSINESS UNIT COMPARISONS

The undisputable leader in business process benchmarks is the Xerox Corporation. The process of benchmarking against the leaders in the industry, as well as against direct competitors, has been a major part of the corporate culture at Xerox from its earliest days.

Part of the reason for this leadership has to do with the diverse technology developed and marketed by Xerox and the large number of other companies that Xerox has been directly competitive with. Clearly, Xerox raised benchmarking to a new art primarily because it had to in order to survive. However, it is also important to note that Xerox has a close association with Battelle Labs, an organization that fosters and invests in new technology. This requires a precise determination of competitive market potential and continuous improvement of production processes in order to successfully bring new technology to the marketplace and preserve dominant market share.

The Xerox approach is aggressive and almost military in its orientation toward intensive tactical and strategic analysis of direct competitors and noncompetitive industry leaders. This analysis includes financial, operational, quality units of measure, and information about external and internal process and product cost.

The Xerox approach involves a heavy reliance upon industrial engineering and operation research techniques to define each production process and operational unit cost, the quality control methods used to isolate defects, and researching industry's best practices. They prototype internal proprietary solutions, which are statistically analyzed and compared in order to determine the most effective fix. One of the most important innovations by Xerox has involved the automatic scanning of online information services

```
PUTNAM MANPOWER BUILDUP INDEX OF LEVELS OF INCREMENTAL
INCREASE IN RAMP RATE FOR SOFTWARE PROJECT DEPLOYMENTS


Deployment Increment      Rate of Delivery      Project Cost       Quality Risks


MBI LEVEL ONE      ===>    Very Slow        /    Very Low        /  Fairly Few Fails

MBI LEVEL TWO      ===>    Moderately Slow  /    Moderately Low  /  Fairly Few Errors

MBI LEVEL THREE    ===>    Moderate         /    Moderate        /  Few Errors

MBI LEVEL FOUR     ===>    Rapid            /    High            /  Higher Error Rates

MBI LEVEL FIVE     ===>    Very Rapid       /    Very High       /  Risk of High Fail Rate

MBI LEVEL SIX      ===>    Extremely Rapid  /    Extremely High  /  Very High Risk of Fails
```

Figure 7-1   Comparison of Putnam's MBI Levels of Manpower Buildup Index Ramp-Up Impact on Software Quality and Costs

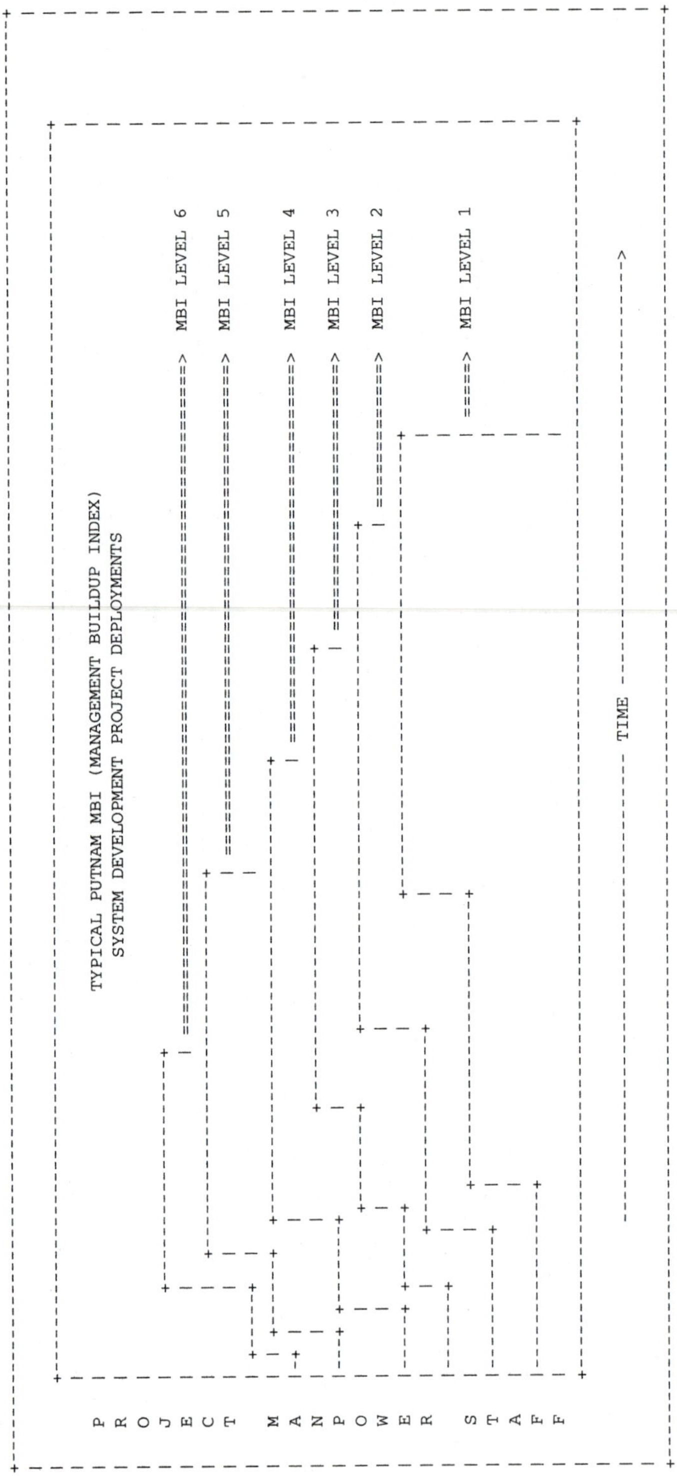

Figure 7-2 Example of Characteristic Putnam MBI (Manpower Buildup Index) Ramp-Up by Deployment Level

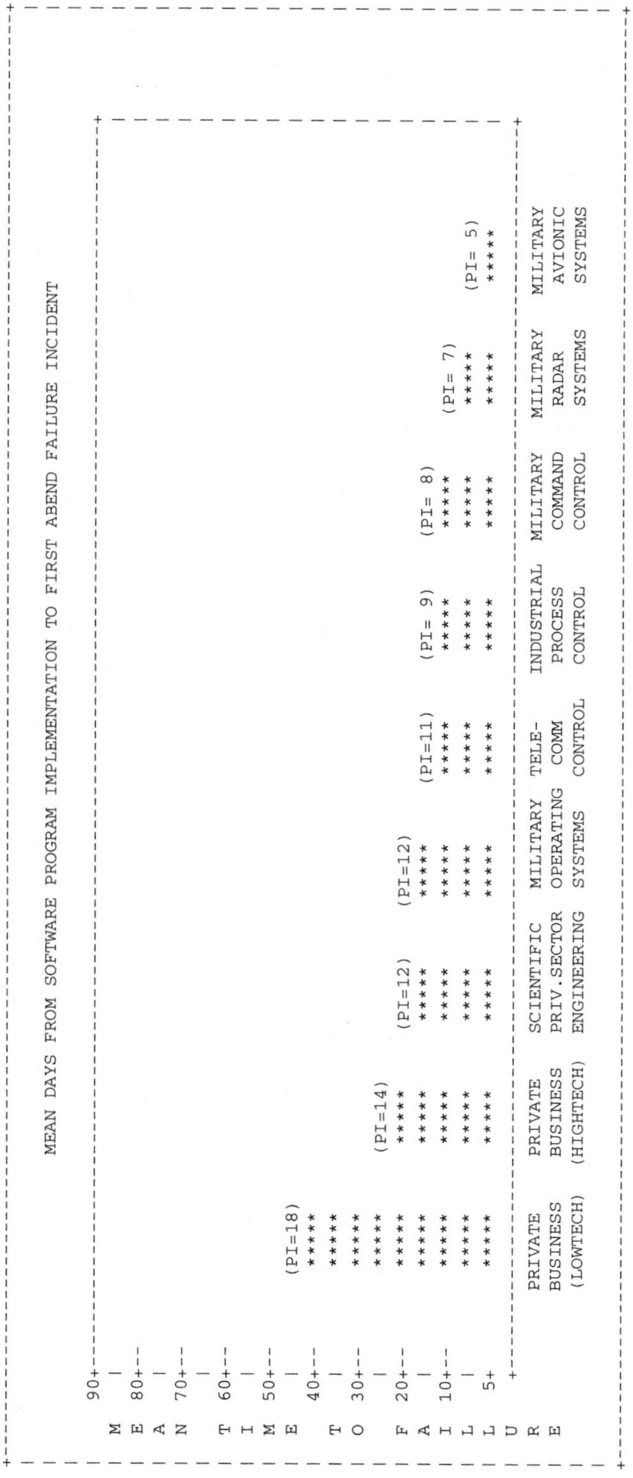

```
              MEAN DAYS FROM SOFTWARE PROGRAM IMPLEMENTATION TO FIRST ABEND FAILURE INCIDENT

M
E
A
N    90+--|
     80+--|
     70+--|
T    60+--|
I    50+--|
M        |(PI=18)
E    40+--| *****
         | ******
T    30+--| ******
O        | ******
     20+--| *****                                                          (PI=14)
F        | ******          (PI=12) (PI=12)
A    10+--| ******  (PI=14) *****   *****  (PI=11) (PI= 9) (PI= 8)
I        | ******  *****    *****   *****   *****   *****   *****   (PI= 7)
L     5+-| ******  *****    *****   *****   *****   *****   *****   *****   (PI= 5)
L        | ******  *****    *****   *****   *****   *****   *****   *****   *****
U     +
R       PRIVATE    PRIVATE  SCIENTIFIC MILITARY MILITARY INDUSTRIAL MILITARY MILITARY MILITARY
E       BUSINESS   BUSINESS PRIV.SECTOR OPERATING TELE-    PROCESS   COMMAND   RADAR    AVIONIC
        (LOWTECH)  (HIGHTECH) ENGINEERING SYSTEMS  COMM     CONTROL   CONTROL  SYSTEMS  SYSTEMS
                                                   CONTROL
```

Figure 7-3   Average of Projects in Putnam PI (Productivity Index) Database and Mean Time to Failure by Application Type

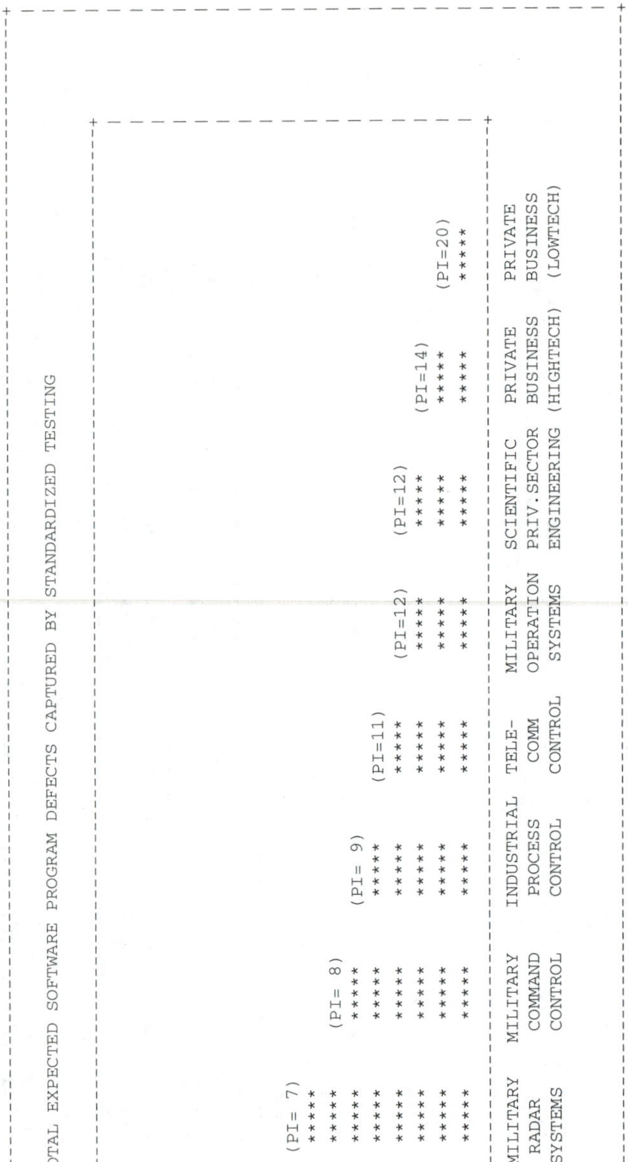

TOTAL EXPECTED SOFTWARE PROGRAM DEFECTS CAPTURED BY STANDARDIZED TESTING

```
         9K+--
F        8K+--
A            |    (PI= 5)
I        7K+--     *****
L            |     ******
U        6K+--     ******
R            |     ******
E        5K+--     ******            (PI= 7)
S            |     ******            *****
         4K+--     ******            *****
I            |     ******            *****          (PI= 8)
S        3K+--     ******            *****          *****
O            |     ******            *****          *****       (PI= 9)
L        2K+--     ******            *****          *****       *****       (PI=11)
A            |     ******            *****          *****       *****       *****       (PI=12)     (PI=12)
T        1K+--     ******            *****          *****       *****       *****       *****       *****       (PI=14)
E            |     ******            *****          *****       *****       *****       *****       *****       *****       (PI=20)
D         0+--     ******            *****          *****       *****       *****       *****       *****       *****       *****
               MILITARY      MILITARY    MILITARY    INDUSTRIAL   TELE-      MILITARY    SCIENTIFIC    PRIVATE      PRIVATE
               AVIONICS      RADAR       COMMAND     PROCESS      COMM       OPERATION   PRIV.SECTOR   BUSINESS     BUSINESS
               SYSTEMS       SYSTEMS     CONTROL     CONTROL      CONTROL    SYSTEMS     ENGINEERING   (HIGHTECH)   (LOWTECH)
```

Figure 7-4   Average of Projects in Putnam PI (Productivity Index) Database and Testing Captured Fails by Application Type

and publications in a manner that supports automated update and management of such competitive marketing data to automate benchmark analysis.

The benchmarking process begins with internal determination of operational process costs and functional business units of measure. Once defined, both of these processes can be fully automated for the data center processing environment based upon SMF or other system logs.

The determination of operational process costs can be directly based upon data center transfer pricing or chargeback billing cost allocation matrix. In other words, each of the major system resources that are measured and charged back to data center customers, can be itemized and used to profile average cost-per-resource type within a given time period. This is done along with the average defect and reliability data for the same time period for each of the operational business units, data center customer groups, or application system areas that are routinely supported.

All of this data, except financial ratios, can be automatically extracted from SMF product–based applications. Even the financial ratios can be automatically accessed and updated from organizational financial analysis or revenue accounting databases.

Determination of functional business units of measure begins with an analysis of all the processes involved in the daily operations of the data center and the business organization that it supports. Each unique process is then defined in operational terms specifying the business operative or deliverable goal that best characterizes the successful completion of a single iteration of a business function process.

For example, the business function of an airline gate agent is to board passengers onto the plane within a given time period prior to departure. Among the functional business units measure would be such items as "passengers boarded per open departure gate hour," "percent of ticketed passengers issued a boarding pass," or "number of passengers sold tickets at the gate," all of which indicate some portion of the business process that is normally performed by the gate agent function. Another example would be business units measuring the completion of an insurance claim processor function, including such items as "number of claims filed per day," "percent of claims approved in initial review," or "number of claims passed to utilization review," all of which involve part of the claims processor function.

Every form of business will normally collect and store functional business process measurements such as this. These measurements are used to estimate manpower requirements, redeployed headcount, and improved efficiency of business operations. By combining these measurements with the automated operational process unit costs calculated from resources in the system log data, it is possible to determine the unit cost as a metric that is useful for analyzing the direct cost benefit of the data center support function to the operations of the business.

For example, the "passengers boarded per hour" statistic can be combined with the equivalent time period cost to process the application software products that support the gate agent. The resulting business unit cost can then be segmented and monitored as part of the overall cost of business functions related to the average cost of boarding each passenger.

The segmented business unit cost can also be monitored over time and compared to alternatives for delivering the same function in a manner that can reduce costs and improve quality. Changes in the unit cost can determine whether the individual gate agent station, or all gate agent stations, have become more or less productive. It can determine the effect that discrete operational, procedural, or functional software changes make in the productivity of the customer business area that is being supported. The same method can be used to determine business units for quality service levels, in which a functional business process measurement is divided by a quality indicator. Indicators include failures, downtime, on-time deliveries, and process throughput, rather than a unit cost.

It is sometimes necessary to segment the operational unit costs from the system log data, or to consolidate resource usage line items, to achieve a functional business unit measure that is understandable and useful to the data center customer being served. For example, the claims processor function may involve order entry of several specific online forms, which are essential to the proprietary business operation or are a governmental regulatory requirement.

The SMF system log data can be used in order to automatically segment the unit cost. This is done by providing a count and associated cost of an online transaction in which to enter the form data, the number of forms printed, and the unit cost to print a particular form number. This information can become particularly important in a service bureau or carrier arrangement in which it is necessary to track a benchmark objective. Or, perhaps it is a contractual obligation to provide functional business services or products at a particular unit cost level or per unit functional business transaction rate. The same approach can be used to track service level agreements which are operationally defined as business units. Examples include that no more than a specified number of defects or periods of downtime will occur subject to a penalty or rebate against a base billing rate.

Obviously, these are serious business management practices that should not be attempted until there is suitable historical performance data to make accurate quality and productivity predictions. The rigors associated with running a data center like a manufacturing operation or an airline have been the exception rather than the rule in the past. This was the case since most data centers were cost centers and not subject to the same direct cost analysis methods used by revenue-related, functional business operations. However, as more business operations seek to convert their data centers into service bureaus or profit centers, and because more businesses are demanding better quality and efficiency from their internal data centers, it is clear that more rigorous internal process benchmarking will become prevalent in the future. Due to the relative ease and efficiency of their implementation, as well as low functional data processing internal functional process costs, the automated quality measurement products and system log-based applications will also surely become more prevalent over time.

Examples of some typical reports which will familiarize you with functional business unit costs and service levels are shown in Figure 7-5.

PROCESS BENCHMARK INDEX FOR COMPARISON TO EXTERNAL BUSINESS UNITS

Many of the automated benchmarking techniques originally pioneered by Xerox have been adapted and further automated by American Airlines using automated software quality measurement tools and analysis methods. The American Airlines approach is also oriented toward advanced operations research and industrial engineering methods, especially since these techniques are used in the yield management process optimizing aircraft maintenance and flight schedules, as well as conserving jet fuel, labor, and other operational resources.

The SABRE Computer Services subsidiary of American Airlines has adapted many of these techniques for the optimization of the largest, nonmilitary computer reservation system network in the world. Application of techniques that improve the quality and efficiency of airline transportation service via the operation of a large-scale computer data center network has been a major innovation of SABRE. American Airlines has established an automated link between the operational quality and performance monitoring of its systems using operating system log. In this way, it becomes possible for SABRE personnel to have real-time access to information about the current operational quality, efficiency, and unit costs of their SABRE network data centers. Also provided are comparative industry "best practice" and direct competitors' benchmark information and data.

XYZ CORPORATION BENCHMARK ACHIEVEMENT PLAN

UNIT COST	1990	1991	1992	BENCHMARK OBJECTIVE	BENCHMARK ACHIEVEMENT
APPLICATION-A					
$/INVOICE	$2.20	EXCEEDED	EXCEEDED	$2.00	DONE
$/STATEMENT	$4.40	$3.20	$2.90	$2.00	1993
$/COLLECTION	$16.60	$12.90	$11.40	$10.00	1994
APPLICATION-B					
$/PAYCHECK	$2.20	$2.10	EXCEEDED	$2.00	DONE
$/TAX CALC	$1.10	$2.30	$2.10	$2.00	1995
CUSTOMER SATISFACTION					
APPLICATION-A					
ZERO DEFECTS	95%	98%	99%	100%	1994
APPLICATION-B					
1ST-DAY-OF-MO	99%	99%	EXCEEDED	99.5%	DONE
INVENTORY TURNOVER					
APPLICATION-A					
PGM REUSE RATIO	1:2.3	1:1.9	1:1.2	1:1	1994
APPLICATION-B					
CHGS PER KLOC	122	105	EXCEEDED	50	DONE

Figure 7-5   Benchmarking Comparison of Year-over-Year Achievement in Data Center Process Quality Variables

First of all, it is necessary to identify the major competitors and noncompetitors that are most desirable to routinely track and benchmark against. If the number of benchmark partners is kept to a relatively small number, it is easy to enter the key financial ratios and operational statistics from public information sources into a workstation spreadsheet. This can occur at least once every year; if more frequent comparisons are desirable, it becomes increasingly feasible to automate a routine online information service inquiry that can be downloaded to an application on a LAN workstation overnight.

Once the download from the information service is combined with the software quality measurements from the performance history database, it is relatively simple to automatically route appropriate levels of exception or routine summary update reports to the relevant area of management or customer services administration. It is also possible to automatically analyze the data and search for critical patterns that have been defined using process rules in an expert system or neural network application.

Despite the existence of some established industry indexes, it is often desirable to create an internal indexing method that can be used to quickly scan comparative benchmark data. A number of alternative methods can be used, including a standardized score with 100 as the average (like an IQ score) or an arbitrary scaled index against a unit or service level achieved at a particular historical date (like a Dow Jones stock index). Any arbitrary standardized score can be used against a scaled maximum and minimum value (such as an SAT test score). However, if it is desirable to make the benchmark easily understood, or, if the potential audience is not always known, a simple percent period-over-period unit variance will probably suffice in most cases.

Examples of some typical automated benchmarking report formats which show external as well as internal software quality and unit cost performance are shown in Figure 7-6.

FORECASTING FUTURE INTERNAL AND EXTERNAL SOFTWARE QUALITY COSTS

Once the most critical business units and their associated operational costs have been determined, and automated methods implemented, it is possible to begin to forecast trends in software quality or cost performance improvements (or decrements) using charting methods. Charting methods are commonly used in financial analysis and in industrial engineering. The two most important types of benchmarking charts are the key financial ratios and performance gap charting methods.

The financial ratios charts always compare some macro-level accounting unit—such as total revenues—to a component accounting unit—such as a segmented component cost. For example, the total revenue of the business organization, or the estimated revenue share contributed by a department or divisional business unit, are normally used as a macro-level unit. The operating expenses of the data center, or costs of developing and maintaining an application software package, are usually the most common segmented component that is compared as a ratio of the total revenue variables. Other common financial ratios relate to the return on investment, or the ratio of the proportion of the overall application system environment that is turned over, by replacing, or developing, new application systems. These ratios are normally expressed as a component percentage of macro-level business operations or data center segmented financial expenditure and operational spending performance category breakouts.

There is a need to develop general estimates of comparable key financial ratios about direct competitors and industry leaders. This is achieved either from industry magazines' annual statistical issues, industry trade almanacs, or a private consulting firm. These ratios are then compared to internal operations and specific software packages.

PROCESS UNIT COST COMPARISON

| | EXTERNAL BENCHMARK DATA CENTERS | | | | INTERNAL |
| | CORPORATION | | | SERVICE BUREAUS | Process Costs |
	A	B	C		
INVOICE PREPARATION PROCESSING	$2	$4	$3	$ 3	$ 2
ACCOUNT STATEMENT PROCESSING	$2	$4	$6	$ 3	$ 3
COLLECTION ACTION PROCESSING	$2	$4	$9	$ 3	$ 4
TOTAL PROCESS PER ACCOUNT	$2.43	$6.34	$9.45	$ 6.72	$ 6.78

Figure 7-6   Benchmarking Comparison of Internal versus External Data Center Productive Process Unit Costs

The next step is to use industrial engineering techniques to develop performance gap trending charts, which give an indication of how the internal data center operations compare to the competition. This is done by plotting one of the functional business unit cost estimates, or a key financial ratio, against a time dimension. Trendlines should be extrapolated to characterize an internal projection, as well as a projection of an industry standard derived from the industry almanac or a specific competitor or industry leader that has been measured by a software productivity analyst.

If there is a cross-over in trendlines, it is possible to estimate when internal productivity or quality will become (or has become) better or worse than the industry average or a particular competitor of interest. This cross-over can be used to estimate the parity achieved, or the benchmark performance gap, that is most likely to occur at a particular point in the future if things remain static.

Another kind of benchmark performance gap chart, known as the *Z-chart*, shows the *quantum* changes that are expected or have occurred in a comparative trendline. The Z-chart looks like a single-line version of a benchmark performance gap cross-over chart. It splits to two levels at a point where an expected or known innovation in technology or productivity levels creates a new trendline. This trendline can be expected to be the dominant benchmark level in the future. Z-charts are thus one of the most important methods of identifying and communicating to financial management the need for changes in technology and operating procedures. This involves particular lead times in order to stage the new technology or organizational changes in a way that provides for their most effective implementation.

Examples of benchmark performance gap cross-over charts and Z-charts are shown in Figure 7-7. These charts can be automatically generated out of financial and system log performance databases using SAS/GRAPH software and the SAS/QC application product which will be covered in the next chapter.

PARETO RANKING METHOD FOR COMPARING
PREDOMINANT PROCESS INFLUENCE

It often becomes desirable to analyze an existing process in order to determine predominant factors—that is, the classes and categories of products or problems. This is done to develop new methods or control procedures which improve the quality or productivity of an operational process. This becomes particularly important if a benchmark performance chart shows a growing gap between internal data center operations and an industry standard or competitor.

One way to simplify this analysis is to use *Pareto* diagrams or ranking methods which *break out* a process into component steps or product characteristics and then measure them according to a critical functional business unit. The measurements are then sorted and compared as component percentages of the whole. The results are normally plotted as contiguous vertical bar charts, in rank order from the left, and overlaid with a line graph indicating the cumulative percentage of the whole associated with each consecutive rank order item.

The Pareto chart will show if there is a small number of common problems, product characteristics, or procedures, or if the divisions are evenly distributed across all the possibilities. The 80/20 rule provides a general indicator for the analysis of Pareto charts. If 80 percent of the total measurement units are concentrated in 20 percent or less of the items that are measured, then a *selective* intervention is required to make an improvement in quality or productivity. This involves either a change in the quality of the input materials or level of service skills or a specific automated control or standard operating procedure that eliminates an undesirable service problem or product characteristic. However, if there is not an 80/20 loading on the predominant high-order Pareto rank items, and the measurements are more or less equal

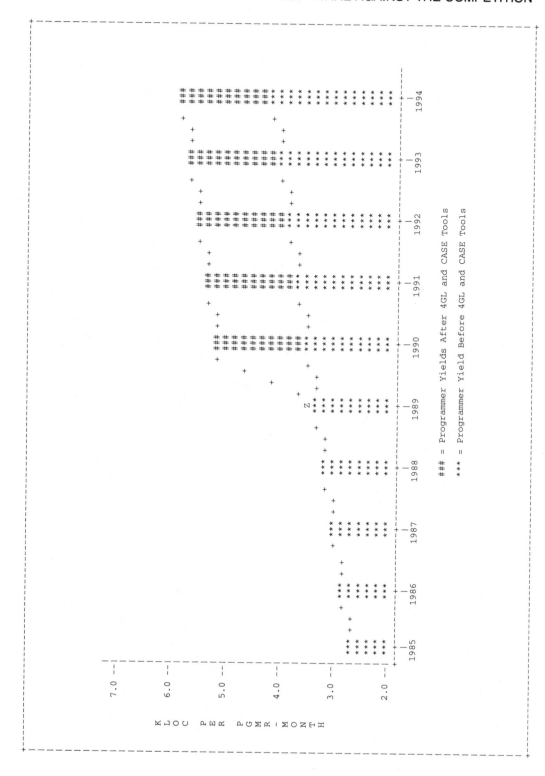

Figure 7-7   Z–Chart Benchmarking Plot Projection of Productivity Improvement Trend after 4GL and CASE Tools

across all rank items, then *global* intervention is needed and must be applied equally across the entire environment. The intervention must be directed at some problem or characteristic that all rank items share equally in order to decrease or increase a critical functional metric across the board.

Additionally, cross-linked Pareto charts can be used to compare internal versus external productivity and quality or to compare two internal products or applications. This method uses side-by-side bar charts indicating the relative percent of each rank item in two comparable environments or performance groups.

This method is useful, especially in combination with the Ishikawa "Fishbone" cause and effect charts used in TQM programs, to provide more detailed process analysis between the internal data center operation and an industry leader or major competitor.

All of these methods can be automated since Pareto ranking reports and charts can be routinely outputted.

An example of a simple Pareto chart with descending ranks and a side-by-side Pareto chart is shown in Figure 7-8.

SOFTWARE DEMOGRAPHICS TO DESCRIBE BUSINESS UNIT PROCESS COSTS

As in any business-related activity, it is essential for the effective and productive data center operation to understand the needs and concerns of its customers. Just as a profit-oriented business operation must conduct market research to determine where and how its products and services are being used, the data center must also conduct market research to analyze its effectiveness in serving business unit customers.

This must be done in terms that business unit customers can directly relate to their own functional operations, primarily in order to demonstrate to the data center customers that the products and services provided are an important part of their functional operations, and also to assure that the customer is able to manage the direct costs of providing a revenue-generating product or service, which indirectly supports the ongoing operations of the information data center.

To a large degree, market research is comparable to the same kinds of quality dimensions surveyed by business marketing consultants. They can all be automatically derived in the form of time-dimensioned "snapshots." These sample data snapshots involve information that includes the identity of each individual or production application system using the output processed by a particular application product and each product that is used from a particular terminal or business unit area. Snapshots also include usage statistics, such as how long, how many times within a particular period, what types of input or output are involved, and other information that must be accounted for in transfer pricing, chargeback cost allocation, and data center capacity planning data. In addition, it is possible to use the system logs, along with the data set storage catalogs and other machine-readable system directory information, to obtain information about the products in the data center's in-house software inventory.

This kind of information, which can be used to characterize the customer as well as to detect discrete patterns or changes in the customer base, is commonly known in marketing as *demographics*. Demographics are simple, statistical data descriptions that measure various characteristics of the users or potential users of a product or service. Analysis and planning of software quality and productivity data center support operations require detailed statistical demographic profiles of products, services, and customer trends. This information must be kept in the historical system performance database to provide a basis for calibrating demographic and performance snapshots over time, across software environments, and internal versus external boundaries.

Figure 7-8   Example of a Pareto Ranking of a Program Production Operational Process Ranking Cumulative Trend

These demographics can be used to prepare comparative bar charts, pie charts, or trendlines and as the basis for Z-chart or performance gap benchmark charting. A substantial number of software demographics can be collected based on system logs accumulated to a historical demographic snapshot database.

DEMOGRAPHIC PENETRATION DATA FOR GAUGING SPREAD OF NEW TECHNOLOGY

One of the most important uses of the demographics data involves the automated tracking of the penetration of new technology from the time it is first introduced and made available to the data center customers. This data can include the number of customers, amount of time that a new technology is used relative to traditional methods, the amount of data, product, or report output that is generated by the new technology, and comparison between alternative forms or usages of the new technology.

This information can be used to model the impact of growth in new technology usage to set goals for the new technology penetration and to compare costs and quality gains that can be expected from the technology. This modeling technique makes use of operations research and the related fields of queueing theory and yield management.

Basically, statistics and probability theory are applied to test assumptions about the continuance, discontinuance, or particular patterns in the use of a specific technology, product, or service, based on carefully defined quantifiable demographic levels. Although this is a relatively new area of software metrics and analysis, it is growing rapidly as an extension of the same methods that are used in data center capacity planning.

SYSTEM PROCESS QUALITY INDEX FOR INTERNAL COMPARISON OF SOFTWARE

Once a software demographics database and a software quality performance history database have been developed and accumulated for a sufficiently long period of time (preferably three years or more, but at least six months or more), it is possible to make comparisons across application software systems using *Analysis of Variance* (ANOVA) techniques. This statistical method is supported by several standard procedures provided with the Base SAS 4GL reporting language product marketed by the SAS Institute. The ANOVA method can help identify systems that have a high level of commonality or dissimilarity, which can be used to standardize workloads and target common process problems by a standard or operating procedure change.

Another method is to index all of the application systems from the same system environment (such as MVS batch, TSO, CICS, IMS, etc.) based upon grouping by their application system name in a job card accounting code or rollup by a cross-reference table based on the job name or session ID. The next step is to identify a managable number of factors (normally between six and twenty), which can be measured using SMF system logs and which have been converted to operational business units that are relevant to management of the data center. Examples of such units might include:

- Average fully allocated process cost per job or session execution
- Ratio of program failure incidents per new module or change

- Percent of production executions completing without failures
- Percent of program inventory that failed per a unit of time
- Percent of production programs modified per a unit of time
- Average CPU time between application program failures

These values can be extracted directly from the performance history database accumulated from the SMF system logs according to grouping assignments based on common software demographics and automatically downloaded on a routine basis to a PC spreadsheet program. Such a spreadsheet can be organized with application system name or group as the first column, against a matrix of quality and performance measurements in the following columns.

The raw data can then be individually ranked and indexed for each variable, and a score can be assigned based on either the rank or an indexed standard score. The sum of indexed scores across all quality and performance factors can provide a composite score reflecting a robust variety of indicators of software quality and performance. The indexed scores can be ranked to identify the application systems with the greatest potential for quality improvement in the greatest number of quality dimensions. The individual factor ranks can be examined in order to find the most critical factors that can be improved upon.

This is a technique that is similar to the method used by several of the standardized college entrance examinations. It is the method used in the Airline Quality Index developed by the U.S. Department of Transportation, which ranks commercial airlines according to a variety of important quality and performance factors. Although there is no similar national index for the computer industry, there probably will be someday. Airlines are, after all, a largely deregulated industry—yet the FAA requires federal reporting. It is likely that federal reporting for the computer industry will be mandated in the future.

8

VENDOR SERVICES
TO INTEGRATE
BENCHMARK DATABASES

There are several "Big-6" U.S. national accounting firms that provide technical consulting services, which include alternatives for the establishment and integration of vendor system performance database and software benchmark management configurations. This includes either MXG or MICS, or a similar proprietary product, as well as support of the customization of any system log EDP audit product to integrate various hardware vendors' operating system logs and data storage catalogs not directly supported by MXG or MICS or which must be collected in particular ways outside the standard configuration supplied by the vendor.

One example is the *Airline Control Program* (ACP) operating system or the banking industry's *Transaction Control Program* (TCP) operating system. Both are based on user-defined system log record customizations under IBM's VM high-level operating system. Because they involve operating system modifications not directly supported by IBM under the general prevailing maintenance agreements, such specialized operating systems are not usually available in the base set of components offered by MXG or MICS—although both MICS and MXG make provisions for integrating customer-defined external files and database into the central performance database complex. Each of these two major PDB systems have users' groups, which often share user-defined specialized system log components. Yet, in some cases, details of the customized system log records for individual industries or individual corporations are so proprietary that details of their system log record layouts are confidential and not released outside of their own companies.

Almost all of the Big-6 accounting firms have their own individual programs for EDP audit and confidential peer group benchmark comparison programs. Several have been particularly successful at integrating various configurations of the MXG and MICS products for clients that have customized operating systems and user-defined system logs. They also have been relatively successful at arranging some confidential and cooperative data sharing between firms and organizations that may benefit from strategic alliances or are not directly competitive. This is particularly true across functionally related industries, such as airlines and hotel chains or banks and investment firms. Therefore, it is certainly worth discussing potential for such confidential benchmark data sharing with each of the Big-6 accounting firms if there is a serious interest in, or management awareness of, the substantial benefit of such an arrangement. The first place to start is probably the office of the financial controller for the data center, who can discuss the options with the local accounting office currently performing the external independent audits of the data center's accounting. Both the data center financial controller and external auditor should certainly be involved in the selection of an EDP system log audit or confidential peer group comparison benchmarking service.

VENDOR SERVICE TO ASSIST DATA CENTER BENCHMARKING: KPMG

One of the most effective and efficient ways to initiate an automated software process quality and productivity benchmarking program is to subscribe to one of the comparative data center benchmarking consulting services, such as KPMG Peat Marwick Advanced Technology's Automated Peer Group Comparison. This specialized consulting service allows a data center to receive confidential and automated statistical profiles, which benchmark the performance of internal data center operations, against national DP industry leader data centers or competitive data centers, based on staffing levels and hardware capacity in available CPU Million Instructions Per Second (MIPS).

Comparative environmental configuration profiles, software demographics, and software quality and performance benchmarks are provided with respect to:

- Hardware configuration and utilization by device type
- Number of staff by primary DP function
- Expenses and unit costs by process type
- Technology and product type utilization levels

KPMG Peat Marwick Advanced Technology Peer Group Comparison Service for hardware usage in an MVS environment is fully automated using its own proprietary SAS language programs, which take snapshots of SMF logs and system catalog data. For mixed or non-MVS environments, data is collected manually by interviews and surveys, which are analyzed and reported in a similar fashion along with MVS environment benchmarks by SAS analysis procedures. The price of this benchmark analysis and peer comparison service is dependent on the size of the data center and the number of years of the subscription.

This service evolved out of many years of data center consulting experience by KPMG Peat Marwick assisting clients in evaluating the productivity, efficiency, and quality of internal data center operations and the common desire of data center management to know how their internal operations compare to other data centers. Based upon agreements that KPMG Peat Marwick was able to arrange with many of its clients to support confidential data-sharing, and based on the fact that almost all of their client data centers have MVS with SAS Base language products installed, KPMG Peat Marwick has been able to accumulate one of the most extensive software and data center operational performance benchmark databases in the United States. Over 300 major Fortune 500 data centers are currently in their benchmark unit cost performance database, representing some of the nation's largest banking, finance, insurance, transportation, utilities, and major manufacturing companies.

Among the systems, software, and data center performance quality metrics that are supported by the KPMG Peat Marwick Automated Peer Group Comparison are the following:

- Hardware usage and service level indicators:
  - CPU (total versus used capacity)
  - DASD (capacity allocated versus used and data set aging)
  - Tape (size of library, mounts, and usage)
  - Print (hardcopy, online view, and other)
  - Response time and transaction volume
  - Number of batch jobs processed and average throughput
  - Number of production job failures
- Organization and staffing by functional support category
- Expense for salaries, technology, and data center supplies
- Degree to which automation products are utilized

Automated analysis for hardware usage data in an MVS operating environment is based upon the on-site processing of thirty days of peak SMF and RMF system log tape archives, DASD VTOCs, and tape management catalogs, and the entire analysis is normally completed in less than five days. Hardware usage data in a non-MVS operating environment is collected manually and can take somewhat longer, depending on complexity of the configuration.

When the service was first introduced several years ago, each data center was required to be an MXG-licensed site, assured that all necessary system log data collection mechanisms were in place and that the technical staff were already well versed in computer performance evaluation methods and data collection procedures, which greatly expedited the SMF system log extraction process. However, this is no longer a requirement, and KPMG Peat Marwick Advanced Technology offers their peer group comparison benchmarking service to any data center, regardless of whether they have MXG. In fact, KPMG is increasing use of MICS and related Legent products to support its integrated Data Center Management services.

Analysis is presented in a series of benchmark reports comparing key financial indicators and their related software quality and performance measurement indicators for the internal data center and those in competing businesses. If multiple-year subscriptions are purchased, the data is trended, and discrete improvements or dropoffs in system performance and quality are identified and analyzed.

An individualized efficiency analysis and strategic recommendations report is provided to help data centers make decisions about potential changes in technology, utilization, or configuration which result in the greatest possible improvement. Of particular value in improving data center product service quality are the automated benchmark and diagnostic analysis of opportunities for:

- Reduced paper and increased service levels by online viewing
- Enhanced DASD management by migration of datasets to tape
- Moving small tape files to DASD to reduce tape mount waits
- Increased job throughput by eliminating redundant activities
- Reducing staff by consolidating overlapping job functions

This service is probably one of the most valuable investments that a data center can make in order to get maximum benefit out of implementing automated software quality measurement methods. Once this type of comparative DP industry statistical software benchmarking data is available, it can be used for continuous quality and productivity improvements. Initial implementation of an automated peer comparison subscription service often pays for itself, or even an entire automated software quality measurement program, within the initial cycle of analysis.

More information about the KPMG Peat Marwick Advanced Technology's Automated Peer Group Comparison services can be found in Figures 8-1a through 8-1j and in Appendix B.

ABC Company
PEER GROUP COMPARISON STATISTICS

BENCHMARK CATEGORY	PREVIOUS STUDY	LAST YEAR	Current Benchmark Data			
			ABC Company	Benchmark Average	Variance fr/Benchmark	BEST PRACTICES
CPU STATISTICS						
INSTALLED CPU MIPS	999.99	999.99	+9.9%	9.9%	9.9%	9.9%
USED CPU MIPS	999.99	999.99	+9.9%	9.9%	9.9%	9.9%
OVERALL % USED						
% USED BY ON-LINE	9.99	9.99	+9.9%	9.9%	9.9%	9.9%
% USED BY DBMS	9.99	9.99	+9.9%	9.9%	9.9%	9.9%
% USED BY TSO	9.99	9.99	+9.9%	9.9%	9.9%	9.9%
% USED BY BATCH	9.99	9.99	+9.9%	9.9%	9.9%	9.9%
% USED BY TEST	9.99	9.99	+9.9%	9.9%	9.9%	9.9%
% USED BY OTHER	9.99	9.99	+9.9%	9.9%	9.9%	9.9%
PRIME SHIFT % USED						
% USED BY ON-LINE	9.99	9.99	+9.9%	9.9%	9.9%	9.9%
% USED BY DBMS	9.99	9.99	+9.9%	9.9%	9.9%	9.9%
% USED BY TSO	9.99	9.99	+9.9%	9.9%	9.9%	9.9%
% USED BY BATCH	9.99	9.99	+9.9%	9.9%	9.9%	9.9%
% USED BY TEST	9.99	9.99	+9.9%	9.9%	9.9%	9.9%
% USED BY OTHER	9.99	9.99	+9.9%	9.9%	9.9%	9.9%
NON-PRIME SHIFT % USED						
% USED BY ON-LINE	9.99	9.99	+9.9%	9.9%	9.9%	9.9%
% USED BY DBMS	9.99	9.99	+9.9%	9.9%	9.9%	9.9%
% USED BY TSO	9.99	9.99	+9.9%	9.9%	9.9%	9.9%
% USED BY BATCH	9.99	9.99	+9.9%	9.9%	9.9%	9.9%
% USED BY TEST	9.99	9.99	+9.9%	9.9%	9.9%	9.9%
% USED BY OTHER	9.99	9.99	+9.9%	9.9%	9.9%	9.9%

Figure 8-1a   Example of KPMG Data Center CPU Benchmark Comparison

ABC Company
PEER GROUP COMPARISON STATISTICS

BENCHMARK CATEGORY	PREVIOUS STUDY	LAST YEAR	ABC Company	Current Benchmark Data		
				Benchmark Average	Variance fr/Benchmark	BEST PRACTICES
DASD SUB-SYSTEM						
INSTALLED GIGABYTES	999.99	999.99	+9.9%	9.9%	9.9%	9.9%
ALLOCATED GIGABYTES	999.99	999.99	+9.9%	9.9%	9.9%	9.9%
USED GIGABYTES	999.99	999.99	+9.9%	9.9%	9.9%	9.9%
ALLOC. % OF INSTALLED	999.99	999.99	+9.9%	9.9%	9.9%	9.9%
USED % OF ALLOCATED	999.99	999.99	+9.9%	9.9%	9.9%	9.9%
INSTALLED POOLS						
% PRODUCTION POOL	9.99	9.99	+9.9%	9.9%	9.9%	9.9%
% SYSTEM POOL	9.99	9.99	+9.9%	9.9%	9.9%	9.9%
% TEST POOL	9.99	9.99	+9.9%	9.9%	9.9%	9.9%
% WORK POOL	9.99	9.99	+9.9%	9.9%	9.9%	9.9%
ALLOCATED SPACE % REF'D						
0 - 15 DAYS	999.99	999.99	+9.9%	9.9%	9.9%	9.9%
16 - 30 DAYS	999.99	999.99	+9.9%	9.9%	9.9%	9.9%
31 - 60 DAYS	999.99	999.99	+9.9%	9.9%	9.9%	9.9%
61 - 120 DAYS	999.99	999.99	+9.9%	9.9%	9.9%	9.9%
121 - 365 DAYS	999.99	999.99	+9.9%	9.9%	9.9%	9.9%
> 365 DAYS	999.99	999.99	+9.9%	9.9%	9.9%	9.9%
% ALLOCATED SPACE OPTIMALLY BLOCKED	999.99	999.99	+9.9%	9.9%	9.9%	9.9%

Figure 8-1b   Example of KPMG Data Center DASD Subsystem Benchmark Comparison

ABC Company
PEER GROUP COMPARISON STATISTICS

BENCHMARK CATEGORY	PREVIOUS STUDY	LAST YEAR	ABC Company	Current Benchmark Data		
				Benchmark Average	Variance fr/Benchmark	BEST PRACTICES
TAPE SUB-SYSTEM						
TAPE DRIVE CONFIGURATION						
REEL DRIVES	999.99	999.99	+9.9%	9.9%	9.9%	9.9%
CARTRIDGE DRIVES	999.99	999.99	+9.9%	9.9%	9.9%	9.9%
SILO TRANSPORTS	999.99	999.99	+9.9%	9.9%	9.9%	9.9%
TOTAL MONTHLY MOUNTS						
% SPECIFIC MOUNTS	9.99	9.99	+9.9%	9.9%	9.9%	9.9%
% NON-SPECIFIC MOUNTS	9.99	9.99	+9.9%	9.9%	9.9%	9.9%
TAPE LIBRARY STATUS						
AVAILABLE LIBRARY SLOTS	9.99	9.99	+9.9%	9.9%	9.9%	9.9%
% MULTI-FILE VOLUMES	9.99	9.99	+9.9%	9.9%	9.9%	9.9%
% LESS THAN 10 MEGABYTES	9.99	9.99	+9.9%	9.9%	9.9%	9.9%
% OPTIMALLY BLOCKED	9.99	9.99	+9.9%	9.9%	9.9%	9.9%
% CREATED/NEVER REF'D	9.99	9.99	+9.9%	9.9%	9.9%	9.9%
% HELD 0 - 3 MONTHS	9.99	9.99	+9.9%	9.9%	9.9%	9.9%
% HELD 4 - 6 MONTHS	9.99	9.99	+9.9%	9.9%	9.9%	9.9%
% HELD 7 - 12 MONTHS	9.99	9.99	+9.9%	9.9%	9.9%	9.9%
% HELD 1 - 7 YEARS	9.99	9.99	+9.9%	9.9%	9.9%	9.9%
% HELD > 7 YEARS	9.99	9.99	+9.9%	9.9%	9.9%	9.9%
% CYCLE CONTROL	9.99	9.99	+9.9%	9.9%	9.9%	9.9%
% PERMANENT RETENTION	9.99	9.99	+9.9%	9.9%	9.9%	9.9%

Figure 8-1c   Example of KPMG Data Center Tape Subsystem Benchmark Comparison

ABC Company
PEER GROUP COMPARISON STATISTICS

BENCHMARK CATEGORY	PREVIOUS STUDY	LAST YEAR	ABC Company	Current Benchmark Data		
				Benchmark Average	Variance fr/Benchmark	BEST PRACTICES
ON-LINE STATISTICS						
PRODUCT TP REGIONS	999.99	999.99	+9.9%	9.9%	9.9%	9.9%
TEST TP REGIONS	999.99	999.99	+9.9%	9.9%	9.9%	9.9%
MAXIMUM NO. OF CONNECTS	999.99	999.99	+9.9%	9.9%	9.9%	9.9%
ONLINE RESPONSE TIME						
TSO TRIVIAL RESPONSE	999.99	999.99	+9.9%	9.9%	9.9%	9.9%
TSO NON-TRIVIAL RESPONSE	999.99	999.99	+9.9%	9.9%	9.9%	9.9%
MONTHLY TRANSACTIONS						
% TRIVIAL TRANSACTIONS	9.99	9.99	+9.9%	9.9%	9.9%	9.9%
% NON-TRIVIAL TRANSACTNS	9.99	9.99	+9.9%	9.9%	9.9%	9.9%
BATCH STATISTICS						
TOTAL MONTHLY JOBS	999.99	999.99	+9.9%	9.9%	9.9%	9.9%
% PRODUCTION	9.99	9.99	+9.9%	9.9%	9.9%	9.9%
% TEST	9.99	9.99	+9.9%	9.9%	9.9%	9.9%
EXECUTION ELAPSED TIMES						
AVG. PROD ELAPSED TIME	999.99	999.99	+9.9%	9.9%	9.9%	9.9%
AVG TEST ELAPSED TIME	999.99	999.99	+9.9%	9.9%	9.9%	9.9%
PROD PROGRAM FAILURES						
% PRODUCTION FAILURES	9.99	9.99	+9.9%	9.9%	9.9%	9.9%
REASONS FOR FAILURES						
% DASD RELATED FAILURES	9.99	9.99	+9.9%	9.9%	9.9%	9.9%
% OPERATOR CANCELS	9.99	9.99	+9.9%	9.9%	9.9%	9.9%
% PROBLEM PROGRAM ERRORS	9.99	9.99	+9.9%	9.9%	9.9%	9.9%
% USER ERRORS	9.99	9.99	+9.9%	9.9%	9.9%	9.9%
% OTHER FAILURES	9.99	9.99	+9.9%	9.9%	9.9%	9.9%

Figure 8-1d   Example of KPMG Data Center Online Benchmark Comparison

ABC Company
PEER GROUP COMPARISON STATISTICS

BENCHMARK CATEGORY	PREVIOUS STUDY	LAST YEAR	Current Benchmark Data			
			ABC Company	Benchmark Average	Variance fr/Benchmark	BEST PRACTICES
PRINT STATISTICS						
LOCAL LASER PRINTERS	999.99	999.99	+9.9%	9.9%	9.9%	9.9%
DEFAULT IMAGES PER PAGE	999.99	999.99	+9.9%	9.9%	9.9%	9.9%
LOCAL IMPACT PRINTERS	999.99	999.99	+9.9%	9.9%	9.9%	9.9%
TOTAL MONTHLY PRINTOUT						
% PAGES PRINTED LOCALLY	9.99	9.99	+9.9%	9.9%	9.9%	9.9%
% PAGES PRINTED REMOTE	9.99	9.99	+9.9%	9.9%	9.9%	9.9%
PRINT CLASS STATISTICS						
% PAGES PRODUCTION	9.99	9.99	+9.9%	9.9%	9.9%	9.9%
% PAGES TEST	9.99	9.99	+9.9%	9.9%	9.9%	9.9%
PRINT FORM STATISTICS						
% PAGES STANDARD FORMS	9.99	9.99	+9.9%	9.9%	9.9%	9.9%
% PAGES NON-STD FORMS	9.99	9.99	+9.9%	9.9%	9.9%	9.9%
PRINT TECHNOLOGY STATS						
PAGES VIEWED ON-LINE	999.99	999.99	+9.9%	9.9%	9.9%	9.9%
PAGES ON MICROFICHE	999.99	999.99	+9.9%	9.9%	9.9%	9.9%

Figure 8-1e Example of KPMG Data Center Printer Benchmark Comparison

ABC Company
PEER GROUP COMPARISON STATISTICS

BENCHMARK CATEGORY	PREVIOUS STUDY	LAST YEAR	ABC Company	Current Benchmark Data		
				Benchmark Average	Variance fr/Benchmark	BEST PRACTICES
PERSONNEL STATISTICS (FTE)						
TOTAL DATA CNTR PERSONNEL						
DIRECT OPERATIONS						
CONSOLE	999.99	999.99	+9.9%	9.9%	9.9%	9.9%
TAPE OPERATORS & LIBRNS	999.99	999.99	+9.9%	9.9%	9.9%	9.9%
PRINT DISTRIBUTION	999.99	999.99	+9.9%	9.9%	9.9%	9.9%
OTHER	999.99	999.99	+9.9%	9.9%	9.9%	9.9%
TOTAL	999.99	999.99	+9.9%	9.9%	9.9%	9.9%
OPERATIONS SUPPORT						
SCHEDULERS	999.99	999.99	+9.9%	9.9%	9.9%	9.9%
JOB SETUP	999.99	999.99	+9.9%	9.9%	9.9%	9.9%
I/O BALANCING	999.99	999.99	+9.9%	9.9%	9.9%	9.9%
AUTOMATION SPECIALISTS	999.99	999.99	+9.9%	9.9%	9.9%	9.9%
CUSTOMER SERVICE	999.99	999.99	+9.9%	9.9%	9.9%	9.9%
PROBLEM/CHANGE MGMT.	999.99	999.99	+9.9%	9.9%	9.9%	9.9%
OTHER	999.99	999.99	+9.9%	9.9%	9.9%	9.9%
TOTAL	999.99	999.99	+9.9%	9.9%	9.9%	9.9%
TECHNICAL SUPPORT						
CAPACITY PLANNING	999.99	999.99	+9.9%	9.9%	9.9%	9.9%
SYSTEMS PROGRAMMING	999.99	999.99	+9.9%	9.9%	9.9%	9.9%
DASD MANAGEMENT	999.99	999.99	+9.9%	9.9%	9.9%	9.9%
NETWORK SUPPORT	999.99	999.99	+9.9%	9.9%	9.9%	9.9%
DATABASE SUPPORT	999.99	999.99	+9.9%	9.9%	9.9%	9.9%
OTHER	999.99	999.99	+9.9%	9.9%	9.9%	9.9%
TOTAL	999.99	999.99	+9.9%	9.9%	9.9%	9.9%
DATA ADMINISTRATION / MANAGEMENT & PLANNING	999.99	999.99	+9.9%	9.9%	9.9%	9.9%
TOTAL SOFTWARE APPLICATION DEVELOPMENT PERSONNEL	999.99	999.99	+9.9%	9.9%	9.9%	9.9%

Figure 8-1f Example of KPMG Data Center Personnel Benchmark Comparison

ABC Company
PEER GROUP COMPARISON STATISTICS

BENCHMARK CATEGORY	PREVIOUS STUDY	LAST YEAR	ABC Company	Current Benchmark Data		
				Benchmark Average	Variance fr/Benchmark	BEST PRACTICES
PERSONNEL TO SYSTEM RATIO						
PER USED MIP						
DATA CENTER STAFF	999.99	999.99	+9.9%	9.9%	9.9%	9.9%
CONSOLE OPERATORS	999.99	999.99	+9.9%	9.9%	9.9%	9.9%
SYSTEMS PROGRAMMERS	999.99	999.99	+9.9%	9.9%	9.9%	9.9%
CAPACITY PLANNERS	999.99	999.99	+9.9%	9.9%	9.9%	9.9%
NON-DIRECT STAFF	999.99	999.99	+9.9%	9.9%	9.9%	9.9%
PER INSTALLED MIP						
DATA CENTER STAFF	999.99	999.99	+9.9%	9.9%	9.9%	9.9%
CONSOLE OPERATORS	999.99	999.99	+9.9%	9.9%	9.9%	9.9%
SYSTEMS PROGRAMMERS	999.99	999.99	+9.9%	9.9%	9.9%	9.9%
CAPACITY PLANNERS	999.99	999.99	+9.9%	9.9%	9.9%	9.9%
NON-DIRECT STAFF	999.99	999.99	+9.9%	9.9%	9.9%	9.9%
BASED ON WORKLOAD						
TAPE STAFF/10K MOUNTS	999.99	999.99	+9.9%	9.9%	9.9%	9.9%
DASD MANAGER/50 GBYTES	999.99	999.99	+9.9%	9.9%	9.9%	9.9%
PRINT STAFF/100K PAGES	999.99	999.99	+9.9%	9.9%	9.9%	9.9%
SCHEDULERS/10K JOBS	999.99	999.99	+9.9%	9.9%	9.9%	9.9%
I/O STAFF/10K JOBS	999.99	999.99	+9.9%	9.9%	9.9%	9.9%
USED MIPS/CONNECTION	999.99	999.99	+9.9%	9.9%	9.9%	9.9%
USED ONLINE MIPS/LINKAGE	999.99	999.99	+9.9%	9.9%	9.9%	9.9%
PER APPLICATION PROGRAMMER						
TEST MIPS USED	999.99	999.99	+9.9%	9.9%	9.9%	9.9%
TEST DASD INSTALLED	999.99	999.99	+9.9%	9.9%	9.9%	9.9%
TEST JOBS RUN	999.99	999.99	+9.9%	9.9%	9.9%	9.9%
TEST PAGES PRINTED	999.99	999.99	+9.9%	9.9%	9.9%	9.9%

Figure 8-1g Example of KPMG Data Center Personnel Benchmark Ratio Comparison

ABC Company
PEER GROUP COMPARISON STATISTICS

BENCHMARK CATEGORY	PREVIOUS STUDY	LAST YEAR	ABC Company	Current Benchmark Data		
				Benchmark Average	Variance fr/Benchmark	BEST PRACTICES
SPENDING STATISTICS ($ 000 OMITTED)						
TOTAL SPENDING						
HARDWARE						
CPU	999.99	999.99	+9.9%	9.9%	9.9%	9.9%
DASD	999.99	999.99	+9.9%	9.9%	9.9%	9.9%
TAPE	999.99	999.99	+9.9%	9.9%	9.9%	9.9%
PRINT	999.99	999.99	+9.9%	9.9%	9.9%	9.9%
OTHER	999.99	999.99	+9.9%	9.9%	9.9%	9.9%
TOTAL	999.99	999.99	+9.9%	9.9%	9.9%	9.9%
PERSONNEL						
DIRECT OPERATIONS	999.99	999.99	+9.9%	9.9%	9.9%	9.9%
OPERATIONS SUPPORT	999.99	999.99	+9.9%	9.9%	9.9%	9.9%
TECHNICAL SUPPORT	999.99	999.99	+9.9%	9.9%	9.9%	9.9%
OTHER	999.99	999.99	+9.9%	9.9%	9.9%	9.9%
TOTAL	999.99	999.99	+9.9%	9.9%	9.9%	9.9%
SUPPLIES						
SPECIAL FORMS	999.99	999.99	+9.9%	9.9%	9.9%	9.9%
STANDARD FORMS	999.99	999.99	+9.9%	9.9%	9.9%	9.9%
TAPE REELS & CARTRIDGES	999.99	999.99	+9.9%	9.9%	9.9%	9.9%
OTHER	999.99	999.99	+9.9%	9.9%	9.9%	9.9%
TOTAL	999.99	999.99	+9.9%	9.9%	9.9%	9.9%
SOFTWARE	999.99	999.99	+9.9%	9.9%	9.9%	9.9%
OTHER	999.99	999.99	+9.9%	9.9%	9.9%	9.9%
GRAND TOTAL						
SPENDING BY CATEGORY						
% HARDWARE	999.99	999.99	+9.9%	9.9%	9.9%	9.9%
% SOFTWARE	9.99	9.99	+9.9%	9.9%	9.9%	9.9%
% PERSONNEL	9.99	9.99	+9.9%	9.9%	9.9%	9.9%
% SUPPLIES	9.99	9.99	+9.9%	9.9%	9.9%	9.9%
% OTHER	9.99	9.99	+9.9%	9.9%	9.9%	9.9%

Figure 8-1h Example of KPMG Data Center Spending Benchmark Comparison

ABC Company
PEER GROUP COMPARISON STATISTICS

BENCHMARK CATEGORY	PREVIOUS STUDY	LAST YEAR	Current Benchmark Data			
			ABC Company	Benchmark Average	Variance fr/Benchmark	BEST PRACTICES
COST RATIOS ($)						
AVERAGE PERSONNEL COST	999.99	999.99	+9.9%	9.9%	9.9%	9.9%
AVERAGE DIRECT OPS COST	999.99	999.99	+9.9%	9.9%	9.9%	9.9%
AVERAGE OPS SUPPORT COST	999.99	999.99	+9.9%	9.9%	9.9%	9.9%
AVERAGE TECH SUPPORT COST	999.99	999.99	+9.9%	9.9%	9.9%	9.9%
PER USED MIP						
TOTAL SPENDING	999.99	999.99	+9.9%	9.9%	9.9%	9.9%
HARDWARE SPENDING	999.99	999.99	+9.9%	9.9%	9.9%	9.9%
SOFTWARE SPENDING	999.99	999.99	+9.9%	9.9%	9.9%	9.9%
PERSONNEL	999.99	999.99	+9.9%	9.9%	9.9%	9.9%
PER INSTALLED MIP						
TOTAL SPENDING	999.99	999.99	+9.9%	9.9%	9.9%	9.9%
HARDWARE SPENDING	999.99	999.99	+9.9%	9.9%	9.9%	9.9%
SOFTWARE SPENDING	999.99	999.99	+9.9%	9.9%	9.9%	9.9%
PERSONNEL	999.99	999.99	+9.9%	9.9%	9.9%	9.9%
BASED ON WORKLOAD						
COST TO MOUNT A TAPE	999.99	999.99	+9.9%	9.9%	9.9%	9.9%
COST TO STORE GB OF DASD	999.99	999.99	+9.9%	9.9%	9.9%	9.9%
COST TO PRINT PAGE LOCAL	999.99	999.99	+9.9%	9.9%	9.9%	9.9%

Figure 8-1i Example of KPMG Data Center Cost Ratio Benchmark Comparison

ABC Company
PEER GROUP COMPARISON STATISTICS

BENCHMARK CATEGORY	PREVIOUS STUDY	LAST YEAR	Current Benchmark Data			
			ABC Company	Benchmark Average	Variance fr/Benchmark	BEST PRACTICES
CONTROL SOFTWARE ADVANCES (DEGREE IMPLEMENTED ON SCALE OF 1 – 100)						
CONSOLE MANAGMENT	99.99	99.99	+9.9%	9.9%	9.9%	9.9%
TAPE MANAGEMENT	99.99	99.99	+9.9%	9.9%	9.9%	9.9%
DASD MANAGEMENT	99.99	99.99	+9.9%	9.9%	9.9%	9.9%
SECURITY	99.99	99.99	+9.9%	9.9%	9.9%	9.9%
SCHEDULING	99.99	99.99	+9.9%	9.9%	9.9%	9.9%
RESTART/RERUN MGMT	99.99	99.99	+9.9%	9.9%	9.9%	9.9%
OUTPUT DISTRIBUTION	99.99	99.99	+9.9%	9.9%	9.9%	9.9%
BALANCING	99.99	99.99	+9.9%	9.9%	9.9%	9.9%
PROBLEM MANAGMENT	99.99	99.99	+9.9%	9.9%	9.9%	9.9%
CHANGE MANAGMENT	99.99	99.99	+9.9%	9.9%	9.9%	9.9%
CONFIGURATION MGMT.	99.99	99.99	+9.9%	9.9%	9.9%	9.9%
SOFTWARE MANAGEMENT	99.99	99.99	+9.9%	9.9%	9.9%	9.9%
DATA CENTER REPORTING	99.99	99.99	+9.9%	9.9%	9.9%	9.9%
HARDWARE ROBOTIC ADVANCES (DEGREE IMPLEMENTED ON SCALE OF 0 – 5)						
TAPE DRIVE AUTOLOADERS	99.99	99.99	+9.9%	9.9%	9.9%	9.9%
AUTOMATED TAPE SILO	99.99	99.99	+9.9%	9.9%	9.9%	9.9%
PRINT ROBOTICS	99.99	99.99	+9.9%	9.9%	9.9%	9.9%

Figure 8-1j   Example of KPMG Data Center Operational Benchmark Comparison

VENDOR SERVICES PROVIDING SYSTEM DEVELOPMENT PROJECT BENCHMARKS

A somewhat different category of benchmarking services is related to the software product development project productivity consulting firms that became commonplace during the time that Computer Performance Evaluation and Software Metrics technologies came into their maturity during the 1980s. Just as there is currently a Big-6 of major nationwide EDP accounting firms, there is a "Little-6" of major nationwide SQM consulting organizations, which has their own proprietary database of software development project statistics, collected either through their own consulting activities or extracted from government and academic sources. The Little-6 Software Quality Metric support organizations are:

- DACS—military system benchmarks, mostly related to COCOMO
- Quantitative Software Measurements (QSM)—mostly military
- Quality Assurance Institute (QAI)—mostly private industry
- Software Engineering Institute (SEI)—diverse applications
- Software Productivity Research (SPR)—by far the largest
- Technology Transfer Institute (TTI)—mostly new technology

There are a number of other highly specialized software quality benchmark databases, which concentrate largely on particular vendor hardware architectures or application software types—such as NASA, AT&T, ACM, IEEE, and DEC Special Interest Groups. However, these SQM databases are the most extensive in both range and detail, and each of these six organizations has some comparative data for calibrating its software development project benchmarks across a wide variety of system environments.

These SQM databases range from an exclusively military systems focus to private business systems, to emphasis on only the latest software technology. This is usually integrated with summary DP industry averages published by the government or academic computer science publications.

DAC, SEI, and SQM databases are being increasingly converted from a military orientation to include a broader base that reflects greater usefulness to private business. QAI, SEI, and TTI databases are mostly oriented toward SQM and SE standards and guidelines, which foster the nurturing of new technologies in order to establish an industrywide common body of knowledge in a manner leading to greater productivity and quality for all. Both SQM and SPR databases are oriented toward confidential services.

The selection of which SQM organization to use is as important as the decision of which EDP accounting firm will do your external auditing. In most cases, it is a good idea to discuss the available options with your data center financial controller as well as your business organization's EDP audit and accounting firm. Your choice should be determined by compatibility to existing data center financial control procedures, and should also be selected based on your business organization's and data center's long-term strategic systems capacity plan, as well as anticipated growth in your data center and any anticipated changes in your technology base.

9

UNDERSTANDING THE LIMITS
OF YOUR SOFTWARE

In order to achieve greater productivity and reliability of software development and operational system processes, quality control must be introduced in a manner that allows for the accommodation of specialized software functions. There are numerous methods and techniques that can be adapted from quality control in manufacturing environments and applied to software development and support operations. However, it is important to distinguish which industrial quality control methods should, and should not, be applied in the software environment.

There are many significant differences between quality control methods used in *mass production* versus *limited production* prototypes. Though there are some notable exceptions, for the most part it is safe to regard routinely scheduled production data processing operations as *mass production* operations. Software development, on the other hand, is normally a more *limited production* operation.

In the former case, the main things that must be controlled are time and materials. In the latter case, any number of quality dimensions may be controlled, such as variation in size or another physically measurable characteristic. This is achieved in both cases by the setting of *control limits* using traditional quality control methods. Acceptable limits are set within a range of software measurements. This chapter will demonstrate how to determine desirable control limit ranges in the software development process or data center operation using system logs.

THE IMPORTANCE OF CONSISTENCY TO INDUSTRIAL
PRODUCTION PROCESSES

The modern industrial manufacturing process has evolved primarily within the past century. Before that time, products may have been manufactured in large production settings, but by different machines or individuals that did not necessarily conform to any precision standard for the end product. Each item produced had the same functions, but there was wide variation in the internal workings and even external appearance of end products produced at the same location and perhaps even by the same individual craftsman or machine. The problem with this method of manufacturing process was that defective products could not be repaired. Each individual component that failed or degraded from normal use had to be remanufactured in a customized manner, which was not always a cost-effective or even technically-feasible alternative.

The American innovation of mass production using standardized components by Henry Ford enabled the replacement of individual parts. This increased the value of the completed product because of the longer life and resilience to obsolescence caused by a single defect or failure. This innovation also made it possible to create economies of scale. Standardized parts could be produced routinely in large quantities, separate from the assembly of individual products or versions of a product. This enabled salvage of large inventories of standardized components, which could be used in other product lines even if a particular assembled version of a product was made obsolete or phased out of continuous production.

This innovation also created significant opportunity to logically structure and analyze each component production process to optimize the materials, time, and labor required to make and assemble components into finished products. This process evolved into an applied science known as *industrial engineering* over the course of the last century.

Although most of the innovations in industrial engineering—such as standardized components, assembly lines, and time study procedures—were primarily originated in the United States, these methods were expanded upon by the Japanese after World War II and the revitalization programs that followed the introduction of these methods by U.S. military occupation forces. The Japanese were able to expand upon the American industrial engineering technology due to the introduction of *Statistical Process Control* (SPC) techniques by Dr. W. Edwards Deming in the 1950s. The Deming methods used statistical tools in order to support a continuous four-step cycle of support to the industrial production process, including market research, design, production, and sales. These four steps were continuously linked as products were developed and optimized.

The SPC methods involved a series of statistical and applied qualitative analysis methods that had not been fully accepted by the manufacturing industries in the United States, but were widely accepted and understood by the Japanese, who made the techniques an integral part of their own nationwide secondary educational curriculum. The Japanese were able to expand upon all of the SPC techniques introduced by Deming, based on the work of innovators such as Kaoru Ishikawa, who introduced the *Total Quality* (TQ) method.

The TQ method, also known as the *Zero Defects* method, was based on the use of SPC techniques to identify production problems and systematically eliminate the factors associated with that problem until it no longer occurred. This method follows a pattern of three sequential steps, which were performed successively until Zero Defects were achieved, and then continuously monitored and regulated in order to detect changes in the level of control over the process. These three steps involved identification of symptoms of the problem, identification of causes of the problem, and identification of the most significant cause of the problem.

The TQ method uses Ishikawa's own "Fishbone" cause and effect charts that document all of the contributing factors or dependent processes connected like "ribs" to "backbone" production assembly procedures. Each factor or dependent process is associated with a list of symptoms indicating potential problems early in the individual component production process, and identifies the causes for that particular symptom. The relative level of occurrence of each problem indicator symptom and related causal factors is measured and ranked using Pareto charts and the 80/20 rule, as described in Chapter 7.

Corrective action or controls are then directed first toward addressing the highest ranking symptom and cause, until it has been eliminated or reduced to an acceptable level of control. After a problem is brought under control, the next most significant problem becomes the predominant cause ranked by the Pareto chart. Each successive predominant problem is addressed until all the problems are under control and all components are standardized and interchangeable.

The success of the TQ method has shown that the most important characteristic of the manufacturing process is that the procedures to produce all components must be uniform, and the resulting product must be consistent according to precise measurable specifications of design and delivery. During the past decade, the United States has begun to integrate the TQ methods based on SPC into an American variation of the Ishikawa techniques, known as *Total Quality Management* (TQM).

There are many similarities between TQ and TQM. Both are based on SPC and share the common use of "Quality Circle" teams. Quality Circle teams empower the subcomponent and assembly line workers to make proactive tactical management decisions about fine-tuning and operational changes in production processes resulting in discrete improvements in the quality of their product. Although the major differences are already being quickly accommodated by the Japanese, the major American improvements in the TQ method have involved independent industrial engineering and operations research techniques and have evolved in the United States parallel to the Japanese innovations.

America's TQM innovations relate to logistics and queueing theory, yield management, risk management, information theory, associative network decision enabling, and the competitive comparison between internal and external processes and products. Due to the proprietary nature of the use of these advanced TQM techniques by the various major American corporations and military organizations that have developed them, and the complex formal mathematical nature of their methodologies, these methods cannot be easily explained other than to characterize that they all are based upon statistical analysis of variance and categorical analysis techniques. Also, all involve the statistical relationship of measurable historical product or service characteristics to normalized probability distributions used to extend verifiable data to make assumptions about areas or events about which little data is known.

The common characteristic across all TQ and TQM techniques is consistency, both in products and services, and the measurement methods by which they are compared. Thus, both TQ and TQM are based on SPC. Examples of the various quality improvement techniques and their historical development by industrial engineering for manufacturing industry applications are shown in Figure 9-1.

IMPORTANCE OF CONSISTENCY TO COMPUTER SYSTEM OPERATION THROUGHPUT

The data processing industry is in many ways comparable to the manufacturing industries in the early part of the century, in which industrial engineering was just beginning to gain acceptance and application in scattered areas across the United States. Although there has been substantial application of many industrial engineering methods ranging from basic SPC and quality control, to advanced TM and even TQM, there is still no widespread acceptance of these techniques by the data processing industry.

The extent to which these techniques have been applied is largely related to the demands placed on internal data centers supporting manufacturing and service delivery businesses or government organizations using SPC, TQ, or TQM techniques. Although IBM and other major vendors have begun to apply quality assurance concepts and technologies, there has been limited application of these techniques because many of these methods involve very time-consuming and labor-intensive manual data collection

```
INDUSTRIAL ENGINEERING AND OPERATION RESEARCH METHOD          SMF MEASUREMENT SOURCES
-------------------------------------------------------      ------------------------

LINEAR PROGRAMMING:      Univariate Forecasting    ==============>   TYPE 30_x - Resource Usage
                                                                     TYPE 38  - Network Capacity
                                                                     TYPE 7xx - CPU Capacity

QUEUEING THEORY:         Arrival Rate Analysis     ==============>   TYPE 2xx - Job/Session Start
                                                                     TYPE 22_x - Channel Arrival
                                                                     TYPE 38  - Network Arrivals

GAME THEORY:             Resource Contention Analysis ===========>   TYPE 30_x - Resource Usage
                                                                     TYPE 40  - Dynamic Allocation
                                                                     TYPE 75  - Swap Resource Action

SYMBOLIC LOGIC:          Expert System Heuristics  ==============>   SMF User Exits

INFORMATION THEORY:      Effective Throughput Analysis ==========>   TYPE 30_x - Resource Usage
                                                                     TYPE 38  - Network Flow
                                                                     TYPE 7xx - CPU Work Loadings

VALUE ANALYSIS:          Utilization Review Analysis ============>   TYPE 0 - Initial Program Load
                                                                     TYPE 2xx - CPU Configuration
                                                                     TYPE 30_x - Job Accounting
```

Figure 9-1 Categories of Industrial Engineering and Operations Research Data Captured by SMF

to support software quality measurement. This is changing, however, as more and more technical personnel and management staff become aware of the relatively low cost and ease of collecting software quality data by automated accumulation of system log measurements which can be used in TQ and TQM methods.

Although the advanced TQ and TQM methods such as statistical yield management, risk management, and *Just-In-Time* (JIT) dynamic inventory control technology may not be available as off-the-shelf software products for some time, it is almost certain that eventually such products will be available and widely used. In the meantime, the existing automated software quality measurement tools and products can be used as the basis for developing in-house applications which support advanced TQM applications. These applications are often based on the same proprietary techniques used by the customers of the data center to maximize profitability and revenues of their own product manufacturing or service delivery operations.

One area which has already received substantial attention by vendor development and marketing involves SPC and methods of statistical analysis of production processes and procedures using basic *Operations Research* (OR) and *Quality Control* (QC) methods. These OR and QC methods involve statistical analysis and graphing of normalized standard measurements to monitor and regulate the consistency of the products and services from which an organization gets its revenues.

The most common application of these methods has been in the area of data center problem management and resource recovery—both in regard to eliminating program defects and fine-tuning system configuration and resource allocation controls in order to get maximum responsiveness and throughput for all application systems. The immediate benefits have been in the areas of reducing costs of reruns and system resource spoilage, as well as achieving significant optimization of available system resource utilization and system capacity planning, which approaches economies of scale. Examples of various sources and applications of quality improvement data that can be extracted from system logs are shown in Figure 9-2.

MANAGING MASS PRODUCTION TO ACHIEVE SYSTEMATIC ECONOMIES OF SCALE

The production operations environment has been the first area where data processing has applied industrial engineering and operations research methods. In this way, most of the concepts and methods supporting a mass production process operation, such as queueing theory, critical path analysis, and basic categorical or classification analysis, are largely understood and more or less universally applied in some form in all U.S. data centers, including both mainframe batch production and online teleprocessing networks environments.

Most conventional IBM mainframe data centers are already quite proficient at defining batch production classes or online stages for job queues and service-level workload. The procedures for defining and assigning batch initiator classes and online transaction or session categories are well documented in vendor manuals and taught extensively.

There is also substantial training, vendor documentation, and support products in the areas of operational scheduling and variance analysis that help identify and eliminate reoccurring processing bottlenecks and assign workloads to open windows of availability.

However, the grouping of routinely processed application systems into consistent workloads or common performance groupings is a complicated process, which is covered in much less detail by vendor documentation and which still can be characterized as more of an art than a science.

TOTAL QUALITY MANAGMENT AND STATISTICAL PROCESS CONTROL METHOD	SMF MEASUREMENT SOURCES
CONTROL CHARTS: Process Capability Analysis ===========>	TYPE 30_x - Job Process Waits TYPE 38 - Network Process Wait TYPE 7xx - CPU Process Waits
PARETO DIAGRAMS: Cumulative Ranking Analysis ===========>	TYPE 2xx - Job/Session Account TYPE 22_x - Device Load Factor TYPE 38 - Network Load Factors
ISHIKAWA/FISHBONE DIAGRAMS: Cause-and-Effect Analysis ===========>	TYPE 30_x - Failure Causals TYPE 40 - Access Bottlenecks TYPE 75 - Workload Comparison
HIERARCHICAL TREE DIAGRAMS: Nested Process Path Analysis ===========>	TYPE 30_x - Event Process Path TYPE 38 - Network Process Path TYPE 76 - CPU Process Trace
CHECK SHEETS: Linear Process Path Analysis ===========>	TYPE 30_x - Sched. -vs- Actual TYPE 38 - Send -vs- Actual TYPE 7xx - Request -vs- Actual
AFFINITY MATRIX: Bivariate Cross-Correlation ===========>	TYPE 30_x - Device Contention TYPE 38 - Path Contention TYPE 7xx - Workload Contention

Figure 9-2   Categories of Total Quality Management and Statistical Process Control Data in SMF

Various methods exist for assigning the best mix of databases to be actively executed in the same multiprocessing partition or system environment. But few are widely detailed outside of highly specialized and often very expensive training seminars taught by advanced data processing technology consultants.

Although it is often desirable to manage complex workloads in multiprocessing environments using advanced capacity planning methods and tools, it is possible to analyze basic workload problems involving overall system environments, production shifts, or peak activity within particular application areas or customer access pathways. This involves using some variation of basic quality control comparisons of group mean averages or a time-sequenced quality control method, which can be graphed as a control chart.

The use of quality control charts is one of the most effective ways to plot and quickly analyze nonexponential processes. These processes are not subject to a forecastable growth function, yet are subject to some seasonal and random variation within a reasonably controllable range. There are basically three types of quality control charts:

- Box mean charts (also known as *cat whisker* charts)
- Cumulative sum charts (also known as *arrow* or *V-charts*)
- Shewhart charts (also known as *middle-of-the-road* charts)

The wide variety and number of discrete variations in the methods of calculating and graphing each of the types of control charts has led to some confusion in their interpretation and probably to some reluctance in applying them outside of manufacturing environments. Even in factory settings, most manufacturing personnel are normally acquainted with only one particular type of control chart and may not even recognize the other types as being control charts.

However, because of the fact that each type of control chart focuses on a particular functional type of problem, it is important for data center quality support personnel to recognize and understand each of the three basic control charts. These are covered in more detail later on in this chapter. Although there are a large variety of statistics that can be calculated and plotted in order to generate a control chart, there is a common method used in all control charting techniques.

The purpose of all control charts is to show three statistics in an x-y coordinate plot of a time series against a significant operational process measurement. These three statistics are:

1. the average measurement value across the entire time series that is plotted,
2. a continuous plot of the individual measurement values against specific time series coordinates, and
3. the demarcation of the most extreme range within which the individual measurements can fall and still be regarded as normal or as a randomized variation.

The statistic that is used to establish the normal range of variation is itself the source of some of the greatest variation between each of the different methods of control charting and can include standard deviations, standard error, or other statistical variance.

Any of the quality measurements accumulated from system logs to a performance history database can be plotted and analyzed to determine the consistency of the systematic batch production process throughput and contingent responsiveness of online host teleprocessing systems. This basically involves the tracking of measurements over time to determine when and why peak maximum and extreme minimum drop-offs occur. This kind of analysis combines a basic time series analysis within the specification of critical control limits that serve to monitor and regulate process quality and keep resource usage levels low.

DETERMINING CRITICAL DESCRIPTIVE SOFTWARE QUALITY CONTROL LIMITS

The most common type of control chart used for graphing the most basic descriptive statistics over time, or to show snapshots of the comparative descriptive statistics for several demographic classes or categories of data, involves *Box* control charts. These are also known as *cat whisker* control charts and involve an x-y coordinate plot with a continuous measurement along the y-axis and categorical grouping data segmented on the x-axis.

A vertical box is plotted for each categorical level or classification grouping, in order to show the range of normal variance, such as within 1.0, or up to 3.0 standard deviations, or within a particular value range that has been established as within an acceptable in-house or industry standard for that measurement. The box is overlaid against cat whiskers, or an I-bar line, extending beyond the top and bottom of the standard range box in order to show the most extreme minimum and maximum values of statistical *outliers*. These outlier values should not be ignored. Yet, they cannot be regarded as statistically significant values within the normal range of the distribution of values which occur within the box average for a given class or category.

This type of control chart is a quick way to compare the normal range of variation. In the case of a time series analysis, it is possible to quickly determine if there is a widening gap in extreme outlier cases which do not conform to the normal case or which are increasing outside the existing standards or methods of regulatory control. In the case of categorical or descriptive class comparisons, it is easy to quickly determine if there is any particular group that is harder to control or is more likely to have extreme variation than the other classes or categorical groupings.

Examples of Box control charts, for both a time series and categorical analysis, are shown in Figure 9-3.

MEASURING CRITICAL TRENDING LIMITS FOR SYSTEM MANAGEMENT CONTROL

Another type of control chart, known as a *Cumulative Sum* or *V-mask chart*, can be used as a standardized test to determine whether or not a process can be reasonably regarded as under control. In this test, "under control" is assumed to be within the bounds of what can be statistically regarded as a stable process. A stable process is subject to normal, random variation. It must be determined if the process has come under the influence of a particular independent variable, or group of variables, which are causing it to destabilize outside of the normal limits of the existing controls. This type of control chart, also known as an *arrow chart*, involves the x-y plotting of a measurement value on the y-axis, against a time series of values on the x-axis, with an overlay of a V-mask. A V-mask is more like an ">" pointing to future, as yet unplotted time series values extending to the right of an x-y plot. The "upper arm" and "lower arm" projected by the V-mask are projected backward statistically, based on a reverse geometric series of calculated values, which either contain or intersect a line plot of real-time series values.

If the plot of real values is contained within the ">" of calculated reverse geometric values, then the process can be considered as stable and within normal limits of variation and control. However, if the

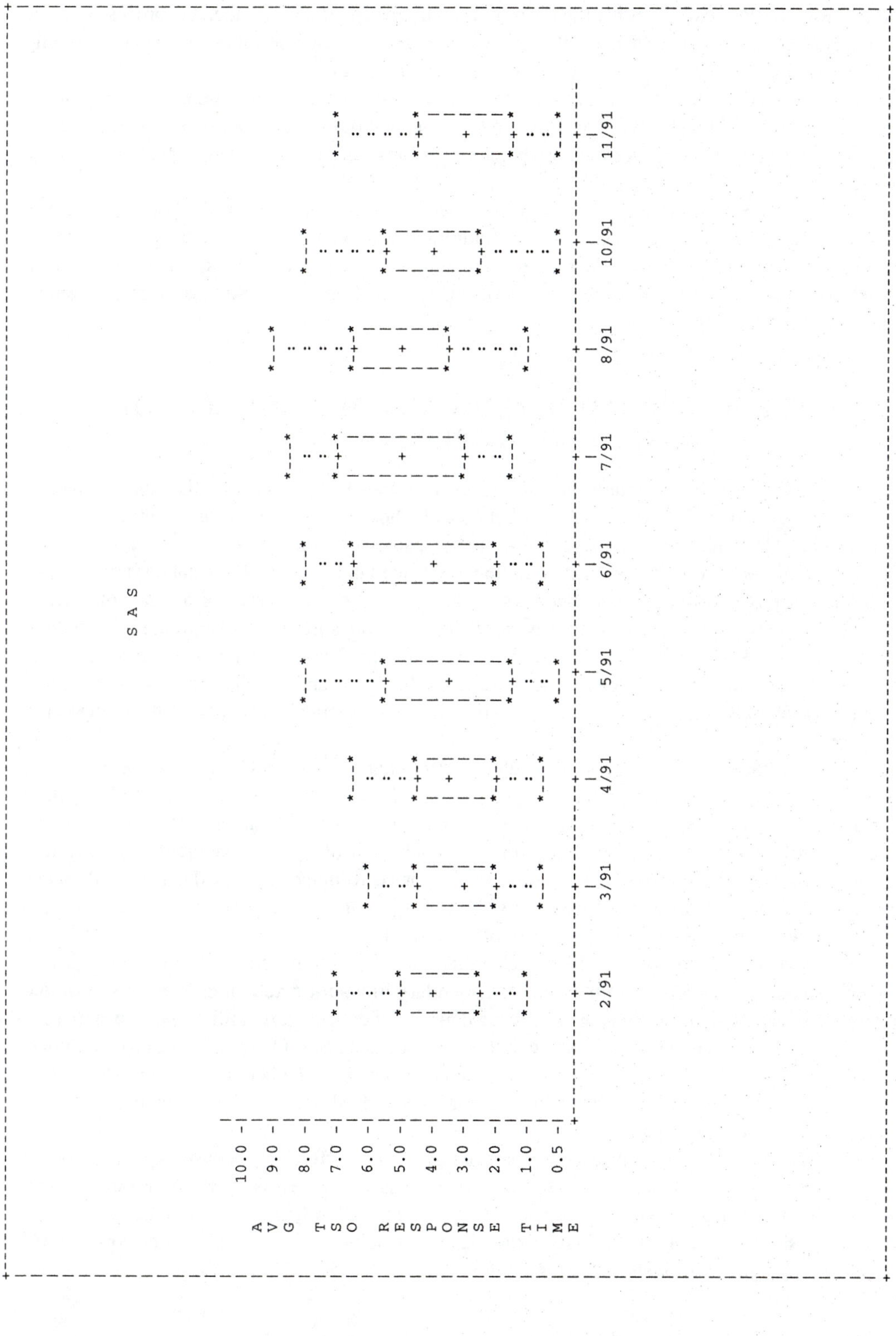

Figure 9-3   Example of a Box, or Cat Whiskers, Monthly Average Time Series Plot of Online Response Time Meaures

time series plotted values exceed either the top or bottom boundary of the ">," then the process must be considered as out of control, that is, unstable with regard to the existing control procedures or normally acceptable variation in the product or services which are being measured.

The severity of the destabilization condition is regarded as being directly proportional to the geometric area that exceeds the ">" boundary. Thus, a single spike outside of the boundary would be regarded as less critical than several peak values outside the boundary or peak values exceeding both arms of the ">" boundary.

Since the final value of the series is used as the geometric point of the ">," this method emphasizes a new critical exception to a process that has been traditionally stabilized and is often used as a critical exception reporting method signaling the need to begin monitoring a process which had previously been reasonably regarded as under control. Examples of this type of Cumulative Sum, or V-mask, control chart are shown in Figure 9-4.

CONTROL-DELIMITED THRESHOLD MANAGEMENT OF COMPUTER OPERATIONS

The most common type of control charts, *bar-delimited* or *middle-of-the-road*, actually consist of a large number of different types of specialized control charts, all showing the extreme and central statistical distribution value. This may include either a series of bars, such as in the case of −3, −2, −1, +1, +2, +3 standard deviations, or plotting of extreme delimiters only, as in the case of −4, +4 standard deviations.

The former case is known as *bar-delimited*, since the control chart consists of a series of vertical stripes, or bars, and the latter case is known as *middle-of-the-road*, since the two extreme lines and the central bar tend to look somewhat like the lines on a highway. In all cases, there is a central vertical bar in the center of the control chart which extends parallel to the x-axis and which measures the statistical variation from a central distribution statistic selected to indicate statistical normality for the group being measured.

Among some of the many types of bar-delimited control charts are: Cpk, Cp, 1/Cp, X, X-Bar, R, P, C, and U charts. Each of these specialized types of control charts involves normalized distribution statistics indicating specialized control conditions and types of variance which relate to particular types of process control problems. Each of these control charts makes use of data that is extracted from system log data organized as a time series in a software quality or performance history database and makes determinations of the normal range of variability. It is also possible to identify extreme peak system resource usage which should be further analyzed or monitored.

These control charts are most often used to track online sessions, or transaction response times, device wait, other resource-contention wait times, and the boundary limits for batch initiator classes or online queue staging types. Several of the specialized bar-delimited control charts utilize specific statistical methods, which can be used to further analyze outliers or special causes. Others involve cross-comparison of related measurement control charts and are used to determine whether effects are related and to obtain some indication of whether there are trade-offs which should be further analyzed before attempting new regulatory controls.

These control charts are commonly used to characterize critical differences between system resource users or categories of hardware devices and to detect critical changes in levels of system resource usage. The bar-delimited control charts are very similar to the types of monitoring involved in capacity planning, utilization analysis, and availability analysis. Examples of bar-delimited and middle-of-the-road control charts using system log data are shown in Figure 9-5.

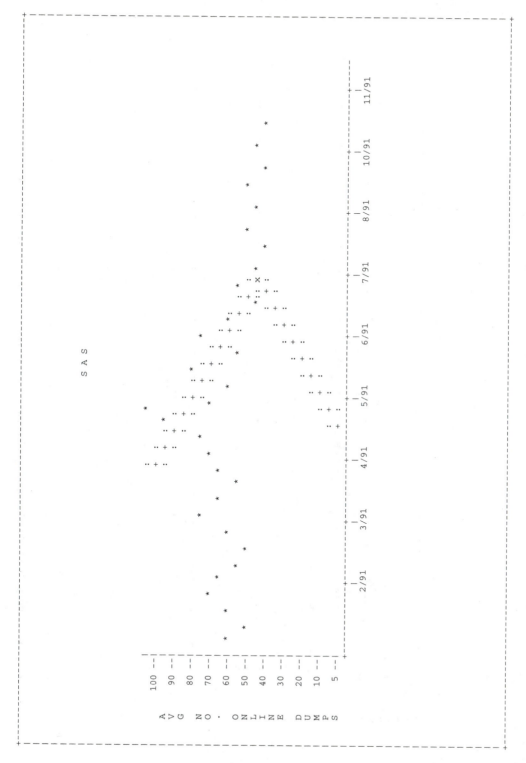

Figure 9-4 Example of a V-Mask Cumulative Sum Control Chart Time Series Plot of Number of Online Dumps

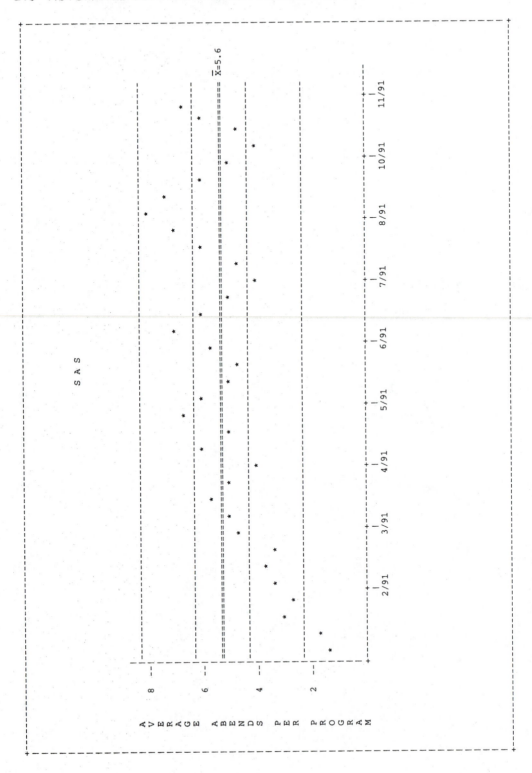

Figure 9-5 Example of a PROC SHEWHART Test for Special Causes Time Series Plot Average Abends per Program

MEASURING PRODUCTION OPERATIONS TO ACHIEVE SCALED EFFICIENCY

Once a control chart has determined whether a system resource or routine production process measurement is within normal control limits, it may be desirable to determine the relative trade-offs which need to be regulated in order to achieve the best mix of regulatory parameter values that will result in the optimum balance of resource usage variables.

One common example of this is the system regulatory control trade-offs between data-I/O buffer and CPU-region virtual paging space that is requested and allocated for particular programs. Batch jobs or sessions which have process characteristics that are particularly unusual for a given system environment may have to be adjusted significantly.

If control charts of the CPU paging or swaps, or the maximum available data buffer pools, show a characteristic peak value when a particular system, program, or database is active, then it may be necessary to adjust the competing values. This must be done according to the ratios or formulas for regulating the competing application software trade-off processes according to the SMF performance data and specifications in vendor manuals.

Another area where this kind of system control trade-off may become important is in the input and output buffer space allocated for network-attached, virtual terminal control. This is normally the case in fine-tuning *Virtual Terminal Access Method* (VTAM) tables according to IBM procedures and specifications. This is an area that is particularly well documented by IBM and can easily be regarded as more straightforward than the tuning of I/O buffer pools versus CPU region size. However, this becomes more complicated in the increasingly common environments that utilize multiprocessing or even parallel processors, as well as some level of advanced or automated CPU supervisory control (such as under the installation of MVS/ESA operating systems).

After identifying a significant control limit variance in the terminal I/O or network response time waits, it may be necessary to calculate the optimum trade-offs of I/O buffer pools based on a range of hypothetical data packets or I/O message size values. This is normally done by plotting the number and size of prospective buffers against the number and size of known terminal I/O message packets. These most often involve either two-dimensional region plots or three-dimensional contour plots which show the relative concentration of particular sizes or levels of data mask buffer pool space versus data packets or messages that easily fit into space allocated at a given level. This kind of plot not only gives a representation that explains the current situation or control condition, but also gives an indication of how much better or worse the situation is likely to become as either of the two or three interrelated process trade-off values are increased or decreased.

Examples of such region plot and contour plot graphical representations of a fine-tuning regulatory control problem are shown in Figure 9-6.

MANAGING LIMITED PRODUCTION TO ACHIEVE SPECIAL PROCESS FUNCTION

One of the most common examples of a limited production process involving a specialized function is the program testing that is commonly performed before a new application is approved. The amount of testing needed and related test resource usage is not easily predicted. The number of times that the new application program or changes to a program may need to be tested is a highly variable situation. This is often based on factors such as the relative experience of the application programmer, contention for resources available

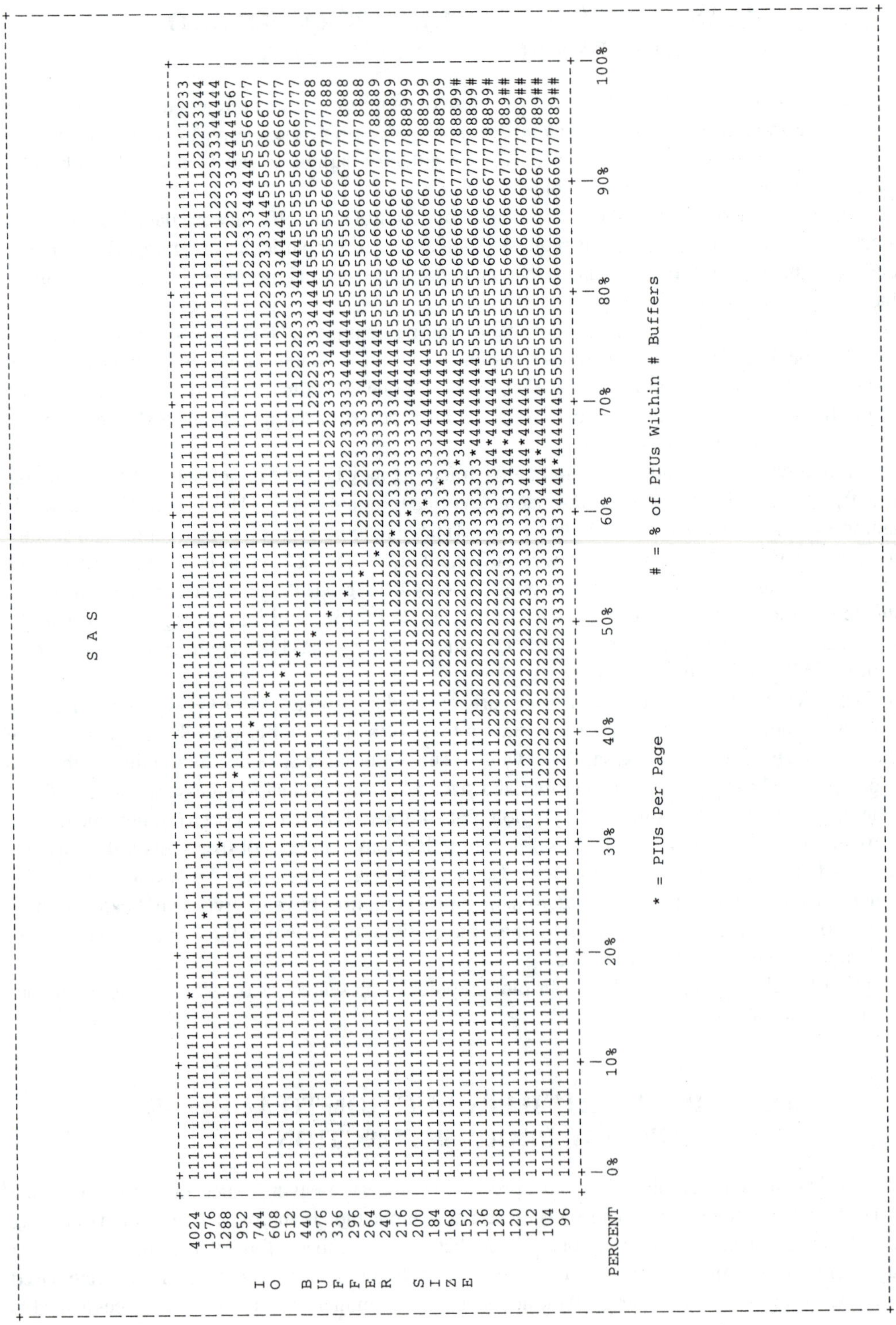

Figure 9-6   Example of a Contour Plot Demonstrating the Optimum Performance Surface for Number of I/O Buffers

for the testing, the standards and procedures of an individual data center, and the application area involved in the system development project. However, if there is sufficient historical performance data available about past testing in individual application development areas, there should be some basis for estimating test resource demands within particular ranges and within particular time periods.

This assumes that project management and programmer task scheduling data are available as starting points for each block of projected resource usage, along with reliability data indicating whether testing activities are likely to begin and end on given dates. Another requirement is that the system development process can be characterized by specific test resource usage levels that correspond to a routine and structured system development life cycle methodology, with emphasis placed on *ramped* or *staged* levels of manpower and support staff specialization, which test system-related functions at points in time relative to project scheduling dates.

Control charts can be used in combination with system log data segmented by appropriate job accounts. Both help identify those testing activities that do not fall within the normal range, whether compared to the rest of the programs tested as part of a particular project or as a whole compared to related system development projects for a specific customer or application area, these extreme outlier cases can be audited or further analyzed to determine why they are requiring either more extensive or less rigorous test time and resources. This can suggest that the related programs be treated differently when they are first implemented into production or else that increased testing or delay implementation is needed if system log data cross-checks indicate a high-level of test program abend failures and high usage. The use of control charts to indicate progress or potential problems in the system development process is especially beneficial.

MEASURING *AD HOC* WORKLOADS FOR STANDARDIZING NONCONVENTIONAL TASKS

Control charts are similarly used in the analysis of limited production as it relates to *ad hoc* reporting environments or segmented portions of a system environment in which surplus or underutilized resources are available for *ad hoc* usage by internal business customers. This type of workload becomes particularly important in being able to monitor and control resources at a level that makes underutilized system resources available to external service bureaus.

Whereas test system resource usage is commonly monitored using bar-delimited control charts, this is not normally possible in tracking nonconventional *ad hoc* resource usage. With the exception of clearly stepped and seasonal system resource demands, most *ad hoc* system resource usage cannot by definition be forecast with the same reliability as production system resources or even test system resources.

Although it is possible to control access to *ad hoc* resources at predetermined levels, for the most part it is much more common to use V-chart or Cumulative Sum control charts to track nonconventional, *ad hoc* resource usage. The most important objective in this case is to detect a major shift in the level of demand for and availability of the surplus resources. This is done in order to make tactical changes in regulatory parameters and configuration controls, before there is any undesirable impact upon the normally more critical production system resources.

10

VENDOR PRODUCTS TO CONTROL SOFTWARE QUALITY

One of the most common uses of control charts in the analysis of software quality involves measuring the incidence of program abends or system failures occurring in particular application system environments or even in individual software programs within the system environment. In this case, the statistical distribution of the number of program abends within particular categories of software failures is plotted over time, within the constraints of the control limits defined by standards of minimum acceptable performance. Or, they can be plotted against average defect densities for a particular application system or group of application systems, such as in the support of a particular customer business area or function.

The system log data in the historical performance database normally includes abend error and problem condition codes. These can be counted and grouped by severity so a series of control charts can be generated which graph changes in failure rates for individual programs or entire system workload environments. Most of the automated quality measurement and performance history database management products have special tools and facilities for extracting and maintaining separate historical dataset records. These are kept in the form of time series as needed for generation of control charts. Several even provide control charting facilities as well.

In such cases, any of the three major types of control charts, including box charts, V-mask charts, or bar-delimited control charts, can be used relative to the type of desired information in each problem detection or service-level monitoring situation. These charts can easily be placed into a routinely scheduled production batch job in order to automatically generate software quality measurement plots characterizing the overall systems environment as well as red flag software products or programs. SAS Institute has several products supporting these software quality measurements, such as SAS/*Operations Research* (OR) and SAS/*Econometric Time Series* (ETS). But SAS/QC is particularly useful in this regard.

VENDOR STATISTICAL QUALITY CONTROL
REPORTING PRODUCT: SAS/QC

The SAS Institute vendor offers a statistical quality control analysis and reporting product that supports basic and specialized control charting methods on the IBM host mainframe, PC/DOS, and OS/2 PC workstations, as well as UNIX workstations. SAS/QC software, a key component of the *SAS System for Quality Improvement*, offers a variety of specialized tools for quality management. A wealth of tools is included for establishing statistical quality control and reducing variability. A complete, full-screen environment is provided for producing Shewhart charts, performing process capability analysis, and pinpointing manufacturing problems with Pareto and Ishikawa diagrams. Complete online help and an online tutorial are included.

For quality engineering applications, a complete environment for designing and analyzing industrial experiments is also included. A variety of designs can be constructed, including two-level factorial, response surface, orthogonal array, and mixture designs. Facilities are also included for Taguchi and QFD applications, providing ready access to state-of-the-art techniques. Even users with limited statistical training can get results quickly. An introductory tutorial and extensive help features provide an excellent way to learn about experimental design and analysis.

The output from SAS/QC software can be viewed interactively or saved for standard compliant archival. It is designed with impressive capabilities for color-coding quality dimensions to aid in rapid SQM anaysis, and the colors of the output can put new life in TQM analysis sessions or presentations.

The cost of the SAS/QC host-based product varies from about $2,000 up to about $20,000, depending on the size of the data center installation and if there are other SAS Institute products on site. Cost of the PC versions vary from about $500 per workstation to less than $100 per workstation, depending on the number of copies of SAS/QC for the PC licensed at a particular work site. Examples of SAS/QC facilities are shown in Figures 10-1a to 10-1d.

VENDOR STATISTICAL PROCESS CONTROL
REPORTING PRODUCT: SPC-PC

All of the specialized control charts and descriptive statistical methods are available for graphical analysis on a PC workstation by the *Statistical Process Control for the PC* (SPC-PC) software product line developed and marketed by Quality America, Inc. of Tucson, Arizona. Demonstration demo disks are available for the product series for the PC-DOS and Microsoft Windows environments. The product covers the statistical process control charts and descriptive statistics described in this chapter, as well as the widest variety of advanced TQM process analysis tools available in any TQM or SPC professional's toolkit to date. Although it is the only PC product highlighted in this book, it is a "host-friendly" product easily adapted to SMF-based ASQM programs.

The SPC-PC product line can receive downloaded ASCII files or input from a variety of spreadsheet formats. Although the SPC-PC toolkits are limited to PC workstations, they support programmer workstation configurations such as Texas Instruments IEF, Knowledgeware IEW, and the Microfocus COBOL platform in a complementary fashion. SPC-PC truly links software engineering to automated software quality metrics in ways that bring to mind visions of the distributed networked platform software factories of the future. SPC-PC easily supports most of the more advanced statistical process control and total quality management methodologies, such as automated generation of Ishikawa "Fishbone" Cause-

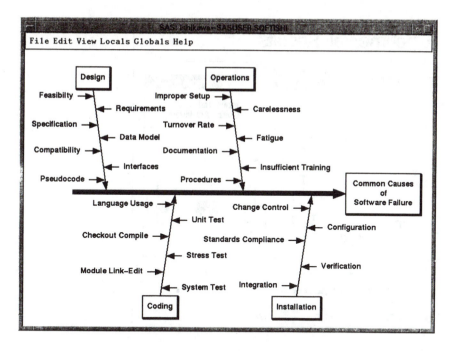

Figure 10-1a   SAS/QC Ishikawa Cause-and-Effect Chart for Software Errors

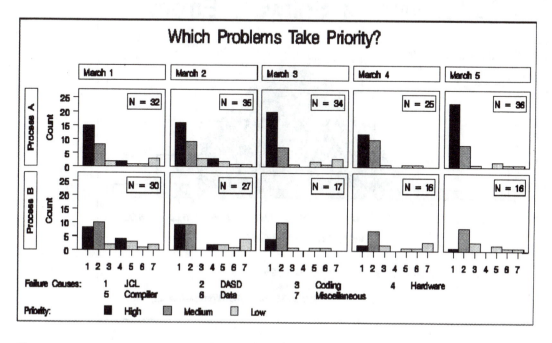

Figure 10-1b   SAS/QC Pareto Ranking of Dominant Software Error Causes

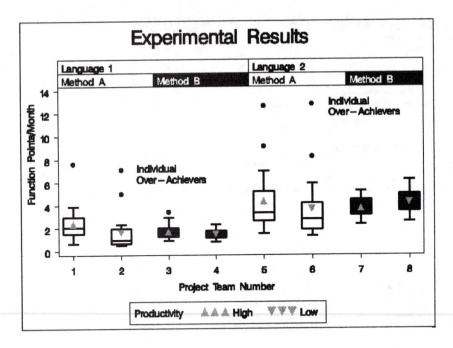

Figure 10-1c   SAS/QC Box, or Cat Whiskers, Plot of Software Productivity by Language

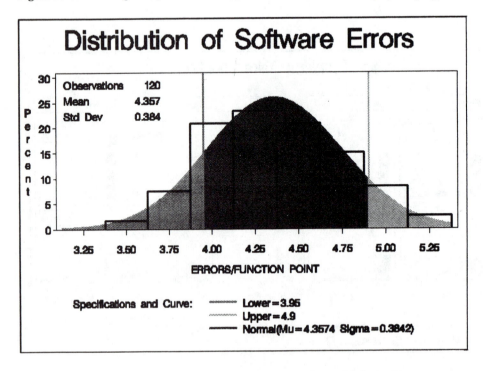

Figure 10-1d   SAS/QC Normalized Distribution Capability Chart of Software Errors

and-Effect diagrams, *Quality Function Deployment* (QFD) matrix methods, and Functional Process Control Flow diagrams, which are not as easily supported by any major, host-based software quality metrics product (including SAS/QC).

The complete SPC-PC product family includes SPC-PC EZ, menu selections generate X-Bar and R, X-Bar and Sigma, U, C, P, and Np control charts, Pareto analysis, histograms, and capability analysis; SPC-PC II and SPC-PC III, which are both increasingly advanced toolkits for PC-DOS environments and include all the functions of SPC-PC EZ, plus multivariate analysis, cumulative sum charts, regression analysis, scatterplots, and moving average by range and sigma; and SPC-PC IV-Windows and SPC-PC Advanced IV-Windows, the corresponding versions for Microsoft Windows environment and the most compatible with the more advanced software engineering workstations and programmer productivity platform environments. The costs range from just over $500 for the first workstation license for SPC-PC EZ, to several thousand dollars for unlimited site licenses across LAN workstation networks. Examples of some of the many SPC-PC software quality measurement analysis facilities and reports are shown in Figures 10-2a to 10-2d. The demo evaluation diskettes can be obtained from Quality America, as listed in Appendix B.

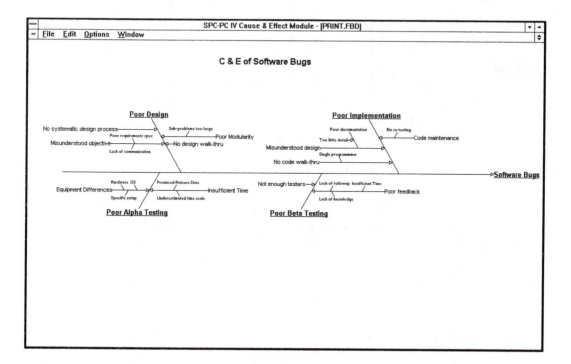

Figure 10-2a   SPC-PC Cause-and-Effect Chart of Software "Bug" Introduction

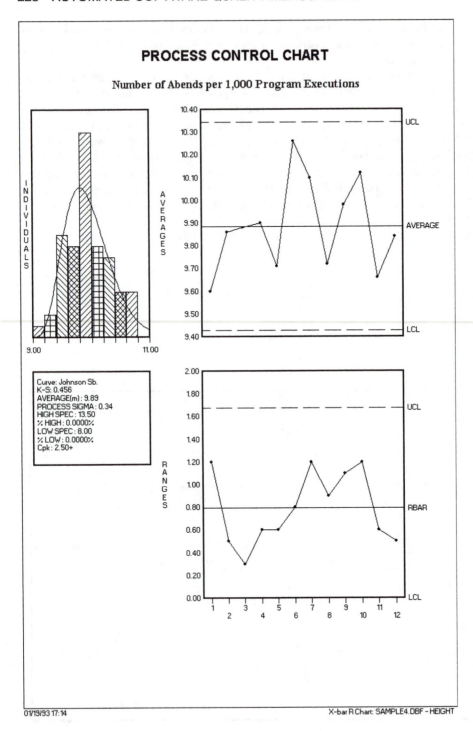

Figure 10-2b SPC/PC Control Chart of Errors by Software Process Rate

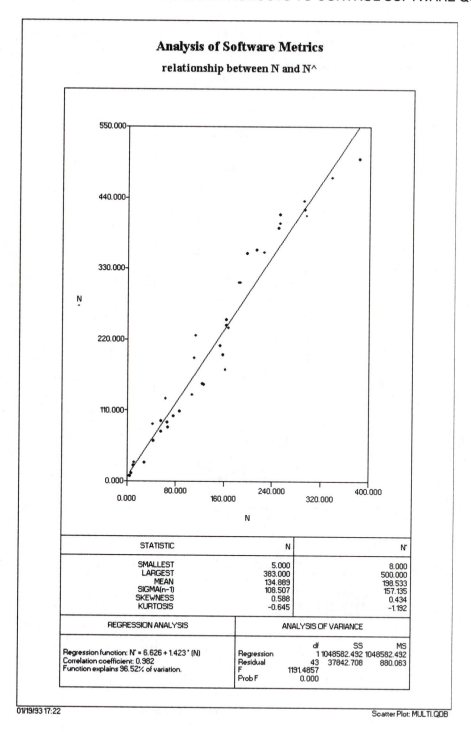

Figure 10-2c SPC/PC Regression Analysis of Software Metric Productivity Factor

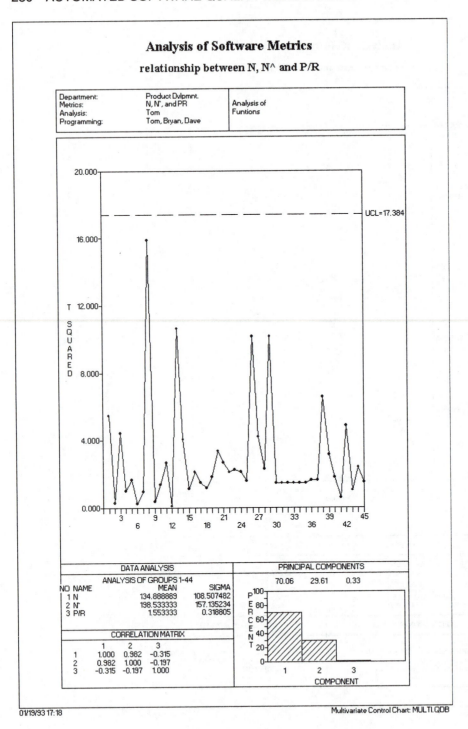

Figure 10-2d   SPC/PC Principal Component Correlation Analysis of Software Metric Factors

11

VALUING SOFTWARE IN
YOUR IN-HOUSE
SYSTEM INVENTORY

Determining the value of in-house software can be a very subjective and time-consuming task. If your data center is in the business of selling software as a vendor, software value is a pricing issue that will vary based on consumer demand.

The value of software developed in house for internal business use may be impacted by vendor markets for similar applications and the pervasive influence of new technology. But since a portion of such in-house software may be custom designed and usable only by the business that developed it, the value of an in-house inventory is more often determined by factors such as original cost to process or maintain.

Ultimately, value is determined by how much the product contributes to profitability or other organizational goals versus the cost to enhance or redevelop the system to take advantage of new technology or to replace it with software purchased from a vendor. Depending on the availability of technology such as CASE program generators or SQL database tools, and the in-house expertise to use them, the value of existing software may be greater than the cost of a full replacement. In such cases, selective enhancement can be justified to improve a capital facility. In the future, such evaluation may be similar to real estate appraisal. In the meantime, software metric estimators can provide the best guidelines. This chapter will cover how value can be estimated automatically based on system logs.

HISTORICAL PERSPECTIVE OF VALUING AND
PRICING IN-HOUSE SOFTWARE

In the early days of data processing, most application software systems were developed within academic environments, because mainframe systems were so expensive that only a few business organizations could afford them. Universities and government organizations developed most of the software because early applications were the result of R&D efforts supported by public funds. In fact, even after IBM, DEC, and other major mainframe vendors had made their systems affordable, and many business

231

organizations had their own software development departments, most of the utility or specialized system support functions were obtained from major university or government organizations. A large number of such products were adopted from the public domain by IBM, DEC, and the others, improved upon and made available as part of their standard maintenance support agreements or for a nominal fee.

The software that originated in universities, other public funding institutions, or vendor user groups were either placed in public domain, licensed, or even sold outright for an administrative fee. There was rarely any attempt to recover the costs of programmer labor or system test resources as part of the pricing of such software products.

One example of this pricing philosophy was the SAS-based MXG system log management product, which was originally priced and continues to be marketed at a relatively nominal cost to data center customers, reflecting the low cost of system development and test resources available in academic and research development environments. Although Dr. Barry Merrill, who developed MXG, was under no obligation to follow this philosophy, MXG pricing is typical of such thinking.

The reason for this philosophy relates to the belief that software developed by vendor user groups, universities, or other public institutions are public domain and equal property of all citizens or organizations within the country, since their combined revenues have contributed to the development of the software. In some cases, this provision was even included in contracts or directives to develop software at public expense.

Since then, especially in the military systems sector, the government retains the option to sell or license software developed at public expense. This is done in order to recover development costs or fully pay back the government for funding the costs of system development. The main advantage to private firms developing such software was that they would have an assured early market for the software; the main advantage to the government was that they were able to share in some of the public market revenues generated by software after expensive research and development costs were completed, and economies of scale made it possible to generate greater revenues.

This arrangement reflects the trend to manage the government like a business, which is mutually beneficial to the taxpayers as well as the software vendors. However, it has raised the costs businesses must pay for commercial software.

This trend continued even as the mainframe systems hardware costs dropped and as intelligent workstation CASE tools and methods provided greater leverage of programmer labor costs. This has resulted in higher costs for commercial software developed with the assistance of public funds.

The rising cost of programmer labor has also served to raise the prices of privately developed software. As IBM and other hardware, as well as commercial software, vendors developed new application systems using their own programmers and system test resources, it became necessary for them to recover their development costs with prices higher than those available for modified public domain products.

Although there was a relatively short period in the early 1980s when software vendors were able to "name their own price," the "boom" in computer software, which involved customer willingness to pay almost any price, was quickly normalized by the rise in competition. Such competitive forces caused the prices for most computer software to be reduced to near the actual cost of software development, and by the late 1980s competition in the commercial software industry had become so intense that a major effort was underway to greatly reduce development costs as well.

These trends have placed the full burden of commercial software costs with the individual customer. Although many businesses were buying off-the-shelf software at high prices in the early 1980s, by the next decade most commercial business software was either developed or procured according to precise internal customer specifications by in-house data center staff.

In addition, business customers have become increasingly knowledgeable and demanding as to the price performance of the software they pay for. This includes both a greater emphasis upon the quality and the functional business value of the software that they buy and operate to support their business.

Traditional business analysis methods are being applied more rigorously than ever before in decision making related to *fix, build, or buy* methods to meet software needs. Increasingly, this analysis involves EDP audit-quality system resource usage, transfer pricing, and direct costing data based on analysis of SMF and other software measurement logs. As this happens, the data center business analysis becomes more and more precise.

MEDIATING INFLUENCES THAT ADJUST THE VALUE OF SOFTWARE

Ultimately, the value of any software program is related to the resulting corporate advantage. This may involve support to the sustained cash flow or profits of a business operation or the performance of functional objectives of a public organization.

This value is determined based upon the same evaluation criteria used in any business management assessment. This involves a wide variety of business factors, ranging from the investment costs of obtaining the software to the operating costs of using the software after it has been fully integrated into the data center systems environment and functional business user areas. For the most part, operating costs can be taken directly from the data center chargeback, transfer pricing, or other cost allocation system and supported by resource usage activity. However, investing in the various options of obtaining and financing ongoing support may involve a financial analysis that takes into account the nature of the pertinent business operations and the impact it could have on that organization's revenue. This must involve some integration of the system resource usage and software performance history data related to any existing systems currently providing support to the business function along with financial projections of future costs as they relate to the potential benefits of business operations.

This analysis is simplified substantially if functional business unit costs and benefits of existing software, as well as benchmark estimates of competitive or industry leader costs, have been calculated and are automatically updated to a data center software performance database. It is also easier if risk related costs of existing software, and related labor-intensive terminal data entry or technical support procedures, are quantified and stored with system reliability and dependability databases. However, regardless of the availability of data center operation expense pools and system log-based software performance history data, it is necessary to provide estimates of the long-term impact of any software change or new software acquisition on the performance of the existing data center environment as well as the efficiency of the customer business operations.

In many cases, particular software programs may be a requirement in order to operate the business. In the case of highly proprietary business functions, the value of the software is determined exclusively by the business trade-offs of having or not having a particular level of software capability.

IMPORTANCE OF PROPRIETARY INFLUENCES
UPON VALUE OF SOFTWARE

The value of any software product must be determined by the level of importance that its customers place upon both its functional capabilities and performance quality. These are factors which must be determined by each organization as part of their own internal strategic business planning and management objectives. The increasing opportunity for new informational technology to provide a competitive edge, or even a necessary tactical hold, in a tightening business market can heighten the importance of the valuation of software as it impacts future business growth and even survival.

The effectiveness of software valuation and the estimation of system operational costs must be based upon historical performance data as well as real-time data that is precise and up-to-the-minute.

Since there is rarely commercially available software for most proprietary business functions, software valuations of this type must be based upon benchmark comparison methods which involve data from internal sources. This usually involves *Value Engineering* (VE) or *Quality Function Deployment* (QFD) techniques, which are commonly part of TQM initiatives.

These techniques involve a standardized process, which is undertaken by a data center in order to analyze and document every function and internal operational process, and then each functional operation is measured with a precision that can only be reliably performed in an automated fashion by the computer itself in the form of SMF or other similar system log data. The VE and QFD techniques then assign direct process unit costs and quality cost benefits to each step in a function or process. TQM methods are then used to determine if the process can be made more efficient by introducing an alternative procedure or sequence of process steps.

All of the available options for optimizing the performance or quality of the business process can be used as a basis for determining strategic benefit relative to the competition and the organization's long-term objectives. When VE and QFD techniques are used in combination with automated software quality measurements and system log-based performance history data, the proprietary business benefits and potential risks can be accurately predicted in a manner that provides a useful basis for comparative valuation of alternatives for obtaining and supporting proprietary application software.

Basically, these procedures involve creating another dimension to the system resource cost pool allocation or chargeback billing and transfer pricing matrix. There are a number of PC workstation–based spreadsheets, as well as SAS-based host spreadsheets and host relational database products, which can be linked in 3-D in order to support such analysis. The products covered in Chapter 5 are particularly useful here.

RELATIONSHIP OF VALUE TO FINANCING OF
SOFTWARE ACQUISITIONS

Essentially, financing of any capital acquisition involves the analysis of potential *Return on Investment* (ROI), relative to the risk that any potential ROI will be fully achieved. In the case of pricing-based valuations, the risk is calculated in the form of the statistical probabilities that levels of market potential can be achieved within specific time frames in order to recover levels of incremental investment and ongoing costs. This is relative to the trade-offs of comparative software product alternatives in terms of business profitability and quality objectives. In the case of proprietary valuations, risk is calculated based upon the potential strategic market dominance that can be achieved by particular proprietary software solutions relative to nonproprietary commercial software alternatives and the overall nature of the business sector that is involved.

In other words, financing of software acquisitions involves an internal financial analysis by data center financial control analysts in order to determine the economic justification for either borrowing funds or committing to service-level agreement to provide data center access to a prospective business customer over a long term. This analysis can have very significant impact on the long-term viability of the data center operation; and due to the rising cost of programmer and technical support labor related to routine data center operations, this type of financial feasibility analysis is becoming just as important, if not more important, than traditional system hardware capacity planning.

The impact of each software acquisition upon long-term data center operations and technical support costs must be monitored on an ongoing basis using management accounting reports. Much of this type of data can be provided by consolidating project management history data with the software performance database based on system logs.

Another consideration that can be addressed by system logs is the statistical risk assessment of particular key financial ratios and assumptions which must be substantiated in order to justify a software development project or commercial software purchase. To a large degree, this can be supported by existing system performance history and comparable existing system reliability and dependability data, along with competitor and industry leader benchmark process unit cost estimates, as were discussed in Chapter 7.

The SMF-based software performance history data, as well as individual software program execution *snapshots* and benchmark analysis utility programs, can provide important substantiation to support software *fix, build, or buy* decisions. This should include a *what-if* procedure for automatically linking SMF-based software baseline measurements to financial ratios and forecasting of system resource cost impact projections.

FUNCTIONALITY AND USE OF SOFTWARE SIZE METRICS TO ASSIGN VALUE

One of the most important ways to assign realistic valuation to a software product is to determine internal transfer pricing impact estimates of the relative costs to develop functionally equivalent application software. Said software would be of comparable size, complexity, and quality, and its value would be based upon past data center system development project performance history and performance characteristics of similar existing in-house software products. This involves more of an emphasis upon the aggregate size and complexity of all the programs comprising a software product, rather than the previous emphasis on comparative analysis of the detailed process unit costs and comparative quality trade-offs of particular functional process steps. But this level of estimation is normally more suitable to decisions that lean more heavily toward proprietary in-house software development decisions, rather than situations that will probably involve a software purchase. The proprietary software development alternatives must be estimated and compared using conventional productivity analysis and system life-cycle manpower support buildup indexes or ratios as were discussed in Chapter 7.

One of the easiest ways to assign valuation by comparing relative costs and time frames to deliver equivalent aggregate size and complexity of competing proprietary software alternatives is based upon comparative estimates of function points to develop or enhance in-house software applications, relative to commercially marketed vendor software. This is very easy if there is a significant in-house software inventory which has been measured using manual function point calculation procedures.

It is arguably preferable to automate the scanning and calculation of function point estimates based on lines of sourcecode, using the SPR backfire method. Backfire method estimates have been shown to be consistently within 15 percent of the manual function point estimates, at less than 10 percent of the manual function point data collection labor costs.

Examples of SMF system log record types and variables that can be used in order to estimate software size and complexity have been covered in Chapter 5.

THE TABLE-OF-ELEMENTS MODEL OF ASSIGNING VALUE BASED ON LANGUAGE

By using the backfire method, in combination with one or more of the automated software size scanning techniques for estimating function points using SMF system logs, the effort and costs to inventory and the value of in-house software inventories can be greatly reduced. When used in combination with procedures to spot-check and calibrate the automated function point estimates, there is usually no significant reduction in accuracy of the function point counts obtained at greatly reduced costs.

The backfire method also involves the SPR proposal that the function point estimation language leverage ratios are comparable to a "table of elements" in chemistry. Each new language and technology that is developed in the future can be added to the "table of programming language elements," along with characteristic valuation and productivity estimation ratios and leverage factors used to calibrate or adjust estimates for a particular software module up or down based on the statistical characteristics describing the manner in which the language was used in the program. These estimates can then be used to generate comparative application software valuation based on relative internal data center costs or for comparison to "out source" vendor development service costs. An example of the table-of-elements schema proposed by Capers Jones for general function point sizing based on language conversion factor weights was covered earlier in Chapter 5.

AUTOMATED METHODS OF COLLECTING AND UPDATING SOFTWARE INVENTORIES

As was discussed in Chapter 5, automated scans of sourcecode library *partition dataset* (PDS) directories can be used in order to reliably estimate the function points in extensive software inventories, especially if the estimates are calibrated by weighted adjustments based on randomized spot-check manual function point calculations by language and customer functional application area. It is also possible to automatically scan and estimate function points in individual software programs using similar methods based on SMF-based capture of the number of SYSIN records read into compilers that create load modules or the number of SYSIN records read into a Fourth-Generation Language or program interpreter such as the SAS language product.

These approaches are based on application of automated counting of *lines-of-code* (LOC) in program sourcecode module files within partition dataset libraries, using the backfire method, industry-tested calibration ratio equivalents for each major programming language, and data center–specific weights and calibration ratios corresponding to the sourcecode format and internal comment documentation standards. Basically, the greater the rigor of the in-house system development standards for coding and documenting software, the greater the accuracy of the automated function point calculation estimates based on SMF data.

The accuracy of the estimates may also vary somewhat based on the conformity of the in-house programming staff to DP industry standards and practices for each particular programming language. The language-leverage ratios and statement-based function point estimation equivalents determined by Capers Jones and other researchers to best match common language coding practices are nonetheless entirely sufficient for most inventory and valuation by conventional data centers sensitive to rising labor costs. Although there are as many definitions and conventions as to what constitutes a single sourcecode statement as there are methods of manually calculating function points, the automated estimations based upon SMF log data or scans of PDS library directories are accurate enough for most conventional data centers. Estimates should be routinely validated and calibrated using manual calculation or spot-checks based upon an automated parsing scan product such as Q/AUDITOR. This is especially true in large data centers where the cost of technical support manpower to manually collect function point counts may be prohibitive, while an automated procedure using SMF-based line counts and the backfire method can assign reasonable valuation for thousands of programs in less time and cost than may be required to manually measure just one.

It is equally important to update program inventories, as well as changes in software valuations, on an automated basis. This includes both the automated scanning to identify new programs compiled or added to production sourcecode libraries and changes in benchmark unit costs, productivity conversion factors, and rates used for calculations.

An example of an automated inventory report based on SMF system logs and using the backfire method to estimate function point value is shown in Figures 11-1 through 11-3. This report rates actual development cost versus average commercial vendor benchmark cost.

CAPITAL PROPERTY IMPROVEMENT MODELS
BASED ON REAL ESTATE

In a large sense, the valuations and changes in valuations for in-house software inventories can be automatically assigned and managed in a manner that is very similar to the methods used by real estate analysts to appraise and manage changes in the valuation of capital properties. In fact, there is an increasing need for this approach due to an ongoing trend made necessary by tax regulations related to the development and acquisition of computer software.

There are indications that software valuation appraisers may be trained and licensed like real estate appraisers in the future. Although most of the software valuation methods can probably be automated, the differences between the alternative methods will focus on the best tax advantages relative to whether proprietary software is developed anew or if it involves sourcecode reuse, program generator technology, or a discrete improvement to a particular program. These considerations will make it all the more important to consistently classify and value in-house proprietary software in an automated manner, in order to obtain the fastest possible measurement of discrete changes in large inventories.

There is still some flexibility in the manner in which the government tax agencies allow application software inventories either to be expensed or amortized over their useful system life cycle; however, it is increasingly clear that this may not always be the case. Although many of the manual and automated techniques of measurement and inventory are equally new and controversial within the agencies responsible for ruling on the various tax codes, the Big-6 accounting firms increasingly indicate that

```
REPORT ASQ00221:  WEEKLY COMMERCIAL BATCH << PROGRAM DELIVERY ACTIVITY >> DEVELOPMENT LIBS UPDATE LOG < WEEK ENDING 10/19/92 >
                                          ABC MGMT=VP1    :DIR1    :MGR1
```

OBS	SYSTEM NAME	PROGRAM MODULE	LANGUAGE TYPE	SYSTEM DESCRIPTION	DATE UPDATED	PROGRAMS DELIVERED	CHANGES TO PGM	TOTAL STATEMENTS	ESTIMATED FUNC PTS	EST TOTAL 1991 VALUE
12	AAP	AAP107	PL/1	ACCT ACTIVITY PROCESS	10/16/92	1	115	4,482	63	$75,752
13	AAP	AAP003	COBOL	ACCT ACTIVITY PROCESS	10/12/92	1	26	4,073	39	$46,549
14	AAP	AAP111	COBOL	ACCT ACTIVITY PROCESS	10/13/92	1	79	2,650	25	$30,286
15	AAP	AAP029	PL/1	ACCT ACTIVITY PROCESS	10/13/92	1	23	622	9	$10,513
16	AAP	AAP035	ASMB	ACCT ACTIVITY PROCESS	10/18/92	1	47	1,723	8	$9,707
17	BRP	BRP00902	ASMB	BACKUP RECOVER PROCESS	10/14/92	1	15	541	3	$3,048
18	BRP	BRP00901	ASMB	BACKUP RECOVER PROCESS	10/16/92	1	52	475	2	$2,676

Figure 11-1   Sample SMF-Based Weekly In-house Software Program Inventory Update and Current Valuation Estimates

```
** MOST CURRENT VERSION OF ALL ABC APPLICATION PROGRAMS RESIDING IN BOTH PROD AND TEST DEVELOPMENT PDSLIB SORTED BY NAME **
```

OBS	SYSTEM NAME	DESCRIPTION	TOTAL PGMS	PROGRAM CHANGES TO DATE	NUMBER OF SOURCECODE STATEMENTS	NUMBER OF ESTIMATED FUNC PNTS	EST ORIGINAL DEVELOPMENT FP-BASE COST	EST 1991 $$ FUNC PT COST ABC REWRITE	EST EXTERNAL REWRITE COST IN 1991 $$
1	AAA1XXX	AUTO ACCT ACTION PROCESS	156	5,655	149,685	2,090	$1,068,156	$1,276,589	$2,508,034
2	AAB1XXX	AUTO ACCTG BALANCE PROCS	17	1,144	18,941	267	$135,788	$162,946	$320,130
3	AAC1XXX	AUTO ACTIVITY CNTL PROCS	1	4	833	12	$5,972	$7,166	$14,079
4	AAD1XXX	AUTO AREA DIST PROCESS	3	210	3,898	51	$26,123	$31,347	$61,586
5	AAE1XXX	AUTO ACCT DISB PROCESS	10	29	3,377	48	$24,435	$29,052	$57,076
6	BAA1XXX	BANK AUTO ASSIGN PROCESS	25	545	12,758	195	$91,632	$118,966	$233,726
7	BAB1XXX	BALANCE ACTUAL BOOKINGS	10	220	7,128	100	$51,101	$61,321	$120,473
8	BAC1XXX	BREAKEVEN ACTION CNTL	25	39	12,374	58	$29,761	$35,484	$69,713
9	BAD1XXX	BENEFIT ASSIGN DEC SYS	164	3,155	91,210	1,288	$653,931	$786,851	$1,545,876

Figure 11-2   Sample SMF-Based Automated Accumulated In-house Software Application System Product Valuation Summary

		FUNCTION PTS		PROGRAMS		STATEMENTS		CHANGES	
		SUM	%	SUM	%	SUM	%	SUM	%
SYSTEM	LANGUAGE								
JJJ1XXX	ASMB	16	100	4	100	3424	100	31	100
	ALL	16	100	4	100	3424	100	31	100
KKK1XXX	LANGUAGE								
	PL/1	349	100	72	100	24808	100	1162	100
	ALL	349	100	72	100	24808	100	1162	100

Figure 11-3   Sample SMF-Based Software Program Inventory and System Development Productivity Reporting Using SPR Method

software inventory value estimations and adjustments based on data center transfer pricing and cost pool allocations are going to be the safest option in the long term, relative to exclusive reliance upon manual inventory and valuations based on manual function point calculations. Although some manual function point counting for calibration and verification may be necessary, it is increasingly likely that this will be an external auditor task, and most of the internal function point counting and related software valuation will be performed by EDP audit-quality automated procedures such as Q/AUDITOR, PDS directory scans, or automated software sizing estimation based on SYSIN record counts in SMF.

Regardless of the automated method used, it is critical that the information be timely and consistently calculated, in a manner that can be reproduced, or globally changed, in the event of major year-to-year changes in the tax regulations concerning proprietary in-house computer application software inventories. Equally important will be the ability to archive and audit past methods of software valuation, regardless of whether it involved in-house data center development expenses or vendor product purchase.

TYING AUTOMATED SOFTWARE VALUATIONS TO LIFE-CYCLE DECISION MAKING

Once an automated system for inventory and valuation of all in-house data center production of application software has been implemented, it is possible to accumulate in-house software inventory history in a database which can be linked to system development project planning and scheduling databases or reporting. This will support the entire life cycle of mission-critical data center application systems and can include both the estimation of comparative costs of proprietary software as well as analysis of alternatives for enhancement or consolidation of application software that share some common functional or procedural characteristics.

Value Engineering and Quality Function Deployment analysis can also be automated to some extent, if sufficient data models and corporate enterprise meta-data as well as functional business process models have been defined in a machine-readable manner and are accessible to interface with the automated software inventory and program valuation reporting. This capability depends on the commitment of the data center and its customers to TQM procedures and the availability of a corporate data model repository or an in-house data dictionary.

To some extent, SMF system log data can be used in order to automatically build cross-references of system resources and dataset interrelationships, as well as corporate meta-data and enterprise process relationship models, based on SMF job account activity in combination with SMF dataset access activity records. To an extent, SMF can also be used in order to automatically populate and update a data dictionary or system repository with critical software profile descriptors, as well as performance and quality statistics and the relationships between key application system resources.

These relationships are also essential to audit a data center chargeback billing or transfer pricing system and the functional relationships between data center customer areas. Patterns of usage of key corporate data resources as well as application systems should also be routinely evaluated using SMF job account identity and suspense activity exception reports, in order to determine when and if changes should be made to billing assignment for particular system resources or application software usage costs.

To a large degree, the integration of the automated software inventory and valuation data automatically collected, updated, and audited using SMF system logs, can also be used by data centers in order to support *Just-In-Time* (JIT) inventory methods used by Japanese and American automobile manufacturers. Automated software measurement and reporting can provide the real-time feedback mechanism necessary for data center staff and management to more closely track the number of software programs that require system resources and technical support within shorter time frames. It is also possible to reduce data center costs by matching orders for paper and other supplies and scheduling of operations staff according to precise monitoring of active software inventory.

Use of external vendor out sourcing for portions of system development projects or short-term, labor-intensive system support efforts can be based on evidence from SMF system logs as to whether software development programs are being added to inventory on schedule and within estimated variance for functional program size and complexity as specified in the original system design. This method can be particularly useful when SMF-based project validation audits are combined with automated scans by products like Q/AUDITOR, covered in Chapter 5.

VENDORS THAT CAN ASSIST IN INVENTORY MANAGEMENT OF SOFTWARE

Although this is another one of the commercial application areas with the greatest potential benefit from automated software measurements based upon SMF and other system logs, it is still not an area where major vendor marketing activity has begun. Industry standards and government regulations, which will undoubtedly impact it, are yet to be defined. Until additional developments occur, it is best to seek out the advice and assistance of a Big-6 certified public accounting firm with considerable EDP audit expertise and resources, such as Price Waterhouse or KPMG Peat Marwick Advanced Technology group.

One notable exception is the Q/AUDITOR product described earlier. This vendor product is particularly useful when it is used to support an automated software inventory along with SMF log-based system resource cross-reference and performance history database in order to support software tuning and reengineering. Another product that is worth noting is the ENDEVOR software available from Legent. This product supports automated software inventory management across all host, network, and PC workstation platforms. It is especially powerful when used in conjunction with the Legent MICS Performance Database product.

12

MANAGING AUTOMATED SOFTWARE FACTORIES OF THE FUTURE

There is growing acceptance of the view that, in the future, information data centers may be operated as automated software development factories. The belief has shaped the strategic technology initiatives of hardware vendors such as IBM, DEC, and HP—as well as their Japanese competitors.

Yet, almost a decade after these initiatives were first announced, it has become very clear to data center customers that there is no environment with the automatic capability to dramatically transform a data center into a software factory. Only the individual management and technical staff of each data center can create a software factory—by virtue of using basic software engineering methods to develop a more efficient, productive, and functional operation and using the hardware, tools, and other resources that they already have.

It was always a bit misleading when hardware vendors gave the impression that they could automatically transform the information industry from an art to an engineering science. Hardware vendors can only provide the tools—and for the most part, they already have. Just as there are good factories and bad factories, success of a software factory will depend on skills of its data center management, as progress is made in individual data centers as well as in industrywide developments, including new technology.

The key to managing software factories of the future will be the use of precision software quality measurement. There may never be a more precise and cost-effective source of software measurements than system logs. This chapter will discuss future trends in automated data processing related to the methods previously explained in this book.

WHAT SOFTWARE FACTORIES OF THE FUTURE MAY LOOK LIKE

The software factories of the future will not be physically structured like industrial factories of the past. However, all of the functional areas and logical divisions will be very similar, within the limits of the network connectivity and processing capability of the system architectures that support them. This will create some changes in the physical layout of what we now know as a data center. But the changes will be largely a matter of distributed capability provided by multiple parallel process arrangements, involving what will probably relate more to the evolution of Local Area Networks (LANs) to Wide Area Networks (WANs), rather than simply the offloading of mission critical application software processing from host mainframes to PCs and attached intelligent workstation processors.

The software factory of the future will in effect be largely a "data center without walls," in which the traditional physical computer operational facility will be distributed in function across a wide-ranging interconnected processor network. It will have multiple platform levels and be able to integrate a variety of vendor architectures and protocols within each platform level. The data center technical support functions will increasingly involve "telecommuting" as well as distributed arrangements for technical support and as customer interaction with the host data center resources.

The "assembly line" in software factories of the future will exist in a variety of different locations. The procedural flow of the human activities required to develop application software and decision-enabling utilities will involve precisely sequenced operational procedure tasks and form "conceptual assembly lines" in the post-industrial information society, which directly correspond to industrial engineering and operations research arrangements used during the present industrial era. The "abstract" factories and conceptual assembly lines that are evolving for manufacture of software products and technologies of the future are already just as real as the concrete and steel physical manufacturing plants that were the mainstay of the economies of the developing world through most of this century.

However, as we move into the next century, and a new information-oriented Post-Industrial Era, the software factories of the future will in many ways establish the seminal groundwork for a management organization, and a way of life, that will be the model upon which all of the business economics and productive work functions of the future will be based. Even as traditional industrial manufacturing facilities are fully automated into robotic and numerical control operations characterized increasingly in the direction of unattended operations, the software factory assembly lines which characterize the future will be applied in order to achieve increasing economies of scale and operational reliability in heavy manufacturing.

Although it is likely that there also will continue to be many industrial sectors which are more appropriate *not* to fully automate and will continue to essentially depend upon human labor to carry out the manufacturing process, even these factory settings are likely to be managed over distributed data center network arrangements. Most likely this will involve complete "semi-automated cottage industry" shops and "short-order" self-sufficient physical assembly lines, across diverse geographical areas, in order to benefit from delocalized economics of distribution and lower product transportation costs. As this happens, many of the traditional in-house business information functions will also undoubtedly be out sourced and contracted locally according to market-driven value-pricing factors and competitive forces, which are driven as much by technology trade-offs as by supply and demand.

The typical traditional information data center will be hard pressed to convert to the organizational structure needed to support a software factory environment. However, it is clear that those data centers which do so will become much more competitive.

VISIONS OF THE SOFTWARE FACTORY
OF THE FUTURE

Not everyone is going to welcome the end of the industrial era and the beginning of the information era with open arms. Already, many people openly express concern and resentment about the impact computers have been having, and continue to have, upon their lives.

However, the transition is already driven by economic and social forces which cannot be averted or impeded in any major way. Every change in the organization of civilized society has been an uncomfortable process and resisted until the benefits of the change are widely recognized. The changes that we are undergoing as the information age begins, are no exception.

In many ways, these forces of resistance are curiously greatest even within the software technology sector where all of these changes have first been realized. In spite of the fact that the software sector is based on technology, it is difficult for many within the software industry to adapt to the new tools and the new organizational changes. This experience has been most pronounced with the early beta versions of each of the new forefront information technologies, including *Computer-Assisted Software Engineering* (CASE), *Fourth-Generation Language* (4GL), *Relational Database*, *Expert Systems*, *Artificial Intelligence*, and *Premise Engineering*. Any of a number of new technology watchwords of the early nineties, will most assuredly become the status quo, will be replaced by new technology watchwords by the end of the decade.

The nature of change is such that all new technology and new ways of thinking almost guarantee that every vision of the future will be controversial and subject to criticism until it has not only been fully realized but demonstrated to have proven worth. This is certainly true with each vision of the software factories of the future which have been put forth by major vendors as well as academic and research environments. Ultimately, the real potential for success of any vision of the future is not so much the characteristics that it offers as a world view unto itself, but rather by the realistic ways that it provides for a bridge from problems of the past to opportunities to improve the quality of life in the future.

IBM'S HOST-BASED INFORMATION WAREHOUSE OF THE FUTURE

Before any major strategic directives by any major vendor had mentioned software development factories of the future, IBM issued a series of new product releases and strategic technology directives which related large host mainframe business databases and enterprise data repositories to "*Information Warehouses.*" This analogy was a natural extension of the incredible growth in large-scale mainframe CPU processing power and direct access data storage technology, which began in the late seventies and began to increase rapidly throughout the eighties.

The various high-speed, high-volume data access devices and developments in database technology provided numerous new markets for the storage of previously unimagined volumes of data. This was readily accepted by IBM customers with growing appetites for online real-time access to incredible volumes of information, beyond what even IBM had dreamed of a decade before. IBM began to market its mainframe hardware with the admonition of "why settle for a warehouse of paper and filing cabinets when you can have an Information Warehouse at your fingertips."

The purpose of this analogy was pure Madison Avenue and image-based marketing. But it successfully sold a whole new generation of computer technology, the first to be oriented more toward the data than the process. The basic objective was to convey the *size* that was involved, rather than a change in the concept of data center organization. However, this conceptual link, established between the structure of a distributed system architecture and the physical facilities, is the underlying foundation of traditional industrial era manufacturing business. It undoubtedly had a permanent impact on the way business executives regarded computer systems within the overall framework of their business organization.

The analogy IBM presented of the information warehouse continues to be expanded and revised over time. As new software factory analogies to physical business facilities are introduced, it is updated and revitalized.

IBM'S APPLICATION DEVELOPMENT FACTORY
OF THE FUTURE: AD/CYCLE

By the mid-eighties, IBM was undergoing a major internal revolutionary upheaval of its own that would foreshadow the direction that technology would take in the nation and the world. Because of the unanticipated success of Apple, and other personal computer vendors, IBM was forced to abruptly reconsider its long-range marketing strategies and their predominant focus for system architecture development. Ultimately, IBM would have to emulate its competition.

IBM was no longer able to depend solely upon the concept of increasing size as the driving force behind its business. Since the major business customer executives and managers making decisions about corporate information processing resource investments were using desktop personal computers in their offices, less businesses relied solely upon host-attached terminals and hardcopy printout.

As IBM moved to the lead in the personal computer business sector by the end of the eighties, it had become more important to reduce its predominant emphasis upon size and increase its emphasis upon accessibility. The changing information systems marketplace also required that the relative roles of desktop computers and their traditional host mainframe business be reconciled in a way that would continue pre-eminence of their primary business—mainframes.

The result was the issuance of a series of new strategic technology directives by IBM, followed quickly by other major system vendors, throughout the late eighties and early nineties. This included a revitalized packaging of "*distributed* information warehouses" of the future and related distributed storage devices and distributed decision-enabling database technology. It heralded a new conceptualization of delocalized support to decentralized business organization functions across many diverse hardware platforms.

This new concept of an information center matched the growing trend of horizontal rather than vertical business organizations and related business application software. It was founded upon a new technology initiative that came to be known as "System Application Architecture" (SAA), which indicated the increasingly interdependence of the system architecture and the business applications it was designed to support.

The new SAA architecture consisted of a series of structured levels for platform system architectures and application software data communication protocols, ranging from DOS and OS/2 operating systems at intelligent network-attached desktop PC workstation levels, to midsize minicomputers as well as traditional host mainframe operating systems such as MVS and VM. The new SAA arrangement created the framework for an integration of the information processing infrastructure that consolidated and merged support to business terminal end users, as well as application software programmers and other data center technical support personnel.

This integration made possible a more direct and common data linkage between business functions and the support of those business functions by data center staff. This included the support of both the decision-enabling process as well as traditional "information warehouse" databases and more traditional data processing application software development.

During this same time period, IBM began to encourage the concept of distributed system application networks as equivalent to a "*virtual assembly line*." Complementary business decision functions were increasingly interrelated with the data center technical support to decision-enabling database functions, and there was increasing integration of the traditional software development life-cycle methodology with involvement of internal business customer application end users in the in-house proprietary application software development process. This use of an assembly-line analogy was formalized as the IBM strategic initiative known as "*Automated Development Life Cycle*" and was a major component of the AD/CYCLE line of strategic IBM products.

The early products related to IBM's AD/CYCLE were largely ISPF order-entry interfaces to traditional CICS, IMS, and some DB2 database technology. But there was a renewed emphasis upon the productivity measurement and management accounting methods based on industrial engineering and manufacturing operations research. Although this involved techniques based on manually entered observation or measurements and conventional administrative record keeping, it was clear IBM's long-term goal was to increase support to automated AD/CYCLE process based on ASQM and automated validation of manual entry data based on system logs.

Although SMF was expanded to support host-based distributed network measurement, LANs and especially stand-alone PCs would need local system log facilities as well. Exactly how this would take place (and to a large degree, still remains to take place) had to await further developments in software engineering.

SOFTWARE FACTORIES OF THE FUTURE AND SOFTWARE ENGINEERING

The formalization of the concept of a software factory of the future has become more than just a marketing initiative by a system vendor, and it is now the focus of an industrywide software development discipline based on the systematic application of industrial engineering methods to the management of information data centers. This new discipline has become known as software engineering and is now being taught along with computer science in most university information science professional programs of instruction.

There has been some resistance to this new concept of a software factory. Traditional data processing does not feel that programming can be regimented or managed like a factory assembly line, in which routine tasks in the software development life-cycle process become more highly specialized and are passed from one specialist worker to another. In this traditional view, programming is more of a skilled craft, in which an individual programmer is assigned requirements for a particular application, and that same programmer is directly involved in the entire development process—from design specifications through coding, testing, documentation, implementation, and customer training—as well as ongoing maintenance and enhancement of the software that the individual craftsman programmer has developed.

In reality, there is a place for both approaches. Computer software is a diverse enough commodity that there probably always will be software craftsmen guild shops, as well as software engineering and program manufacturing organizations that are more in step with the concept of a software factory.

For more than three generations after the marketplace for automobiles was revolutionized by the mass-production techniques of Henry Ford, there continued to be markets for limited-production automobiles built by small auto shop craftsmen to meet exceptionally high-end standards of excellence for speed, comfort, and style—but at a premium price affordable by only a few who appreciate, and pay for, the efforts of individual skilled craftsmen. Yet, after the automobile factory assembly-line process was first introduced by Ford, and adopted by other major manufacturing companies, the demand for automobiles built by skilled craftsmen clearly dwindled relative to growing demand for assembly-line products.

More American consumers were able to afford an automobile, and the overall American economy prospered for two decades as a result. In many ways, the American software industry is in a critical period of transition that parallels many of the same economic conditions during the early days when Ford first introduced his assembly-line concept. If the United States is able to advance software engineering and the software factory concept—the same way that the United States led the world in applying industrial engineering to the automobile industry in the early part of this century—there is no reason why it cannot extend its strategic international software business advantage into the next century. Software engineering is the key to applying industrial engineering to software manufacture and taking fullest advantage of ASQM and system logs such as IBM's SMF.

Software engineering is also the driving force behind the application of Total Quality Management, Statistical Process Control, and other production-quality control techniques to the continuous improvement of programmer productivity and software product quality. All of these techniques are based on measurement of application software development products and human effort to support the software development life-cycle process, using industrial engineering and manufacturing operations research measurement techniques.

The first software engineer to formally define how these techniques would be used in the software factory of the future was James R. Johnson, of Hallmark Cards. In various books and articles, Johnson has documented guidelines, based upon his own experience, which can help create software factories of the future across the United States, with dramatic implications to expansion of international marketing of American software products and services throughout the world. Examples of his fundamental parallels between the nature of the measurement functions for traditional manufacturing businesses and software factories of the future, are shown in Figures 12-1 and 12-2.

Although system logs are not by any means the only source of software quality and programmer productivity measurement data, they are an increasingly popular software metric data source. This is because of the relatively low cost of collection and the relatively high level of reliability and standardized measures. Throughout this book, examples have been given for the use of SMF and related system logs as an automated source of software quality measurement and the basis for automated support to all of the major technical support functions to support the creation and maintenance of a software factory of the future. These are by no means the final word in potential applications of automated software quality measurement based on system logs, and rapidly developing technology poses new opportunities and new measurement techniques every day. The nature of system logs within the IBM vendor environment, as well as all related logs to monitor activity of computer users, is constantly expanding. It is undergoing constant change as a result of ongoing developments in operating systems and system architectures, as well as developments in software engineering and Total Quality Management technology as it is applied to software development.

The software factory model presented by Johnson also covered detailed business planning and quality measures that continue to evolve. Examples of some measures as they are currently recommended by Johnson, QAI, and others, are shown in Figure 12-3. Most of these measures can be automated based on SMF.

TELECOMMUNICATIONS INDUSTRY IMPACT
UPON TRADITIONAL DATA CENTERS

One of the great software industry visionaries who has been most responsible for popularizing software engineering and CASE tools as a panacea for increasing programmer productivity has been James Martin. There is no living author who has written more extensively on more computer application programming topics or anyone who has been more successful at forecasting the future of the software industry. Among the most successful areas of his long-range visions of the future has been the impact of telecommunications upon the software industry, and Martin was notably the first to foresee the potential impact of satellite-based, public-access, value-added data communications and local area PC

PROCESS	MEASUREMENT VALUE	
STRUCTURED	LOW Software Design Process Control Quality Control Capacity Planning Forecasting	HIGH Project Management Project Control Utilization Review Chargeback Billing Methods and Standards
UNSTRUCTURED	VERY LOW Project Deployment Technical Training Data Security Software Inventory Data Administration	LOW Purchased Products Software Demographics Technical Communications Software Valuation Program Maintenance
	FEW <=== OUTPUTS ===> MANY	

Figure 12-1 Functional Process Paradigm for an Information Data Center Software Factory Measurement

```
                              MEASUREMENT VALUE
                              =================

                    LOW               HIGH                LOW
                    ---               ----                ---

STRUCTURED      Engineering       Management          Purchasing
                Operations        Manufacturing       Marketing
                Quality           Distribution        Advertising
                Finance           Accounting          Inventory
                Budget            Regulations         Maintenance

                    VERY LOW
                    --------

UNSTRUCTURED    Personnel
                Recruitment
                Legal
                Benefits
                Administration

                    FEW  <=== OUTPUTS ===>  MANY
```

Figure 12-2   Functional Process Paradigm for General Business Enterprise Organizational Measurements

PERFORMANCE MEASURMENT	METRIC FORMULATION	1993 OBJECTIVE	1993 SPECIFIC GOAL	1993 ACTUAL MEASURE
A. PRODUCTIVITY				
1. Support Productivity =	Total LOC / Total Staff	Increase	99,999	99,999
2. Project Productivity =	LOC per Project / Project Manyears	Maintain	9,999	9,999
3. Function Point Yield =	FP's / Project Mandays	Increase	.9	.9
4. LOC Productivity =	LOC Attempted / Project Staff	Increase	9,999	9,999
5. Data Center Productivity =	FP's / Programming Days	Increase	9	9
B. QUALITY				
1. Maintenance Incidents =	Total LOC / Existing Program Abends	Maintain	9,999	9,999
2. Project Incidents =	New Program LOC / New Program Abends	Maintain	9,999	9,999
C. ESTIMATING				
1. Scheduling Efficiency =	Projects On Schedule / Total Projects	Maintain	99%	99%
2. Budgeting Efficiency =	Projects Under Budget / Total Projects	Maintain	99%	99%

Figure 12-3 Functional Process Performance Objective Measurements for a Data Center Software Factory

networks, as well as wide area packet-switching networks, which have already revolutionized the computer industry almost as much as the personal computer itself.

Martin continues to see beyond the immediate and apparent impact of automated data and telecommunications technology upon the software development industry. One of these areas is the impact of teletext, teleconferencing, and telecommuting technology upon the future of a highly specialized software factory, in which individual tasks are assigned from a central virtual software assembly line to workers across the nation or even around the world.

This is still considered a fairly far fetched idea. The main problem is the unfortunate lack of sufficient telecommunications infrastructure to support cost-effective management of such an arrangement and the lack of common data communications standards to make it technically feasible. Yet, the concept is beginning to take hold, and other visionaries are making similar predictions about virtual distributed computer network places.

Already, telecommuting is becoming a common practice for many large corporation data centers. However, the limits of telecommuting are still largely within the same local metropolitan area. Yet, there is no reason why a national "interstate" telecommunications infrastructure could not be built, similar to the interstate highway system, with central high-speed fiber-optic pipelines and high-density transmission corridors providing unprecedented economies of scale for American business and creating opportunities for "long haul" data network communication conducive to interstate computer services business.

Although other nations, such as Japan, France, and Germany, will undoubtedly be fiercely competitive in the development of new software engineering technology to support automated software factories of the future, a telecommunications corridor to support distributed data centers and virtual software assembly lines will be a superset of technologies that would more directly benefit the geographic, economic, and cultural factors unique to the United States. It may thus be a more fruitful technology niche and one of the best strategies for focusing national R&D policy for reinvestment of "Peace Dividend" dollars.

This kind of national technology initiative would not have been possible during the Cold War. However, there is now a clearly growing consensus that this is one of the most productive and strategic ways America can reinvest the so-called "Peace Dividend."

If such an effort is undertaken, it will also clearly require considerable involvement by SEI and the military system establishment, since a telecommunications interstate corridor would require design and development of new technologies to support strategic and tactical protection of such a national resource, so that American business security interests depending on it could never be challenged. This approach would help to ease the transition from a defense-oriented economy and slow the painful, and potentially counter-productive, wholesale elimination of critical defense system contract establishments. It would be able to truly reap the "Peace Dividend" by applying much of the defense system's work in progress to more nonmilitary applications with a payback that may even include preservation of peacetime military resources, which may still be needed in order to guard American communication resources strategic to American business interests around the world.

A lot of radical changes would also be necessary in the federal regulations related to the communications industry and, more importantly, in the definition of the status of corporate business entities as they exist and operate across interstate and even international boundaries. However, these problems are no greater than the challenges and opportunities that were posed by the establishment of the American interstate highway system or the design of the first international telephone network.

Clearly, ASQM technology and telecommunication network billing measurement technology will both have to be integrated along common lines and according to common standards (as well as common goals and objectives) in order to assure the benefits of such a national telecommunications highway to provide for virtual distributed computer business network places for the American people. But it is a vision that can be and should be realized. However, it may require a strategic alignment from two industries based on two different technologies that have not always mixed well together, as well as an alignment between two corporate mega-rivals—IBM and AT&T—who would have to equally share in this vision or it may not be possible to achieve. In some ways, this may be more like the great transnational railroad project, with IBM and AT&T leading their respective technologies toward a single shared vision, which must meet like the rails that ended with a "Golden Spike" at the center of the nation.

UPCOMING CHANGES IN THE NATURE OF PROGRAMS AND PROGRAMMING

Aside from an increasing probability that the nature of the physical layout of data centers will change, the traditional work environment for software programmers is almost certain to change radically as software factories of the future become commonplace over the next decade. It is also very likely that the nature of software programs, and the process by which programming is performed, will also change radically in at least two major ways as software engineering matures into a standardized professional discipline.

First, the structure of computer program sourcecode will become less dependent on traditional process-oriented design methods and language architectures and increasingly dependent on reusable object-oriented program design methods and architectures. Second, the manner in which programmers are compensated for their efforts will undoubtedly change radically over the next decade, which is certain to have immediate and far-reaching impact on the manner in which software is valued and programmer labor costs recovered.

The first trend is already largely underway, as reusable GUI and *Object-Oriented Programming* (OOP) computer science methods gradually replace more and more application areas dominated in the past by traditional procedural data processing languages. However, the object-oriented methodologies will probably not completely replace procedural language methods. There are both strengths and weaknesses associated with each of these two divergent approaches, and each will find its niche.

The most important consideration of the impact of this trend upon ASQM and software engineering, is that up until this point in time, no really adequate method of measuring and valuing OOP and GUI program source modules has yet been devised. Function points do not yet provide any range or precision to support OOP and GUI software measurement—even SPR groups all OOP and GUI together in the same region of the language-equivalent table of elements, at an unreasonably high productivity factor weight which does little to distinguish between OOP program quality or productivity.

Perhaps this will change over the course of the next decade, as the various methods of OOP and GUI become more clearly divergent, and there are more precise productivity leverage factors that can be associated with each. New software metrics methods and even possibly new measurements are yet to be defined, and considerable work must be done in order to make ASQM data for the new program technologies comparable and convenient to collect. To some degree this can be implemented directly into the CASE tools and SE developer platform environments, yet is also going to be necessary to integrate these measurements according to some consistent national software quality measurement standard, in order to assure that the data will be comparable and consistent across vendor architectures.

The traditional data processing profession has enjoyed almost half a century of unmatched financial opportunity, and the level of programmer compensation has grown faster than any other labor market sector in the world. For the past four decades, to be a "highly paid computer professional" has meant to be the envy of all other professions. Computer science degree programs have become the number one choice of academic major for university freshmen for over two decades. Yet the situation has clearly begun to change and is likely to change even more drastically before the computer profession and the American economy are fully stabilized.

Already, many DP industry analysts are predicting that, if there are no major changes made in quality and productivity of the American programmer, the traditional world dominance of the American computer software industry could be lost to other nations such as Germany and Japan—much the same as dominance of the American automobile industry was lost over a decade ago. Barring some unforeseen development, such as massive unionization of the computer programmer labor force (which is very unlikely to happen), the number of programmers, and the average market point salaries for computer professions, will probably begin to drop throughout the next decade. As fewer programmers are employed than in the past, the few programmers employed actively in the software development industry will all use advanced CASE toolkits and program generators, or reusable program module developer integration products, to build software—rather than directly writing or customizing procedural language sourcecode as in the past (SAS language may be one exception, but even SAS may give way to statistical GUI and OOP methodologies in the future).

James Martin first used the analogy of "Application Development without Programmers" to popularize software engineering and CASE tools. It now appears that the next decade could be more appropriately defined as "Application Development without Programming Managers" (or data centers)—let alone programmers.

POTENTIAL IMPACT OF INCREASING REGULATION OF INFORMATION INDUSTRY

If any one lesson has been learned by American business over the past two decades, it is that too much government regulation of business, and not enough regulation of business, can both be equally bad for business. There has to be a "happy medium." During the nineties, one of the great challenges for the American government will be to devise a new process to measure the value and effectiveness of various levels of national regulatory powers and to monitor the economy to determine when and where to make changes to "fine-tune" the regulatory process.

The traditional process defined for legislative and judicial control of regulatory actions is simply too slow. Because of the time sync differences between the short cycle of technology shifts or seasonal economic disruptions versus the long cycle of judicial process, the courts have confounded many of the well-intentioned and otherwise constructive efforts of both the executive and legislative branches. This must be corrected or our entire democratic system will increasingly fail where technology is concerned.

There are growing indications that more extensive government regulation is to be expected in the computer software and information industry in the future. This could be good or bad depending on how well the government listens to the needs and desires of American business and technology user groups, as well as the American people.

So far, the computer industry has fared far better than any other business sector has ever fared in the past with regard to governmental regulatory discretion. Because it is a new industry, and because the executive regulatory process has in fact been steadily improved over the past several decades, the level of computer industry regulation has been very consistent with what the computer industry and its customers have wanted and needed.

Hopefully, this will continue to be the case. Hopefully, ASQM will be one tool which will be able to provide both business and government with an increased level of computer industry measurement standardization and detail in order to provide continuous improvement in the quality of computer systems and value-added influence of computer technology on our economy.

Although far-reaching technology directions and funding initiatives should be formalized into laws and precedents by legal minds, the executive branch should have the exclusive power to work out the details—but with more direct (and immediate) accountability to the business leaders and the employees who make up the tax-paying public. Because of the accelerated pace of society, and the speed at which technology can result in drastic changes in our economy, the time span to get a legislative bill passed into law, let alone the time span between elections, must be considered to have possibly become too long relative to the kind of tactical "midterm" corrections modern businesses must make. In the days when the constitution was first written, most businesses only took account of themselves every two to five years, and that was sufficient. Today, every viable business must normally reevaluate itself and make policy corrections or staff changes every quarter; perhaps the government needs to do the same.

In many ways, the governmental regulatory process needs to be more like the operating system of a computer, with supervisor polling, management accounting measurements, and sampling rates that are increased or decreased depending on how many critical problems are detected. This includes more powers for mobilizing reserve resources when needed, controls to guarantee reserve resources will be replenished after the critical situation is recovered, and more timely procedures and measures for swapping out inactive or counterproductive process units. Government could learn a lot about system regulatory processes by studying the design of SMF.

HOW SYSTEM LOG MEASUREMENT DATA MAY CHANGE IN THE FUTURE

Although there have been recurring rumors that IBM has been considering replacing SMF system log architectures with a more relational *"DB2-like"* measurement architecture, it is unlikely that this will happen because of the better performance that the SMF system log integrated control block architecture has over any known architecture that involves external I/O processing. This is definitely something that could change overnight by the introduction of some unprecedented new technology, but the prospect is extremely limited.

IBM has always denied such a far-fetched possibility, yet the rumors continue to persist. Most likely this is the result of some wishful thinking by some DB2 fans. It is most likely that IBM would have far more unhappy customers if SMF was withdrawn from support, than more happy customers if DB2 replaced it.

According to Dr. Barry Merrill, it is most likely that the SMF system log architecture will be continuously improved upon, and that the SMF refinements by IBM will eventually become the standard for every vendor in the industry. Merrill believes that the number of system logs will continue to grow as long as there are new hardware vendors and new system architectures. He also believes that all of the vendors who have not yet provided the same level of software performance measurement detail as IBM will eventually do so, and that the positive experience the Computer Measurement Group has had with IBM in the recommendation and specifications for enhancement to SMF will be similarly positive, as the CMG approaches all other vendors to request more system log performance measurement detail.

The positive experience that CMG and other software metrics support groups have had with IBM and other vendors would be a good lesson for the government regulators during this critical period of transition from the Industrial Age to the Information Age. The United States should develop more national software engineering standards and technology to support a strategic communications infrastructure and distributed network place software factories of the future, in a manner that will foster and sustain American dominance of the computer software industry in the international marketplace. The best approach for regulating the computer software industry, as well as other major American business sectors, would be for government to respond to their requests for more measurement accountability and regulatory standards according to its own "user group" recommendations and specifications and emulate the successful and positive customer-oriented procedural model that IBM has established.

HOW SYSTEM LOGS WILL FIT INTO SOFTWARE FACTORIES OF THE FUTURE

Aside from minor differences between information visionaries over whether traditional host mainframes or "desktop" personal computer–based networks will be the main focus of the software factories of the future, it is most likely that the technology and conventional system architectures will change over time, and it will be increasingly difficult for the terminal user to distinguish where the host mainframe computer network ends and the local personal computer network begins. The fact remains that the transition between past centralized organizations to more delocalized organizational structures and locally administered operations will continue to be based upon the traditional dictum, "you can't manage what you can't measure."

Since SMF and other host mainframe system logs are the most advanced methods of measuring software quality and computer processing power, performance, and quality available today, it is most likely that this technology will be advanced over time. It will be increasingly delocalized in function as distributed host-based System Network Architectures (SNA) are monitored and measured from the mainframe processors. The local networks will undoubtedly be increasingly accessible and compatible with mainframe system log automated software quality and system operation monitoring tools.

It is also likely that software factories of the future will use system logs as a basis for real-time monitoring of unattended data center operations and control similar to those used in automated manufacturing systems. This will include consolidation of all information related to the status of each step in the application software development process, including both human and automated system effort to support software product creation. It will also include automated monitoring and control of software products and in-house application program inventories and optimize access to information center data and process resources. All operations within the central data center, as well as all activity on attached information networks, will be automatically measured and continuously improved in quality and service to delocalized data center customers.

Automated software quality measurement based on computer system logs clearly will be an essential tool of the future for the management control of the Information Age. The future of system logs may not only be involved with the automated measurement of software quality in distributed software factories, but they also may be involved in control and management of the protocols and procedures with which we interact with software factories and each other. ASQM and system logs will undoubtedly be key technologies of the future Information Age, and the only limitations will be the imagination and creativity with which they are applied.

Appendix A

AUTOMATED SOFTWARE QUALITY METRICS PRODUCT AND SERVICE VENDORS

ABEND-AID

Compuware Corporation
31440 Northwestern Highway
P.O. Box 9080
Farmington Hills, MI 48333
Tel: 313/737-7300
FAX: 313/737-7108

The *ABEND-AID* and *FILE-AID* line of automated operational data center support products is constantly being enhanced and expanded to provide additional functionality and capability to handle a growing number of operating system control programs and system architectures. This vendor will continue to be a major source of automated software quality metrics products and programmer productivity software innovation.

APGC (AUTOMATED PEER GROUP COMPARISON SERVICE)

KPMG Peat Marwick Advanced Technology
One Cranberry Hill
Lexington, MA 02173
Tel: 617/863-2700
FAX: 617/863-2715

The Automated Peer Group Comparison service can be one of the most fruitful investments that a data center makes. There are currently almost 200 data centers in the APGC database, all representing major corporations in a wide variety of business sectors: manufacturing, finance, insurance, real estate, health care, education, transportation, retail, energy and utilities, as well as some major agencies of the U.S. government. The *APGC* comparison benchmark data is among the most precise and reliable of its kind, since every confidential profile is automatically collected using the same proprietary SAS programs and is both measured and analyzed according to the same automated procedures. Every major business sector can be benchmarked anonymously against computer industry leaders as well as benchmark partners from your own business category, according to your specifications of criteria for benchmark pairing. In the initial years of subscribing to this service, considerable optimization and cost savings can be identified by *APGC*, as the client data center approaches the national average. In ensuing years, the *APGC* helps to assure that the data center continues to rank well against national standards of software quality. As the *APGC* database grows, this will become an increasingly valuable service that should be renewed year after year. In the future, vendor services such as *APGC* may become as prevalent as the use of external EDP auditors to confirm internal audit findings. *APGC* metrics may also be the standard benchmarking method for software factories of the future.

BATTLE-MAP

McCabe Associates
Twin Knolls Professional Park
Suite 111
Columbia, MD 21045
Tel: 1-800-638-6316

Although the McCabe Cyclomatic Complexity metric has in many ways rivaled function points as the premier software metric developed over the past two decades, it has probably been more intimidating to data center operational analysts and application programmers because it does not fit as easily into a procedural process model as function points do (i.e., function points correspond to things that can be pointed to in JCL or sourcecode statements, whereas Cyclomatic Complexity is more abstract and only remotely ties back to procedure-level blocks of program sourcecode). Yet, over the past several years, McCabe Associates have developed a series of products, which generate network maps directly from sourcecode scans, for most conventional procedural as well as object-oriented programming languages. These network displays can be printed and compared against the sourcecode path networks generated by ongoing program maintenance changes, which will clearly be seen to make the program simpler or more complex, with a corresponding higher risk of failure incidents as complexity of the program increases. Although the Cyclomatic Complexity metric is probably going to continue to be included in traditional sets of available software metric tools (Q/AUDITOR offers the option to calculate Cyclomatic Complexity along with Halstead metrics), it is doubtful if it will ever approach function points as a major industry standard software measurement. However, the McCabe network maps generated by sourcecode scans could become more popular and useful in the future as more procedural language applications are replaced with object-oriented program language sourcecode, since McCabe Battle-Map and related program coding maps seem to help explain "oops" calls. Send for their free demo diskette to get the full effect of this impressive ASQM technology.

BEST/1

BEST/1 North American Marketing
BGS Systems Incorporated
128 Technology Drive
Waltham, MA 02254-9111
Tel: 617/891-0000
FAX: 617/890-0000

The BEST/1 family of automated system capacity planning and data center cost-quality improvement model analysis products are unmatched in the area of advanced software performance systems engineering. They are increasingly recognized as the leader in the area of planning for complex data center CPU upgrades and the analysis of overall strategy for implementing Storage Management Systems (SMS). They support implementation of System Application Architecture (SAA) in multiplatform IBM host-attached system networks, especially with regard to design and optimization of DASD cache management. BGS Systems also has extensive training programs in system performance evaluation methods and skills and performs onsite performance consulting.

BRS/Search Service

Maxwell Online
800 Westpark Drive
McLean, VA 22102
Tel: 1-800-955-0906
FAX: 703/893-4632

The BRS online search service is a part of the Maxwell Communications empire of Great Britain. It contains over 150 separate databases covering quality topics in education, sciences, engineering, and business. It has over 20,000 subscribers. The *BRS* online division also markets a sophisticated *Text Information Management System* (TIMS), offering the fastest online search capability available anywhere due to a proprietary high-speed internal indexing technology (which is somewhat related to the software architecture used by SAS database language procedures). BRS software and services can be automated to scan hundreds of wire services and publications based on a selected set of keywords, which can help assure that any new information about a business competitor or new technology of interest will not escape capture and archival by in-house data center quality benchmark analysts.

CA-JARS

Computer Associates
711 Stewart Avenue
Garden City, NY 11530
Tel: 1-800-645-3003

The *CA-JARS* chargeback billing system is a classic. It has been one of the originals, and continues to be a mainstay, in the SMF and system log management facility arena. It is based on some proprietary high-level procedural language compiled code, as well as SAS language database reporting facilities, so in many ways it is the best of both worlds—a 4GL database manager and a highly efficient processing component for handling even the largest data center's volume of SMF system log detail data. CA also offers a long line of Automated Computer Center control integration vendor products, which are worth looking into when considering Automated System Operations.

D-CAF

System Software Alternatives
1010 W. Fremont Avenue, Suite E
Sunnyvale, CA 94087
Tel: 1-800-888-0478
FAX: 408/720-0250

The *Data Center Administration Facility* (D-CAF) is another comprehensive SMF and system log-based software performance quality management product. The *D-CAF* product line has a growing customer base who are extremely satisfied with the selective power and economy of *D-CAF* as compared to a more full-featured ASQM product like MICS. The main difference between MICS and *D-CAF* is that you don't get the thousands of MICS "canned query" standardized reports or the enormous TSO workstation facility that comes with MICS. The control center for *D-CAF* is *LONGVIEW*, a PC-based workload forecasting product, which is even more user-friendly than the competition's TSO menu screens, without the often irregular response time of TSO applications. The other enticing feature about D-CAF is the fact that it uses a proprietary host performance database expansion/contraction algorithm to reduce the storage to about one-half what would be required to store the same level of software measurement detail in an SAS database format.

DIALOG

Dialog Information Services
3460 Hillview Avenue
Palo Alto, CA 94304
Tel: 415/858-3785
FAX: 415/858-7069

The DIALOG online database services are based upon a proprietary advanced search technology developed by the Lockheed Corporation. The DIALOG service provides access to 370 online databases, including many specialized government agency data stores and the databases of many large professional and technical organizations, as well as online business information and abstracts of academic and professional journals of interest to quality analysts. DIALOG has over 120,000 subscribers.

I-METRICS TOOLKIT

Compumetrics Inc.
67 Wall Street
New York, NY 10005
Tel: 212/323-8150

The Compumetrics organization provides consulting and automated software performance measurement and analysis tools development assistance, including capacity planning, system modeling, workload modeling and forecasting, and application software product inventory sizing. Compumetrics is one of the most experienced consulting organizations of its kind in providing assistance for planning and installing MXG, MICS, or BEST/1 software performance databases. They are a good source of ongoing assistance in SMF data analysis, including setting of service levels, exception reporting, system migration, system maintenance planning and productivity, as well as onsite training in the use of MICS and the SAS application language products. They offer consultation to assist in integrating the SMF-based system log measurement and analysis products such as MICS, MXG, or BEST/1 with the real-time system monitors such as OMEGAMON or offline software monitors such as STROBE. The Compumetrics organization has also developed a proprietary, PC-based capacity planning and performance analysis product that offers a lot of powerful software quality measurement features and capabilities, named *I-Metrics*. They will send a demo to qualified data centers requesting it.

IMF

Boole & Babbage
510 Oakmead Parkway
Sunnyvale, CA 94086
Tel: 408/735-9550

The *IMF* product is an enhanced version of the IMS system log. It can replace the standard Control/IMS logs that were originally developed by Dr. Mario Marino, who also developed MICS. The IMF log also can be used as an alternative input to MICS, instead of the standard IBM system log for IMS. IMF provides considerably more detail at the individual transaction program statistics and database I/O level, since it samples a broader range of system events impacted by the online system programs and system network queueing controls.

IPS/OPT

Chicago Soft, Ltd.
6232 North Pulaski Road
Chicago, IL 60646
Tel: 312/525-6400

The *IPS/OPT* product runs on an intelligent PC workstation that can receive downloaded SMF system data from MICS, MXG, or BEST/1. Data also can be extracted from SMF using Chicago Soft utility software programs. This product can be used to determine the optimum system tuning parameters for the master control IEAIPS and IEAOPT members. It can automatically generate host-tuning parameter specification cards, including checking for correct parameter syntax, and make the necessary updates to a file that can be uploaded from a PC.

ISM/CPPM

Information Systems Manager
301 Broadway
Bethlehem, PA 18105
Tel: 215/865-0300

The *Information Systems Manager* (ISM) is a product and service vendor supporting system performance analysis. ISM features a *Capacity Planning & Performance Manager* (CPPM) program, offering systems professionals a way to improve their capacity and performance efforts while reducing the overall time and expense to process the raw data into usable system resource measurement statistics. The service supports SMF analysis and offers PC-based software products with in-depth planning and modeling capabilities. Each month ISM customers send an SMF or RMF tape, and within about a week they receive an up-to-date analysis on more than forty color charts that enable trending and identification of trouble spots which require the immediate attention of data center technical staff. Also shipped is a PC diskette preloaded to customer specifications with customized data center analysis to support tactical and strategic capacity planning. The service enables offsite processing to relieve critical capacity or fully utilized peak demand periods when all resources are dedicated to meeting priority customer turnaround and availability needs. Services can also be arranged as part of contingency planning for *post mortems* after an unforeseen outage.

KOMMAND

PACE Applied Technology
7900 Sudley Road
Manassas, VA 22110
Tel: 703/369-3200

The *KOMMAND* product is one of the more popular chargeback billing systems on the market today. It supports data center break-even or profit-centered chargeback billing, as well as memo billing arrangements. It provides information on utilization of data center resources and services, cost recovery, year-to-date revenue analysis, budgeting, and invoicing at five levels, and it also supports cost redistribution or prioritization methodologies. User-specified rates drive pricing based on standard formulas. The *KOMMAND* reporting system is menu-driven, which gives online access to a master repository of chargeback system debits and credits, budget status, customer file maintenance, job costing at job termination, and online confirmation of process completion.

MICS

Legent Corporation
8615 Westwood Center Drive
Vienna, VA 22182
Tel: 708/734-9494

The *MVS Integrated Control System* (MICS) has been the dominant automated software quality measurement tool for almost a decade. The Legent Corporation is constantly developing new technology and advanced application products based upon the SAS language and database management facilities and operating system logs and system control program internals for all major hardware vendors' system architectures. They are particularly strong in two new application areas: automated data center unattended operations and automated data center in-house software inventory management. Legent is also highly competitive in the area of expert systems and automated support to *Systems Managed Storage* (SMS) in large SAA (Systems Application Architecture) integrated cross-platform data center environments. They continue to lead all other major commercial application vendors in the area of automated software measurement technology and they have extensive in-house training programs. They routinely present new methods and strategic industry analysis at *SAS Users Group International* (SUGI) and *IBM Computer Measurement Group* (CMG) meetings.

MXG

Dr. H. W. Barry Merrill
Merrill Consultants
10717 Cromwell Drive
Dallas, TX 75229-5112
Tel: 214/351-1966
FAX: 214/350-3694

MXG was the first major SAS product and the first major Computer Performance Evaluation product. It continues to lead the industry as the first vendor to decode and implement software to read and manage each new operating system log technology. Merrill Consultants is the organization that Dr. Barry Merrill established after he originally developed the *MXG* system log management and performance database facilities product line. Merrill Consultants continues to support ongoing enhancement and expansion of the *MXG* product line and coordinates releases and upgrades to accommodate new operating system technology via an *MXG* newsletter and *MXG* users' group. Merrill Consultants can also assist in locating qualified and experienced *CPE* technical support personnel. Barry Merrill continues to be very active in the *SAS Users Group International* (SUGI) and the *IBM Computer Measurement Group* (CMG) and routinely appears at their annual conventions. Barry is a powerhouse technical staff of one and rivals the giants of the mainframe software industry who have staffs numbering in the thousands. If there is a technical problem or usage question, Barry handles it personally, and every *MXG* customer, who either identifies a problem or supplies documentation on a new operating system technology or new system log, always gets his or her name listed in the next *MXG* newsletter. Barry is devoted to the goal of working with all system vendor user groups the way CMG has done with IBM. Barry helped make SMF what it is today. He believes the number of system logs will continue to grow, and *MXG* will always handle them all first.

NEXIS

Mead Data Central
9443 Springboro Pike
P.O. Box 933
Dayton, OH 45401
Tel: 513/865-6800
FAX: 513/865-1350

The NEXIS online database service is the first organization of its kind (it even predates COMPUSERVE). For almost a quarter century, NEXIS has been the confidential source of choice for business and financial analysts. The technology has stayed at the forefront, and there are currently over 2,600 individual databases—which is more databases than most online database services have customers.

OMEGAMON

Candle Corporation
1999 Bundy Drive
Los Angeles, CA 90025
Tel: 213/207-1400

Although it was mentioned only briefly in this book, the *OMEGAMON* line of real-time system performance monitors is one of the most important tools that systems programmers and operations analysts have in their troubleshooting toolkit. *OMEGAMON* gives hundreds of real-time system process operational and utilization statistics in the form of a TSO or VTAM attached terminal display. The same statistics that come up on the *OMEGAMON* screens will be logged to SMF. Candle also has been an industry leader in the development of performance-tuning techniques and works closely with IBM to define diagnostic procedures and metrics to tune SRM.

PERFORMANCE ADVISOR

Domanski Sciences
100 Craig Road
Suit 101
Freehold, NJ 07728
Tel: 201/303-1500

The Domanksi *PERFORMANCE ADVISOR* is an advanced heuristic knowledge-based expert system for troubleshooting, performance analysis, diagnosis, and tuning of MVS mainframe environments. The *PERFORMANCE ADVISOR* software is PC-based and provides expert advice and technical skill cross-training to data center managers and analysts responsible for software quality and operational system engineering. *PERFORMANCE ADVISOR* comes with extensive software performance and system tuning rules of thumb, which can be adjusted or redefined to account for site-specific data center standards or new technology configurations. In addition to providing expert MVS tuning advice, *PERFORMANCE ADVISOR* comes with a complete Knowledge Engineering shell and knowledge base development toolkit environment, supporting the creation and customization of expert rule systems for environments other than MVS. The Domanski Sciences vendor offers a PC bulletin board service for its clients, so they can exchange their in-house expert systems with each other. The *PERFORMANCE ADVISOR* is priced at the level of most PC software, which makes it one of the best ASQM bargains on the market today. Send for their demo disk, or call to access their customer support PC bulletin board.

Q/AUDITOR

Eden Systems Corporation
14950 Greyhound Court
Carmel, IN 46032
Tel: 317/848-9600
FAX: 317/843-2271

Eden Systems continues to offer quality automated software measurement products in functional areas where there are no major competitors providing exactly the same type or level of new application tools support. This is one of the most innovative, practical, and affordable sources of software engineering tools which can be implemented quickly and easily in order to support comprehensive Total Quality Management programs. Eden continues to release new products in specialized areas of system development productivity and software quality every year, including multiple high-level languages and integrated platform support. It is also one of the most important strategic vendors in the area of software reengineering, as well as automated methods for conversion and standardation across generational technology. The Q/AUDITOR and Q/ARTISAN products and technology are changing so rapidly that it is difficult to relate all of the late-breaking developments. It's a good idea to write the vendor to request the latest literature, as well as a free product demo diskette.

SAS/QC

SAS Institute
SAS Campus Drive
Cary, NC 27511
Tel: 919/677-8000
FAX: 919/677-8123

The SAS Institute was the original developer of the Statistical Analysis System language and the database management facilities. SAS is a true Fourth Generation Language and has been shown to routinely result in productivity gains five times greater than procedural high-level languages such as PL/1 or COBOL. The SAS Institute markets its language and database management systems, as well as over a dozen specialized software application support products for enhancing the functionality and capability of the SAS Base procedural library. SAS/QC is a powerful data center automated management support system product and is available with extensive graphic and online data analysis functions for both IBM host mainframe and PC workstation platforms. Related products also support project managment and operations research, as well as computer performance evaluation and numerous programmer productivity applications. The SAS Institute is an academic research and computer systems training institution with a wide range of available in-house or onsite training courses, video training, and technical publications. The *SAS Users Group International* (SUGI) is an organization with national and regional affiliates worldwide, which meets yearly or even monthly in some areas to present technical assistance and tutorial training in a wide range of SAS application areas, including Quality Assurance and Management Information Systems.

SLIM

Quantitative Software Management, Inc.
1057 Waverly Way
McLean, VA 22101
Tel: 703/790-0055
FAX: 703/749-3795

The *SLIM* system is an automated software development estimating and planning tool designed by Lawrence Putnam. The *SLIM* system has been used for many years by the U.S. and British military system commands, as well as several large U.S. telecommunications companies. It is the software measurement and project planning platform of choice for NCR and Unisys system architectures. The *SLIM* product is based upon the *Productivity Index* (PI) and the *Manpower Buildup Index* (MBI) devised by Putnam and has been used successfully to develop some of the most complex military weapons systems ever designed. The *SLIM* system is available on a variety of operating systems, including a PC platform base. The *SLIM* system has been used to accumulate one of the largest software development productivity databases in the world, containing over 2,200 software projects, which represent 208 million lines of code, in over eighty languages, and involves over 50,000 years of programming effort. This database can be used as a benchmark comparison *Productivity Analysis Database System* (PADS), which was designed as a companion to *SLIM* and a related family of products. Although the *SLIM* system has been identified primarily with military applications, it is being used increasingly by large corporation data centers, especially in the telecommunications, engineering, and manufacturing industries.

SPC-PC

Quality America Inc.
7659 E. Broadway, Suite 208
Tucson, AZ
Tel: 1-800-729-0867
FAX: 602/722-6705

Quality America's Statistical Process Control product line for personal computers is an industry standard for both operational research process measurement analysis and graphical process documentation aids needed for even the most comprehensive TQM support. Although the product has been for the most part a PC-workstation product in the past, increasing usage among software quality measurement analysts who use SAS software performance database management tools has resulted in a number of automated methods for interfacing SPC-PCs to host SAS databases. In the meantime, SPC-PC continues to add statistical analysis and TQM functionality, which serve to support new automated software engineering methods and standards.

SPQR

Software Productivity Research, Inc.
77 South Bedford
Burlington, MA 01803
Tel: 617/273-0140

The *Software Productivity, Quality and Reliability* (SPQR) product was designed and developed by Dr. Capers Jones, as the first fully automated method of estimating software complexity and size and the corresponding manpower effort required to deliver a particular software product. The SPR organization established by Capers Jones has more recently developed a second product, CHECKPOINT, which standardizes and automates many of the procedures for administering a complete software project audit, including software quality assurance, standards compliance, and productive programmer yield analysis, at a level of detail that is suitable to support software development services chargeback or transfer pricing according to a highly specified chart of accounts. The SPR organization also markets access to the largest existing software project productivity benchmark database in the world, with detailed history and statistics on over 4,000 system development projects conducted over the past forty years.

STROBE

Programart
120 Massachusetts Avenue
Cambridge, MA 02138
Tel: 617/661-3020

The Programart organization supports application of its products to apply practical operational process troubleshooting and software error diagnostic using reengineering methods. It is also involved in training application programmers and other technical support staff in software-tuning methods, as well as consulting related to software program coding standards and conventions for optimizing the efficiency of the data center in-house program inventory management operations. The *STROBE* product line is undergoing a significant evolution in the nature of its technology, from products which support traditional object load modules compiler generated from third-generation procedural high-language sourcecode module files, to run-time *Structured Query Language* (SQL) and *Object-Oriented Programming Structures* (OOPS), which make up the major portion of fourth-generation system architecture and application software development of the future.

UNIX SYSTEM TOOLKIT

AT&T Bell Labs
Whippany Road
Whippany, NJ 07981-0903
Tel: 1-800-828-UNIX

The Software Reliability Engineering methods developed by AT&T and John Musa can be demonstrated using sample programs that Bell Labs will make available to any interested data center. These programs are written in FORTRAN, but can be easily converted to the SAS language and used as an external database interface for MICS or MXG. The sample programs provided by AT&T are fully tested on an IBM 370/168 and can be executed on an OS/VS or MVS processor, with some modifications for upward system compatibility to match language-compiler versions. The most significant application of the SRE methodology, however, has been in the UNIX environment. Bell Labs offers consulting services on using the UNIX system toolkit, which provides the best available equivalent of system log measurement tools for UNIX software.

VIEWPOINT

Datametrics Systems Corp.
Burke Professional Center
5270 Lungate Court
Burke, VA 22015-1600
Tel: 703/385-7700
FAX: 703/385-7711

The *VIEWPOINT* online performance monitor features advanced statistical auto-correlation technology to quickly discriminate overlapping or interrelated workloads or performance problems. *VIEWPOINT* has been shown to cut software quality measurement analysis time in half by automatically finding and classifying probable causes of response-time bottlenecks, throughput problems, or network hardware failures. The *VIEWPOINT* statistical analysis component product is PC-based and can run under Microsoft Windows, which allows display and toggling between multiple graphical views of system resource impact factors or workload measures in order to narrow the search to factors which have corresponding rates of change. The *VIEWPOINT* performance monitor data collection software supports automated notification of operational process problems via automated electronic message sending based on threshold management and early warning alert parameters, which are user specified and stored in a system table. *VIEWPOINT* has a lot of interesting features which approach the most advanced state-of-the-art technology and herald future ASQM directions.

Appendix B

AUTOMATED SOFTWARE QUALITY MEASUREMENT SUPPORT ORGANIZATIONS

COMPUTER DESIGN

PennWell Publishing Co.
One Technology Park Drive
Westford, MA 01886
Tel: 508/692-0700
FAX: 508/692-0525

The *Computer Design* journal is a biweekly professional publication about computer systems design, development, and systems integration. A complimentary subscription is available to all qualified system development professionals who request it.

COMPUTER MEASUREMENT GROUP (CMG)

CMG Headquarters
111 E. Wacker Drive, Suite 600
Chicago, IL 60601
Tel: 312/938-1228

The CMG is widely regarded as the birthplace of modern *Computer Performance Evaluation* (CPE) and has been largely responsible for elevating CPE from an art to the status of applied science and technology. The CMG originated as the Boole and Babbage User's Group, in the early days when Dr. Mario Marino was designing the first Control/IMS system log and building the foundations for what later became MICS in the 1970s. In 1975, the B&B/UG became the CMG, and the membership was expanded to include all areas of CPE interest and professional expertise. There is an annual CMG conference, which is attended by most ASQM as well as CPE vendors and is one of the most important national events of the year for DP capacity planners and software performance analysts. CMG awards the A. A. Michelson award annually for the year's most significant professional contribution to computer metrics. The national chapter also publishes a yearly *CMG Transactions*, which presents critical and timely computer measurement topics.

DACS NEWSLETTER

Data Analysis Center for Software (DACS)
Kaman Sciences Corporation / RADC
258 Genesee Street, Suite 103
Utica, NY 13502
Tel: 315/734-3696

Although the *DACS Newsletter* is the result of U.S. Army and U.S. Air Force software standardization initiatives, it has been converted for nonmilitary access and administration by the Kaman Sciences contractor firm. It may not always be clear unless the newsletter is read closely, but it is in fact still the premier informational bulletin for military systems standardization and technology transfer. Every ASQM professional should request the gratis subscription from DACS.

DATA CENTER MANAGER

ICP Publishing Company
9100 Keystone Crossing, Suite 200
Indianapolis, IN 46240
Tel: 317/844-7461
FAX: 317/574-0571

The *Data Center Manager* journal is a complimentary publication for MIS and DP managers. It has excellent articles summarizing quality issues and technology in easy to understand terms.

DATA CENTER OPERATIONS MANAGEMENT

Auerbach Publishers
One Penn Plaza
New York, NY 10119
Tel: 212/971-5000
FAX: 212/971-5025

The Auerbach *Data Center Operations Management* series is a subscription service of comprehensive guidelines and expert recommendations for improved efficiency and quality of data center service operations. It is available in looseleaf binders, which are routinely updated with new technical recommendations. The cost is currently $375 per year.

DATAPRO

Datapro Research
600 Delran Parkway
Delran, NJ 08705
Tel: 609/764-0100

The *DataPro* series is another looseleaf subscription service, with a wide variety of software and vendor rating analysis information. Several different topics are available, and the cost is currently about $1,000 per year for each topic area.

ENTERPRISE SYSTEMS JOURNAL

Thomas Publications
10935 Estate Lane
Suite 375
Dallas, TX 75238
Tel: 214/343-3717
FAX: 214/553-5603

The *Enterprise Systems Journal* is another gratis monthly magazine for qualified data center management and technical analyst staff. It is one of the best sources of practical applications software performance-tuning and system programming advice available (including IBM GUIDE/SHARE). The articles are all top-notch, by the best MVS software quality and system performance experts in the world today. This is an extremely useful publication, which should be distributed to all members of your data center staff and then kept on the reserved shelf of your data center technical library.

GARTNER GROUP

Saatchi & Saatchi
56 Top Gallant Road
Stamford, CT 06904
Tel: 203/964-0096
FAX: 203/324-7901

The Gartner Group is another high-powered computer industry analysis subscription service, with a wide range of specialties, including mainframe, mini and PCs, LANs, software, office automation, and telecommunications. The cost varies depending on the category and level of subscription service support. Current pricing is around $1,000 per year, per major topic area.

IBM GUIDE/SHARE USER'S GROUPS

IBM Guide Inc. / IBM Share Inc.
111 E. Wacker Drive
Chicago, IL 60601
Tel: 312/644/6610
FAX: 312/565-4658

There are two IBM User's Groups. Both groups require that the members be representatives selected from data center installation sites that are substantial commercial customers of IBM. The two groups were originally organized, and traditionally administered, with the intention that IBM Guide would be an organization primarily directed toward interests of data center managers, and IBM Share would support data center technical staff including capacity planners, application software performance tuners, and other CPE professionals. In recent years, the two organizations have increasingly addressed topics that overlap. Although it is not normally possible to be a concurrent member of both organizations, it is important that each data center is actively involved in each of the two groups and that the two reps meet regularly to compare notes.

INFOTEXT

Infotext Publishing Company
347000 Coast Highway, Suite 309
Capistrano, CA 92624
Tel: 714/493-2434
FAX: 714/493-3018

The *Infotext* journal is a monthly guide for finding and using online database information by remote dial-up access. It is one of the best sources of specialized online information services to support your corporate benchmarking efforts. It is available free to qualified computer professionals upon request.

INSTITUTE FOR INFORMATION MANAGEMENT (IIM)

Institute for Information Management
Applied Computer Research, Inc.
Phoenix, AZ 85068-9280
Tel: 602/995-5928

Since 1971, Applied Computer Research has been affiliated with the Institute for Information Management. ACR publishes the prestigious *EDP Performance Review*, *EDP Performance Management*, and the *Computer Literature Index*. IIM sponsors a series of ongoing seminars, workshops, and forums exclusively for computer industry professionals and is active in the support of computer performance management and capacity planning fields. IIM will send a complimentary copy of *EDP Performance Review* and their upcoming course schedule to all who write to request them.

NETWORK COMPUTING

CMP Publications, Inc.
Attn: Network Computing Circulation Department
600 Community Drive
Manhasset, NY 11030-9789
Tel: 516/562-5071
FAX: 516/562-7293

Network Computing is a monthly technical magazine that is available gratis to qualified data center technical and management professionals. This is a good source on software quality standards and issues that impact both host and network environments and should also help to bridge some of the gaps between IBM and UNIX.

QUALITY

Hitchcock Publishing Co.
191 S. Gary Avenue
Carolstream, IL 60188
Tel: 708/665-1000
FAX: 708/462-2225

Quality journal is a complimentary informational publication about applications of Quality Assurance technology in the data processing industry. A subscription is available free of charge to qualified professionals and libraries that request it. This journal is a "must" for AQSM professionals who read to stay on top of new software quality standards and methodologies.

QUALITY ASSURANCE INSTITUTE (QAI)

Software Quality Analysis Programs
Suite 350, 7575 Dr. Phillips Boulevard
Orlando, FL 32819-7273
Tel: 407/363-1111
FAX: 407/363-1112

QAI sponsors a *Certified Quality Analyst* (CQA) program, which prepares software quality professionals for a certification test and C.Q.A. licensure, based on academic education, continuing education seminars, and "Software Quality Analyst Professional's Body of Knowledge," a self-paced independent study course. The C.Q.A. certification and licensure procedure is being considered as a prerequisite for ISO 9000 auditors by the governments of most of the British Commonwealth nations, such as Australia, Singapore, and India, as well as Saudi Arabia, Bahrain, and most other Arabic nations, Mexico, Brazil, and most South American nations. In the United States, QAI's C.Q.A. certification is now required in order to work in the software quality departments of IBM, GTE, Pacific-Bell, and other large Fortune

500 companies. Once a candidate is awarded the C.Q.A., recertification depends on yearly registration and completion of forty Continuing Education units in Software Quality Metrics coursework every year. There are individual and corporate memberships to the QA Institute and its many activities, and QAI also publishes a quarterly journal. The QAI is the premier organization for software quality metrics professionals. QAI was founded by William Perry, who has been one of the most prolific and renowned authors in the area of software quality measurement for several decades. QA Institute sponsors a continuing series of weekly seminars and training on a very wide variety of software quality measurement, testing, and productivity improvement. Timely SQM topics are discussed, and practical SQM knowledge is presented by a wide range of experts in the SQM field. It may be your best chance to get a personal consultation with the nation's expert on any specialized SQM topic. There are a series of annual conferences on major SQM topics held throughout the year. QAI also sponsors a "C.Q.E." certification program, which trains and standardizes Malcolm Baldridge Award application evaluators.

SAS USER'S GROUP INTERNATIONAL (SUGI)

SAS Institute Inc.
Box 8000
Cary, NC 27511-8000
Tel: 919/467-8000
FAX: 919/677-8123

The *Statistical Analysis System* (SAS) 4GL programming language is the data analysis tool of choice for all computer performance and software metrics professionals who make extensive use of computer operating system logs and software monitors. The annual SUGI convention devotes several days of seminars and SAS User presentations in topics of quality control, computer performance evaluation, management information systems, and applied statistical methods, as well as tutorials in using and applying SAS Language, which span from beginner to advanced user levels. In addition, numerous vendors that interface to SAS databases and SAS Language products demonstrate their latest wares and provide a series of hands-on tutorials for interested CPE and ASQM professionals. SUGI convention announcements and schedule of events, as well as articles highlighting some interesting or unusual applications of SAS Language products at SAS customer installations around the world, are published in the *SAS Communications* quarterly magazine. This magazine is free and available to qualified CPE and ASQM professionals by writing to SAS on company letterhead to request a subscription. Each year, all of the papers and presentations at the annual SUGI events are published in a large volume, which usually contains hundreds of SAS programs and well over 1,000 pages of good SAS coding tricks—it is definitely a "must" for your data center technical library.

SOFTWARE ENGINEERING INSTITUTE (SEI)

Software Engineering Institute
Carnegie-Mellon University
Frew Avenue & Margaret Morrison
Pittsburgh, PA 15213
Tel: 412/268-7700

Software Engineering Institute (SEI) was established in 1983 as part of the national *Software Technology for Adaptibility and Reliability* (STAR) initiative of the U.S. Department of Defense. In spite of its early military funding, SEI has not focused exclusively on military system technology (unlike DAC/RADC) and is instead a national repository of project productivity and quality benchmark data for business and government alike. SEI was chartered as a clearinghouse of information about all public and private software technologies of potential strategic significance to help the United States achieve a more competitive international business advantage. For this reason SEI may be increasingly important, as more defense funding is redirected toward revitalizing our technology infrastructure and creating a more competitive national technology policy. SEI is best known for its Software Engineering Maturity Scale (SEMS) for benchmarking data center's "STAR Quality."

SOFTWARE QUALITY ENGINEERING (SQE)

Software Quality Engineering
3000-2 Hartley Road
Jacksonville, FL 32257
Tel: 904/268-8639

The Software Quality Engineering consulting firm manages many special interest groups, including co-sponsorship of an annual International Conference on Applications of Software Measurement. This conference often has presentations by such renowned leaders in the ASQM field as A. J. Albrecht, Capers Jones, John Musa, and many others. In the past, SQE has co-sponsored this event along with the national chapters of the *American Society for Quality Control* (ASQC) and *Data Processing Management Association* (DPMA), and they continue to have a strong cooperative relationship with working committees of the ASQC and DPMA. SQE is also very active in coordinating groups responsible for consolidating proposed new or revised national software engineering standards, which may eventually become a part of federal regulatory codes. Like QAI, SQE also offers consulting services to corporate data centers interested in starting TQM programs or in preparing an application for the prestigious Malcolm Baldridge Quality Award. This consultation includes critique of data center TQM procedure, as well as assistance in development of a local TQM or Software Metrics function. It is a good idea to ask to be added to their mailing list, since this is likely to be one of the most important organizations to foster growth of ASQM.

SPECIAL INTEREST GROUP ON METRICS (SIGMETRICS)

Association for Computing Machinery (ACM)
1133 Avenue of the Americas
New York, NY 10036
Tel: 212/869-7440

The SIGMETRICS group is active in many areas of new technology information distribution and management. ACM is a supporter of professional seminars and conferences on ASQM.

TECHNOLOGY TRANSFER INSTITUTE (TTI)

System Performance Programs
Technology Transfer Institute
741 Tenth Street
Santa Monica, CA 90402
Tel: 213/394-8305

The TTI is one of the leading providers of quality training and continuing education for the computer industry. It is associated with such well-known software engineering and software quality performance evaluation experts as Bernard Domanski, Tom DeMarco, and the world renowned James Martin. TTI offers training at the customer site, or at its own facilities, and also assists in the organization and administration of technical presentations.

WATSON & WALKER TUNING LETTER

Watson & Walker
814 Sandringham Lane
Lutz, FL 33549-6801
Tel: 1-800-553-4562
FAX: 813/949-3674

The *Cheryl Watson's Tuning Letter* is a newsletter subscription service of practical MVS software tuning and measurement advice. It offers pragmatic suggestions for improving the performance of all MVS systems and software applications based on software quality measurements that are available directly from SMF and RMF system log utilities and IBM product reporting facilities, without any commitment to long-term historical performance database products. Cheryl Watson has worked as a systems programmer and performance-tuning trainer for EDS and Amdahl and as a consulting trainer for Legent. She is a regular speaker at CMG and SHARE. This newsletter is one of the best investments your data center can make so as not to miss a single tuning trick. The subscription price of the newsletter is currently $295 per year ($345 outside the United States).

Appendix C

AUTOMATED SOFTWARE QUALITY MEASUREMENT BASIC SAS LANGUAGE TOOLKIT

Since most SAS language-based performance measurement products, such as MICS and MXG, provide advanced SAS language coding hints and basic SAS tutorial assistance, it is expected that the ASQM professional can learn the fundamentals of SAS programming from these sources—as well as from the basic SAS language manuals available from SAS Institute. It is also advisable that every data center that licenses SAS language products should keep a full set of SAS manuals in the data center technical library, in addition to ordering a complete set of SAS Institute annual *SUGI Proceedings*. Another source not to be overlooked is the User's Group Libraries for MICS and MXG, which share complete SAS language programs for specialized software measurement applications. SAS also provides a user-submitted SAS program library, as well as user-written SAS macros and procedures, which provide specialized SAS toolkit functions which apply SAS Base language products. Beyond these important sources of critical SAS toolkit items, here are ten little-known "SAS tricks" that are useful to SAS programmers as they apply TQM and ASQM techniques to their analysis of SMF data using SAS.

1. **Time Plots to Graphically Present Relative Time-Base Metrics:**

   One of the most overlooked and underutilized SAS procedures is PROC TIMEPLOT. This procedure is useful to ASQM analysts who need to stretch out and compare a time series for a particular environmental domain or application workload area. The PROC TIMEPLOT procedure is particularly useful in the monitoring of a deadline for either a customer *Service-Level Agreement* (SLA), data center *Management-By-Objective* (MBO), or *Service-Level Objective* (SLO). This procedure can be specified to monitor a twenty-four hour period, over the course of a month, or even a year, depending on SAS time-base specifications. The TIMEPLOT procedure is also very useful in monitoring the effectiveness of a chargeback billing rate at fully recovering anticipated data center costs or monitoring the variance of expected capacity planning levels of system utilization or response time against actual results. The basic format for an SAS PROC TIMEPLOT procedure is:

```
PROC TIMEPLOT    <UNIFORM   column alignment on all pages >
                 <MAXDEC=   n maximum decimal positions    >;

PLOT             <OVERLAY   to place all series on 1 plot>
                 <HILOC     to connect points by a hyphen>
                 <JOINREF   to join extreme points by ref>
                 <REVERSE   to rotate the axis of a plot >
                 <POS=      n to print to n chars wide    >
                 <AXIS=     to specify units or time-base>
                 <REF=      to specify a midline ref      >
                 <REFCHAR=  char used as ref (default=|) >
                 <OVPCHAR=  char to plot if data converge>;

CLASS            <breakout variable names>;
BY               <grouping variable names>;
ID               <descriptive variable>;
```

The PROC TIMEPLOT procedure can also be combined with SAS DATA steps and PUT statements to customize reports by outputting conditional demarcation lines to spread out or separate the series of unit values, to create "*Gant*-like" plots.

2.   **Expert System Heuristic Rules-of-Thumb Conditional Coding:**

The basic trick to coding knowledge rules in SAS is similar to the case or condition statement in traditional structured programming. The basic format is commonly used in an SAS DATA step, either as a conditional "OR" statement or as a traditional "IF-THEN-ELSE," as found in other procedural languages such as PL/I or COBOL, as well as SAS. An example of a complex structured *unconditional* SAS case statement is:

```
IF SUBSTR(PGM_NAME,1,3)='IEF' OR
   SUBSTR(PGM_NAME,1,3)='IEH' OR
   SUBSTR(PGM_NAME,1,3)='IEJ' THEN.<rule action>;
```

An example of a *conditional* "IF-THEN-ELSE" would be:

```
IF SUBSTR(PGM_NAME,1,3)='IEF' OR
   SUBSTR(PGM_NAME,1,3)='IEH' OR
   SUBSTR(PGM_NAME,1,3)='IEJ' THEN.<process 1>;
ELSE
     <process 2>;
```

This simple technique can be the basis of a multitude of special exception condition checks or automated diagnostic notifications, which can increase the power of the automated software quality measurement tools and reduce the effort required to analyze the incredible volume of data that SMF system logs can generate. There are notably more efficient ways to code SAS case and condition statements, but this method is the most suitable for online "what-if" query coding using the SAS online display manager, which is similar to the function QMF provides for DB2 programmers on TSO.

3.   QA-AUTO Assignment of Exception Condition Diagnostic Group:

The key to a QA-AUTO automatic assignment of exception condition or diagnostic grouping codes based on an expert rules definition using SAS case or condition statements is to optimize the code by converting the conditional edits or ranges into a permanent numeric-indexed value using PROC FORMAT. This SAS procedure allows the programmer to associate a descriptive label, or even a short message (generally less than thirty characters), to a prescribed numeric value or range of values. The general format of the PROC FORMAT procedure is:

```
PROC FORMAT    <LIBRARY= name of SAS format lib>;
      VALUE    <format name>
               <value-(range)>;
      PICTURE  <mask name/fill char/prefix char/hival>;
```

This simple procedure can be used to define an efficient means of providing standardized labels and messages for prescribed qualitative conditions, which can be changed or adjusted at any time by simply resubmitting the PROC FORMAT procedure against the indicated SAS format library, along with the new specifications. As an example, the following PROC FORMAT code would make it possible to associate a QA-AUTO diagnostic message with a software quality measurement variable scanned from incoming SMF:

```
PROC FORMAT LIBRARY=QA-AUTO.FORMAT.LIB;
      VALUE RESPTIME (FUZZ=.5)
            0-1='** GOOD WORK - SUBSECOND RESPONSE **'
            2-3='-- RESPONSE TIME OK - KEEP ITASIS --'
            4-90='\\ SUB-STD ALERT - CALL SWAT TEAM //'
            90-200='!! MAJOR CRISIS-CALL IBM REP !!';
```

This message can then be "pulled in" and applied to individual SAS observations on the SAS report by use of the following code when the PROC PRINT procedure is invoked:

```
PROC PRINT.
      FORMAT <<var name>> RESPTIME;
```

Using this technique, there is no need to carry the additional data storage and process overhead of keeping the diagnostic message or category label in every database where response time data occurs. Furthermore, by keeping service-level time limits or software quality measurement standard data in a PROC FORMAT library in this way, it is possible to make application-specific or data center wide "across-the-board" changes in values that are assigned for particular workloads or customer agreements (i.e., define separate ranges for RESPTIM1, RESPTIM2, etc.). It is also worth noting that many methods can be used to actually automate the generation of the SAS code that resets or recalibrates PROC FORMAT service-level standard descriptions, such as the automated standard exception level recommendation that is provided by the MICS Base product facilities.

4.   Pareto Ranking Analysis of Predominant Cause and Effect:

There should be nothing particularly magical about Pareto charts for SAS programmers, since most SAS programmers have been using the Pareto *80/20* rule for years, possibly without ever really knowing its name. One of the most commonly used SAS Base procedures is PROC FREQ. This frequency ranking procedure takes input as tabular datasets (i.e., spreadsheets) and outputs the number of occurrences for each group, the percent of the overall population input, as well as cumulative frequency (the running total occurrences), and cumulative percent. If the number of groupings are small enough, it is usually possible to visually determine if the *80/20* rule applies to the data. If not, the groups can be recombined or redistributed as many times as necessary in order to determine the best focus for efforts to eliminate or reduce a particular software quality problem of concern. There is only one catch here, which is a critical item that determines whether or not the PROC FREQ output will be usable as input to a Pareto diagram. The general format for PROC FREQ is as follows:

```
PROC FREQ    <DATA= input SAS file name          >
             <ORDER= FREQ/DATA/INTERNAL/FORMATTED>;
      TABLES <(count) variable names             >
             <LIST/or cross-tab default           >
             <OUT= output SAS file name          >
             <specialized statistics request list>;
      WEIGHT <(multiplier) variable name>;
      BY     <(subgroups) variable names>;
```

The critical item is that ORDER=FREQ must be specified to receive the output ranked from highest frequency to lowest frequency, as needed for Pareto chart input; otherwise, the default is the SAS internal value (which can be confounding if you try to relate the output to any logical order or pattern you can see).

5.   Comparison of Current to Previous Version Software Controls:

The SAS Base language product provides a PROC COMPARE procedure that is extremely efficient and takes full advantage of all the internally indexed capabilities of the SAS database format. Since it is often desirable for the ASQM analyst to make rapid comparison between current versus previous versions of software program source coding modules, as well as two contiguous versions of JCL members or even an input data file, it is often easiest to accomplish this task by use of PROC COMPARE. This procedure is so efficient that it is possible to scan current versus previous versions of entire JCL libraries, sourcecode libraries, or even SMF Type 14 Data Set Access and Attributes (DCB specifications such as LRECL, BLKSIZE, DSORG, etc.). It can even compare the number of EXCPs or I/Os recorded against individual datasets for a given time period and output a file of percent-variance by individual member or dataset. While it might be expected that such an incredible task would take enormous CPU resources, depending on the number of sorts and sort variables involved, a simple, one-way PROC COMPARE procedure usually only takes a relatively few CPU seconds. The general format for the PROC COMPARE procedure is as follows:

```
PROC COMPARE     <DATA=       input 'current' dataset  >
                 <COMPARE=    input 'previous' dataset >
                 <OUT=        output (compare results) >
                 <statistics/OUTPERCENT/OUTNOEQUAL    >
                 <METHOD=     RELATIVE/PERCENT/ABSOLUTE>
                 <ALLOBS/NOBS/ALLVARS/ALLSTATS/etc.   >;

        VAR      <variable names to compare 'C-vs-P' >;
        WITH     <to equate variable names across ds >;
        ID       <to carry forward a noncompare var  >;
        BY       <to order subgroup (sorted by) vars >;
```

Examples of the kind of output that can be achieved from the use of this procedure in a daily JCL configuration DCB audit check function were shown in Chapter 1. This kind of procedure can be applied to any number of other software quality measurement and software standards audit functions and, when monitored along with an appropriate variance notification and followup process, the PROC COMPARE procedure can provide a valuable tool to the AQSM professional, as well as traditional EDP auditors. One small caveat that goes with the use of this SAS procedure is that although it is extremely efficient when the number of comparative variables per PROC COMPARE execution is kept to a minimum, the specification of several compare variables at once can actually overload most CPU memory region maximums (i.e., keep the number of compares small!).

6. **Merging Cross-System Log Records to Relate Concurrent Events:**

This is probably one of the most important capabilities that the SAS language provides, giving it an advantage over all other methods of reading and summarizing SMF system log records. Each SMF record observation carries the full set of job accounting codes, as well as either the start or stop SMF-timestamp, which is just about as unique as a fingerprint. When it becomes desirable to cross-link the functional information to two different SMF log record times, the following applies. First, the two SAS record types are sorted by a single critical identifier or account code and a common timestamp that is shared by both records (either a process start or end time). Second, in order to eliminate duplicate SMF records for the same event, it is a good idea to add one additional metric variable that accumulates during the SMF collection process, and sort in descending order to keep the most recent value. It is also a good idea to specify "NODUPLICATES" in the PROC SORT procedure options. However, the basic match merge process can normally be achieved as follows:

```
PROC SORT DATA=SMF_REC1; BY ACCT1 SMFTIME;
PROC SORT DATA=SMF_REC2; BY ACCT1 SMFTIME;
DATA SMF_COMB; MERGE SMF_REC1 SMF_REC2:
        BY ACCT1 SMFTIME;
```

The result is a single, summarized dataset that contains the functional data from two separate types of SMF log records, which reduces storage requirements and makes it possible to quickly retrieve specialized conditional datasets (similar to the way DB2 user view tables are created by "JOIN" query statements). It is also a good idea to use "KEEP= " in order to specify only the variables that you want to store for any permanent SAS dataset that is created; otherwise, SAS will keep every variable that was common to both datasets, which can waste considerable storage.

7. Line Plots of Common Year-over-Year Seasonal Cyclic Trends:

There are a lot of tricks involved in applying the SAS/GRAPH and SAS/PLOT procedures, and a whole book could be written about the intricate ins and outs of SAS graphing and plotting. Most novice SAS programmers don't take long to move from basic SAS reporting to generating hundreds and hundreds of SAS graphs and plots that show the same data broken out a thousand different ways. The point is that one good picture is probably worth a thousand *so-so* pictures, and most data center managers would rather have everything said in one graph than have all the graphs in the world when it comes time to making critical decisions. So it's important for the ASQM professional to "get it all on one chart." The facility that SAS provides for this purpose is an SAS/GRAPH "OVERLAY" function. This parameter is specified in different ways for each SAS/GRAPH or SAS/PLOT procedure, so you have to check each of the individual SAS manuals, but the basic format is:

```
PROC PLOT <or GRAPHx>     <DATA= input SAS dataset name   >
                          <UNIFORM if same scale all pp    >
                          <NOLEGEND to drop varnames at top>;

        BY                <group variable (for breakouts)  >;
        PLOT              <var1 * var2/axis vars//OVERLAY//>;
```

When you specify "/OVERLAY" at the end of the "PLOT" statement, all of the data will be plotted within the confines of the same time-base dimension or functional group variable defined in the "BY" group statement. This technique is particularly useful with ASQM data used in capacity planning or forecasting analysis of time series data. It should be noted that the OVERLAY technique does not work as effectively if there is no common dimension that can realistically be "stretched out" so that the overlaid data either falls along the same line or plots to several "levels" one above the other (as in the case of the "Y-O-Y" time series data); otherwise, what you get is a "scatterplot."

8. T-Test Comparative Analysis of Alternative Process or Method:

The comparative t-test experimental analysis of two alternative methods or competing application workloads as presented in Chapter 3, is easily generated without very much special preparation by use of the PROC UNIVARIATE procedure. The two test condition datasets ("experiment" versus "control") are usually processed by concurrent PROC UNIVARIATE procedure statements. The general format is as follows:

```
PROC UNIVARIATE DATA=EXP_DATA FREQ PLOT NORMAL;
     VAR NO_FAILS;
     ID PGM_NAME;
PROC UNIVARIATE DATA=CTL_DATA FREQ PLOT NORMAL;
     VAR NO_FAILS;
     ID PGM_NAME:
```

Although there are considerably more available PROC UNIVARIATE procedure options than those shown, this particular specification (i.e., "FREQ PLOT NORMAL") is most commonly preferred. These options produce the complete set of univariate frequency and confidence interval statistics and normalized distribution with both histogram and "box-and-whisker" plots. Any other options that are specified for this procedure will restrict the PROC UNIVARIATE output to particular statistics rather than print all statistics, and excluding any of these three option keywords will not produce the full report as shown earlier in Chapters 2 and 3. This is an extremely useful procedure for ASQM analysts, since it is the best way to prove whether a specific method, standard, or process has actually improved software quality.

9. **Reading and Unloading Partitioned Dataset Lib Directories:**

Examples of code for unloading a partitioned dataset using PROC SOURCE was presented earlier in Chapter 5. The main point to make here is that PROC SOURCE can also be used to print the PDS directory, or unload PDS members to a sequential file, or to print out and provide line and member count statistics on a hardcopy report. This can be done for selected members by a common module name prefix (again, the importance of standardized application and program naming conventions). The basic format for this procedure is as follows:

```
PROC SOURCE      <DIRDD=  dsn to unload directory to >
                 <INDD=   dsn of pds to be unloaded  >
                 <OUTDD=  dsn of ps file to unload to>
                 <NOALIAS/NODATA/NOPRINT/NOSORT/NOSUM>;

        SELECT   <xxx:-yyy:>;
        EXCLUDE  <xxx:-yyy:>;
        FIRST    <'literal string used as header rec'>;
        LAST     <'literal string used as trailer rec'>;
        BEFORE   <'literal string before x member rec'>;
        AFTER    <'literal string after x member rec'>;
```

It should be clear that the "FIRST/LAST/BEFORE/AFTER" statements also give PROC SOURCE the capability to read a PDS directory and to automatically generate SYSIN control statements to utility programs such as IEBCOPY or SYNCSORT. This can be a very useful tool for managing software libraries. Although PROC SOURCE does not have the scan capability found in FILE-AID Batch or Q/AUDITOR, when used in combination with many of the SAS Character Edit Function statements, and some of the specialized User-Written SAS procedures in the SAS User Group Library, it is possible to globally edit JCL or reformat program sourcecode according to changes in data center standards, in a single execution pass. Even though it is more desirable to procure FILE-AID or Q/AUDITOR for more specialized program sourcecode scanning and global standards management tasks, PROC SOURCE provides a powerful alternative when you need to quickly develop automated software management solutions.

10. **Tallying Software Metric Units into Classes or Time Blocks:**

By far, the most overlooked SAS procedure is probably the extended capabilities of PROC TABULATE. Output from this procedure was shown in Chapters 2, 3, and 11 and can always be identified by the following characteristic PROC TABULATE matrix pattern:

```
          +-----+-----+-----+-----+-----+-----+
          |  a  |  b  |  c  |  d  |  e  | ... | ALL |
+---------+-----+-----+-----+-----+-----+-----+-----+
|    A    |  9  |  9  |  9  |  9  |  9  | ... | 99  |
+---------+-----+-----+-----+-----+-----+-----+-----+
|    B    |  9  |  9  |  9  |  9  |  9  | ... | 99  |
+---------+-----+-----+-----+-----+-----+-----+-----+
|    C    |  9  |  9  |  9  |  9  |  9  | ... | 99  |
+---------+-----+-----+-----+-----+-----+-----+-----+
|   ...   | ... | ... | ... | ... | ... | ... | ... |
+---------+-----+-----+-----+-----+-----+-----+-----+
|   ALL   | 999 | 999 | 999 | 999 | 999 | ... | 9999|
+---------+-----+-----+-----+-----+-----+-----+-----+
```

The various options for this procedure tend to be fairly complex relative to all the other SAS procedures, which is probably why it isn't used more extensively by SAS programmers (and also probably why SAS Institute has devoted an entire manual to this one Base SAS procedure). The basic format for PROC TABULATE is a little more complicated than with most other SAS procedures, as can be seen in the following:

```
PROC TABULATE   <DATA= input SAS dataset name        >
                <FORMAT=SAS format for all cells      >
                <ORDER= FREQ/DATA/INTERNAL/FORMATTED  >
                <FORMCHAR= char to put around boxes   >
                <DEPTH= maximum dimensions across page>;
        CLASS   <group variables                >;
        VAR     <all numeric vars to be used    >;
        FREQ    <numeric var to group by        >;
        WEIGHT  <numeric var to mult by         >;
        BY      <variables to break out by      >;
        FORMAT  <names/size of ea. var format   >;
        LABEL   <descriptive labels ea. var     >;
        KEYLABEL <label to give to statistics   >;
```

```
TABLE      <var1*stats,var2*stats          >
           <MISSTEXT/FUZZ/CONDENSE/RTSPACE>
           <BOX= _PAGE_/var/string          >
           <ROW= FLOAT/CONSTANT             >;
```

In spite of this, it is well worth the effort to learn to use PROC TABULATE, in order to quickly prepare matrix reports or tally qualitative software metrics. It is a good idea to get the SAS manual for PROC TABULATE procedure, since it includes a large variety of examples which can be used as models for almost any application of the procedure that you will ever need. One last note is that the PROC TABULATE "ORDER=" statement is similar in nature to the same statement in PROC FREQ. The two most important options are "ORDER=FREQ," which will list the largest values or percentages first (in descending order, like a Pareto ranking), and "ORDER=DATA," which will list in the order it was sorted for input. Otherwise, if no "ORDER=" is specified, the default is "ORDER=INTERNAL," which is the SAS data internal indexed order (a.k.a. "ORDER=INFERNAL," since you can try from now until doomsday to find a logical pattern in the output resulting from even the most innocent specification of this PROC option).

Appendix D

SOFTWARE PROBLEM MANAGEMENT AND PROGRAM FAILURE CODES

The MICS product builds several performance database files derived automatically from the SMF system log operational process records and provides the data entry facilities that a technical staff can use to update additional problem management information. Comments can be added to performance data and permanently archived in order to support fully standardized and comparative analysis of trends in operations management and forecasting of the impact of discrete changes in standards or procedures. It supports problem management according to the following software error categories and system failure reason codes, which conform to recommendations of IBM's problem management user task force.

Reason Code	Software Problem Management and Program Failure Category
1XXX	Processor Hardware Failure
1100	Central Processor Failure
1110	Processor Storage Error
1200	Channel Failure
1300	Control Unit Failure
1400	Tape Drive Failure
1500	DASD Device Failure
1550	Mass Storage Failure
2XXX	Teleprocessing Equipment
2150	Multiplexor Failure
2160	Control Unit Failure
2200	Communications Line Outage
2300	Communications Processor Failure

(continued)

Reason Code	Software Problem Management and Program Failure Category
2400	Local Area Network Failure
2500	Microwave Transmission Failure
2600	Satellite Transmission Failure
3XXX	Hardcopy I/O Devices
3100	Mechanical Printer Error
3110	Laser Printer Failure
3120	Card Reader Error
3130	Card Punch Error
3150	OCR Reader Error
3160	Plotter Failure
5XXX	Software
51XX	System Software
5100	Operating System Failure
5200	JES2 Failure
5300	JES3 Failure
5400	Utility Failure
5500	Application Programming Error
55XX	Application Software
5600	Media Date in Error
5650	IMS Failure
5700	DB2 Failure
5750	Documentation Error
58XX	Communication Software
5800	TCAM Failure
5850	VTAM Failure
5900	NCP Failure
5950	Netview Failure
5800	TCAM Failure
5850	VTAM Failure
5900	NCP Failure
5950	Netview Failure
6XXX	Personnel
6400	Console Operators Error
6410	I/O Personnel Error
6420	Scheduler Error
6430	Data Control Personnel Error
6440	Tape Librarian Error
6450	DASD Manager Error
6500	Data Entry Error
6700	Hardware Installation Error
6800	Clerical Error
8XXX	Facilities
8130	Power Outage
8140	Air Conditioning Failure

Reason Code	Software Problem Management and Program Failure Category
9XXX	Scheduled Outage
9100	Systems Software
9200	Hardware Installation
9300	Hardware Maintenance

The following IBM Abend Error Code descriptions and general category of software or operational process problems can be used to automatically assign the initial diagnostic category for purposes of software quality reporting, for data center methods and standards process analysis. The final problem resolution and diagnostic category can be determined after consideration of the system message or operational product system log codes are also taken into account.

(*NOTE: Snnn=System Abend Codes; Unnn=User-Defined Program Abend Codes.*)

Abend Code	General Software Error Description	Initial Error Cause Category
SACC	FORTRAN Accounting Error	Language Error
SA00	EXCP Processing Error	System Error
SA0A	FREEMAIN Exec Error	Program Defect
SA03	Return Prior Subtask	Program Defect
SA13	Open Execution Errors	JCL Errors
SA22	Force Command Entry	Program Defect
SA37	Open File Request Error	Input Data
SA78	FREEMAIN Exec Usage Error	Program Defect
SB0A	GETMAIN/FREEMAIN Error	Program Defect
SB00	False Error Condition Error	Program Defect
SB14	Close Execution Error	Program Defect
SB37	End-of-Volume Error	Input Data
SC03	Task Close Error	Program Defect
SC13	Concatenate Dataset Errors	JCL Errors
SD0D	Abend Request Overlays	Program Defect
SD13	Invalid Graphic Device	Program Defect
SD2D	Invalid Link Edit Address	Program Defect
SD23	Invalid Transmit Request	Program Defect
SD37	Output Request Task Fail	Input Data
SE37	Output Request System Fail	Input Data
SDFB	JES3 Error	System Error
SF2D	Invalid Overlay Request	Program Defect
SF37	Irrecoverable Device Fail	System Error
S0B0	System Workarea Error	System Error
S0CA	Decimal Exceeds Field	Program Defect
S0CB	Decimal Divide Exception	Program Defect
S0CC	Calculation over High Value	Program Defect

(*continued*)

Abend Code	General Software Error Description	Initial Error Cause Category
S0CD	Calculation under Low Value	Program Defect
S0CE	Program Division by Zero	Program Defect
S0CF	Program Multiply by Zero	Program Defect
S0C1	Operation Exception	Program Defect
S0C2	Privileged Operation Request	Program Defect
S0C3	Address Points to Self	Program Defect
S0C4	Protection Exceptions	Input Data
S0C5	Address Space Exceptions	Input Data
S0C6	Data Handling Exceptions	Input Data
S0C7	Data Definition Exceptions	Input Data
S0C8	Binary Field Entry Error	Input Data
S0C9	Fixed-Point Divide	Program Defect
S0D2	Program Checkpoint Invalid	Program Defect
S0D3	Checkpoint System Call	Program Defect
S0D7	PT or SSAR Error	Program Defect
S0E3	Program Virtual I/O Error	Program Defect
S0F1	Program I/O in OS Handler	Program Defect
S0F2	JCL I/O Logic Error	JCL Errors
S0F3	DASD I/O Controller Errors	System Error
S0F8	Disabled OS/SVC Error	System Error
S000	Unresolved I/O Wait	Input Data
S001	Input/Output Error	Input Data
S002	File Error	Input Data
S003	Error in End-of-Block	Input Data
S004	Input DCB Conflicts	Input Data
S005	Invalid BSAM Decimal Return	Program Defect
S006	Invalid Service Request	Program Defect
S008	Invalid SYNAD Error	Program Defect
S013	Process Sequence Errors	JCL Errors
S014	Process Out-of-Sequence	JCL Errors
S02A	JES2 Control Block Invalid	System Error
S02B	Program Exit Parm over Max	Program Defect
S02C	JES2 Function Address Space	System Error
S020	Invalid BDAM Allocation	JCL Errors
S021	Invalid ASCB Address	System Error
S022	VPSS Returned Bad Device	System Error
S024	Invalid Print Service Task	System Error
S027	Invalid Print Service Error	System Error
S028	Program Damaged by Pageswap	System Error
S03A	ISAM Dataset Error	Input Data
S03B	ISAM Invalid LRECL	JCL Errors
S03D	Open Error with Bad DD	JCL Errors
S03E	QISAM Insufficent Space	JCL Errors
S030	I/O Error in BSAM DSN	Input Data

Abend Code	General Software Error Description	Initial Error Cause Category
S031	I/O Errors in ISAM Dataset	Input Data
S032	BISAM/QISAM Open Error	Input Data
S033	Error in ISAM Open	Input Data
S034	Error in BISAM Open	Input Data
S035	Error in BISAM Open	Input Data
S036	Error in BISAM Open	Input Data
S037	Insufficient BSAM Buffers	JCL Errors
S038	Insufficient DD Space	JCL Errors
S039	QISAM EOF Flag Errors	Program Defect
S04C	Invalid Terminal Return	System Error
S04D	GETMAIN Macro Error	Program Defect
S04E	DB2 Internal System Error	System Error
S040	Error in TCAM Group	System Error
S041	Error in TCAM Queue	System Error
S042	IPL Abended Activation	System Error
S043	No Abend DCB in Procedure	JCL Errors
S044	Missing DD Statement	JCL Errors
S045	Insufficient TCAM Message	System Error
S046	Insufficient TCAM Space	System Error
S047	Invalid Subprogram Call	Program Defect
S047	Unauthorized Service Request	Program Defect
S048	Invalid Recovery Return	System Error
S049	Invalid Recovery Service	System Error
S05A	Invalid FREESRB Return Code	System Error
S05B	Invalid SRB Timing	System Error
S05C	Invalid Allocation Model	System Error
S05D	CALLDISP Entry Fail	Program Defect
S05E	SRBSTAT Macro Fail	Program Defect
S05F	VSPC Address Space Error	Program Defect
S052	Invalid Program Call Request	Program Defect
S053	Invalid Program SVC Request	Program Defect
S054	Unrecoverable SVC Routine	Program Defect
S055	Event Notify Errors	Program Defect
S056	Program Modified DCB Block	Program Defect
S057	Wrong DVC in DEB Table	Program Defect
S058	Invalid OS Service Call	Program Defect
S059	Stop/Reset Service Call	System Error
S06A	SRB Function Recovery Fail	System Error
S06C	LSQA GETMAIN Loop	System Error
S06D	RTM Slip Monitor Error	System Error
S06E	RTM Free Cell Error	System Error
S06F	RTM Recovery Failure	System Error
S061	Graphic Macro Fail	Program Defect

(continued)

Abend Code	General Software Error Description	Initial Error Cause Category
S062	Graphics Language Error	Program Defect
S063	Graphic Terminal Cancel	Operation Controls
S064	Address Space CML Lock	System Error
S065	SS AFFIN Macro Lock	System Error
S066	MVS Dispatcher Lock	System Error
S069	Remote Terminal Call Fail	System Error
S07A	Serious Swapout Error	System Error
S07B	Program Address Load Errors	Program Defect
S07C	OS Command-Level Conflict	Program Defect
S07D	Stack Overflow Fail	System Error
S07E	Device Path Invalid	System Error
S07F	Wrong TCB Address Space	System Error
S070	Suspend Macro Lock	Program Defect
S071	Program in Loop or Wait	Program Defect
S072	Unavailable System Resource	System Error
S073	Invalid SETLOCK Error	Program Defect
S074	Invalid Program Lock	Program Defect
S075	Invalid OP System Request	Program Defect
S076	Invalid System Address	System Error
S077	Invalid Console Request	System Error
S078	Invalid Subroutine Return	Program Defect
S079	Invalid Terminal Message	Program Defect
S08F	Changekey Operation Fail	System Error
S081	SQA Storage Frame Fail	System Error
S082	SET LOCKWORD Failed	System Error
S083	Auxiliary Storage Failure	System Error
S084	Auxiliary Storage I/O Fail	System Error
S085	Virtual I/O Page Entry	System Error
S086	Virtual I/O Operation Fail	System Error
S087	FREEMAIN Operation Fail	System Error
S09A	Invalid Global Resource	Program Defect
S090	BSAM DD Unit PARM	JCL Errors
S091	Internal BTAM Controls	Program Defect
S092	Improper BTAM DCB	Program Defect
S093	Improper BTAM Open	Program Defect
S094	Invalid Open Controls	Program Defect
S095	BTAM Terminal GEN Error	System Error
S096	Insufficient Buffer Space	JCL Errors
S097	Insufficient I/O DIR Space	JCL Errors
S098	Invalid BTAM Errors	Program Defect
S099	Invalid BTAM Address	JCL Errors
S1FA	System Crash from JES2	System Error
S1FB	System Crash from JES3	System Error
S1F1	System Crash (Unknown)	System Error

Abend Code	General Software Error Description	Initial Error Cause Category
S100	Invalid Device Request	Program Defect
S102	Invalid CTLBLK Address	Program Defect
S106	LINK, LOAD, XCTL Errors	Program Defect
S113	TYPE=J Open Error	JCL Errors
S117	TYPE=T BASM Close Error	JCL Errors
S12D	Invalid Data Overlay	Input Data
S122	Operator Cancel W/D	Input Data
S13E	System Task Premature End	Program Defect
S130	DEQ Macro Instruction Error	Program Defect
S137	Tape Hardware Error	System Error
S138	Duplicate Device Request	Program Defect
S14F	Status Request Interrupt	Program Defect
S16E	Control Program Request	Program Defect
S171	Paging Request Overlay	System Error
S18A	RSM Invalid Request	System Error
S2F3	System Crash during Execute	System Error
S206	Invalid Parameters	Program Defect
S213	Open Error	JCL Errors
S214	Close Error	JCL Errors
S222	Operation Cancel WO/Dump	Input Data
S228	EXTRACT Execution Errors	Program Defect
S23E	DETACH Macro Instruction	Program Defect
S233	Invalid Dump Requests	Program Defect
S237	End-of-Volume Error	Input Data
S240	RJE Transaction Format Error	Input Data
S30A	Loaded Program Not Found	Change Control
S300	Program Fail during I/O	Input Data
S301	Program Request Exceeds Wait	Input Data
S305	Program FREEMAIN Errors	Program Defect
S306	Get Program Request Error	Program Defect
S313	I/O Errors Getting DCB	System Error
S314	I/O Errors Reading DCB	System Error
S32D	Address Exceeds REGION	Program Defect
S322	Time Limit Exceeded	Input Data
S328	EXTRACT Macro Overloaded	Input Data
S337	EXTRACT Exec Overloaded	Input Data
S338	Wrong Subprogram Called	Program Defect
S378	Request Exceeds MAXCPU	Program Defect
S4F1	Insufficient System Space	System Error
S40D	ATTN Request Overlays	Input Data
S400	EXCP Processing Error	Input Data
S406	Bad Exec LINK/XCTL	Program Defect
S413	Open Execution Errors	Input Data

(continued)

Abend Code	General Software Error Description	Initial Error Cause Category
S414	I/O Error in DASD Volume	Input Data
S422	JCL Exceeded MAX DD	JCL Errors
S437	I/O Error at EOV	Input Data
S482	Invalid RACF Message	Data Security
S483	Invalid RACF Return Code	Data Security
S50D	I/O Error in Unit Control	DASD Storage Mgmt.
S506	Insufficient REGION	JCL Errors
S513	Tape DS Open Error	Program Defect
S522	Wait State Time Limit	Input Data
S537	Tape VOLSER in Use	Scheduling
S60A	No Task Workspace	JCL Errors
S604	GETMAIN Request Fail	Program Defect
S605	FREEMAIN Request Fail	Program Defect
S613	Open Execution Errors	Input Data
S614	Close Execution Error	Input Data
S622	I/O Volume Exceeded	Input Data
S637	End-of-Volume Error	Input Data
S7F1	System Abend	System Error
S700	Program Interrupted I/O	Program Defect
S706	Bad LOADMOD Request	Program Defect
S713	Failed DS Read Request	Input Data
S714	Tape Label/DS Error	Input Data
S722	Output Limit Exceeded	Input Data
S737	End-of-Volume Error	Input Data
S738	Unexpected Queue Message	Program Defect
S80A	GETMAIN/FREEMAIN Error	Program Defect
S800	System Override Error	Program Defect
S801	Program Wait Limit Errors	Program Defect
S804	Program Exceeded Region	Program Defect
S806	Requested Program Not Found	Program Defect
S813	Wrong Open Macro Error	Program Defect
S822	Excess Requested REGION Parm	JCL Errors
S837	I/O Error at EOV	Input Data
S878	GETMAIN/FREEMAIN Error	Program Defect
S9F1	System Abend Failed Task	System Error
S90A	Program Closed File Two Times	Program Defect
S900	System Abend Failure	System Error
S906	Program Macro Exec Loop	Program Defect
S913	RACF-Protection Error	Data Security
S922	RACF-Protection Override	Data Security
S937	Invalid Dataset Password	Data Security
U0000	MTO Control Recovery	Program Defect
U0001	LOGDS Data Conflict	Program Defect
U0002	Control Region Lockout	Program Defect

Abend Code	General Software Error Description	Initial Error Cause Category
U0004	Control Region Lockout Loop	Program Defect
U0005	LOGDS Close Errors	Program Defect
U0006	LOGDS Close Loop Error	Program Defect
U0008	Insufficient Working Storage	Program Defect
U0010	Invalid Data Format	Input Data
U0011	Invalid Console Message	Input Data
U0012	Invalid Block Size	Input Data
U0013	Invalid Data Logged	Input Data
U0014	Invalid Subprogram Parm	Input Data
U0015	Incomplete PDS Directory	Input Data
U0016	DCB/DSCB Conflicts	Program Defect
U0017	Out-of-Sequence VS Buffer	Program Defect
U0018	Out-of-Sequence Log Control	Program Defect
U0019	Module Count Sequence Error	Program Defect
U0020	Illegal Data Modify	Program Defect
U0021	Log Master Task Error	Program Defect
U0022	Session Control Errors	Program Defect
U0023	DLI Address Process Error	Program Defect
U0024	DBRC Region Control Error	Program Defect
U0025	Duplicate DBRC Control	Program Defect
U0026	System Task Usage Fail	Program Defect
U0027	Abnormal Dump Request	Program Defect
U0028	OP Console Data Request Fail	Program Defect
U0029	DLI Program-Requested Dump	Program Defect
U0030	Invalid Procedure Override	Program Defect
U0031	Log Block Check Error	System Error
U0036	Invalid VT Polling Error	System Error
U0037	Invalid SYS ACK Error	System Error
U0038	Failed Emergency Restart	System Error
U0039	VTAM ID Request Failed	System Error
U0040	Share SYSCMD Lock Fail	System Error
U0041	DBRC Sign On Request Fail	System Error
U0042	Backout Sign On Errors	System Error
U0043	Stop Recovery Fails	System Error
U0044	Started W/O Checkpoint	System Error
U0045	Restart W/O Checkpoint	System Error
U0046	Incompatibile PCB Parms	JCL Errors
U0047	Insufficient PCB Storage	JCL Errors
U0048	INIT Recovery Error	System Error
U0049	OS Storage Exceeded	System Error
U0050	Storage Device Incompatible	JCL Errors
U0064	Invalid JCL Comment Line	JCL Errors
U0069	No FAST PATH Defined	Program Defect

(continued)

Abend Code	General Software Error Description	Initial Error Cause Category
U0070	IMOD Return Code Error	Program Defect
U0071	SYSMOD Compatibility Error	Program Defect
U0072	LOG DS DCB Error	JCL Errors
U0073	Insufficient INIT Log Space	JCL Errors
U0074	LOG DS I/O Errors	System Error
U0075	Invalid DCB Received	System Error
U0077	Invalid DELETE Errors	Program Defect
U0078	Insufficient CNTLBLK Space	Program Defect
U0079	IMOD Nucleus Load Error	System Error
U0080	OSAM I/O Table Errors	System Error
U0081	SUBSYS Control Table Errors	System Error
U0082	Invalid Security Action	Data Security
U0084	BMP Call Data Missing	System Error
U0085	Message Format Changed	System Error
U0088	Initialize Storage Failure	System Error
U0090	Data Posting Block Failure	System Error
U0092	Overloaded System Area	System Error
U0097	Overloaded VSAMPOOL	System Error
U0099	Overloaded WORKPOOL	System Error
U0100	Bad Checkpoint Restarts	Program Defect
U0102	Missing/Invalid PCB	Program Defect
U0103	ZERO/NEG Checkpoint Parm	Program Defect
U0104	Invalid Checkpoint LRECL	Program Defect
U0106	IMOD Load Failures	Program Defect
U0107	RACF Table DS Error	Data Security
U0111	Invalid Data Declare	Program Defect
U0113	DLI PROC Call Error	Program Defect
U0120	Incompatible Region Address	Program Defect
U0121	Invalid Linkage Control	Program Defect
U0124	Invalid Pointer Control	Program Defect
U0132	Invalid Clock Store	Program Defect
U0134	Region ID Lock Fail	Program Defect
U0135	Invalid Program Request	Program Defect
U0136	Duplicate Region ID Request	Program Defect
U0139	System Event Task Tables	Program Defect
U0140	Dependent Region Not in PST	Program Defect
U0141	Signon Token Not Found	Program Defect
U0142	Insufficient PST Storage	Program Defect
U0143	Insufficient PST Virtual	Program Defect
U0144	No ID Table Available	Program Defect
U0145	Dependent Call Table Error	Program Defect
U0147	Signed Off with Active Call	Program Defect
U0148	IMOD During Sign Off	Program Defect
U0149	Invalid Dump Switch	Program Defect

Abend Code	General Software Error Description	Initial Error Cause Category
U0150	DLI/DBRC Conflicts	Program Defect
U0151	Invalid DFS Control Dataset	Program Defect
U0152	Sequence Buffer Compare Fail	Program Defect
U0153	Invalid System Call	Program Defect
U0154	Sequence Buffer Access Error	Program Defect
U0155	Sequence Buffer Test Error	Program Defect
U0156	Illegal DL/I Calls	Program Defect
U0157	DLI Call w/Wrong Key	Program Defect
U0160	Dependent Call w/o Sign On	Program Defect
U0166	RACF Not Available	Data Security
U0168	Checkpoint Change since GEN	Data Security
U0171	RACF Tables Not Available	Data Security
U0172	Insufficient Restart Space	System Error
U0175	Irrecoverable LOG I/O Error	System Error
U0176	System Recovery Error	System Error
U0200	Task Internal Control Error	Program Defect
U0203	Task Subroutine Errors	Program Defect
U0204	DLI Call Trace Logs	Program Defect
U0206	Wrong PSB DD Name	JCL Errors
U0209	Wrong DCB DD Name	JCL Errors
U0214	Wrong Region Type Parm	JCL Errors
U0215	Logical Log DS Errors	JCL Errors
U0216	Invalid Log Procedure	JCL Errors
U0219	Terminal Command Fail	Program Defect
U0222	Request Obsolete Instruction	Program Defect
U0230	Work Area Pool Fails	Program Defect
U0240	BMP Task Time-Outs	JCL Errors
U0242	Low PCB Exec Parms	JCL Errors
U0250	Excess DLI Region Request	JCL Errors
U0251	Missing PRINT DD	JCL Errors
U0252	Abnormal Status Calls	Program Defect
U0253	PCB Does Not Match PSB	Program Defect
U0254	Output DS Open Errors	Program Defect
U0255	DLI Test Compare Limit	Program Defect
U0256	Bad PSB during Compare	Program Defect
U0257	VT Control Block Scan Error	Program Defect
U0258	Permanent I/O Check Error	Program Defect
U0259	Invalid Parm Passed	Program Defect
U0260	Parms Exceed Limits	Program Defect
U0261	Invalid Call Parms	Program Defect
U0262	FAST PATH DLI Parms	Program Defect
U0270	GSAM Checkpoint Invalid	Input Data
U0271	Checkpoint Buffer I/O Error	Input Data

(continued)

Abend Code	General Software Error Description	Initial Error Cause Category
U0272	BSAM to GSAM Incompatible	Input Data
U0273	GSAM DCB Control Block Error	Input Data
U0274	Bad Interface Error	Input Data
U0275	DUMPAREA Overloaded	Input Data
U0300	Program Requested Dump	Program Defect
U0302	Irreconcilable DBRC Error	Program Defect
U0303	Invalid Program Exit	Program Defect
U0305	Invalid Segment Span	Program Defect
U0306	Invalid Accumulator	Program Defect
U0310	Previous Status Conflict	Program Defect
U0311	Survey Status Error	Program Defect
U0315	Invalid Authorization Code	Program Defect
U0347	Missing SYSUDUMP DD	JCL Errors
U0355	Unavailable Access Method	JCL Errors
U0359	HISAM Utility Call Fail	System Error
U0360	Access Method Failed	System Error
U0400	DEDS Error in SVC I/O	Program Defect
U0402	Invalid I/O SVC Calls	Program Defect
U0403	OSAM BATCH I/O Controls	Program Defect
U0407	Invalid Queue Method	Program Defect
U0408	Invalid Queue Attempt	Program Defect
U0411	Bad Transaction Log Test	Program Defect
U0413	SYSTBL Limit Exceeded	Program Defect
U0415	Bad Exec Statement Parm	Program Defect
U0427	Invalid Logical DLI	Program Defect
U0428	Undefined PSB Parms	Program Defect
U0430	DLI Buffer SVC PARM	Program Defect
U0432	BMP PSBDEF Conflict	Program Defect
U0436	Wrong Exec PARM Defined	Program Defect
U0437	System GRPNAME Invalid	Program Defect
U0440	Bad TRNXNM Exec Parm	Program Defect
U0444	Bad TRMLNM Exec Parm	Program Defect
U0448	Bad Remote TRML Parm	Program Defect
U0451	Bad PSB GEN Parm	Program Defect
U0452	BMP Schedule Conflict	Program Defect
U0453	Incompatible Schedule Parm	Program Defect
U0454	BMP/MPP Checkpoint Schedule	Program Defect
U0456	BMP Issued Program Call	Program Defect
U0457	BMP by Same Active PSB	Program Defect
U0458	Prior Program Lockouts	Program Defect
U0462	No GET UNIQUE Call	Program Defect
U0474	Programmer Requested Dump	Program Defect
U0476	No Valid PCB Address	Program Defect
U0477	Exceeds WORKPOOL Space	Program Defect

Abend Code	General Software Error Description	Initial Error Cause Category
U0499	Exceeded INSERT Limit	Program Defect
U0500	Invalid Program Linkage	Program Defect
U0501	Bad Terminal Device Calls	Program Defect
U0502	Bad Graphics Call	Program Defect
U0503	Wrong PTERM Calls	Program Defect
U0504	Queue Switch Errors	Program Defect
U0505	Insufficient Control Region	Program Defect
U0506	LOG DS Out-of-Sequence	Program Defect
U0509	Invalid SYSID Controls	Program Defect
U0511	Invalid Buffer Control	Program Defect
U0512	Bad Queue Manager Control	Program Defect
U0513	Program Exit Subroutine	Program Defect
U0514	LTERM Controls Invalid	Program Defect
U0516	LTERM Control Conflict	Program Defect
U0517	Invalid Data Conversion	Program Defect
U0519	Message Queue Repeated	Program Defect
U0520	Invalid PCB or DBD	Program Defect
U0522	Invalid LT or PT Defined	Program Defect
U0525	SYSCLOCK Usage Errors	Program Defect
U0528	Missing GSAM DD Reference	JCL Errors
U0551	Invalid PCBDEF Parm	JCL Errors
U0552	No MPP SYSID Names	JCL Errors
U0553	Invalid LINKAGE Request	Program Defect
U0554	Invalid ATTN Requests	Program Defect
U0555	Invalid I/O Request	Program Defect
U0556	Invalid PREV Request	Program Defect
U0557	CNTLBLK Directory Address	Program Defect
U0558	No Message Destination	Program Defect
U0559	Queue Not Available	System Error
U0560	Queue Manager Failed	System Error
U0561	Program Changed Control Block	Program Defect
U0562	Incompatible I/O Buffer	Program Defect
U0563	Incompatible Link Control	Program Defect
U0564	Redundant I/O Buffer	Program Defect
U0565	Insufficient I/O Pools	Program Defect
U0566	Message Queue Failure	System Error
U0567	Console I/O Errors	System Error
U0568	SYSQUEUE Manager Failure	System Error
U0569	Incompatible Message Parm	System Error
U0570	Bad Message Destination	System Error
U0571	Unexplained Shutdown	System Error
U0572	Invalid Segment Size Parm	Program Defect
U0573	Incompatible Segment Label	Program Defect

(continued)

Abend Code	General Software Error Description	Initial Error Cause Category
U0578	Bad Device INIT	Program Defect
U0579	Bad Control Block Linkage	Program Defect
U0580	Exceeded Available CSA	Program Defect
U0581	No VTAM System Control	System Error
U0582	Insufficient VTAM Buffer	System Error
U0583	No SCD Control Nucleus	System Error
U0584	Bad Console Message GEN	System Error
U0585	IBM Control Region Fail	System Error
U0586	IBM Control Library Failed	System Error
U0587	FAST PATH Control Fail	System Error
U0588	Bad System Subroutine Exit	System Error
U0589	FAST PATH System Error	System Error
U0590	VTAM I/O Failure	System Error
U0599	Pageswap Control Fail	System Error
U0600	Diagnose Test Fail	System Error
U0601	System Control Overwrite	System Error
U0602	I/O Management Service Error	System Error
U0605	Program Status Control Fail	Program Defect
U0606	Invalid Cross Memory Call	Program Defect
U0611	Invalid Message Descriptor	Input Data
U0612	Skipped Record Lock	Input Data
U0616	Permanent I/O Error	Input Data
U0618	Invalid Overflow DD	JCL Errors
U0622	Invalid System Control	JCL Errors
U0623	Invalid PARM	JCL Errors
U0630	IMOD Control Errors	JCL Errors
U0631	ITASK Control Errors	JCL Errors
U0632	Too Many Exec Parms	JCL Errors
U0633	Bad DBRC Member Parms	JCL Errors
U0634	Blanks in Exec Parm	JCL Errors
U0636	Truncation of Exec Parms	JCL Errors
U0638	Alignment of Parms	JCL Errors
U0640	Incompatible JCL Parms	JCL Errors
U0642	Excess Pass Parm Length	JCL Errors
U0643	Invalid Parm Character	JCL Errors
U0644	Destination List Delimitor	JCL Errors
U0646	Invalid SPIE Parm	JCL Errors
U0648	Invalid CHK Parm	JCL Errors
U0650	Invalid CLASS PARM	JCL Errors
U0652	Missing Parm Field	JCL Errors
U0654	Invalid Exec Parm	JCL Errors
U0658	No Symbolic Program Name	JCL Errors
U0662	No First-Exec Parm	JCL Errors
U0676	Invalid IF3 Handling	JCL Errors

Abend Code	General Software Error Description	Initial Error Cause Category
U0677	Optimizer Not Consistent	JCL Errors
U0678	Missing DD Library Reference	JCL Errors
U0684	Duplicate IMS ID Parm	JCL Errors
U0688	Wrong DBRC Specified	JCL Errors
U0689	Invalid DBRC Specified	JCL Errors
U0701	Invalid Control Block Parm	JCL Errors
U0702	Invalid DEQ Specified	JCL Errors
U0704	Invalid Pool Name	JCL Errors
U0709	Buffer Request Exceeds Pool	JCL Errors
U0710	Save Area Failure	System Error
U0711	Buffer Control Failure	System Error
U0712	Invalid Transaction Control	System Error
U0713	Invalid ENQUEUE Message	System Error
U0714	Invalid ENQUEUE Request	System Error
U0716	Irrecoverable Message Queue	System Error
U0717	Insufficient CSA Pool	System Error
U0718	System INIT Failure	System Error
U0719	INIT Line Failure	System Error
U0720	INIT Process Fail	System Error
U0721	INIT Buffer Failure	System Error
U0722	INIT ECB Failure	System Error
U0723	Incompatible System Version	System Error
U0725	Insufficient CSA Area	System Error
U0728	Insufficient OS Swap Region	System Error
U0736	Insufficient Restart Region	System Error
U0738	System Cancelled Region	System Error
U0739	Insufficient Message Region	System Error
U0741	System Linkage Attempt Fail	Program Defect
U0742	DLI Date SVC Usage Error	Program Defect
U0743	DLI Logical Usage Fault	Program Defect
U0744	Invalid Call Attempt	Program Defect
U0745	Invalid Function Attempt	Program Defect
U0746	Invalid Close Attempt	Program Defect
U0747	Invalid TCB Call Attempt	Program Defect
U0748	IMOD Macro Usage Fail	Program Defect
U0749	ISYS Override Attempted	Program Defect
U0750	Wrong Length Return Code	System Error
U0751	ISAM SYNAD Failure	System Error
U0752	Bad DSCB Control Reference	System Error
U0753	GET SYNC General Fail	System Error
U0754	GET SYNC System Fail	System Error
U0755	Invalid COND Return Code	System Error
U0755	Invalid STATUS Return Code	System Error

(continued)

Abend Code	General Software Error Description	Initial Error Cause Category
U0756	Invalid DCB Parm Passed	System Error
U0757	Invalid SYSQUE Parm Passed	System Error
U0763	QUEUE Manager Failed	System Error
U0765	OSAM Access System Fail	System Error
U0766	ITask Dispatch Fail	System Error
U0768	Switch Dispatch Error	System Error
U0770	Data Switch Error	System Error
U0773	PCB to PSB Conflict	Program Defect
U0775	Insufficient MAX ENQ Parms	Program Defect
U0776	Insufficient DBLOAD Area	Program Defect
U0777	RSRC Control Deadlock	Program Defect
U0778	Backout Method Failed	Program Defect
U0779	Insufficient MAXQUEUE Area	Program Defect
U0780	Latch Lockout Error	Program Defect
U0781	DLI Lost Last Transaction	System Error
U0783	PSB Not on PDIR Chain	System Error
U0793	Log Link Reference Invalid	System Error
U0794	System Sort Link Error	System Error
U0795	System Sort Link Failure	System Error
U0796	REPL Return Link Not Locked	System Error
U0797	Unrequested Segment Return	System Error
U0799	Edit Logic Failure	Program Defect
U0800	Edits Exceeded Workspace	Program Defect
U0801	Concatenated Key Lockout	Program Defect
U0802	Variable Segment Key Lockout	Program Defect
U0803	Read Logic Errors	Program Defect
U0804	Insufficient DLI Logic	Program Defect
U0806	Invalid Buffer Mark	Program Defect
U0807	Invalid Path Errors	Program Defect
U0808	DEL/REPL Logic Errors	Program Defect
U0810	Invalid PSB GEN	Program Defect
U0811	Bad Pointer Passed	Program Defect
U0816	DB Index SYNC Error	Program Defect
U0819	Index SYNC Controls	Program Defect
U0824	Invalid Program EXIT	Program Defect
U0825	PLI Handling Errors	Program Defect
U0826	Exec Parm I/O Index	Program Defect
U0827	Latch Library Failure	Program Defect
U0828	INSERT Sequence Errors	Program Defect
U0829	VSAM Delete Errors	Program Defect
U0832	Dump PB Control Failure	System Error
U0833	Invalid SYSID Error	System Error
U0834	I/O Message Errors	System Error
U0835	I/O Message Failure	System Error

Abend Code	General Software Error Description	Initial Error Cause Category
U0843	Randomizer Logic Failure	System Error
U0844	Null Input DB Space	System Error
U0845	Unexpected Status	System Error
U0846	Unexpected Post I/O	System Error
U0847	Unexpected Access	System Error
U0848	Subpool I/O Locked	System Error
U0849	Subpool I/O Locked	System Error
U0850	Invalid Pointers in DB	Program Defect
U0851	Invalid DB Pointer Init	Program Defect
U0852	Invalid Pointer Reset	Program Defect
U0853	Bad DB Invalid Segment Code	Program Defect
U0854	Invalid Pointer	Program Defect
U0855	Invalid Lock Request	Program Defect
U0856	Invalid Latch Request	Program Defect
U0857	Invalid Insert Request	Program Defect
U0858	Invalid Segment Pairing	Program Defect
U0859	Missing Logical Path	Program Defect
U0860	Bad Insert Pointer	Program Defect
U0863	Bad Key Compression	Program Defect
U0864	Bad ENQ/DEQ Controls	Program Defect
U0865	Exceeds Insert Space	Program Defect
U0867	Insert Logical Errors	Program Defect
U0868	Backward Chain Errors	Program Defect
U0869	DLI Buffer Routing	Program Defect
U0876	Input DCB Inconsistent	Program Defect
U0888	No Default DB Format	Program Defect
U0889	Invalid Device Type	Program Defect
U0890	No Format DD Reference	JCL Errors
U0891	Missing Format Dataset	JCL Errors
U0892	Insufficient Buffer Pool Size	JCL Errors
U0893	Directory Name Missing	JCL Errors
U0894	Directory Name Error	JCL Errors
U0895	Insufficient External Space	JCL Errors
U0896	Invalid DUMMY DD	JCL Errors
U0897	Insufficient Stage Pool Size	JCL Errors
U0900	Incompatible DUMMY DD	JCL Errors
U0901	Security Maintenance Parm	JCL Errors
U0902	Wrong Transaction Name	JCL Errors
U0902	Bad Transaction Name	JCL Errors
U0904	Invalid Directory Entry	JCL Errors
U0905	Insufficient REGION Size	JCL Errors
U0906	Invalid REGION Size	JCL Errors
U0907	PSB to PCB Conflict	JCL Errors

(continued)

Abend Code	General Software Error Description	Initial Error Cause Category
U0908	PSB Name Not Valid	JCL Errors
U0909	PCB Name Not Valid	JCL Errors
U0910	Bad PSB in Register	Program Defect
U0911	PSB Length Invalid	Program Defect
U0912	Invalid PSB or DBD	Program Defect
U0916	Invalid DBD Defined	Program Defect
U0918	Invalid PSB Defined	Program Defect
U0925	Invalid Sequence Parms	Program Defect
U0945	Invalid Message Format	Program Defect
U0947	Bad DBD Received	Program Defect
U0948	Invalid DBD Format	Program Defect
U0949	Bad SYSID Format	Program Defect
U0950	No Working Control DS DD	JCL Errors
U0951	Dynamic Limit Parm	JCL Errors
U0953	No BLKSIZE for DB	JCL Errors
U0955	Abend on Statement in SYSIN	JCL Errors
U0956	Illogical Parent Key	Program Defect
U0957	Entry Lengths Not Equal	Program Defect
U0958	PSB Refers to Wrong Index	Program Defect
U0959	Invalid Logical Pointer	Program Defect
U0961	Shared Index Conflict	Program Defect
U0962	PSB Hierarchy Sequence Fail	Program Defect
U0963	Wrong System Checkpoint	Program Defect
U0965	Segment Definition Conflict	Program Defect
U0969	Header Record Sequence Error	Program Defect
U0970	Checkpoint SYSIN Errors	Program Defect
U0971	Restart Sequence Errors	Program Defect
U0979	Process Sequence Errors	Program Defect
U0986	Segment Path out of DB	Program Defect
U0987	Wrong Segment DBD Index	Program Defect
U0989	DBD Indexed to Bad Segment	Program Defect
U0990	DBD Linked to Wrong Segment	Program Defect
U0991	Wrong Logical Child	Program Defect
U0993	Invalid SEGMENTNAME	Program Defect
U0994	Invalid PSB Field MAP	Program Defect
U0996	Invalid PSB-Level Field	Program Defect
U0997	Excessive Logical Levels	Program Defect
U0998	Logical Segment Limit	Program Defect
U0999	Dynamic Allocation Reclaim	JCL Errors
U1001	Wrong PSB Exec PARM	JCL Errors
U1002	Bad Path Control PARMS	JCL Errors
U1003	Wrong PATH Control PARM	JCL Errors
U1006	Buffer PARM over Maximum	JCL Errors
U1008	Code Did Not Release Buffer	Program Defect

Abend Code	General Software Error Description	Initial Error Cause Category
U1009	Path GEN Conflicts	Program Defect
U1010	Segment Pointer Limit	Program Defect
U1011	Path INIT Failure	Program Defect
U1012	IMSVS PROCLIB Error	System Error
U1013	PSB To DBD Conflict	System Error
U1014	Region Action Sequence	System Error
U1016	Wrong SYSACTION Sequence	System Error
U1017	Address Conversion Failure	Program Defect
U1019	Invalid PATH Calls	Program Defect
U1020	IFP Task Failure	System Error
U1021	System Randomizer Failed	System Error
U1022	System Linkage Failed	System Error
U1023	Excessive Edit Length	System Error
U1024	IFP System Task Error	System Error
U1032	Address Conversion Failure	System Error
U1033	Excess Message Region Buffer	System Error
U1034	IBM ISWITCH Errors	System Error
U1035	IBM DBSWITCH Errors	System Error
U1036	IBM DBSWITCH Errors	System Error
U1037	DEDB Log I/O Failed	System Error
U1038	VSAM GEN Failure	System Error
U1041	DLI Help Logic Lock	System Error
U1050	Bad Vertical CONFIG Defined	System Error
U1111	Product Internal Error	System Error
U1168	Database Sequence Controls	System Error
U1188	IBM I/O Device Fail	System Error
U1222	Database Control Failed	System Error
U1301	Database Out of Space	JCL Errors
U1500	SKDTIO Table Conflict	JCL Errors
U1501	Bad Library DD	JCL Errors
U1506	Lost System Pass Data	Program Defect
U1973	Recovery Completion Error	Program Defect
U1977	Language Coding Error	Program Defect
U2017	System Function Recovery	System Error
U2018	IRLM INIT Failure	System Error
U2201	Lock on Parm Control	Program Defect
U2222	Control Pass Error	Program Defect
U2476	DBRC RECON Failure	System Error
U2478	MAXPST Limit Failed	System Error
U2479	MPP Availability Fail	System Error
U2480	DBRC Task Failure	System Error
U2484	Insufficient CSA for IFP	System Error
U2485	DMAC Latch Failure	System Error

(continued)

Abend Code	General Software Error Description	Initial Error Cause Category
U2486	IRLM Latch Failure	System Error
U2487	Invalid System Date	System Error
U2488	DBRC Status Code Lost	System Error
U2489	ITask Stop Failure	System Error
U2496	IRLM Stop Failure	System Error
U2763	Checkpoints Not in Log	Program Defect
U2821	Bad DBD CONFIG Lock	Program Defect
U2828	DB Insert Pointer Lock	Program Defect
U2849	Invalid DB Control Pointer	Program Defect
U2860	DB Insert Pointer Fail	Program Defect
U3001	Program Forced System Call	Program Defect
U3002	Failed PL/1 Editcode	Program Defect
U3004	Invalid Parm Format	JCL Errors
U3005	Obsolete Proc Format	JCL Errors
U3006	Directory LRECL over 256	JCL Errors
U3007	FAST PATH Stat Fail	System Error
U3008	FAST PATH Open Fail	System Error
U3009	Invalid Sequence Block DD	JCL Errors
U3010	Insufficient Working Storage	JCL Errors
U3011	Invalid OUTMSG Parms	Program Defect
U3012	Invalid INMSG Parms	Program Defect
U3013	Message Stack Overflows	Program Defect
U3014	Literal Pool over 32K	Program Defect
U3015	Literal Work Stack Limit	Program Defect
U3016	Internal Symbol Logic	Program Defect
U3017	Internal Binary Logic	Program Defect
U3018	Internal Literals	Program Defect
U3021	Field Description Logic	Program Defect
U3022	Format Description Over 32K	Program Defect
U3025	Internal Table Logic	Program Defect
U3030	Invalid MFS Library Member	System Error
U3040	IMOD INIT Failure	System Error
U3041	TCB Return Code Invalid	System Error
U3050	Pseudo Abend	System Error
U3055	DB2 Link Not Available	System Error
U3058	TCB Return Code Invalid	System Error
U3059	IPAGE Format Failed	System Error
U3060	Invalid Input Record	Input Data
U3077	Recovery Task Error	Program Defect
U3098	Invalid Transmit On Code	Program Defect
U3099	Invalid Input Header	Input Data
U3100	MFS Parser Failure	System Error
U3101	Invalid Logical Statement	Program Defect
U3102	Invalid ITB Message Pass	Program Defect

Abend Code	General Software Error Description	Initial Error Cause Category
U3105	Invalid Continuation Char	Program Defect
U3106	Invalid Device Request	Program Defect
U3110	Invalid System SVC Logic	Program Defect
U3111	Invalid Source Statement	Program Defect
U3115	MFS Stack Process Fail	System Error
U3116	MFS External Sort Fail	System Error
U3120	MSC Controller Unavailable	System Error
U3141	Log Dataset I/O Failure	System Error
U3199	Tape Sequence Mount Errors	Operation Controls
U3200	Duplicate I/O Tasks	Operation Controls
U3265	Log Record Utility Failure	System Error
U3274	Log Archiver Failure	System Error
U3275	DBRC Request Failure	System Error
U3287	DB Permanent I/O Error	System Error
U3297	Table Wait Lockout	Program Defect
U3300	Command Request Lockout	Program Defect
U3305	Task Request Lockout	Program Defect
U3312	DBRC Request Failure	Program Defect
U3333	Virtual System Failure	Program Defect
U3400	Status Code Handling Error	Program Defect
U3411	Bad MODSTAT DD	JCL Errors
U3412	MODSTAT I/O Errors	System Error
U3500	Data I/O Address Overlay	System Error
U3501	I/O Device Transfer Error	System Error
U3502	DB2 Resources Unavailable	System Error
U3503	Internal Table Overlay	Program Defect
U3504	Dynamic Data Growth Overlay	Program Defect
U3505	Invalid System Pass Data	Program Defect
U3506	Control Statement Error	Program Defect
U3507	Duplicate Entry Call	Program Defect
U3508	Insufficient Work Area Fail	Program Defect
U3509	Recovery SYNC Control Area	Program Defect
U3510	Recovery Checkpoint Area	Program Defect
U3511	Bad Input Data Passed	Program Defect
U3512	Bad Input Data Reception	Program Defect
U3513	Buffer Pool Overlay Failure	Program Defect
U3514	Transmission Edit Violation	Program Defect
U3517	Problem in Input File	Input Data
U3521	Problem in Transaction Input	Input Data
U3600	Insufficient Workspace Size	Program Defect
U3601	Insufficient Array Handling	Program Defect
U3771	Table Overflow Errors	Program Defect
U3902	Data Entry Edit Error	Program Defect

(continued)

Abend Code	General Software Error Description	Initial Error Cause Category
U3904	Hardcoded Table Error	Program Defect
U3905	Defective Counter Error	Program Defect
U3909	Wrong Input Header	Input Data
U3913	Corrupted Control File	Input Data
U3917	Bad ID or Key Passed	Input Data
U3919	Insufficient Table Size Area	Program Defect
U3920	PSB or DCB Conflict	Program Defect
U3930	Transaction Washout	Program Defect
U3960	Insufficient Data I/O Area	Program Defect
U3999	Insufficient Table Pool	Program Defect
U4000	On Code Convert Error	Program Defect
U4001	On Code Transmit Error	Program Defect
U4013	Input Data Damaged	Input Data
U4036	Unexpected Table SYNC	Input Data
U4044	Unexpected Dataset LRECL	Input Data
U4090	Insufficient Virtual to Exec	Program Defect
U4095	Virtual System Failures	Program Defect
U5000	Invalid SYSIN Error	JCL Errors
U5020	SYSIN Control Parm Errors	JCL Errors
U6000	Invalid Access Method	Program Defect
U6400	QSAM Access I/O Error	Program Defect
U8000	Missing Program DD Reference	JCL Errors
U8880	SYSPRINT Disposition Error	JCL Errors
U9000	Program-Default Error	Usage Errors
U9900	Product-Default Error	Usage Errors
U9990	Product Command Error	Usage Errors
U9999	Utility Procedure Error	Usage Errors

Appendix E

AUTOMATED SOFTWARE QUALITY MEASUREMENTS ANNOTATED BIBLIOGRAPHY

BINDER, ROBERT. *Application Debugging: An MVS Abend Handbook for COBOL, Assembly, PL/I, and FOR-TRAN Programmers*. Englewood Cliffs, NJ: Prentice Hall, 1985.

This book provides an in-depth treatment of the complex process that has traditionally been required in order for applications or systems programmers to diagnose and solve a software program dump abend problem. The book focuses on traditional labor-intensive software debugging procedures and does not mention the use of ABEND-AID or other new expert system technology tools that can help speed up and increase productivity of software diagnostic troubleshooting analysis. Nonetheless, it provides an excellent comprehensive reference of the individual application program debugging procedures and data entities that need to be understood and accounted for in order to automate the software quality measurement function and support to program debugging.

BOEHM, BARRY W. *Software Engineering Economics*. Englewood Cliffs, NJ: Prentice Hall, 1981.

This book was first published over a decade ago. It has not been cited earlier. It is regarded as a classic and has in many ways influenced the rising interest in software metrics over the past decade, possibly even as much as Function Points have. Boehm's COCOMO (COnstuctive COst MOdel) method for software project estimation and productivity evaluation is explained in comprehensive detail in this book, along with a wealth of other useful software metric models and analysis, which can be applied to any data center's Total Quality Management program. Boehm had developed the model for TRW and it was applied at Boeing. Several versions were used in military system development. Boehm is now even more associated with the Department of Defense and the DARPA agency, where COCOMO has been refined and applied to a large number of mission-critical advanced military projects. There is little doubt that Boehm was far ahead of his time, and the econonmic theories that are explained in this book will probably become more important than the COCOMO model descriptions, as society advances further along into the transition between an Industrial Era to an Information Era. As for the COCOMO model itself, it is rigorous enough that it can be applied with great precision to any application type and for any software customer. However, it involves some relatively complicated statistics in comparison to Putnam's models, which tend to be more intuitive and easily accepted by most data center management. However, they are both likely to be refined as the software industry moves from militarily focused models in the wake of the Cold War years.

CAMPBELL, ROBERT C. *Benchmarking*. New York: ASQC Press, 1989.

This book is already regarded as something of a classic for the many companies interested in competing for the U.S. Department of Commerce Malcolm Baldridge Quality Award. The benchmarking tools and techniques discussed in this book are not exactly the same as what system programmers traditionally think of as benchmarks for a given CPU with a given MIPS rating. Campbell is talking about using the same general method to benchmark an internal business organization process against itself over time and against the most critical competition external to the organization. These techniques were developed by Xerox Corporation and demonstrated to be extremely useful at surviving in a competitive marketplace. One method that Campbell recommends is to identify the industry leader's method or process and estimate their process unit costs regardless of whether or not your business is in direct market competition with them, as well as to set goals for improving efficiency and unit costs while keeping a watchful eye out for strategic advantage. This is probably going to be a major direction-setting technique that will help redefine the future of TQM as a unique American process.

CARRICO, MICHAEL; GIRARD, JOHN; JONES, JENNIFER. *Building Knowledge Systems: Developing and Maintaining Rule-Based Applications*. New York: McGraw-Hill/Intertext, 1989.

This is an excellent tutorial in the practical aspects of the development of knowledge-base expert systems using standardized exception rules of thumb (a.k.a. "heuristics"). The book walks the reader through the entire development prototyping process for an automated auto repair expert system application. The general design easily can be adapted to quickly prototype a very similar diagnostic expert system to "troubleshoot" and debug software problems by substituting SMF input for auto diagnostics.

CHARETTE, ROBERT N. *Software Engineering Risk Analysis and Management*. New York: McGraw-Hill/Intertext, 1989.

This is another book that has a decided military focus, but, in spite of the many references to MIL-STDs and military operations, it is also clearly applicable to nonmilitary government agencies as well as large corporate software development risk assessment and data center operations management. Most of the methods that are discussed in this book involve the same techniques that are used in risk management science, which is the insurance industry industrial underwriting equivalent to the annuity statistics used in life insurance underwriting. There has always been a close relationship between the methods used by industrial insurance risk management underwriters and military intelligence analysts, going back to the days when the British firm Lloyds of London had a virtual revolving door with the British military intelligence organizations. The book also gives one of the best treatments of basic probability statistics, and how they can be used to make decisions and plan for all possible contingencies, that is available in any book of its kind. There are also case studies and advanced software engineering risk models and methods, which directly apply to automating of SQM. This book reflects on one area of military software development that is probably more readily adaptable to nonmilitary software than any other (except possibly MIL-STD test plans).

CONTE, S. D.; DUNSMORE, H. E.; SHEN, V. Y. *Software Engineering Metrics and Models*. Menlo Park, CA: Benjamin/Cummings, 1986.

Conte, Dunsmore, and Shen have written the definitive work on software metrics which has compared and redefined each of the historical models and methods used in software quality and productivity analysis. This book involves some fairly heady topics and complicated statistical concepts, but is well written and very easily understood, compared to the original writings of Boehm or Putnam, or many other important SQM theorists and practitioners summarized in this book. Although it is best to keep original works by the leading theorists as references for analysis of some esoteric ASQM applications, this is the one single most useful book on SQM.

DEITEL, HARVEY M. *An Introduction to Operating Systems: Including Case Studies in UNIX, VAX, CP/M, MVS, and VM.* Reading, MA: Addison-Wesley, 1984.

This is a somewhat dated classic, which is probably evident by the equal billing to CP/M; yet it has enjoyed a long tenure as a textbook of choice for computer science programs. It is a good reference on how comparative operating systems developed, back in the days when there were few overlaps in techniques used in the then relatively fewer number of possible system architectures and system control program designs. The situation is considerably more complex now, with multilevel parallel platforms and open system architectures, and a lot has happened in the VM and MVS worlds since 1984 (let alone UNIX and VAX). But it is a good idea to keep this book as a reference in order to refer back to the basic operating system strategies that have been "hybridized" and recombined in creative ways to build the new generation OS.

DHILLON, BALBIR S. *Reliability Engineering in Systems Design and Operation.* New York: Van Nostrand Reinhold, 1983.

This is yet another classic, this time on the application of all the best lessons learned by industrial engineering over the past century, in order to improve the efficiency of software design and the reliability of fault-tolerant (and not-so-fault-tolerant) computer systems. Although this is another work that was the result of substantial (Canadian) military support, it does not directly mention any military systems and even devotes a large part of the work to discussion of medical and power equipment control systems. This book is definitely the most statistically rigorous treatment of all the books listed in this bibliography, but it is also very useful as a reference work that can provide many proven software reliability conversion formulas, applied models, and practical rules of thumb, which can be plugged directly into the MICS or BEST/1 capacity planning tools (with much broader application than Conte, Dunsmore, and Shen, or even Boehm or Musa).

ISHIKAWA, KAORU. *What Is Total Quality Control? The Japanese Way.* Englewood Cliffs, NJ: Prentice Hall, 1985.

This is an important book to add to your library, since it is the best available source to describe the Japanese view of their Total Quality initiative (i.e., SPC), its history, and processes. There are many differences here between the Japanese approach and what has been evolving in the United States, as our much more widely understood Total Quality Management movement, which is based more on horizontal empowerment of employees in all operational decision making and benchmarking against competitor operations rather than the TQC focus on product QC. Basically, the Japanese are closer to Demming and the original Statistical Process Control techniques, which were taught in high school and applied to production assembly lines. Much of the common view held by Americans is that the fundamental process of Japanese TQ programs is the quality circle. Although this is certainly one part of the Japanese approach, it is clear that the quality circle is more a part of the Japanese culture than any kind of industrial process secret. What made the Japanese so competitive so fast was quality control methods, which were taught to all employees; yet the application of those techniques was not only encouraged, but required, by the use of "foolproof" automation of the quality measurement process, in order to guarantee precision and standardization of the measures. This book is a must in order to understand why some U.S. quality programs work and others don't, and why data centers should very carefully consider fully automating all their software metrics.

JAIN, RAJ. *The Art of Computer Systems Performance Analysis: Techniques for Experimental Design, Measurement, Simulation, and Modeling.* New York: John Wiley & Sons, 1991.

This is the first book of its kind, and it is definitely going to be a regarded as a classic, as Computer Systems Performance Analysis goes through the transition from being a somewhat haphazard art to a true engineering science. This book covers all the advanced statistical opportunities for continuous quality improvement of computer systems and software, after you have a comprehensive performance history database such as MICS or

MXG. It deals with sophisticated statistical methods, but it provides a good primer on each topic and serves as a good statistical tutorial as well as a source of many good applied tuning methods.

JOHNSON, JAMES R. *The Software Factory: Managing Software Development and Maintenance*. Wellesley, MA: QED, 1991.

The Johnson series of books and articles on the Software Factory concept are already classics. They are also controversial and clearly ahead of their time. The reaction from many programmers and data center managers has been, "but computer data centers are not a factory and you can't manage programmers like factory workers." Although some aspects of the Software Factory take some imagination in order to see the possibilities, it is clear that this is the way of the future; it's what data center customers want and expect, and the organizations that are best able to accommodate the ideas in this book are the companies that will grow and thrive in the increasingly competitive world marketplace. Automated software measures based on system logs is one tool that can be used to make it happen.

JONES, CAPERS. *Applied Software Measurement: Assuring Productivity and Quality*. New York: McGraw-Hill, 1991.

If any one individual could be singled out for recognition as the father of modern software metrics, Capers Jones would easily be at the head of the line. He has been involved from the beginning in the development and refinement of Function Point method and other methods to measure software complexity and size impact on the system development life-cycle process. Capers Jones has also developed his own Software Productivity Research (SPR) Function Points, Feature Points, and "backfire" estimation methods. This book provides a detailed history of the development of Function Points and related software metrics, as well as an extensive analysis of the "State of the Union" for the U.S. software industry, including both average quality and productivity trends over the past four decades. This is a very good reference book as well as an interesting history of how software metrics have progressed since first-generation computing. It is also a source of numerous ideas that can be applied to ASQM.

JULIUSSEN, KAREN; JULIUSSEN, EGIL. *The Computer Industry Almanac*. New York: Brady Books/Simon and Shuster, 1991.

This publication has been updated and reprinted yearly since 1988. It includes a complete directory of computer hardware and software vendors as well as major corporate users of computer services, including names, addresses, and both current and historical statistics. It is probably the one single most important source for locating and tracking DP industy leaders to monitor as your own data center "benchmark partners." It also provides potential sources of additional information as needed.

McCLURE, CARMA. *CASE Is Software Automation*. Englewood Cliffs, NJ: Prentice Hall, 1989.

Carma McClure is closely associated with James Martin, who has done more to popularize Computer-Aided Software Engineering and its tools than probably any other author. McClure and Martin are always on top of the latest software development and productivity tools. James Martin Associates also perform consulting services, and the results of their research are regularly featured in such publications as *Computerworld*. This particular book is the most recent update of the status of the state of the art in software engineering methods and tools. CASE is continually evolving, and it must be watched closely in order to be able to develop more automated ways of capturing CASE software measures. This is because it is often developed on platforms not always directly accessible to mainframe system log and performance management systems. However, vendors such as Legent and others, already offer some cross-platform tools that link to CASE repository.

MERRILL, H. W. ("BARRY"). *Merrill's Expanded Guide to Computer Performance Evaluation Using the SAS System*. Cary, NC: SAS Institute, 1984.

This is "The Guide" that became the handbook for CPE professionals and practitioners alike, as CPE matured to an advanced technical science over the past decade. This is a very hefty, comprehensive reference, over half of which is a detailed data dictionary of the original 10,000 or so system log metrics that were first made available to users of MXG. A second volume was published by SAS Institute, which is just as big and devoted entirely to the description of another 10,000 or so data items added since the original Merrill guide was published. At least half of each volume is devoted to practical discussion of a wide variety of advanced CPE topics, including application software quality improvement. The MXG/HIUSAGE report is particularly worth noting, since it is often used to develop a composite "System Health" index, which can be used to prioritize software programs and problem areas that may benefit from STROBE tuning or new data center standards. Both volumes of the Merrill CPE guide should be ordered directly from Merrill Consultants, since MXG is now supported by the SAS Institute only in international markets. The combined set costs $100 and is truly a bargain considering the number of software performance tips provided. Merrill has plans to supplement the guides with online MXG documentation that will include detailed descriptions of over 40,000 new metrics.

MILLER, HOWARD W. *How to Automate Your Computer Center: Achieving Unattended Operations*. Wellesley, MA: QED, 1990.

This book does not address software quality, but it does address system operational process quality, and the use of system logs as one of the essential tools needed in order to automate any data center. Miller believes that no operational staff necessarily need to be at consoles all night to submit or even monitor production process scheduled batch or "24x7" online database processing support. Between this book, J. R. Johnson's books, Charette's book on system risk analysis, and the tools to manage automated software quality measurement, any data center can accomplish the same "Just-In-Time" management of technical labor and resources the the Japanese accomplish in unattended factory automation.

MUSA, JOHN; IANNINO, ANTHONY; OKUMUTO, KAZUHIRA. *Software Reliability Measurement, Prediction, Application*. New York: McGraw-Hill, 1987.

AT&T Bell Laboratories have developed more sophisticated as well as practical methods for measuring and managing software quality and reliability than any other organization except IBM itself. Although most of the applications and techniques are geared for UNIX networks and the related characteristics of software programs executing in that environment, the SQM methods and reporting schemes developed by John Musa also have applicability to the IBM world, especially as the nature of open architectures make it difficult to tell where SNA ended and TCP/IP took over. This book is the best technical treatment of software reliability theory and statistical analysis methods, and it is also a good idea for IBM analysts to become more acquainted with the UNIX technology, as the two worlds become closer over time.

PERRY, WILLIAM E. *Data Processing Budgets: How to Develop and Use Budgets Effectively (A Management Perspective)*. Englewood Cliffs, NJ: Prentice Hall, 1985.

If Capers Jones can be regarded as the father of modern SQM, William Perry must be regarded as the father of modern software quality assurance. No one has written and published more on SQA and related subjects. Bill Perry helped found the QA Institute for the data processing profession, and he continues to be the driving force in spreading the message of the benefits of software development process standardization and the need for international procedures to train and certify software quality analysis professionals. This particular book is most useful as a discussion of high-level data center management budget decision support needs. It provides many examples of areas where the process can be expedited and made more effective by use of automated system resource usage measurement systems, combined with chargeback billing, or transfer pricing, which are directly interfaced to Budget-vs.-Actuals variance reporting.

PIRSIG, ROBERT M. *Zen and the Art of Motorcycle Maintenance*. New York: William Morrow, 1974.

This book should be in the library of every ASQM professional, as it has been cited by the likes of Capers Jones and many other SQM leaders as a major "cultural alignment milestone," which helped to create renewed interest in, and understanding of, the impact of considerations of quality on our everyday lives. Although the book has little to do with motorcycles, and even less to do with Zen, it has a lot to do with the meaning of quality and how it has come to be viewed by Western civilization (which is very much different from the Eastern views of quality that have received so much attention because of the competitive business success of the Japanese quality programs). This is a literary work, but it also can be viewed as an ASQM reference work in the years to come. There are a lot of things said in this book about the nature of how the Western world has approached the issue of quality throughout the history of civilization, as well as some insight into the areas where Western approaches can be vulnerable to Eastern views. It can help the wise data center manager to more fully understand why it is a good idea to obtain MXG as well as MICS. It should also help provide insights as to why systems programmers are more interested in the "guts of the machine," and applications programmers don't often want to know how machine internals work and are most concerned with how the screen displays will look and how the reports are formatted. It might also help put a lot of rapidly changing technology and economic conditions into a much broader, gentler perspective.

PUTNAM, LAWRENCE H.; MYERS, WARE. *Measures for Excellence: Reliable Software on Time, within Budget*. Englewood Cliffs, NJ: Yourdon Press, 1992.

Although this book was clearly the product of the military model of software development planning and performance evaluation, there is enough practical business applicability here that it should be very useful to data center management for private enterprise organizations as well. The software quality and productivity models seem to be highly intuitive and can easily be applied to any data center's operations. The book also provides a good solid introduction to many applied operations research methods and techniques, which can increase the critical success potential of any data center Total Quality Management program. The Quantitative Software Management consulting organization that was started by Lawrence Putnam is likely to have an increasing role in transfer of many military software development methods and software engineering technologies to the private sector. Putnam also highlights many of the QSM software quality metrics analysis and system development project management tools in his book, and many can use direct input from system logs in their analysis.

SAMSON, STEPHEN L. *MVS Performance Management: Mechanisms and Methods*. New York: McGraw-Hill, 1990.

This book is an extremely valuable reference, both as an update of the most current enhancements to the MVS operating system, such as ESA and SAA, as well as detailed procedures for tuning the MVS system control program parameters and application software JCL and database access controls. It can be used along with the software quality metrics in the MICS or MXG performance database in order to achieve continuous quality improvements in efficiency and performance of applications and system software.

SCHULMEYER, GORDON. *Zero Defect Software*. New York: McGraw-Hill, 1990.

This is an extremely useful book as a reference to the techniques that have been applied from Japanese approaches to Total Quality, which have been successfully adapted by the military and by major U.S. corporations. Although the focus of this book is more related to real-time monitoring and process control than host or network transaction processing software, the techniques discussed in this book can all be applied to MVS and VM systems using

SMF and other system logs as automated software quality metrics input to the statistical error prediction and program test verification coverage technologies that are presented in detail.

SEADLE, MICHAEL S. *Automating Mainframe Management Using Expert Systems with Examples from VM and MVS.* New York: McGraw-Hill/Intertext, 1991.

Although this book presents a hypothetical mainframe operations management system, the examples and sample pseudo-code clearly can be applied to an actual implementation by converting to any major procedural object language, including C, C++, C370, Pascal, Lisp, Prolog, or even SAS. The key to applying this book is to understand the potential of knowledge-based, expert system procedural "rules" techniques in order to automate and control operational processes. The techniques in this book are similar to the techniques that have already been used in computer-aided manufacturing. This book can be used most effectively along with Miller's book on unattended data center operations. Both make use of automated software quality measurements and system performance measurement history databases in order to implement such a system in a manner that is effective, cost-efficient, and reliable, while providing high levels of quality and service.

SMITH, CONNIE U. *Performance Engineering of Software Systems.* Reading, MA: Addison-Wesley, 1990.

This book presents software quality performance analysis methods and techniques which were used by NASA, among others. Most of the approaches are oriented toward real-time monitoring and process control systems; however, many have direct application to the MVS and VM transaction or message-switching environments, especially in the area of network contention and service patterns involving remote access to host process service. This book also presents Software Performance Engineering (SPE) as a new area of professional specialization, which will probably be the basis of academic technology professional eduction programs in the future, as well as methodological process models, which may be the basis for future national standards similar to those which the NBS adapted from NASA in the field of Software Engineering. As this happens, it is likely that additional standards will be specified for the use of automated system logs such as SMF as direct input to SPE or other Software Engineering performance methods.

INDEX